Women of a Certain Age

Women of a Certain Age

Contemporary Italian Fictions
of Female Aging

Rita C. Cavigioli

Madison • Teaneck
Fairleigh Dickinson University Press

© 2005 by Rosemont Publishing & Printing Corp.

All rights reserved. Authorization to photocopy items for internal or personal use, or the internal or personal use of specific clients, is granted by the copyright owner, provided that a base fee of $10.00, plus eight cents per page, per copy is paid directly to the Copyright Clearance Center, 222 Rosewood Drive, Danvers, Massachusetts 01923. [0-8386-4065-6/05 $10.00 + 8¢ pp, pc.]

Associated University Presses
2010 Eastpark Boulevard
Cranbury, NJ 08512

The paper used in this publication meets the requirements of the American National Standard for Permanence of Paper for Printed Library Materials Z39.48-1984.

Library of Congress Cataloging-in-Publication Data

Cavigioli, Rita.
  Women of a certain age : contemporary Italian fictions of female aging / Rita C. Cavigioli.
     p. cm.
  Includes bibliographical references and index.
  ISBN 0-8386-4065-6 (alk. paper)
    1. Italian fiction—20th century—History and criticism. 2. Italian fiction—21st century—History and criticism. 3. Aging in literature. 4. Women in literature. I. Title.
PQ4088.C38 2005
850.9′354—dc22
                                2005005794

PRINTED IN THE UNITED STATES OF AMERICA

In memory of my mother

Contents

Acknowledgments	9
Introduction	15
Scope and Plan for a Cultural Study of Italian Women's Narratives of Aging	15
Overview of Related American Research on Gender and Aging	18
Age Consciousness and Narrative Strategies	25
Theories, Contexts, and Texts	30

Part I. Contexts

1. Representations of Italian Women's Life Courses: A Historical Perspective	35
Cultural- and Social-History Approaches to Women's Life Courses	35
Age Roles and the Dynamics of Domesticity	37
Age Models and Codes: Toward a Definition of a National Female Identity	42
New Bodies for New Women	44
2. Aging in Italy Today	50
Living Conditions and Life Quality of Older People	50
Emerging Trends in Italian Old-Age Culture	54
3. Older Italian Women: Between Tradition and Transition	60
Gendered Images of Aging Across the Media	60
Patriarchal Discourses of Aging: A Close Reading	64
Women's Debate on Gender- and Aging-Related Issues	70
Italian Feminism and Age Studies	73
Demographics	76
Life Quality and Patterns	77
Older Women's Relationships to Time and Space	78
Low-Profile Old-Age Identities	80

Part II. Texts

4. Female Lines in Family Narratives	87
Introduction	87

Susanna Tamaro's *Va' dove ti porta il cuore*	90
Margaret Mazzantini's *Il catino di zinco*	99
Isabella Bossi Fedrigotti's *Di buona famiglia*	111
5. Ripening and Completion in Women's Old-Age Novels	128
Introduction	128
Luce D'Eramo's *Ultima luna*	132
Elena Gianini Belotti's *Apri le porte all'alba*	153
6. A Case Study: The 1968 Generation	172
Introduction	172
Luisa Passerini's *La fontana della giovinezza*	176
Conclusion	194
Notes	199
Works Cited	246
Index	261

Acknowledgments

I WISH TO EXPRESS MY GRATITUDE TO THE PEOPLE AND ORGANIZAtions that have encouraged me along the way.

I would like to acknowledge the support of my colleagues at the University of Missouri-Columbia during my tenure-track career, in particular of my senior colleague in the Italian program, the late Glenn Pierce, a man who deeply believed in my work, both as a literary scholar and as a teacher. I miss his presence in the office next door and our daily informal exchanges over students' papers, Italian politics, gourmet recipes, and cats. I am grateful to the Chair of my department, Carol Lazzaro-Weis, for her thorough reading of my manuscript and helpful editing suggestions. As an expert in Italian gender studies, Carol has been very supportive of my research in feminist age studies. I would also like to thank those colleagues who read and commented on individual chapters of my book: Mary Jo Muratore for her comments on the first draft of the introduction, and Catherine Parke and Magdalena Garcia Pinto for their critique of the chapter "A Case Study: The 1968 Generation." Special thanks go to Linda Reeder, whose meticulous and extensive written comments on the chapter "Representations of Italian Women's Life Courses: A Historical Perspective" were critical to the development of my age-history perspective.

I am grateful to the University of Missouri Research Board for providing financial support for my library research in Rome and Milan in summer 2000, and to the university's Center of Excellence on Aging. In particular, I want to thank Rebecca Johnson, Marilyn Rantz, and Jay Gubrium, for making me feel a welcomed and essential part of their team of gerontology specialists and for encouraging me to contribute my expertise as a humanist and as a teacher educator.

I want to express my deep gratitude to the most recent and enthusiastic supporter of my work in Italian age studies, Millicent (Penny) Marcus, for her rewarding comments on my manuscript and her insightful grasp of what I like to believe are the strongest aspects of my critical methodology, as well as for suggesting the final title of my book.

I am deeply indebted to the mentors whom I have been fortunate to meet in my academic studies and career. Some of them, like my UCLA dissertation director, Marga Cottino-Jones, and two teachers and advisors at the University of Washington in Seattle, Martha Banta and Pia Friedrich, have become everlasting friends. They have read and commented on my work-in-progress, shared long telephone conversations during the years I spent teaching and researching in Italy, and encouraged my decision to relocate in my early forties and take up an academic career in the United States.

My most supportive long-term mentor-friend in Italy has been Edda Melon, one of my *laurea* dissertation advisors, whom I would like to thank for encouraging and promoting my work in feminist age studies in Italy. A great inspirer and guide in this pioneering field of Italian cultural studies has been Luisa Passerini, both as author of the book *La fontana della giovinezza*, which I have had the opportunity to discuss with her, and as a mentor in the methodology of historical research in a Turin women's reading group in which I took part some years ago. I am also indebted to Maria Teresa Marziali, president of the Italian chapter of OWN (Older Women's Network)-Europe and to the Associazione De Banfield in Trieste for sending me publications relevant to the Italian debate on old-age cultures. In the field of American feminist age studies, I have benefited from verbal and written exchanges with two experts, Anne Wyatt-Brown and Devoney Looser, the latter a new colleague at the University of Missouri.

My affectionate gratitude goes to Evelyn Somers, who has helped me polish my non-native English style in a respectful and at the same time participating way. As the first editor of my drafts, she more than anyone else has entered the texture of my work-in-progress. I would like to thank Harry Keyishian, director, and the editorial committee of Fairleigh Dickinson University Press for having graciously accepted my study. I am also indebted to the anonymous readers of my manuscript and to the editorial staff of the Associated University Presses, in particular to Christine Retz, managing editor, whom I thank for her kind replies to my editorial queries.

After investigating Italian women writers' female genealogies and legacies throughout this book, I would like to end this section with two personal acknowledgments to my own female genealogy and legacy. This book is dedicated to Maddalena, my mother, who passed away on November 7, 2002. Even if she could not read a word of English, she would have boasted about my published book, which kept me so inexplicably busy during my summer visits in Turin and took so much quality time away from her longed-for reunions with her lost-abroad daughter. "Are you still working on your book?" she would ask. I wish I could whisper to her: "Il libro è finito, ce l'ho fatta, mamma." The book cover is dedicated to my recently acquired daughter, Chiara Bi

Feng, and acknowledges the place where she was found, the Taogong temple. When my husband Giovanni and I went to China to adopt her in October 2004, we visited this temple, located in Langli Town, a suburb of Changsha, Hunan. We were told that this Taoist temple is dedicated to two local officers who were so beneficial to the town as to become semi-deities. While looking at the frescoes inside the quite dilapidated temple, I was impressed by two details I saw on the same wall: a younger woman riding a tiger, and an older woman walking out of her house toward a kneeling man. The first detail represents a daughter fighting a wild animal to save her father, the second an officer who gives up his appointment to look for his mother. For me, at that time precariously balancing myself on the verge of a momentous life passage, equally distant from, and close to, the memory of my mother in her old age and the expectations about my infant daughter's self-construction as a woman, the two details, if combined together, represented two tesserae in an ideal female life-span mosaic inspired by courage and self-respect. I am proud and surprised to have come to the decision of proposing the wall of a rural temple in the heart of China as the cover for a book on Italian age cultures.

I greatly appreciate the consent of the following authors, literary agents, publishers, and journals to my request to use these materials in my book:

- Earlier versions of chapter 4 originally appeared in Italian as "Paradosso, risarcimento e sovversione: La figura della nonna nella genealogia femminile in Susanna Tamaro e Margaret Mazzantini" in *Essays in Honor of Marga Cottino-Jones*, edited by L. Sanguineti White, A. Baldi, and K. Phillips (Florence: Edizioni Cadmo, 2003), 187–203; and as "Sorelle nel tempo: Ritratti di donne che invecchiano insieme in *Di buona famiglia* di I. Bossi Fedrigotti" in *Italian Quarterly* 40, no. 155–156 (2003): 37–47.
- An earlier version of chapter 6 appeared as "Generation, Gender, and Cultural Genealogies: The Aging of the '68ers in Luisa Passerini's *La fontana della giovinezza*" in *Women's Studies: An Interdisciplinary Journal* 32, no. 5 (2003): 603–39.
- Selections from Susanna Tamaro's *Va' dove ti porta il cuore* and its English translation, *Follow Your Heart*, appear with the permission of the author's literary agent, Vicki Satlow, and of Random House, Inc.
- Selections from Margaret Mazzantini's *Il catino di zinco* appear with the permission of the author and her literary agency, TNA.

- Selections from Isabella Bossi Fedrigotti's *Di buona famiglia* appear with the permission of Longanesi Editore.
- Selections from Luce D'Eramo's *Ultima luna* appear with the permission of Marco D'Eramo.
- Selections from Elena Gianini Belotti's *Apri le porte all'alba* appear with the permission of Giangiacomo Feltrinelli Editore.
- Selections from Luisa Passerini's *La fontana della giovinezza* appear with the permission of the author.
- Selections from students' essays on old age in *I nonni secondo i ragazzi delle scuole di Trieste* appear with the permission of Campanotto Editore.

With the exception of Susanna Tamaro's *Va' dove ti porta il cuore* and *Per voce sola*, all the English translations of the Italian texts cited in this book are mine.

Women of a Certain Age

Introduction

SCOPE AND PLAN FOR A CULTURAL STUDY OF ITALIAN WOMEN'S NARRATIVES OF AGING

SITUATED AT THE CROSSROADS OF GENDER STUDIES, NARRATOLOGY, and cultural studies, this book investigates the impact that the demographic and cultural revolutions of the last century have had on Italian women's life courses and on their literary imaginations. In light of large-scale changes in Italian demography and culture, it is not surprising that a survey of contemporary women's fiction should reveal a growing awareness of intersecting age identities and of old-age issues.

As an Italian scholar whose fields of expertise are twentieth-century literature and women writers, I have chosen Italy of the 1990s as the geographic and chronological focus of this study. The 1990s is a decade heavily invested on the symbolic level with an end-of-millennium climate, emphasizing epoch-making transformations. In addition, the decade is located at the end of a century deeply marked by women's search for identity, by their growth as historical subjects, and by the demographic explosion of older women in Italy's population. Since the beginning of the twentieth century, women's life expectancy has doubled in a European country that competes with Spain for the world's lowest birth rate and that today counts more elderly than young people.

Italian gerontologists have so far showed little interest in gender-related issues, and interpretive frameworks for late-life creativity and narratives of aging are seldom debated among literary scholars. If the study of aging experiences and issues pertaining uniquely to Italian women has been limited, the possibility of an Italian woman outliving her reproductive years has opened up a sort of uncharted territory, potentially subversive in its "anachronism"[1] and particularly fertile for the literary imagination. A significant number of recently published Italian women's novels delineate and characterize aging, life passages, and intergenerational relations. In addition to a new sensitivity to older women's subjectivity and to their relationships to social institutions, an increased attention to female characters maturing across the life span, more inclusive analyses of generational models within and outside of the family, and a wide-ranging view of the micro-historical developments of the twentieth century are evident in many narratives. Since some of these narratives are bestsellers, the growth—and composition—of a new reading audience and publishers' target market must also be assessed.

My "age-conscious" critique of contemporary narratives is directed toward sensitizing readers of Italian women's fiction to a life-course perspective and guiding their responses to the age-based constructions that pervade the Italian cultural imaginary. In *Declining to Decline: Cultural Combat and the Politics of the Midlife* (1997), Margaret Morganroth Gullette uses the term "age consciousness-raising" and insists that it should be developed and taught at home and in the schools.[2] In her most recent essay, *Aged by Culture* (2004), she encourages "true age consciousness" as a form of "active self-reflection" that reaches beyond the analysis of "discrepancies in the official story."[3] This means considering whether "alterations in 'temporality'" have affected our individual stories and whether we "feel more like reporting or hiding them"; whether decline discourses have invaded our jokes, our vocabulary, and our secret autobiographies, and whether these discourses have "aged" more vulnerable parts of our bodies while "making other unchanged or improved parts invisible."[4]

My assumption is that age consciousness affects narrative strategies; the critical questions and concerns that I address are incentives and guidelines to age-conscious reading and literary criticism. My own critical consciousness has grown as I have approached a new theoretical debate that originates in a field—gerontology—where the literary concerns of my own fields of expertise play a minor role. The additional critical insight that I have acquired has allowed me to recognize my own "research genealogy." In the wake of my new familiarity with humanistic gerontology, my earlier work—a study of Italian writer Sibilla Aleramo's diary that investigated a particular form of female autobiography—is clearly, to my new critical self, a study in women's late-life creativity.[5] By the same token, I see now that the cohesion that I traced in Aleramo's diary is analogous to the search by some humanistic gerontologists for autobiographical consciousness in the life review, a re-integrative narrative prompted by the realization of impending death.[6] The literary authority issues with which Aleramo struggled as a woman writer in male-dominated intellectual circles become entwined with older people's "attempt to construct some final 'authorized' version" of their life narratives.[7]

My present study is divided into two parts that represent an ideal progression from contexts to texts. "Part I: Contexts" consists of three chapters. The first chapter, "Representations of Italian Women's Life

Courses: A Historical Perspective," traces changes in the representations of women's aging bodies during different phases of Italian history in connection with women's social status, geographical locations, educational and professional opportunities, and marriage prospects. The historical survey is not comprehensive; the focus is on modern and contemporary history and on the age models that most affect the novels examined in this book. The following two chapters—"Aging in Italy Today" and "Older Italian Women: Between Tradition and Transition"—present both statistical information about and analysis of the social presence, cultural impact, and gender identity of older people in present-day Italy. The chapter "Aging in Italy Today" discusses the effect of Italian demographic patterns in various areas, ranging from personal to political to economic. "Older Italian Women: Between Tradition and Transition" investigates patriarchal constructions, as well as women's present experiences and projections for their future ones. The aim of this chapter is to bring together, in a comprehensive picture, media images, public initiatives, generational debates, monographic studies, interviews, and survey results. I hope, with these numerous fragments of gendered discourses, to encourage age-conscious sociocultural critique among Italian women.

"Part II: Texts" is also divided into three chapters, each devoted to the analysis of two to three novels; the third chapter employs one text as a case study. The novels are grouped under three main headings relevant to Italian cultural studies of age and gender. "Female Lines in Family Narratives" (chapter 4) is concerned with inter- and intragenerational patterns within the family—i.e., the grandmother-mother-granddaughter line, and sister plots examined from a life-course perspective. "Ripening and Completion in Women's Old-Age Novels" (chapter 5) focuses on older characters' communities outside the family. Two typical contemporary scenarios are examined: urban condos and geriatric institutions. "A Case Study: The 1968 Generation" (chapter 6) deals with the most interesting aging group in contemporary Italy: that of women who are, at the time of this writing, in their fifties, whose *Bildung* was affected by the 1968 cultural revolution and the rise of the women's movement in the 1970s. Each chapter in Part II is introduced by brief general observations on the thematic emphases and narrative strategies that characterize the novels and justify their grouping as a unit.

With one exception, the novels that I analyze have not been published in English, and non-Italian readers are not likely to be familiar with them. For this reason, in addition to translating quotations, I have provided introductory information for each novel on plot, circumstances of publication, and critical and popular reception. I also frequently refer to interviews with the authors, reviews in newspapers or literary journals, and debates on age-related issues possibly raised by these books. Following an explanation of the background of each novel and of its structural and stylistic features, the textual analysis is divided into sections organized according to dominant themes; in accordance with my close-reading approach, these sections are subtitled with significant quotes from the texts. The analysis of each novel looks at narrative structure, narrative technique, characterization, setting, and choice of themes and imagery, and asks how and to what degree narrative strategies are affected by age consciousness.

My critical methodology is illustrated in detail in the introduction, first by situating my approach in relation to the most significant contributions in humanistic gerontology, particularly the American debates regarding literary representations and cultural studies of gender and aging, second by outlining the criteria that have guided my narrative analysis. In the conclusion I make suggestions for future research in Italian age studies.

Overview of Related American Research on Gender and Aging

The central contribution of the humanities to gerontology is the recognition that age is a cultural construct. For literary critics, aging is "not only an objective reality but an act of the imagination, its meaning a crafted dialectic of 'fact' and 'fiction.'"[8] As demonstrated by the following overview of the critical frameworks that I have found most stimulating, and to which this book responds quite eclectically, my approach to gerontology is that of a close reader of literature who is intrigued by the relations that women establish with time. Discussing the approach of "critical gerontology," Harry Moody claims that "it is time to 'reinvent' old age" and that "gerontology must properly be the study of human time."[9] Steven Weiland, another proponent of critical gerontology, writes that "narrative is the point of connection between literature and gerontology."[10] If gerontology is the study of human time, and narrative can be defined as "the representation of real or fictive events and situations in a time sequence,"[11] "time consciousness" is where literary criticism and gerontology can ultimately find a common ground. In a life-course perspective that dialogues with the literary imagination, time is, as Kathleen Woodward points out, "prospective as well as retrospective," a story can be both "prophecy and remembrance,"[12] and emerging or projected age scenarios must interrogate aging experiences of the past.

The American debate in the new cross-disciplinary area that Gullette calls "age studies" has helped immensely to ground my insights. I concur with Gullette about the relevance of identifying an "age studies zone" and with her definition of age studies and of their scope as:

> a large interdisciplinary zone where practitioners are becoming increasingly aware of age as a category and increasingly skillful at using it in their very different kinds of work. The zone includes women's studies, gender studies, literary gerontology, life-course studies in developmental psychology, sociology, family and social history, and anthropology. The field should expand; eventually—and the sooner the better—age studies should influence cultural studies, narratology, the history of sexuality.[13]

Gullette's emphasis on a gendered perspective is on target. Age studies and gender studies do share contiguous spaces in cultural studies; both are cultural discourses of difference. The consciousness of "intersecting age identities" to which I refer in the first paragraph of this introduction is a reminder of difference at many levels, both within the gendered subject, who is not identical to herself through time, and across the plurality of bodies, generations, and sociohistorical contexts.[14] The peculiarity of age as a discourse of difference is that it "is the one difference we are all likely to live into."[15] Since individual experiences of age and aging are always relative and relational, being old and young are not absolutes but temporary realities of the self that are measured against age identities and the aging processes of others. The notion of "age identity," Gullette argues, adds "temporality to static postmodern identity theory" and makes us aware, for example, that "'girl' or 'woman' doesn't mean what it meant at 20 in 1960 to the same female person in 1998."[16]

Woodward's notion of "figuring age" is particularly intriguing because it confirms that cultural discourses and social practices that construct the meaning of aging have had a heavier impact on women's life courses. "Figuring age," as Woodward explains the title of her recent collection of essays in feminist age studies, "refers to the representation and self-representation of older women as well as to the figures that they present on the social stage."[17] Since women have been more conditioned than men to "fictionalize" age—by looking younger, acting their age,[18] guessing and comparing other women's ages—the idea of difference in aging discourses includes the multiple reflections of representations and self-representations. To those familiar with Italian culture, the title of Woodward's anthology recalls the myriad of reflecting mirrors that the patriarchal gaze has employed to adapt the *bella figura* mystique—the moral and aesthetic imperative of "making a good impression"—to age-appropriate female behavioral codes. It also recalls the age fictions that have sustained the transmission of religious and sexual practices along female family lines. In creative and regenerative terms, we may also say that the notion of figuring age effectively illustrates contemporary Italian women's "old-age imaginary," which has never been more dramatically different from that of their mothers' generation than it is for the cohort entering the third age today.

If the discovery of age studies and of its intersection with gender studies has motivated me to pursue a new direction among the current and thriving cross-disciplinary debates in Italian cultural studies, Anne Wyatt-Brown's surveys of "literary gerontology" and her critique of recent publications in various subfields of literary gerontology have oriented my reading and my search for a niche in this new field of inquiry. The subfields of literary gerontology whose contributions I have more closely examined are: analyses of literary attitudes toward aging, cultural history surveys, and explorations of new life-course genres from a gendered perspective.[19] I will also mention aspects and trends of literary age studies that I do not find congenial or that do not apply to Italian representations of aging, as well as directions that I find promising yet have left aside for future research.

Regarding the analyses of "portrayals of aging," the contributions that I have found most valuable are those that study the dynamics of literary representation in relation to the cultural imaginary of a given society or historical phase. Early examples of this approach are Barbara and Allan Lefkowitz's essay "Old Age and the Modern Literary Imagination" (1984) and Janice Sokoloff's study of six major British and American novels in *The Margin that Remains: A Study of Aging in Literature* (1987). The Lefkowitzes examine the various ways in which nineteenth- and twentieth-century writers from different western literary traditions "have incorporated the bound and static nature of old age into literary fictions whose forms we expect to turn upon movement, open-endedness, and change."[20] While acknowledging the effects, on literary representations of old age, of "the social and economic stress on progress, or at least change, that has marked western society since the industrial revolution," they investigate four "patterns of narrative response to the static condition of old age."[21] The first portrays older people as models of perseverance, the second as a means of revealing the moral deficiencies of modern society, the third as symptoms of an oppressive social order or of spiritual stagnation, and the fourth as magnifying mirrors of the absurdity of life itself. While identifying distinct modes of characterization, the Lefkowitzes recognize the variety and ambivalence of literary representations of old age. There are in fact no uniquely modern responses to old age in literary terms, as proved by the resurgence of age-related stereotypes and themes across literary history. The only claim that can be made is actually an interesting paradox: "that what might seem on the surface as inimical to narrative development—the bounded, non-teleological condition of old age—has been put to a multiplicity of uses,"[22] some focusing on the condition itself, some on its symbolic possibilities. Particularly interested in female characters, Sokoloff examines the evolution of historical perspectives in the representation of human aging and the relation between the period and the author's attitude toward age. Some of her concerns are the ways "the age of fifty differ[s] in Defoe's eighteenth-century imagination from the thought of the twentieth-century Virginia Woolf"[23] and how *Moll Flanders* combines "understanding of character development with an allegorical vision that moves from wickedness to penitence."[24]

The cultural-history focus seems to prevail in the most recent literary analyses of age. Teresa Mangum's study of representations of older women in Victorian children's literature and conduct narratives argues that the links between children and older women's dependency established by Victorian literature were meant to reinforce the hegemony of middle-class, middle-aged adulthood.[25] An excellent example of how narratives of aging can be interpreted from a cultural-history perspective focusing on a defined time span is Gullette's in-depth cross-disciplinary analysis of the intersection of creativity, aging, and gender issues in medical, journalistic, and literary sources from 1910 to 1935.[26]

In defining age studies and promoting "age-conscious and culturally resistant" criticism, Gullette introduced critical terminology that has helped me in constructing my own discourse on aging. She argues that the parts of the life course should not be called "life stages" (as they are called by those who refuse to regard them as inventions of culture) but "age classes."[27] Her analysis of age fictions and ageist discourses across all age classes—not only old or middle age—in the essay "Age Studies as Cultural Studies" (2000) is extremely astute in pointing out forms of prejudice that lie at the semiconscious level of our collective imaginary.[28] However, despite Gullette's admirable commitment to sociocultural critique from an age-conscious perspective and her intent to discover "progress discourses" that the western "decline mentality about aging"[29] may have suppressed, the militantly "melioristic" stance that she takes in her first book-length study of midlife narratives, *Safe at Last in the Middle Years: The Invention of the Midlife Progress Novel* (1988), seems questionable.[30] I am also uncomfortable with "age utopias": an example is Barbara Frey Waxman's hope of redrawing "the contours of the human species" and translating "into a kind of universal esperanto the language of the 'foreign country' of old age" by fostering new literary genres.[31]

In more general terms, I do not think that literature or literary criticism can or should be used to foster projects or programs. For this reason, I disagree with the emphasis that some critics place on the "benign and affirmative" effect of the humanities on the crude scientific objectivity of gerontology.[32] Inconsistent as it may sound with my choice of research focus and with my intent of raising awareness of Italian age discourses, I have very mixed feelings about the promotion of age studies across the curriculum. The need to foster age-conscious criticism across quite different disciplines, to combine the interests and critical languages of literary scholars and gerontologists, and to construct a solid "pedagogy of aging" for students, researchers, and practitioners has unfortunately encouraged in some studies an instrumental and referential approach to literary portrayals.[33] On one hand, I strongly believe in the usefulness of pedagogical guidelines, bibliographical suggestions, and critical abstracts of novels and poems for course planning.[34] On the other, I agree with Wyatt-Brown when she writes that the pioneering pedagogical drive in a much needed direction—that of introducing literature into academic gerontology programs or raising age consciousness among schoolchildren and adolescents—has produced "'efferent' (instrumental) rather than 'aesthetic' readings (those in which the experience of reading itself is primary)."[35] As a result, Wyatt-Brown adds, "questions of language, genre, style and imagery" have been too often ignored, and insights have seldom been extended into a close reading of selected texts.[36] Also, Weiland observes that the prevailing interpretive approach to literature in gerontology has been to use literary texts for referential value without questioning their epistemological status.[37] "The ironic result of this interpretive strategy," he argues, "has been to fortify the empiricist habit of gerontology so that the humanities become a handmaiden of empiricism. An alternative approach—one recommended by leading theories of literature today—would reveal a text's gaps, inconsistencies, and contradictions."[38]

The attention to narratives of aging has also motivated literary critics to identify new genres that explore character development from a more comprehensive life-course perspective, one that also takes into account later-life development and experiences. The novels I examine do not fit into any of these genres, possibly because no Italian narratives of aging have been examined for the formulation of genre theories. However, the discussion and definition of these genres' structural and thematic traits have helped me to locate hybrid developments of recurring narrative patterns, which will be illustrated in my analyses of individual novels or sets of novels. Significantly, the genre debate is based on studies that have recently questioned established developmental psychology theories, Erikson's in particular, in which the identification of the primary concerns and conflicts of different age classes is based on the study of the *male* life cycle. As Wyatt-Brown warns us, in psychoanalytical approaches to old-age creativity, theories on male cycle, be they Erikson's or Levinson's,[39] "have only limited value in discussion of the journals of a woman writer."[40] Drawing evidence from cross-cultural comparative data, David Gutmann demonstrates that women tend to be more assertive and "agentic" in later life,[41] and that, after experiencing midlife transition in a different way than men, they effectively become "androgynous, sexually bimodal, a mixture, as many observers have put it, of mother and father."[42] Referring to the same phenomenon, Carol Gilligan also emphasizes the continuity with the earlier life stages, in that postreproductive female growth and fulfillment are primarily characterized by affiliation and connection.[43]

Gendered perspectives of the life cycle have affected studies of female *Bildungsromane*, which have, in their turn, questioned the canonical premises of the *Bildungsroman*. It should be acknowledged that this age-conscious genre, concerned with bourgeois male initiation into adulthood and situated in a precise historical and cultural European context—between the French Revolution and World War I, according to Franco Moretti[44]—has been appropriated and redefined by other emerging identities (such as women and ethnic minorities) in the twentieth century. Moreover, the recognition of women's later-life awakening, reengagement, and increased creativity has motivated many explorations of female development to focus on later life rather than on childhood and adolescence, as was the case in the literary tradition of the *Bildungsroman*.

While new names have been coined for narratives of human development—midlife novel, *Reifungsroman*, *Vollendungsroman*, *Altersroman*, novel of senescence,[45] literary autobiography of aging—the most significant aspect of this recent research in genre studies is its focus on women's narratives. Gullette celebrates the "midlife women's progress novel"[46] and Waxman acknowledges the *Reifungsroman*, or "novel of ripening," as a genre that "has been created by women writing about aging women for receptive readers in a rapidly aging society, just as its predecessor, the *Bildungsroman*, was widely read by a more youthful society."[47] Waxman also affirms that she uses two "lenses" for the study of literary autobiographies of aging: one is reader-response theory, the other is the feminist lens.[48] Constance Rooke's description of the features of the *Vollendungsroman*, which she also calls "novel of completion or winding-up," is based on her analysis of a Canadian woman's novel, *The Stone Angel*, by Margaret Laurence.[49] Also, Linda Westervelt, in her introduction to the study of *Altersromane*, identifies feminist scholarship's revision of the *Bildungsroman* as a basis for the exploration and definition of new life-course genres.[50]

Although not concerned with the definition of new genres, Woodward's focus on generations and Wyatt-Brown's on late-life creativity are definitely from a gender perspective. Woodward reminds us in *Figuring Age: Women, Bodies, and Generations* (1999) that the topic of generations is starting to capture people's interest and that therefore women's bodies and generations represent a new, powerful narrative focus.[51] In her introduction to the essay collection *Aging and Gender in Literature: Studies in Creativity* (1993), Wyatt-Brown writes that the essays demonstrate that an analysis of aging's dynamics, in combination with other factors (among them the writer's psychology, gender, sexual orientation, and class), can generate literary insights and theory.[52] As with the studies of female-development narratives, studies of creativity prove the validity of new psychoanthropological theories on women's later-life empowerment. Diana Hume George describes the work of contemporary American women poets aged fifty to seventy as "confrontational, angry, tender, unashamed, naked."[53] While exploring new ways of writing women's lives that have emerged since the 1970s, Carolyn Heilbrun devotes the last chapter of her essay *Writing a Woman's Life* (1988) to past-fifty plots. In these plots she finds new attitudes and a new courage, both linked to the recognition that in a life there is no closure: the acceptance of a new challenge in middle or old age marks, according to Heilbrun, "the end of the dream of closure."[54]

The study of late-life creativity is one of the most promising and fruitful directions of age studies. This approach has encouraged excellent psychoanalytical explorations of literary works and their authors.[55] Critics have used a variety of analytic approaches. Following Wyatt-Brown's classification, research in this field has developed in three main directions: "evidence of creativity and transcendence," "explorations of the writer's psyche," and "the phenomenology of aging." Studies of authors' enhanced creativity and transcendence in old age rely mostly on theories of Jung, Erikson, and Levinson and use journals, memoirs, and novels as primary research material. Explorations of a writer's psyche over the life span are more influenced by theories of Freud, Winnicott, Kohut, and Lacan. One of the most intriguing hypotheses in the third subdivision is Woodward's adaptation of Lacan's theory of the "mirror stage" to old age.[56]

Although I value many contributions in this field, I have not referred to them much in my study because I am more concerned with the relation between text and cultural imaginary than with that between author and text. Besides not finding psychobiographical approaches congenial, I agree with Richard Freedman when he argues that "the enduring power of their [the authors'] art itself suggests that it is founded less on personal psychological idiosyncrasy than on the uncanny ability to perceive and express fairly universal attitudes—at least in the West of the past few centuries—toward the aging which few have the desire or the courage to locate in themselves."[57] In addition, since none of the narratives that I analyze in this book is overtly autobiographical (*La fontana della giovinezza* is more a generational than a personal autobiography), the study of an author's age consciousness is less relevant in my view than other critical concerns. This does not mean that I dismiss authors' views and experiences of aging altogether. On the contrary, I quote and comment on passages from interviews whenever the authors express their opinions on the age-related themes at the center of their novels or mention the real-life models that have inspired their creation of older characters. Moreover, chapter subdivisions in my analyses of the novels reflect to some degree different age identities of the authors at the time of composition, which suggest different levels of identification with themes and characters.

Memoirs, journals, and questions of late-life creativity are not the only areas that I have left aside in my choice of aging discourses. I have also not considered either age-conscious narratives focusing on younger women characters or texts that more explicitly refer to or apply gerontological theories about autobiography, life review, and life transitions. However, I do offer suggestions for future research in these areas, including references to texts and authors particularly worthy of investigation, in the conclusion.

Age Consciousness and Narrative Strategies

When discussing the *Vollendungsroman*, Constance Rooke writes that since they are "running out of time," older characters are often determined to provide a narrative frame to their lives. In this process, "[p]revious versions of a life story may need to be revised in an attempt to construct some final 'authorized' version."[58] The typical structural device of this genre, Rooke adds, is the life review, which is made final by the assumed closeness to the end. I agree that narrative technique may be deeply influenced by the interest in constructing a final authorized version of an existence. Multiple, contradictory discourses may result from conflicting, equally urgent searches for ultimate truths. Multiple internal narrators may be employed. The narrator/narratee or the narrator/implied reader axes may be emphasized: the addressee or alter ego's function is to validate a life version and to be the recipient of a legacy. The reliability of narrative points of view—those of first-person as well as of third-person internal narrators—may be further undermined by a narrator-protagonist's senility or by the fragmentary nature of the narrator's secondhand report of an older protagonist's memories. The narrator's voice may be abruptly silenced by the older character's death or dementia. Older characters' points of view may also be affected by the detachment that they have developed as a result of aging.

Because aging experiences in present-day Italy are diversified, literary portrayals of old age are not confined to a few stereotypes or to flat secondary characters, as they were in the past. Not only are older women the protagonists of the narratives that will be analyzed in this book, but also their relations with other age groups are a central concern. Since age is the basis of character identity in these novels, the stories may focus on the inner development of individual characters through various life stages or on relationships within same-age communities or across generations. This means that age or generational identities may be experienced within a single character or through the relational mirrors of family or the larger society. Age may also function as a powerful agent for deconstructing character identity. The dynamics of disinvestment and reinvestment trigger processes of deconstruction and reconstruction of private and public identity. Furthermore, the fact that from a postmodern perspective the self is never identical to itself through time implies that a single character may be approached as multiple characters at different life stages, or that young characters may incorporate older characters as their future selves.

Narratives of aging usually feature multiple time frames. Recollections, daily routine, present struggles and adjustments, fantasies and projections regarding the future and the afterlife may intersect in various modes and enrich narrative structure. The dialectic of nostalgia and disinvestment, the urgency of the life review or of the last message, the willingness to reinvest and to readjust life rhythms and orientations, the fear of decline and death, and issues of continuity and legacy are central concerns of narratives of aging, and have an impact on story patterns and structure. Besides determining plot, retrospection and projection provide necessary escapes from a dreary old-age present. When the story, as is frequently the case, also contemplates the death of the older protagonist, new plots—those of the survivors—introduce new time frames closely connected with the prospective time of genealogical continuity and of cultural transmission. If one of the survivors is also the narrator, this prospective time may coincide with the time of the narrating.

French philosopher Jean Améry defines old age in terms of "foreignness" to one's own epoch. "The strangers who are guests of former times," he writes, "will constantly find their way around in them [the signs of new times and their relationships] only with difficulty, like the driver of a car in the midst of unknown traffic signs."[59] At the core of narratives of aging we often find not only a preoccupation with adjusting, reconciling, or making sense of the multilayered time frames that result from the accumulation of life experiences, but also a tendency to place relationships and issues in a spatiotemporal perspective. Vertical and horizontal trajectories—almost measurements of one's distance from birth and death—are established by journeys and homecomings, senile wanderings and physical immobility, connections with ancestors and descendants, longing for religious solace and fear of divine punishment. Circular trajectories may, in their turn, underline the seduction of past models, the illusion of escaping the ravages of chronological historical time, or the fear of facing fast-paced change. They clearly demonstrate the repetitiveness of female domestic routines in the past. In narratives of aging, spatial and temporal categories provide powerful metaphors for quest journeys across time. When the character is very old, they may signify the search for ultimate truths, beyond the confines of individual life spans. The conflict between increased awareness of the material aspects of existence (due to physical discomfort or insensitive handling by caregivers,[60] financial restraints or sociocultural alienation) and spiritual interests in death, the afterlife, or in inner resolutions is also the result of a spatiotemporal conceptualization.

In a broader sense, the exploration of age-related issues calls into question historical interpretive frameworks. Although age consciousness is first experienced at the individual or small-group (usually family) level, it translates into an increased sensitivity to collective time-based representations and to their multiple connections: for instance, between tradition and cultural globalization, (pro)creation and survival, generation and genealogy, legacy and mandate; or between the authority and prestige of fashion and the dialectic of power and decline that we tend to associate with conservatism, anachronism or outdatedness, appreciation and ownership of antiques.

The concern with continuity and transmission, decline and completion affects the author's choice of settings, props, and images. Due to the above-mentioned spatiotemporal focus of many narratives of aging, the physical settings and the sociohistorical contexts of these narratives should be analyzed with particular care. Older characters' attachment to memories and their limited mobility or anxiety about coping with the outside world make the home the central setting of their narratives, and may turn everyday relations with the world outside the home into threatening nightmares—or adventurous journeys. In *Vollendungsromane*, Rooke maintains, "the house represents the self in society and contains (through memory and memorabilia) the 'furniture' of identity." Besides being "a marker of belonging or social status," the house can also be a "time capsule" that protects from the social and natural realms. As the house is also a projection of the body, "the dilapidation or disorder of the house is often used to signal the body's decline."[61] Like the house, the body is an important "container-setting," as well as the most powerful vehicle of physical and political awareness. Older women inhabit sexually connotated bodies. Their experiences of frailty, dependence, reification, and death are marked by the increased awareness of their ailing, mishandled, abused, or simply invisible bodies.

In the Italian novels discussed in this book, the home is often located in an undesirable environment, frequently a conglomeration of degraded urban and suburban landscapes that reflects the characters' decline and loss of landmarks in contemporary society as well as their marginal location in this society. When idyllic and regenerating, contact with nature is most often limited to the garden; there it represents an extension of the enclosed protective space of the home and another projection of the character's uneasiness with the "wild" external world. In more than one case, the last home is a nursing home or a hospital.

Inside these container-like settings, older women relate in various ways to objects, animals, and people. Whether they look for contact or not, they often find themselves face to face with other instances of marginalization, alienation, and abuse. The experiences of other older people, immigrants, children, adolescents, or pets may provide analogous examples of their marginalized condition.

Homes are usually crowded with objects: icons of the past that are markers of personal and family property or of female domestic routine, most often reflecting tendencies to collect, pile up, save, amalgamate memories and styles and accept popular, mass-media consumerism quite passively. The disorder that goes along with the undiscriminating domestic collecting of some older people reflects what Aleramo calls "the weight of so much life"[62] in her old-age diary. Waxman observes that the *Reifungsroman*'s focus on "aging's relationship to the domestic environment and the details of household management" reflects what Hélène Cixous describes as women writers' "peculiarly female attentiveness to objects."[63] When discussing the "generational consciousness of older women," Woodward refers to Christopher Bollas's notion of "evocative objects," cultural texts that shape our generational consciousness and help us to imagine our futures.[64] In his essay "The Collector" (1985), Moody attributes older people's interest in collecting to the desire to achieve wholeness and immortality, "create the sense of a bounded or comprehensible universe with an ordering principle," and recapture time and genealogical continuity.[65] This happens because "some objects require the care of many generations extending beyond a single lifetime."[66] He also mentions the childhood-old age bond established by the activity of collecting, which originates in the world of childhood in the "transitional objects" phase that, according to psychoanalytical theorists of Winnicott's school, bridges the gap between fantasy and reality, childhood and adulthood. In fact, collections of memorabilia often represent an idyllic realm where older people's and children's imaginaries can meet.

The objects in our novels—as well as the rooms, foods, and people—have distinctive smells, and smells are powerful memory trails and reminders of physical decay. But along with icons of degradation and captivity, we also find signs of physical and mental awakening: journeys, acknowledgement of long-repressed contents and emotions, meaningful and transforming chance encounters and forms of companionship. Although recurring images and motifs will be analyzed in the chapters devoted to close readings of novels, it should, however, be pointed out that the most interesting images are related to the character's spatiotemporal sensibility. Juxtaposed metaphors abound of horizontality and verticality, material and spiritual realms, immobility and motion.

Animals are quite often sacrificial victims. Rooke writes that animal images may signify a fear of death. Not only do they figure as potential killers: they may also be reminders of our mortality or of the debasement of old age, "as if in old age the human being becomes inevitably a lesser breed."[67] In contrast, children are obviously associated with innocence, and their character and condition is often likened to that of older people. Since family narratives are a widespread genre in contemporary Italian women's literature, children most often represent links in genealogical chains.

The genealogical perspective, in which familial or family-like roles prevail, is the most common pattern of age-based relationship in Italian women's narratives of aging. Within the age identities that these roles have forged, ascendant and descendent relational modes with younger or older versions of the self and mirror projections with same-age doubles are established. The genealogical perspective is central to the discussion of the first three novels: *Va' dove ti porta il cuore [Follow Your Heart]* (1994), *Il catino di zinco* [The Zinc Basin] (1994), and *Di buona famiglia* [From a Good Family] (1991). The analyses of the second set of novels reveal that around and outside of family age chains, a search for new territory, challenges, and freedoms does, in the meantime, take place. In *Apri le porte all'alba* [Open Your Doors to the Dawn] (1999) and *Ultima luna* [Waning Moon] (1993), we meet older female characters who, partly by choice and partly through the force of external circumstances, reengage in new relational modes and residential arrangements, as single dwellers in urban apartment buildings inhabited mostly by older people or when they enter retirement homes. Finally, *La fontana della giovinezza* [The Fountain of Youth] (1999), a study of the early symptoms of aging awareness in a woman who has been deeply affected by her participation in the 1968 and the feminist movements, deals with the most uncharted old-age territory in present-day Italy. This territory is the projected construction of a generation that experienced dramatic changes in women's consciousness and lifestyles and has been called to pioneer social change also in the realm of old-age scenarios.

Theories, Contexts, and Texts

As pointed out earlier in this introduction, my choice of Italian aging narratives and of an age-conscious methodology of literary analysis reflects an interest in investigating the dynamics of literary representation in relation to the cultural imaginary of a given society and in the exploration of wider-ranging life-course genres.

The age-related cultural discourses I discuss in Part I are in dialogue with the aging scenarios presented in the novels analyzed in Part II. The female characters in the novels display a wide and composite spectrum of responses to such discourses and scenarios, ranging from restless discomfort to active criticism. They all struggle with age-appropriateness codes handed down from the past, which regulate their life-course expectations, sexual practices, and roles in the family and in the larger community. They struggle, too, with the legacy of self-deprecating, sacrificial, and guilt-inducing female models. They experience the dramatic impact of feminism and the 1968 movement on generational relations, age- and gender-based power roles, and popular representations of aging. They measure the gap between their recollections of the way things used to be for them as younger selves, as well as for their mothers and grandmothers, and their present condition as older selves—often ailing and socially isolated, sometimes engaged in new patterns of socialization and time management—in a postmodern, postindustrial society. They deal with caregiving and institutionalization issues, and respond to media messages offering packaged solutions for the third age in marketable areas (e.g., rejuvenation, tourism, spiritual healing, retirement planning). Some female characters, particularly the protagonists of the novels in chapter 4, engage in grandparenting; others participate in extrafamilial modes of transmission and aggregation, thus embodying the challenges of a childless society in which the population of older single females grows exponentially.

The novels of aging analyzed in this book represent a noncanonical and quite eclectic use of the narrative possibilities offered by various life-course genres. Following a prevailing trend in contemporary life-course narratives, their focus is on generational relations from a gender perspective. While the novels in chapter 4 can be defined as family or genealogical narratives, the texts examined in chapters 5 and 6—which are more open to the exploration of new, less traditional aging scenarios—combine thematic concerns and stylistic features of *Reifungs-* and *Vollendungsromane*, novels of senility, and mid-life progress narratives.

The investigation of life-course and gerontological theories has proved to be quite beneficial to my narrative analysis. Studies of the life review process, of models of generational continuity, and of sibling relationships in a life-course perspective have definitely inspired my analysis of narrative technique. Theories on the female life cycle have grounded my investigation of women's aging plots. The health professions' views of aging and frailty have enriched my character analysis; likewise, the discussion of caregiving and institutionalization practices has aided my study of the social dynamics of character development. It is important, however, to clarify that the purpose of the overview of research in humanistic gerontology in this introductory chapter is to illustrate the contributions that have motivated and grounded my approach to age studies, not to provide a theoretical foundation for the cultural and literary analysis that follows. As pointed out earlier, while not claiming to apply gerontological theory to literary analysis, I acknowledge the insights that some studies in this field have provided to my reading of women's literature, and make some suggestions for further possible applications of gerontological theory to Italian cultural studies.

Part I
Contexts

1

Representations of Italian Women's Life Courses: A Historical Perspective

Cultural- and Social-History Approaches to Women's Life Courses

A HISTORICAL PERSPECTIVE ON THE LIFE COURSE ENTAILS THE STUDY of material conditions and of cultural representations. It investigates household patterns and the socioeconomic status of age cohorts in different communities, as well as age-based codes and intergenerational power relations. It also attempts to gauge the fears and expectations involved in image construction, consolidation, and preservation, as well as concerns about integrity, purpose, and temporal continuity in both individual lives and lineages.

In addition to using the statistics and broad-scale paradigms of the social sciences, life-course and old-age historians have relied on a variety of sources and methods that reach beyond the results of quantitative analyses. They use census data, wealth surveys, and labor-force statistics to study individual and community developments, and question age-status assumptions in light of the information provided by personal narratives, i.e., diaries, letters, biographies, and literary sources. Although historians acknowledge the socially and culturally constructed nature of age, they differ in their emphases on social experience or on cultural representations.[1]

Social-history methodology is more frequently applied to studies of old age in recent times, and focuses on social policies, career and retirement trajectories, property ownership and transmission of household authority. As social historians have recognized that the location of historical subjects shapes their narratives, a recent trend in western social historiography of aging has been the development of multicultural perspectives. A few comprehensive humanistic gerontology handbooks feature historical sections and, within these sections, include surveys devoted to specific regions or ethnic groups, to migration patterns and non-western traditions. A growing concern with diversity has also encouraged historical studies of women's ages; the main areas of investigation are family and household structures, legal status and social welfare policies.[2] Studies of old age in American history are focusing more and more on diversity—social, ethnic and regional—among aging women.[3]

Cultural historians, more interested in the construction of images and attitudes, have favored the study of the medieval and early-modern life course, for which they have examined prescriptive literature and graphic representations of classic tropes of youth and age. Prescriptive approaches are particularly relevant in investigating gender-based stereotypes of the life course. Normative periodization—the practice of equating age classes with behavioral models—can be traced in a variety of sources: philosophical treatises, sermons, scientific and medical texts, conduct books, paintings. One of the earliest and most renowned treatises on aging in the western world, Cicero's *De senectute* (44 BC), presents us with an ideal male old age, freed from sensual pleasure and dedicated to the cultivation of physical and intellectual health. In medieval and early-modern figurative arts, portrayals of female physical decay were meant to be warnings against the "deformities" of various vices. Some examples of negative allegorization of female old age in Italian figurative arts are Giotto's representation of Envy in the Scrovegni Chapel in Padua, the greedy old nurse who collects golden coins in two versions of Tiziano's *Danae*, and the seventeenth-century painting *La vanità* by Bernardo Strozzi, which represents an old woman dressing in front of a mirror.[4]

Periodization has encompassed various symbolisms throughout European history, from the cyclical view of the life course in medieval iconography to the stepladder stages of the Renaissance. Nineteenth- and twentieth-century iconography has focused not only on an ascending-descending scale of human life most commonly marked in decades, but also on the ascending-descending course of historical events.[5] As a result, we may tend to associate people in their twenties and sixties with different stages in their life careers; similarly we associate politically interventionist or culturally restless periods, such as the 1920s and the 1960s, with youth.

The iconography of a human lifetime has traditionally depicted the archetypal male cycle. Thomas Cole points out that, until the seventeenth century, representations of the ages of life by scholars, writers, moralists, or artists "either subsumed women under the category of man or referred exclusively to men."[6] When *Lebenstreppe* prints began to reach a wider audience in the seventeenth century, they started to feature a woman's and a couple's life stages alongside those of man.[7] If John Bunyan's treatment of the archetypal female journey of Christiana in the second part of *The Pilgrim's Progress* (1684) "reveals the growing stature that Puritanism accorded to women,"[8] modern-age representations of an ideal female life cycle reflect "women's new responsibility for health, beauty, and physical comportment"[9] in male-dominated bourgeois culture.

As for the object of this study, the origins and development of cultural and social constructions of women's life course in Italy, the double jeopardy of ageism and sexism in the periodization of female age classes cannot be overstated. The notion of "age appropriateness" has been instrumental in limiting women's choices by studding their lives with unripe longings and lost opportunities. It has been instrumental, too, in keeping them divided by compartmentalizing generational expectations. Moreover, female bourgeois age-appropriateness codes have been particularly conditioned by the *bella figura* mystique, as will be evident in the discussion of nineteenth-century national stereotypes.

Unfortunately, we cannot rely on systematic and comprehensive histories of the life course in Italy, even less on surveys that map the origins and developments of aging women's life conditions and cultural or literary representations. If we consider Italian age historiography in a European context—reviewing data relevant to the Italian experience in essays on aging in western societies—we can, however, infer information regarding women's age roles in key periods and communities from a number of sources in both cultural-history and social-history research. The most informative types of sources are: studies of household composition; demographic data on medieval and early-modern Italian city-states; research by feminist historians on the construction of Italian female identity and the definition of national models and codes of behavior since the country's unification (1860s).

AGE ROLES AND THE DYNAMICS OF DOMESTICITY

Studies of the Italian family and, in more general terms, of the dynamics of household processes are useful for understanding the nature, characteristics, and limitations of the power that the "mature maternal" carved for itself inside Italian patriarchal organisms. Studies of widowhood are also relevant, in that the mature mother was quite often a widow, and widowhood called for the re-negotiation of gender and age roles and alliances inside the household.

The notion of a strong male leadership over an extended family, transmitted through a system of male seniority, can be traced back to the figure of the *pater familias* in Roman society. His female counterpart, the *matrona*, was a mature mother figure whose capacity to exact obedience from the sturdiest heroes and leaders is celebrated by Latin historians. Livy tells us that Coriolanus's widowed mother convinced him to cease his attack against Rome. In Tacitus's *Annals* we find portraits of influential older women, and learn that emperor Tiberius's mother was his main political counselor until her death at an advanced age.[10]

In medieval and modern Italy a variety of household types coexisted. Historical demographic studies on central Italian municipalities, Florence in particular, show that conjugal households were common in Tuscan cities in the late medieval and early modern periods. The accuracy and wealth of data contained in these studies is due to the fact that population registers were regularly maintained by local authorities for fiscal purposes. In the essay "Growing Old in the Quattrocento" (1982), David Herlihy attributes the importance of the mother in child-raising, and the secondary role of the father in the children's education to a pronounced husband-wife age gap among wealthy families (the average age difference was fourteen years). The urban household typically consisted of a conjugal couple and children, and fathers, being "older and established men . . . preoccupied with affairs of business or of government . . . had not the time, and perhaps not the vigor, to involve themselves deeply in domestic concerns."[11] The mother was the main channel of cultural transmission. Her feminine taste may have had a large role in shaping a society where aesthetic values and refined manners were highly praised, and boys were taught to please women rather than to play with swords or daggers.

As George Minois points out, a consequence of the husband-wife age gap was the fact that "the wife effectively became an eternal minor, whom her elderly husband tended to treat as he did his children."[12] On the other hand, older men often left wealthy widows behind, and "for women with economic means," Lois Banner argues, "widowhood could bring authority and autonomy."[13] Remarriage was discouraged by the fact that widows who remarried were forced to leave their children with their first husband's family.[14] Although in most cases the widows' natal family head took control over the disposition of their dowries, examples of widows' authority have been traced in thirteen-century Siena and Genoa. In Siena, wealthy widows took advantage of the city's expanding economy to make money in various ways: buying and selling real estate, money-lending, managing the agricultural enterprises of their rural estates.[15] In medieval Genoa, artisans' widows were highly prized in the marriage market because they were not subject to the guardianship and inheritance restraints normally imposed on wealthy widows. In fact, they were often their husbands' main beneficiaries, as well as being the lifelong recipients of income from their own dowries.[16]

Older widows sometimes retired to monasteries or hospitals and ended their days there.[17] A unique institution in Renaissance Florence—the object of a study by Richard Trexler—was Orbatello, a lay asylum governed by Florentine women that served as a home for widows and their daughters.[18] In most cases, however, poor widows and unmarried women suffered from great deprivation and could seldom find old-age homes. According to Herlihy, in the Italian Renaissance older women without families were in most cases so poor that they were not listed on the tax rolls and roamed from town to town as beggars.[19]

As for widowers, their remarriages with younger women were encouraged among the upper classes, much like men's late marriages. This made the marriage market desperately competitive: fathers lavished large dowries on their prettiest daughters and placed homely or less healthy ones in convents. Since notions of honor dictated that young women of prominent families be either married or admitted into a convent within a very few years following their puberty, falsification of young women's ages in fifteenth-century Florentine public documents appears to have been quite common. According to Anthony Molho, "this falsification points to the existence of a conscious strategy pursued by fathers and other heads of Florentine households to improve the marriage chances of their nubile female dependents."[20] The practice of marrying off daughters in their early teens was rooted in the conviction that women were morally weak and consequently needed a strong control of their reputation by established patriarchal authority. A nubile daughter over twenty represented a threat to a family's respectability. No matter how innocent and honorable she might be, the older the daughter was, the longer she had been exposed to possible rumors and gossip; an older unmarried daughter, moreover, was evidence of her family's financial difficulties.[21] As for the daughters who took the monastic vows, they would age in religious seclusion. Spared from high child-delivery mortality rates, they often became powerful abbesses and managers of family donations in their later lives.

The sociological and chronological focus of the second set of studies of family and household dynamics is quite different, in that their arguments are based on data from nineteenth- and twentieth-century rural communities, where combined households were (and have continued to be) much more common than in urban settings. According to the standard typology, the presence of widows and/or unmarried relatives has the effect of transforming multiple-family households into extended family ones.[22] Studies of the Italian family's history and household dynamics in the nineteenth and twentieth centuries show that in combined households, the absence, illness, or death of a married male was likely to shift responsibilities onto another male, a married brother or father. This practice reinforced aging women's (both widows' and unmarried women's) security and dependency. Extended-family households also protected aging mothers against the painful experience of the "empty nest," and unmarried women against that of childlessness by allowing them to play maternal roles as grandmothers and aunts.

Research conducted in Europe and the United States shows that kinship relations are strongly "feminized" and that the dominant pattern of kinship is matrilateral.[23] This means that, "in terms of both sentiment and moral obligations," families feel closer "to the female line of kinship than to the male one"; the maternal grandmother is considered more important than the maternal grandfather, and the latter comes before the paternal grandparents.[24] Recent studies show that in most regions of central and northern Italy, on the contrary, the patrilateral system has been the dominant one.[25] According to Kertzer and Karweit, who studied a community outside Bologna, the residence pattern among sharecroppers was definitely patrilocal, "with sons (not just a single son) bringing their brides into their natal household and daughters joining their husbands' households at marriage."[26]

The widespread cultural norm of patrilocal postmarital residence has favored the development of family relational patterns that have been traditionally associated with the "Italian matriarchate" stereotype: a strong mother-son bond and alliance and complex female intergenerational ties, involving younger women both as daughters-in-law and as daughters, as the mature mother's antagonists and as caregivers of older family members. In a patrilocal postmarital residence system, for example, "the community is likely to criticize a daughter-in-law who does not take good care of her father-in-law and mother-in-law."[27] An important study of the Italian family from the nineteenth century to the present gives us a very clear picture of gender and age roles and of the nature and limitations of women's authority in the Italian family tradition:

> This opposition [between mothers-in-law, daughters-in-law, and sisters-in-law] concealed an important stake: it was only through her influence over men that a woman could impose her power and this alliance hardly ever took place between husband and wife, but rather between mother and son. Maternal authority derived from her reproductive role: this authority was exerted through the children, and therefore over their families. Paternal authority, in fact, began to weaken when family units—the son and daughter-in-law couple—were created. These new units stood against one another and against the elderly father, who failed to impose his authority, founded on a public role and on male relationships, inside the family. He necessarily had to accept the mediation of the wife who, through her alliance with the children, corroded the boundaries of the husband's power.[28]

Her existence and identity deeply entwined with those of the other family members in a complex relational web, the "Italian matriarch" had enormous power and responsibility in domestic politics, in granting cohesion and continuity to a family. Outside the family, however, her individual existence was hardly acknowledged by the public collectivity.

In the transition from a rural to a more industrial, urbanized society that gradually took place between the nineteenth and the twentieth centuries, women's life courses came to be heavily tailored to the aesthetic and behavioral status expectations of a developing bourgeoisie. Still lacking an identity both as a worker and as a citizen, the bourgeois woman did not have the peasant mother's productive role in the domestic economy. Idle, perfunctorily educated, devoid of property rights, she had the status of a minor. Public responsibilities belonged to the husband, and household chores and child nursing and care to other women.

Some of these women, hired as servants or governesses when they were very young, would become part of a family's relational web and would age inside that family. In fact, since domestic servants, previously only employed in aristocratic families, became an essential status symbol for bourgeois families, poor country girls, some as young as thirteen or fourteen, were hired in cities and towns across Europe. While approximately one-third of female domestics achieved social promotion through marriage, large numbers of unmarried women continued in service to age fifty and beyond. This suggests that "domestic service could easily take on a permanent character that left thousands upon thousands of women in a celibate state."[29]

As observed by some feminist historians, in the nineteenth century socialization took place mostly in gender-secluded realms.[30] This socialization pattern fostered a high degree of intimacy in both horizontal and vertical family relations, among female age peers and between mothers and daughters. Yvonne Knibiehler claims that the highest degree of intimacy between mother and daughter was achieved in the nineteenth-century European bourgeois family, possibly because gender social roles had never been so differentiated.[31] The issue of a "female legacy," of what a mother could hand down to her daughter in terms of feminine virtues, became therefore relevant.

In post-Unification Italy, the emphasis on mother-daughter transmission of virtuosity was accompanied by a pervasive pedagogical drive. The mission of educating the citizens of a new nation was deeply felt. This mission was highly "feminized"; in fact, it emphasized women's roles as reproducers of the children of the new nation and as their educators. With the establishment of a national school system, a new professional role was made available to lower-middle-class single young women, that of schoolteacher. In a rhetorically charged climate in which ethics were sentimentalized and feminine virtues idealized, there was heavy pressure on women to learn and abide by canons of moral conduct and physical appearance.

AGE MODELS AND CODES: TOWARD A DEFINITION OF A NATIONAL FEMALE IDENTITY

If idealized femininity, which has inspired a large number of edifying publications, is traditionally iconic and atemporal, the definition of a female national character became more and more problematic in the years after the Unification. Regional traits resurfaced under the national mystique, and new sciences, such as anthropometry and *Völkerpsychologie*, identified and studied somatic and psychological physiognomies in relation to geographical location of origin.[32]

As for the definition of age models and codes, the pioneering of new methodologies and the opening of new research fields, such as physiology, psychiatry, the social sciences in general, made the approach to age classes, to psychophysical growth and aging processes appear more scientific. Childhood and adolescence, which were "discovered" in the nineteenth century both as a social concern and as an imaginative resource, started to be associated with early sexual drives. In Italy—a new, demographically young nation with a strong pedagogical mission—a physiognomy of the adolescent woman was sketched, and manuals were devised for her *Bildung*. Significantly, while acknowledging the effect of social components such as class, urban vs. rural upbringing, and work obligations on cultural models, turn-of-the-century humanitarian and socialist rhetoric called for a more democratic, unifying, and dignifying representation of the nation's future generation. In 1900, writer Ida Baccini nostalgically protested: "There used to be young girls, girls and little girls: nowadays there are only *Signorine*. My greengrocer's daughter is a *signorina* like the Marquis of Rudinì's daughter."[33]

Women were called *bambine* until twelve years of age, *giovanette* from thirteen to sixteen, and *signorine* from sixteen to the time they married.[34] These designations are still valid today, except for the term *giovanette*, which has fallen out of use. As a classless marker, the term *signorina* overruled "all the thorny issues of single women's social fitting-in in the aftermath of World War I: 'office *signorine*' . . . 'typist *signorine*' . . . that embodied the illusions of emancipation of many young women."[35] This title has also been the pity-inspiring, ageless label of spinsterhood. Although there were isolated attempts to abolish it as early as the late nineteenth century,[36] the practice of addressing all adult women as *signora* is a fairly recent and not yet generally applied trend.

The use of the title *signorina* to address both teenage and mature unmarried women helps confirm that the main marker of women's initiation into adult life has traditionally been marriage. Marriage is particularly important as an age marker in monogamous societies that do not legitimize divorce.[37] In the essay "Raccontare un matrimonio moderno" (1996), Michela De Giorgio writes that national surveys of marriage-age distribution started in 1865, and that for the next hundred years or so, women's mean age at marriage remained almost stable, fluctuating between twenty-three and twenty-five years, while men's fluctuated between twenty-seven and twenty-eight.[38] Late marriages have been more common in northern and central Italian cities since the seventeenth century, while adolescent marriage has been mainly a southern Italian phenomenon. De Giorgio also remarks that at the beginning of the twentieth century, conventions like anagraphic precedence in the marriages and engagements of sisters were still practiced.[39] The husband-wife age gap has traditionally worked to the benefit of men, whose late marriages were encouraged among the upper classes not only in Renaissance Tuscany, but also in the period between the late eighteenth and the early nineteenth centuries.[40] The reduction of this gap became one of the conditions of a tendency toward the moralization of marriage that started to have some impact in the late nineteenth century.[41]

Late nineteenth-century bourgeois society viewed women's marriage as a behavioral milestone: "the dividing line *before* and *after* the marriage intervened with the force of a rite of passage to settle issues regarding the exploration of wider behavioral possibilities: clothing styles, types of reading matter, management of free time, relationships with the other sex."[42] These codes separated married and single women's experiences and opportunities within different modes of their common "minority status," requiring them, much like children, not to venture beyond the thresholds of life passages. Geography was another powerful marker that acted both to divide and to promote change. A growing web of women's journals contributed to the awareness of different age codes, both within and outside of Italy, regarding women's opportunity for marriage and for independent social activities. Women in southern Italy were known to be subjected to more restrictions than in the north; northern European female models started to be contrasted with those of Mediterranean countries toward the end of the nineteenth century.[43]

From the beginning of the twentieth century to the cultural revolution of the 1960s, age thirty has been generally considered the landmark of women's single status. Anna Vertua Gentile's book of etiquette—in the 1897 first edition as well as in the 1915 eighth edition—advises the thirty-year-old woman to "courageously renounce the young woman's expectations" and to behave in society "like a widow."[44] Female single status has generally been portrayed in Italy, both in fiction and nonfiction texts, as an "imposed, humble, worthless"[45] condition. The origins of this representation, according to an 1895 article that compared Italian and English models, were to be found in the Italian social context, which erected "a rigid and insurmountable barrier" to the "expression of female individuality outside marriage and the family."[46] According to a reader survey conducted by the popular women's magazine *Margherita* in 1911, a woman was old at fifty-four and a girl became a *zitella* at age thirty.[47] At forty, a single woman was not only a *zitella* (the Italian word for "spinster"); she was a *vecchia zitella*. On the positive side, attainment of this age, which coincided with the end of a woman's reproductive phase—thus of her desirability—meant an end to social restrictions. Even in the debate over the age at which women raised in charitable institutions who had neither married nor taken monastic vows could be safely released, early eighteenth- and nineteenth-century church hierarchies agreed on the range between thirty and forty.[48] The idea that aging could coincide with the broadening of social freedom for single women of the urban upper classes started to loom at the beginning of the twentieth century. In 1900, Matilde Serao maintained that forty was the threshold of spinsterhood, past which women could directly administer their properties, travel, and even flirt moderately without being criticized.[49]

The debate about the age at which a *signorina* stopped being considered marriageable—and, consequently, the age at which she could be granted some degree of independence from her parents—is quite interesting, especially if examined in relation to the growth of women's extra-domestic employment. In the course of the twentieth century, the need to protect the honor of both young and adult unmarried women was complicated by their gradual entry into wage work. With the spread of female employment, supporting structures replacing the family had to be created for single women who left their hometowns to work in cities. Since these women, mostly of the lower middle classes, could not afford apartments of their own, some of them were hosted by relatives or in boarding houses run by nuns, while others found accommodation in lay women's hostels, the first of which were opened in Milan and in Rome in the 1910s and '20s.[50]

New Bodies for New Women

It is evident, from this turn-of-the-century survey, that nineteenth-century stereotypes of women's life courses were being corroded in the post-Unification years. However, the real revolution took place in the twentieth century, when women, now much more visible in the public realm, started to be seen as a plurality of bodies and experiences.

The gradual diffusion throughout Italy of northern European and American models brought about a revolution in female appearance based on the idea that healthier, more carefree, less restrictively dressed bodies reflected emancipated, less codified lifestyles, and that physical exercise and hygiene could allow women to control aging processes.

A crucial publication in the development of twentieth-century notions of women's aging in Italy had been Paolo Mantegazza's *Fisiologia della donna* in 1893. While studying the female body in the various stages of its development and decline, the first leading Italian anthropologist maintained that "the duration of beauty will be in proportion to the increased sturdiness."[51] He also pointed out the effects of a classist society on women's physical deterioration: "Today a Lombard peasant woman is old at thirty, an Italian lady is beautiful even at forty; an English woman, who is already a century ahead of us, may be beautiful at fifty, sometimes even at sixty. This is the way the women of the future ought to be."[52]

As Mantegazza's celebration of English women shows, northern European and Anglo-American women were proposed as old-age models. Foreign texts on menopause were also translated at the beginning of the twentieth century: among them, in 1915, Dr. Emma Drake's sexual hygiene manual, *What a Woman of Forty-five Ought to Know* (1902), which advised the mature woman to rest and stay healthy, be more self-centered, and "take up and perfect some of the ambitions of her earlier years."[53] A Danish best-selling novel, Karen Michaelis's *The Dangerous Age* (1911), was translated into Italian in the same year. The novel criticizes double-standard ethical codes regarding the "critical years." The protagonist is forty-three and loves two men, one of whom is eight years her junior. Italian publications were more cautious. In the preface to one of the first hygiene manuals on menopause, readers are warned not to take too seriously the physical and psychological pathologies that rendered mainstream representations threatening.[54] Violations of double-standard age codes were not even contemplated. The only well-known literary example, forty-year-old Foscarina's love for a younger man in D'Annunzio's *Il fuoco* (1900), was inspired by the author's liaison with actress Eleonora Duse.[55]

If in the last hundred years the acknowledgment of new aging modes for women's bodies has been slower in Italy than in other western countries, pressing consumption trends have made it inevitable. In a 1902 article, Ida Baccini used the effective moral association of beauty and decay to warn her young readers against the beauty mystique—by implying that for beautiful women "the undeserved expiation" for their attractiveness started at forty.[56] A few decades later the same beauty mystique was questioned from a similar yet wider perspective. The optimistically wise conclusion on women's aging expressed in a beauty column in the 1936 issue of the *Almanacco della donna italiana* again proposes the topos of the primacy of spiritual over physical youth and reflects an acceptance of physical decline with which we are no longer familiar today; it also encourages women to take control over aging processes and cultural stereotypes:

> Finally, a piece of advice to our older readers: don't try too hard to rejuvenate *externally* through easy means that are of no more use: a spiritually young mental attitude, an environment, a life of understanding and solidarity toward young people (whether they are your children or grandchildren) will rejuvenate more than all the tricks in the world. The tragedy of indestructible beauty is not for our times. Aging is a right, aging serenely is a science and, if we succeed in it, it is no longer "aging": it is living.[57]

A few years later, in 1941, we read in the same beauty column that thanks to changes in women's fashion—shorter skirts, low-heeled shoes, trimmed hairstyles, the use of cosmetics—there seemed not to be a remarkable difference between a twenty-five, a thirty-five, or a forty-year-old Italian woman. It is not a merely "cosmetic issue," the *Almanacco* claims; it is something deeper and more solid, the result of lighter diets, intellectual exercise, and increased mobility.[58]

Not only did women's aging bodies become more mobile and diversified in the twentieth century thanks to revolutions in fashion and hygiene. Age boundaries and definitions were also affected by the last century's dramatic socioeconomic changes and political events, which resulted in new directions of cultural transmission and new patterns of generational relations.

A deeply felt and controversial twentieth-century age-related issue has been that of "generational authority." In the first decades of the century the passage of generational authority started to lose its value. Fathers and heroes were dramatically challenged, in real and symbolic terms, by World War I, psychoanalysis, cultural avant-gardes, and financial downfalls. Nineteenth-century bourgeois mother-daughter intimacy deteriorated as well. As they entered the work market, the daughters started to create horizontal channels for transmitting knowledge about the female body (in particular regarding abortion and contraception practices)[59] that ousted the traditional mother-to-daughter initiation and made the relation between aging, sexuality, and reproduction more complex.

Early twentieth-century victories in the area of female emancipation were overturned by Fascism, under which women's tasks were to procreate, nurture, and manage familial functions in the interest of the state.⁶⁰ The political vision that linked population policy to national power pressured women to comply with family and national interests. Women were expected not only to contribute to the preservation of patriarchal authority but also to be "careful consumers, efficient household managers, and astute clients to squeeze services out of a stinting welfare system, in addition to being part-time and often concealed wage earners to round out family incomes."⁶¹ Not by chance, "the words *sacrifice* and *stinting* recur like a leitmotif in female accounts of maternity and motherhood during the 1930s."⁶²

Fascist culture feared and ostracized the "new woman." According to a short poem published at the height of Fascism in a women's journal, modern behavioral and dress codes might threaten even the most sacred and enduring female stereotypes, among them that of the grandmother. Whereas "grannies of old times" used to wear glasses and bonnets, black or dark clothes, and knew tales and remedies for any ailment, "Today's Granny still dances, / dyes her hair, does her face; / she even falls in love sometimes! / And to be in fashion she has cut her locks (highly praised in the past!). . . . / Time has changed even Grandma."⁶³

As for the impact of Fascism on generational identities, the emphasis on age-compartmentalized socialization discouraged the transmission of experiences across generations.⁶⁴ The practice of rallying Italians in a variety of party organizations and events involving differentiated age, professional, and interest groups was meant to enlist the widest possible basis of popular support for a strong national project. Moreover, the Fascist state was in many ways to take the place of the family in the cultural imaginary. Large-scale mobilization of women started in the early 1930s. Adult women's organizations included the *fasci femminili*, mainly catering to urban middle-class women, the *massaie rurali* for peasant women, and the SOLD, an association of women workers. Younger women could join the *piccole italiane* from age eight to thirteen, and become *giovani italiane* from age fourteen to eighteen. Membership in both associations escalated significantly during the Fascist era.⁶⁵

In line with the Fascist regime and its iconography, the organization of Catholic women's affiliation also followed age-based criteria. Age limits for youth membership were first set by Catholic Action, an organization that had been set up after the country's unification. In 1918, the year of its founding, the Catholic young women's association (*Gioventù femminile cattolica*) did not accept under-fifteen members, because of its "militant character." Over the next fifteen years, four younger age brackets were added: *aspiranti* (from age twelve to sixteen), *beniamine* (six- to twelve-year-old girls), *piccolissime* (age four to five), and *angio-*

letti (from birth to age four).[66] These youth-focused subdivisions were viable as late as the 1960s.

In the second half of the twentieth century, age-based compartmentalization and generational identity were reasserted by the youth protest movements that swept across the western world in the sixties and seventies. In Italy, the *sessantotto* revolution and the women's movement exploded almost at the same time, causing heated debates on seniority- and gender-based power hierarchies. Most importantly, whereas from a historical perspective women's aging is related to reproduction and men's to production, in contemporary times the association of women's aging with their childbearing capability has been undermined. If we review studies of women's age history from the Middle Ages to the nineteenth century, we observe that both adolescent and mature women may have been perceived as threats to the community by virtue of their marginal or liminal position in relation to the reproductive cycle. In the twentieth century, there has been a gradual recognition of women's participation in productive processes; in addition, more complex and flexible criteria of valuing or devaluing women at different stages of their life courses (other than those prescribed by their marital and childbearing statuses) have been introduced. These production-based criteria regard women's education, employment, presence, initiative, and mobility.

Recent developments in Italian cultural history will be discussed from a contemporary perspective in the next two chapters. Although incomplete, this historical survey of age-related issues in Italian history highlights stereotypes and conflicts that still affect Italian women's lives. "Age legacies" handed down from the past affect in various ways the old-age images that women, stronger in numbers, years, and prospects, are renegotiating today. Most importantly, in light of the focus of this book, these legacies are the bases of the plots, themes, and characterization in the novels that will be analyzed in the second part of this essay. We will find, in fact, powerful sacrificial and castrating matriarchs who function as bearers of burdensome family legacies, as well as father figures who are obscured by their emotionally marginal roles. We will see thrifty and repressed homemakers whose passive destructiveness has been triggered by high demands for caregiving and household management, and resentful daughters and granddaughters engaged in life-shattering revolts against those same repressive female models and lifestyles that their mothers and grandmothers embody. We will become privy to unsettled intra- and intergenerational female conflicts over power roles in extended patriarchal families, and encounter women whose relative powerlessness in such families is problematic: maids aging in families that employed them when they were little more than young girls; mature, nubile daughters who falsify their birth certificates to improve their marriage chances; adult bourgeois wives whose dependency has made them childish, lost, and doubtful of their self-worth, and whose education has emphasized propriety and appearances to the point of inhibiting their life energy and inner development. We will also encounter new, often hybrid types whose contradictions reflect today's dramatic shifts in female age roles. The investigation of contemporary conditions and issues in the next two chapters will help us to connect past and present aging modes and to better contextualize Italian narratives of aging.

2
Aging in Italy Today

LIVING CONDITIONS AND LIFE QUALITY OF OLDER PEOPLE

AMONG ALL THE COUNTRIES THAT TOOK PART IN THE SECOND WORLD Assembly on Aging organized by the United Nations in Madrid in April 2002, Italy was the "oldest." Its over-60 population was estimated to be one fourth of its total population and was projected to rise to 37 percent by the middle of this century.[1] In 1901, less than 10 percent of Italians were over 60, while in 1988 this age group represented about 20 percent of the overall population.[2] Life expectancy has increased dramatically in Italy in the last decades of the twentieth century. After experiencing a five-year increase during the period that extended from the end of the nineteenth century to the 1980s, it has doubled since 1980.[3] Today, at the beginning of the twenty-first century, life expectancy is 79 years, the second highest after that of Sweden (79.6).[4]

The most striking demographic feature in present-day Italy is its low fertility rate (1.19 children per woman in 2002, the second-lowest ratio on the planet).[5] As a consequence of the decrease in births, as well as of its high life expectancy, in 1998 Italy hit a new record, as the only country with more old than young people. In that year, it was calculated that 16 Italians out of 100 were above 65, whereas only 15 percent were under 15 years of age.[6] Another projected result of low birth rates is a decrease in the overall Italian population (almost 58 million at the beginning of the twenty-first century) starting with the second decade of the century. In 2030, there will be 4.5 million fewer Italians, and another million will be lost in the subsequent twenty years.

Since the 1980s, Italian demographic figures have been a cause for serious concern. Besides making old-age politics a pressing issue, the progressive increase of older people and the proportional reduction in the numbers of youth and young adults has profound implications for the "demo-psychological" modifications of a collectivity.[7] Although the recent immigration wave is starting to affect birth-rate indexes,[8] Italians are an aging people, and the country features a biological imbalance between the young and the old. Interestingly, the two fastest-growing segments of the Italian population—older people and immigrants from third-world countries—are coming into closer and closer contact (in most cases externally imposed), since *extracomunitari* are often employed as caregivers.[9]

Though experts on demography have emphasized the potential problems of an aging Italian society, policy makers have failed to respond quickly to the changing equilibrium in the labor market among the employed, unemployed, "informal" workers, "baby," and old-age pensioners.[10] In recent years, especially after one of the most radical pension reforms in Europe was approved in 1995,[11] the threat of social security bankruptcy and the demands imposed by European unification have caused volatile discussions among the government, political parties, trade unions, and employers about how to reform pensions. Older people today receive pensions that derive from the Italian unions' powerful and progressive policy of protecting all workers, a protection that extended beyond retirement.[12] Interestingly, the fact that this type of policy is no longer available for the next generation of retirees is bound to antagonize not only the young and the old, but also the "young old" and the "old old."[13] As remarked in an article on the "new revolution" awaiting the 1968 generation, which has been called to pioneer social change even in the case of old-age scenario, "it is not easy to accept working until the age of seventy to support legions of older people who were pre-pensioned in their forties by the old Christian Democratic Party (or by the center-left governments) in order to guarantee social peace and make room for the young baby-boomers."[14]

Although Italian unions forced previous governments to adopt pension criteria that were advantageous for retired workers, the criteria were based on the profile of a "typical" worker: male, main provider, with a steady, upward career.[15] Moreover, if it is true that in Italy more money is spent on the pension system than on other parts of the welfare state, "most spending on pensions should be interpreted as an inappropriate and concealed substitute for other forms of benefit cover."[16] Care services for older people are quite deficient in comparison with the standards of other European countries: 2 percent of the Italian elderly live in retirement homes and only 1 percent benefit from home assistance.[17]

Although the debate on pension reform has placed different generations at loggerheads in terms of public spending quotas, it has not undermined the social image of the older population. The basic infrastructure of Italian society, still very much centered on the family and relying on female caregiving, was able to mitigate the effects of mass aging. As we shall discuss later in more detail, Italian women have retained their traditional caregiving roles. In most cases, those roles have expanded as women have been expected to attend to the needs of the previous generations as well as to those of their children. In addition, it has been estimated recently that the contribution of older people's pensions in households is very high. An article published in the newspaper *La Stampa* in 2000, titled "Grandpa supports one family out of four," challenges the conception that older people live at the expense of their progeny. In fact, 24 percent of Italian families live on the grandfather's pension, and 28 percent of the young unemployed are supported by that monthly allowance.[18] In some areas of the country—for example, the islands and the south—older people contribute more than 50 percent of the income in households of two or three people.[19] In quite a few cases, housing shortages or financial restraints force young couples to start a new family in their parents' home.[20]

As for the living conditions of older Italian people, in a country where regional differences are great, different traditions and varying degrees of industrial development have clearly had an impact on social stratification and attitudes toward older people. Percentages of older people in the overall population also vary significantly: 20 percent of the population in the northern and central regions is over 65 years of age, as compared to only 16 percent in the south.[21] In the northwestern part of the country, where development has been heavily marked by industrialization and the prevailing social unit is a nuclear family whose members spend most of their time outside the home, older people are a "problem" that requires outside intervention and assistance. In this area, the need to fight social isolation has also promoted greater senior interest-group involvement and a greater consciousness of old-age politics, resulting in more cultural opportunities for older people. In the newly affluent regions of northeastern Italy, where small-family production is the economic standard, healthy older family members continue to be part of the production process and are valued, as long as they do not interfere with the intergenerational passage of the means of production and of decision-making. In southern Italy, the islands and the interior regions, where agriculture still prevails, older people either enjoy the affection and respect of the patriarchal extended family or, in the areas affected by migration, may live in isolation.[22]

Apart from regional differences, a growing trend among older Italian people is to remain, after retirement, in the cities where they have spent most of their adult lives. This change from the traditional pattern of returning to the hometown, where family ties and properties are preserved, is connected both to the need to live close to their children and to the fact that three-fourths of older Italian people own their city apartments, which also represent their major financial investments.[23] Although mobility is not high in Italy and parents most often live in the same city as at least one of their adult children, more and more elderly live alone, contrary to stereotypes about Italian extended families and despite the fact that quite a few older people contribute help and financial support to their children's families. In 1999, out of approximately thirteen million over-60 people, almost three million lived alone.[24] The city has become the context of their self-identity: their landmarks are a given shop, an elevator, a public park.[25] As a consequence of their urban isolation, the primary concerns of older Italian people are coping with city crime, traffic, transportation, malfunctioning public services and, in more general terms, with the environmental degradation that affects most Italian cities. The growth of the older urban population only highlights the inadequacy of life quality in Italian cities.

As pointed out above, the economic status of older Italian people, affected by a strong family support system and by former retirement policies, is somewhat contradictory. On one hand, the standard of living for people over sixty-five is usually lower than the average, and older people represent more than 30 percent of the population living below the poverty line.[26] On the other hand, not only is a significant percentage of older people still active in the work market — 7.6 percent in 1998, almost all of them men[27] — but some older Italians are, as discussed earlier, the main source of family income. The poor are mainly those who have social pensions (*pensione minima*), and their numbers are on the rise, particularly in northern Italian cities, where the cost of living is higher. Most of them (80 percent) are women who did not acquire work benefits.[28] This situation is likely to change with the next generation of retired people, as pension reforms and higher job mobility affect current patterns and views of retirement.

Any conclusion regarding the economic status of older people at the beginning of the twenty-first century should, however, be reassessed in light of the introduction of a unified European currency. Although some studies reveal that recent inflation trends in Europe cannot be attributed to the new currency,[29] in Italy the purchasing power of people's incomes has decreased since prices have been converted from liras into euros, owing to the fact that the rising cost of living is not paralleled by an adequate corresponding growth in the country's economic productivity. Low- to middle-income families (among them many households with an older person as head of the family) are facing unprecedented financial difficulties. Moreover, although extensive information campaigns targeted at the third age were organized by local and regional administrations in preparation for the introduction of the euro, many older people, oscillating between extremes of suspicion and ingenuousness, have experienced confusion and anxiety in the transition. According to a warning issued by the City of Rome in 2002, many fraud attempts, perpetrated by would-be social workers and banking consultants offering their door-to-door financial services to older people, were reported in connection with the approaching currency conversion.[30]

Emerging Trends in Italian Old-Age Culture

Today's older Italians have not benefited from the massive democratization of education that has taken place since the 1960s.[31] According to estimates from the late 1990s, only 3.5 percent have a degree, 54 percent have a primary school certificate, and 15.7 percent are without any qualifications.[32] The number of older people who do not have any educational qualification is over 40 percent in the south.[33] Limited education affects the use of free time among older people: though almost all (91.8 percent) declare that they watch TV every day,[34] only 22 percent read books. Yet, reading newspapers is quite a widespread pastime, at least until age seventy-five: 6.5 million older people read them daily.[35] Education is one of the most evident divides between aging generations in Italy, where the young old express more active cultural needs than in the past. The most radical change in this respect should, however, be expected at the end of the first decade of the third millennium, when people who were born in the 1950s and were affected by the democratization of the educational system of the 1960s will enter the third age.

The large older population affects the cultural market immensely, since a rapidly increasing number of healthy and active retired people have time, interest, and resources to invest in a variety of cultural products, ranging from organized tourism[36] to public lectures, from senior associations to the universities of the third age.[37] A small yet growing number of older people are computer literate and communicate using the web.[38] As a consequence of this massive new cultural presence, conceptions and representations of old age are also widely questioned and reassessed. I will conclude this preliminary survey of the new Italian elderly by examining some of the emerging trends in today's third-age culture. Identifying this background will help us place new, updated, and timeless gender stereotypes in perspective.

Older Italian people seem reluctant to organize themselves as an interest group. Possible reasons are the historical weakness of nonpolitical and nonreligious organizations in Italy and the generally low education level of older people. Also, the existence of a tighter family and community fabric than in other western countries and a legacy of leftist culture—the tendency to depreciate corporative communications in favor of public interest—discourage both segregation and lobbying. These may be reasons why the concepts of "ageism" and of a gendered approach to old-age issues do not take root easily. They may also explain why both cultural initiatives for the third age and publications that investigate popular contemporary representations of old age focus on intergenerational communication as much as on specific age-group concerns.

The old-age culture that is spreading in a country where older people form a complex, contradictory entity—marginalized from production yet blocking the demographic, economic, and political takeover by new generations—is necessarily multifaceted. The advice older people receive from gerontologists is often contradictory and hard to put into practice. The most prevailing catch phrases highlight two main ideas: that old age should be the age of ease and freedom, and that older people are the only global resource that is on the uprise in Italy.[39] One wonders what "ease" and "freedom" may mean to people who were young in times of wars and dictatorships, who built their families, in the aftermath of Fascism and of World War II, on foundations of sacrifice and frugality, then experienced, with the 1960s economic boom, the certainty that their children would be spared from the privations that they had to bear. One also wonders what impact the notion of older people as a "resource" might have on parents who are traditionally among the most nurturing in the western world (the stereotype of the Italian parent is one of smothering or authoritarian protectiveness). As grandparents, in particular, they are very often seen as a resource by working parents: whether out of love or out of necessity, over 80 percent take care of grandchildren in a more or less consistent way.[40] Italian grandparents have been estimated to be the most active in Europe: out of the ten hours a day they spend on average in caregiving activities and household-related tasks, four are devoted to their grandchildren.[41] The data on grandparents' support to their families prove that the crisis of grandparenting is only a demographic fact: in reality, an elite number of grandchildren have daily or near-daily contact with grandparents and the number of potential grandparent figures available to children is significantly higher than in the past. More and more children can establish significant bonds with their great-grandparents as well. Expectations about older people's support of their children's families and about children's assistance of their disabled parents show that both ascending and descending intergenerational caregiving roles still hold quite strongly in Italy.

The contradiction, however, lies in the fact that, no matter how willing older people are to offer practical and financial support to their own children, even into their adulthood, they are perceived collectively as the generation that will bankrupt the Italian social security system. In 1999 the number of retired people was calculated to exceed that of employed people (22 vs. 21 million). Thus, the idea of older people as resource may be a response to the collective guilt that mass longevity inspires in a country characterized by low birth rate, overpopulation and traffic density in many areas, and inadequate services. It is a widespread belief that in Italy, more than anywhere else, old-age issues should be approached from a generational equity perspective. From this perspective, the youth vs. old-age conflict is seen in terms of "generational accounting,"[42] and older people are asked to turn from being a collective burden to becoming a resource, through voluntary services and social re-employment.[43]

On the positive side, both emerging representations of old age seem to be oriented toward the enhancement of older people's curiosity and creativity. The ideal of a free-spirited and resourceful older person is likely to become a bridge between the past and the future. This ideal figure would be willing to test new old-age models in the mass longevity scenarios that have been projected and to connect new generations to disappearing values, knowledge, and skills. Moreover, promoting this ideal is a very profitable enterprise: "ease" breeds investments and consumerism, and one of the ways through which older people can be a "resource" is by consuming.

In his famous 1994 lecture at the University of Sassari, titled "De senectute," one of the most reputable champions of older Italian intelligentsia, the late historian Norberto Bobbio, warns that today there is a new old-age rhetoric, "a concealed though very effective form of *captatio benevolentiae* toward new potential consumers."[44] While today's older people represent a powerful section of consumer society and have encountered a wide range of consumer trends and economic scenarios, they are both the beneficiaries and the victims of a global tendency toward the leveling-out of age distinctions and the promotion of youth fashion.[45] The youth mystique and the postmodern denial of aging are phenomena that I do not discuss in this context because they are not specifically Italian. Though rooted in archetypal fears of decay and death, the contemporary "rejuvenation market" reflects, if anything, the success of American models in western societies. In the specific case of older Italian people, self-centeredness and materialism may be partly the result of low fertility rates and of the consequent crisis of grandparenthood discussed above. While on one hand "grandchildlessness" can turn grandparents into idealized collective figures, on the other, it may lead to questioning a whole range of attitudes and values. The importance of legacy, for example, may be disregarded in favor of consumerism or may be reassessed in cultural terms with respect to new heir figures, to be located and chosen outside the traditional genealogies. Both religious and secular approaches to the afterlife may also be affected because the lack of progeny unsettles established notions of transcendence and continuity as well as traditional responses to death and to issues of individual, genetic, and spiritual survival.

It should be obvious from this preliminary survey that age consciousness is at a very transitional stage in Italy today and that strong ascendant and descendant caregiving expectations coexist with intergenerational gaps and conflicts and with an equally strong repression of old age at the collective-unconscious level. It may be surprising to discover that, according to the 2002 Censis report on Italian young people, while 40 percent of the 15 to 30 year-olds define "difference" in terms of sexual orientation, 20 percent indicate age or religion as the second most significant markers of diversity.[46] This is a striking result, considering the high level of intergenerational contacts in Italian social life and the fact that young and young-adult individuals have daily consuetude with and exposure to older people, both at home and in the streets.

In conclusion, I will discuss another important effect of the present demographic imbalance on Italian old-age culture, namely the fact that the growth of the older population promotes the decline of the elitist old-age models of a past, when being old was an honor and a privilege. This decline is not related to a demographic phenomenon only; the association of age and authority has been exposed to significant attacks throughout the twentieth century, especially after World War I and the 1960s. Regarding the 1968 generation entering the third age today, Natalia Ginzburg remarked that, although in their youth they had heard tales about the wisdom and serenity of the aged, they never loved this kind of serenity and wisdom: "[w]e have always loved instead," she writes, "thirst and fever, restless searching and mistakes."[47] The aristocratic old-age culture of the past survives in a few political and intellectual figures whose wisdom, enlightenment, and commitment the '68ers both admired and questioned. They were in many cases among the founders of the Italian Republic in the aftermath of a world war and a civil conflict. For this reason, ideal contemporary old age is often associated with a strong ethical fiber and with political commitment, cast as it is in the heroic mold of the anti-Fascist Resistance. The few survivors of the Resistance generation are well into the fourth age now, and they may represent the last elite of idealized old age.

In the past, Italy has known several illustrious intellectual, artistic, and religious old-age models. In Italian age history, longevity records were held by artists and by religious people.[48] Religious people's longevity in past history was largely due to the fact that convent life sheltered them from epidemics, war, and starvation. The word "retirement," in fact, evokes both the old-age condition and the detachment from worldly pursuits (which is more likely to take place in old age). The association of longevity and religious virtue is a variant of the "wise old man" topos. The appeal and authority of such association in Italian culture is related to the influential roles that older figures in the Catholic Church hierarchies have played in Italian political and spiritual history.[49] The most enduring example of old-age authority in contemporary Italy has been set by Pope John Paul II, who, in the last years of his life, continued to exercise strong public functions in spite of his senility. When a German bishop, Karl Lehmann, suggested, at the beginning of the year 2000, that John Paul II should resign, not only the Italian clergy but also the Italian media in general responded quite critically.[50] Journalist Giorgio Bocca wrote in his *Repubblica* editorial titled "La carne e lo spirito" (2000) that "[t]he Pope's old age and illness is a topic that fascinates both believers and agnostics": it is "the appeal of churches, of religions which last, whereas institutions and ideas of the temporal world keep disappearing."[51] While bravely and defiantly representing, in his own frailty, Christ's preference for the weak and the ailing, Pope Wojtyla's disregard for human age limits also incarnated the unquestionable theocratic patriarchal foundations of the Roman Catholic Church.

The patriarchal perspective does indeed permeate Italian age history, in which the "grand old" are almost exclusively men. While some of today's older public figures have recently published their reflections on old age, the examples they cite to support their reflections are almost exclusively male.[52] The cover title of a 1998 Friday supplement of the newspaper *Repubblica* reads: *La vita comincia a 80 anni* (Life starts at 80). The report was about eighty-year-olds who were still successful in different fields, in the arts, sciences, literature, politics, etc. Around the title, thirty photographs of well-known older people were arranged, and only seven of them were women—a ratio that does not respect longevity indexes, which are to women's advantage.[53] Also, Nobel-prize-winner scientist Rita Levi Montalcini, perhaps the most reputable example of an older female intellectual in Italy, did not herself include a single female in her panorama of distinguished older people in the last part of her essay *L'asso nella manica a brandelli* (1998).[54]

Italian women have had to wait until this century to see a handful of famous older role-model figures come into the limelight, sometimes for their intellectual or political stature, quite often also for their eccentricity. In the first group, only Rita Levi Montalcini and Nilde Iotti stand out; the latter is, however, associated in people's minds with her more famous companion, communist leader Palmiro Togliatti.[55] Significantly, the few other older women that have achieved some degree of notoriety—for example, theater actress Paola Borboni and writers Sibilla Aleramo and Lalla Romano—are also remembered for their violation of sexual age codes, in that they all had much younger partners at a quite advanced age. As writers, Aleramo and Romano are not the only examples of female late-life creativity in contemporary Italian literature; other examples will be mentioned in the conclusion as suggestions for future study on late-life production. Unfortunately, the few and scattered signs of interest in this area, in the form of conferences, art exhibits, and catalogs, are exclusively devoted to the study and appreciation of the late works of men.

In general terms, the Italian intelligentsia seems to be lacking a gender perspective with respect to age-related issues. Frequently it displays overt double standards. In the next chapter, a survey of contemporary forms of prejudice and stereotype—some conveyed through the popular media and some expressed in reputable newspapers or in specific essays on old age—will illustrate the cultural climate in which Italian women are aging today and provide an introduction to the primary focus of this work: Italian women's representations and experiences of aging.

3

Older Italian Women: Between Tradition and Transition

Gendered Images of Aging Across the Media

A SURVEY OF GENDER REFERENCES IN NONFICTION TEXTS CAN SERVE as a fruitful introduction and accompaniment to the narrative analysis I conduct in the second part of my study. While browsing through a variety of visual and written texts, I have traced recurring images, themes, and concerns that may be best illustrated by a cursory overview of the media and popular press. In this section, I will look at some portrayals of female old age in TV spots, cinema, women's magazines, and local news. Then I will apply a closer linguistic analysis to the following text types: children's and adolescents' written and graphic representations of old age; two commentaries from national newspapers; segments devoted to women in gerontological literature and special issues on the third age in social studies journals. Although the focus of this chapter is contemporary popular discourses across a variety of nonfiction texts, one of the two newspaper opinion pieces I have chosen dates back to 1959. The reason for selecting this piece for closer reading is that it features a significant range of patriarchal constructions that have molded the present-day age-class imaginary.

A distinctive trend in TV advertising is the reevaluation of the grandparent-grandchild relationship.[1] These are two powerful consumer categories, whose response to the market has to be weighed against their inversely proportional numeric growth. Most frequently, the spots focus on a playful male bond between grandfather and grandson, as in the famous Italian ad of Philadelphia cream cheese, in which the pair conspire to get more than their share of the best brand of cheese on the table. Another significant group of spots emphasizes youthful spirit and attitude in older people. These ads may present groups of male friends who play soccer or whistle at a young woman walking by the park bench where they are sitting.[2] Women are not portrayed in a positive, youthful light as often. The depiction of older women's sexual prowess is still a taboo in advertising. Instead we see wise grandmothers recommending the best bleach brand to inexperienced daughters or granddaughters—a counterpoint to the childish grandfather-grandson bond.[3] As a sad reminder of changing stereotypes, however, a few recent spots ridicule traditional dignified images of female old age, as in the cases of La Cremeria ice cream and Sigma supermarkets ads. In the first, three gluttonous grandmas join the crowd of children visiting a friend who supposedly keeps a supply of this ice cream in his freezer; in the second, a sprightly old lady is likened to young vandals who destroy the products they touch.[4] The Aprilia motorcycles ad features an older lady who steals a motorbike away from a young couple who are making love.

Women are most often the protagonists in ads for technological devices, in particular telecommunications equipment (e.g., cordless phones and beepers) and hearing aids.[5] The reason is that people in the fourth age who live alone and need to establish a reliable communication system with the outside world are mostly women. As shown by the ad for a hearing center in a Turin newspaper, *La Stampa*'s, special supplement on the third age (a photo shows an older woman using a hearing aid to communicate with a child), hearing-aid technology advertising plays on the assumption that women have a "relational nature."[6] Advertisements for concealed prostheses also tend to use female models, since these products capitalize on female vanity and women's concern with appearance.

While commercials and also documentary programs for older people (mainly on health issues and interpersonal relations) are increasing in TV programming,[7] the same cannot be said about Italian cinema. The few Italian films that feature older protagonists usually focus on a male character—on his old-fashioned dignity, visionary wisdom or eccentricity, or simply on his struggle with decline.[8] A number of studies and surveys of old-age themes and characterization in feature and documentary films have been published in Italy in the last twenty years, mostly in social studies journals.[9]

Older female protagonists are presented almost exclusively as co-protagonists in couple relationships; within the couple, moreover, the husband often plays the leading role. In *La notte di San Lorenzo* (1982), directed by Paolo and Vittorio Taviani, actress Margarita Lozano plays the part of a rich lady who has a chaste and emotionally cathartic one-night love encounter with an older peasant in the devastating scenario of the final days of World War II. *Buon Natale, Buon Anno* (Luigi Comencini, 1989) features Virna Lisi as the wife in an elderly couple forced by financial restraints to live in separate houses, each with a different married daughter's family. This strained arrangement rekindles their passion; after a few secret meetings, they decide to run away together.

Mario Monicelli's *Parenti serpenti* (1991) also deals with older couples experiencing humiliating or even exploitative and abusive treatment by their children's families. Pia Velsi plays the indefatigable grandmother in a couple who have decided to tell their children that they intend to bequeath all their money to the family that is willing to look after them and take them into their home. In response, the children plan to get rid of their older parents in order to collect their inheritance right away. *La casa del sorriso* (Marco Ferreri, 1991) is about love between retirement-home residents. The female protagonist, played by Ingrid Thulin, has a provocative, aggressive role in this film. Seeing that her passion is ridiculed and hampered by both residents and staff—a nurse steals her dentures—she replaces the dentures with vampire teeth. In the science fiction film *I viaggiatori della sera* (Ugo Tognazzi, 1979), Ornella Vanoni is the outspoken feminist wife in a middle-aged couple. In a near future in which society is controlled by the youth, it has been decreed that all citizens must abandon their productive roles once they turn forty-nine and move to vacation resorts—luxury ghettos where they are gradually done away with. A quite different couple is the spinster sister pair played by Emma and Irma Gramatica in an older movie, *Le sorelle Materassi* (Ferdinando M. Poggioli, 1944), based on Aldo Palazzeschi's novel. In this film, two naïve and loving Tuscan embroiderers in their fifties waste their affection and resources on the ungrateful nephew they have raised.

Two fairly significant protagonist roles have been recently played by actress Virna Lisi, a blonde aristocratic beauty who played the "proper old lady" type in both *Va' dove ti porta il cuore* (1996), based on a novel that is analyzed in this study, and *Il giorno più bello della mia vita* (2001). Both movies were directed by Cristina Comencini. While we may observe that female genealogies are a favorite theme of contemporary Italian women writers and also of the (unfortunately few) women film directors,[10] we can also recognize in Virna Lisi's grandmothers a northern Italian upper-middle-class matriarch whose value system clashes with her children's lifestyles and choices. Sexually repressed by her education, she has led a protected life under the wing of a bread-winning husband who was totally unaware of her emotional needs. Now a widow, she is exposed to her descendants' contemporary concerns with homosexuality, feminism, divorce, single parenting, restless grandchildren, engaging careers. In *Il giorno più bello della mia vita* she experiences some sort of mild awakening following this exposure: although her lifestyle does not change a bit, she ultimately comes to terms with her children's choices and learns to accept them.[11]

It should also be noted that some established Italian actresses have engaged in mature seduction roles in their latest films. A couple of examples that come to mind are Sophia Loren's striptease scene in Altman's *Ready to Wear* (1994) — in which she plays an elegant widow who tries to rekindle an old passion with a worn-out Mastroianni—and Stefania Sandrelli's sexually restless fifty-year-old mother trying to escape from marital boredom in Gabriele Muccino's *L'ultimo bacio* (2000). Although this is not the place for thorough investigation of cinematic representations, I would like to conclude by pointing out that the most interesting roles are those that focus on women's interactions in relationships with their contemporaries. Restless, disillusioned, yet resourceful female peer groups often reflect the critical transitional state of the female middle- and young-old-age imaginaries in contemporary Italy. An example by a woman director is *Gentili signore* (Adriana Monti, 1988), about a group of middle-aged housewives who, after starting a craft cooperative, must deal with the mysterious disappearance of the company manager.

Women's magazines generally convey a positive view of women's aging. They underscore the sexual appeal and social aggressiveness of the new mature woman, in accordance with the current trends of the rejuvenation market. While actresses and high-society women are interviewed and photographed as testimonials to modern medicine and plastic surgery, case histories of the success of women managers and entrepreneurs are also brought into the limelight.[12] Some reports cover fifty-plus beauty pageants, others more serious social issues relevant to aging women, such as the burden of caring for older family members or changing roles in female genealogies. Case histories that chronicle overlapping daughter, mother, and grandmother roles or the growing presence of great-grandmothers are presented.[13] An interesting emerging middle-aged female image is that of the *cattiva figlia* (bad daughter), which embodies today's conflicting emotional and practical responses to caregiving responsibilities.[14]

The images conveyed by the local press, which reflects provincial contexts and attitudes, are quite different. An exhaustive survey of an isolated sample — 1994 issues of newspapers from Abruzzi, a central Italian region — was conducted in *Vecchiaia e pregiudizio: La donna anziana nella stampa quotidiana* (1995). According to sociologist Eide Spedicato, the articles feature women in three distinct roles: as "involuntary actresses" in sensational scenarios; as "preferential targets of expressions of violence and insanity, brutality and hideousness"; and as "exceptional subjects," in relation to longevity records or eccentric behavior.[15] The most frequently featured topics are: loneliness, devaluation, marginalization, poverty (19 percent); accidental death (17.2 percent); fragility and social weakness (15.7 percent). They are followed by: suicide attempts, homicide, precarious physical conditions (approx. 9 percent);

longevity (7 percent); road accidents (5 percent); violence and rape (4.3 percent); and late maternity (3.5 percent).[16] The only assertive models that counter the "frail old lady" stereotype are age paradoxes: the centenarian and the *mamma-nonna*, i.e., the postmenopausal mother. It is interesting to note that, although biotechnological experiments are condemned by Catholic public opinion, in 1992 the oldest primipara in the world was a 61-year-old Italian woman.[17] A semantic analysis of local news is also very revealing: the diminutives *vecchietta* and *nonnina* are frequently used to refer to older women, in particular to underline their eccentricity. The paradox between the women's fragility, pointed out by the diminutive, and an action that defies the physical and behavioral limitations imposed by female old age is likely to create a comic effect and to exorcize, through ridicule, readers' fears both of decline and of marginalized individuals.

Patriarchal Discourses of Aging: A Close Reading

Collections of students' essays on aging-related issues and studies of children's drawings are enlightening with respect to patriarchal discourses on old age and grandparenthood. My observations, as well as those of others who have examined children's discourses, are by no means exhaustive; the sample essays and drawings are all by children and adolescents living either in small- to medium-sized towns or in rural areas.

In his commentary on approximately one hundred drawings of grandparent figures by first- and second-grade pupils from a Brescia elementary school, Giancarlo Tamanza argues that some sort of "gender affiliation" can be detected in drawings that represent one grandparent alone. The grandfather alone is chosen as subject by 26.8 percent of the boys and by 7.4 percent of the girls; the ratio is almost reversed for drawings of grandmothers, made for the most part by girls (25.9 percent vs. 9.8 percent boys). According to Tamanza, the prevalence of gender agreement between the represented subject and the author can be read as a result of the fact that "grandfather and grandmother represent for their grandchildren not only substitute parental care figures or occasional play and recreation mates, but also significant landmarks in children's identification process, through which they proceed in the construction of their personality."[18] Gender differentiation tends to be less evident when both grandparents or grandparents and grandchildren appear together in the picture. Gender identity is expressed "through the attribution of the most traditional (perhaps also stereotypical) elements of roles and actions, as well as by placing grandfather and grandmother in different settings."[19] The grandfather is usually placed in a natural setting, or at least outdoors, whereas the grandmother is inside the home, engaged in domestic tasks. A look at the most gender-differentiated results in the observation grids reveals that the grandfather is more often associated with playtime (66.7 percent vs. 5.6 percent for grandmothers). One hundred percent of the drawings representing an older person in a work-related context, however, portray a grandfather. Grandmothers are more often associated with caregiving roles, such as providers of services in 50 percent of the drawings that represent them with their grandchildren or recipients in 40 percent of those drawings. Not a single grandfather appears in drawings that represent caregiving situations. Grandfathers, though, appear twice as often in the "exchange of visits and of presents" category (50 percent vs. 25 percent). Finally, while older women seem to watch TV twice as much as men when grandchildren are not around (33.3 percent vs. 16.7 percent), only grandfathers share TV-viewing with their grandchildren (16.7 percent).

Grandparent figures described in the essays of Trieste area students share similar characteristics and gender-based specificities. The grandfather prevails in children's narrations, both as a compliant playmate with whom minor transgressions can be shared and as a teacher of disappearing crafts and skills, such as mushrooming, fishing, or woodcarving. The activities that engage grandfather and grandchild are most often presented as forms of emotional and technical apprenticeship to still uncontaminated natural wonders and resources. Although grandmothers and grandfathers alike can be sources of anecdotes about war or Partisan resistance times, and grandmothers can be loving figures that, having complete control over food preparation, produce unique treats, a recurring typology portrays them as skittish, irritable, and constantly complaining about their health. Being quite controlling, sometimes vindictive, they represent a potential threat to the harmonious and magic child-grandfather idyll. Too busy with household chores to find the time and desire to play, and made dull and self-deprecating by a lifelong lack of external stimuli and approval, they are, at bottom, insecure about their grandchildren's devotion. These are representative excerpts from essays by two middle-school students—a boy and girl—from a Slovenian-speaking area:

At dusk, we [my grandfather and I] walk back home together.
Dinner is waiting for us on the table. As a punishment for being away for the whole day, we have to set the table and eat everything. Grandpa often winks at me. After dinner, we start to play poker. This is my favorite game. He is the one who has taught me this game. Grandma often gets upset when

we play poker until late. Then Grandpa wishes me good night and we both go to bed.

I think my relationship with him is different from the one I have with Grandma. He understands me, is on my side, and relates to me as a friend and not as family.

I feel quite distant from my grandmother, instead. I notice this also in the way she looks at me. She often seems jealous of me and of Grandpa because she can't put up with the fact that I am closer to him than to her. I think this is true, in that Grandpa takes care of me, while Grandma does not behave the same way to me. I know, however, that I love them both; I often repeat this to Grandma, but she doesn't believe me. She claims that I only love Grandpa and have no consideration for her.[20]

I often play cards with Grandpa. When I was a little girl, he would let me win, but he would often win too. Grandpa is happy almost all the time.

Grandma is different: she is "moodier" and often gets upset. Grandma cooks, washes the dishes, and does the laundry and irons. When she has time, she also sews and gets annoyed at me, because I crack jokes with her, and she doesn't understand them. If I laugh, she doesn't, if I am serious, she is the one who laughs. She often makes mistakes; if I tell her, she replies that she is right and I am wrong....

Grandpa also used to tell me stories and I loved the tale of the rich cats. I knew it by heart. Grandma would never tell me stories. She says that I don't love her. I admit that Grandpa gets all my approval, but I love them both. She doesn't believe me but, let her think what she wants, I love them both.[21]

While both the drawings analyzed by Tamanza and the compositions written for the essay contests sponsored by the Associazione De Banfield reveal that age discourses based on personal experience and familiar elderly models are markedly gendered, the opposite can be said about children's and adolescents' imaginary of old age. When asked to comment on popular prejudice or literary quotes regarding old age or to discuss the status of older people in contemporary society, they most often report stale, secondhand critiques of older people's marginalization from production and of our society's responsibility for disregarding their needs and their wisdom. The underlying patriarchal nature of such generically and neutrally universal discourses on old age is exposed by the fact that, when asked to write or draw exemplary old-age scenarios, children choose to inscribe them in male bodies. The reason primarily lies in the sexist linguistic assumption that the masculine gender defines both male and female roles. In the Italian language the masculine noun *nonno* signifies both "grandfather" and "grandparent" and *vecchio* or *anziano* both "old man" and "elderly person." However, no effort can be traced in the essay and drawing assignments—thus on the part of Italian educators—to compensate for this morphological disregard of gender specificity. It is hardly surprising that in response to essay titles like "What does having a grandfather/grandparent mean to you?" and "Myself as an old man/person," or to a drawing assignment inspired by a real case reported by Abruzzi newspapers, which read "An older man/elderly person has graduated at age 78: What are your impressions?"[22] Italian students, although in daily contact with a primarily female aging society, were much more likely to have male old age than female old age in mind when trying to articulate, possibly for the first time, their own age discourses, thus laying the foundations of their age consciousness.

A close reading of adult patriarchal discourses on aging proves the spectrum of interwoven ageism and sexism in Italian culture to be quite wide-ranging and complex. The first two texts I will examine are concerned with gendered constructions of age classes. Their discourses are strikingly different, in that they are forty years apart in time: the first article was written in 1959, the second in 1999. The second, and far more numerous, group of texts consists of gerontology handbooks or conferences papers and articles on old-age issues. They share an essentialist approach to women's aging: in their effort to stress women's better adjustment to old age, they locate the reasons for this adjustment in women's "nature." Some of them, possibly a third group overlapping with the second, point out the relationship between women's "aging ways" and traditional female roles and life styles.

As stated by its title, which translates as "A long alternating competition: Now the man is older, now the woman is older," the 1959 commentary, published in the newspaper *Corriere della sera*, sees men and women racing in the life marathon, advancing and falling behind in an oscillating pattern of maturation, depending on which sex is "in charge" of the other at which point of the life course. The opinions, frivolously expressed in a fictional drawing-room conversation, are obviously scientifically unfounded. They reflect, nevertheless, established associations of female dependency and childhood and of female maturity and maternal instinct, which have often marked the history of women's life courses, as discussed in the previous historical introduction. According to the journalist Virgilio Lilli "women are born mature"[23] because, as shown by their childhood role-playing with dolls, women instinctively play maternal roles. Precociousness is not confined to their "instinct"; girls are better pupils than boys at school, and their physiological development precedes that of boys. However, "women's mental development definitively stops after age twenty, while men's goes on until past forty."[24] Whatever a woman is instinctively endowed with at birth, a man acquires in the course of life, through his *Bildung*. It is written in "the difference between man's and woman's natures" that the adult woman should carry "residues of childhood that disappear in a man."[25] At a certain point in life, acquired paternal instinct becomes stronger than inborn maternal instinct. As a consequence of this, "an older man can call a woman his age 'my little one' without exposing himself to ridicule, and allow her to indulge in whims and childish displays."[26] As for physical aging, external signs of decay are definitely more precocious in women: a woman's old age is marked by the end of her reproductive phase and an older woman is never an acceptable partner to a man. In advanced old age, however, women seem to recover strength from their maternal roles: in fact, "old wives who hold up old husbands are a common daily sight in the streets."[27] The fact that, at this stage, "women are more charged with maternal instinct than men with paternal instinct,"[28] allows them to cross the finish line as winners.

There is no similar gallant concession to the "gentle sex" in the second article, written by Furio Colombo for *La Repubblica* in 1999. Colombo's argument is that today's "male-female youth universe"[29] is not as "mythical" as the early twentieth-century all-male notion of youth and cannot, therefore, express a youth culture. "The triumph of youth, at the beginning of the century," he writes, "was an exclusively male triumph. 'The aggressive gesture, the feverish insomnia, the athletic stride, the dangerous leap, the beautiful ideas that kill, the contempt of women' in the Futurist manifesto are not fit for the mass of young people who are waiting at the threshold of adulthood, at the end of this century. . . . Now more than half of the mass of waiting young people are women. . . . [Y]outh is no longer the feverish symbol of the world to come and of the action to be accomplished since it is no longer male youth."[30] According to Colombo, the mixed world of youth is a mysterious incoherent conglomerate, incapable of inspiring "art, culture, worldview, anticipation of the future, tension, poetry."[31] As for feminism, it was "an adult revolution"[32] that has not changed our way of looking at the youth myth.

Numerous texts that deal comprehensively with old-age issues have been published recently. An examination of Italian gerontological literature is outside the scope of this study; and the discussion of both the statistical data on older women's conditions and of Italian women's stances on old-age issues is deferred to the following sections of this chapter. But it may be worthwhile here to identify the gender stereotypes that some how-to books on aging convey. Much like the journalist who proclaimed, nearly half a century ago, women's victory at the finish line of human life, there is a tendency today to perceive women's greater longevity as a more adequate way of aging and to associate women's more successful adjustment to old age with the cultural models that inspired contemporary older women's *Bildung*. According to these models—which reflect the transition from a nineteenth-century to a twentieth-century patriarchal order—a woman's "life energy" is attributed, first of all, to her being in tune with natural processes, which explains her better management of concrete, daily details, her instinct for preservation, her better grasp of the life-death cycle. She is also helped by the fact that she has been trained to endure sacrifice and scale down expectations and that, throughout her life, she has been sheltered from the pressures of employment and of the public arena.

In the two pages devoted to "sexual differences," the authors of the essay *Bisogni, opportunità, servizi per la terza età* (1992) suggest that the reason why women live longer, are more active (although in a personal sphere), and maintain a more consistent role handling family responsibilities may lie in the fact that, "being stronger and less hampered by cultural conditioning, they preserve their power, which is more connected to family than to social relationships."[33] According to a study of participation in a Genoa senior center, the women who visit the Social Center present, on the whole, a higher degree of involvement in social life, a higher spirit of initiative and vitality.[34] According to another survey, the reason for women's better adjustment to the third age is that "their not being involved in specialized jobs and not identifying with productive processes, has led them, through a long apprenticeship to sacrifice, to a greater control over little realities that are to be lived and tested."[35] A widespread belief is that the lack of a professional role in their adulthood "would turn into an opportunity and a privilege (in comparison with males) in old age; a woman would therefore be better equipped than a man, because she is in better control of her time."[36] In a special issue on retirement politics that appeared in the leftist newspaper *Il manifesto* in 1987, we read that "[i]t is retirement that makes a man an 'old man.' The same does not happen to a woman, for whom old age has much to do with her physical appearance but also with the loss of her role in the family. When she is expelled from the kitchen, when she can no longer manage the household, that's when a woman ages."[37]

The assumption that women age better is often condescendingly attached to the more ancient mystique of women's superiority. In *La vecchiaia può attendere* (1998), a collection of reflections on old age by Arrigo Levi, the journalist titles the short chapter devoted to women: "Women are better than men." This is how the opening paragraph reads: "One cannot say that they do not think. They do think occasionally; but they rely more on instinct than on reason, and reach instant conclusions on the most complex issues. What's worst is that oftentimes they are even right. Moreover, they pass from one life season to the next with admirable ease. Or perhaps they can lie better to others and to themselves. I decided I had better hear the opinion of a man, a friend, someone my age or even younger."[38] At the conference L'anziano protagonista nella città e nella società (Older people as protagonists in the city and in society), held in Turin in 1999, leading Italian gerontologist Francesco Antonini, referring to the dramatic increase in women's life expectancy in the course of the twentieth century, claimed that "the new century will be made by women, who are creative and will have longer lives to develop their creativity. We will have another Renaissance with an additional fifty percent of creative people."[39]

The emerging myth is that of a "feminized old age," a sort of counterpoint to the old comparison of women's dependency to that of children. This myth is not only based on numbers but also on the belief that women's responses to decline are more effective. Although there may be some truth to this assumption, and women's larger presence in the older population definitely marks old-age culture, in particular that of the fourth age, women lack public old-age models in the arts, sciences, and politics, as discussed in the previous chapter. One might say that there is an ironic parallel between women's mass longevity and their absence from history.[40] Up to the present generation of Italian people over 65–70, most women have aged without substantially modifying their adult life patterns, and their marginality to public responsibilities can be read as marginality to historical time.

The homologizing of male and female life patterns in the direction of women's roles and attitudes (statistics show that Italian men are much more cooperative in household chores in their old age, and more involved in child care, if they have grandchildren) is but another patriarchal myth, whose purpose is to conceal older women's specific needs and daily hardships. As we shall see in more detail shortly, older Italian women, often impaired by poor health, urban isolation, and financial restrictions and unaware, both as housewives or as jugglers of domestic and extra-domestic work, of such notions as "retirement" or "age of ease," may well be superior in their longevity; this does not mean, however, that when they age they are also superior in the "art of living."[41]

Women's Debate on Gender- and Aging-Related Issues

As discussed in the previous section, recent gerontological literature typically features either a chapter on "sexual difference"[42] or gender-differentiated statistical data.[43] The few lengthy publications that focus on women's old-age issues are, for the most part, health education manuals on menopause[44] or sociological surveys based on interviews with a female age cohort. While the gerontological literature on menopause often contains critiques of prejudice and of current medical practices voiced by most western women today, sociological surveys focus on more specifically Italian problems. A significant number call attention to the conditions of middle-aged and young-old women as caregivers of older family members.[45] The leading researcher in this field is Isabella Paoletti, who applies an ethnomethodological framework of discourse analysis to her study of female caregivers, as well as to her wider-ranging research on the social construction of older women's identity. In this second study, titled *Being an Older Woman: A Study in the Social Production of Identity* (1998), she is particularly interested in the conflict between older women's needs and the responses of local institutions. *Vediamo passare le stelle: Storie di vita di donne anziane sole* (1992) is a collection of 142 interviews with women over sixty who live alone in Milan, introduced by a perceptive summary of themes common in them. These interviews, which are a useful instrument for investigating the influence of education on older women's self-representations, expectations, and priorities in the early 1990s, will be analyzed more closely later in this chapter.

The Italian woman in her fifties is the object of several sociological studies. In *Le ragazze di cinquant'anni* (1999), sociologist Marina Piazza focuses on a distinct segment of Italian women. Although the title of her study refers to an entire age cohort, the women that she interviewed are mostly Milan professionals who were born in the late 1940s-early 1950s and whose lives have been bombarded by an extremely wide range of stimuli, challenges, and pressures. Although they married and had children according to traditional expectations, they were affected by the social revolution of the 1970s, campaigned in favor of divorce and abortion laws, and struggled with career, child-raising, and marriage break-ups. Today, they are a "sandwich generation," pressured by the demands of their children and of their older parents, yet molded by such challenging lifestyles into more creative, dynamic, and involved individuals than their male counterparts.[46] Statistical data on the 45–50 age bracket can be found in a document on "women's ages" prepared by DS (Democratic Left Party) Women. According to a survey of both married and cohabiting couples, 80 percent of 45- to 50-year-old women live with a male partner. Many of them, mostly in the north, are separated or divorced; 9 percent are single parents; 5 percent live alone; some are already widowed.[47]

An interesting perspective on women's maturity is offered by *Amore e pregiudizio: Il tabù dell'età nei rapporti sentimentali* (1988), a study of age-role reversal in love relationships, which is based on literary cases and famous couples, as well as on interviews with ordinary people. Pedagogist and writer Elena Gianini Belotti—whose old-age novel is analyzed in the second part of this study—reads today's acknowledgement of mature women's seductiveness as a result of a change in the identities and life choices of fifty-year-old women rather than in female age codes. Even though she views women's claiming the right to love younger men as "a subversive gesture toward the norms that imprison them,"[48] she doubts that this trend will lead to a less image-oriented assessment of women and to the acceptance of older women's sexuality, and, ultimately, of their presence. Gianini Belotti stresses, however, the effects of a decreased social emphasis on fecundity and of new procreation experiments. As a result of the decline of "the patriarchal alliance for the division and the exchange among men of young and fertile women,"[49] and of convenience-based or family-arranged marriage, women's fulfillment is no longer confined to reproduction and to projection on their male offspring, and young men's attraction for mature women will be expressed rather than suffocated by the cultural taboos that label such relationships as incestuous. From this perspective, the younger man-older woman relationship embodies a desirable complementarity and conciliation of masculinity and femininity in balanced individuals.

As for the debate on old-age politics and the organization of older women's interest groups, they take place more at a European level than at the national one.[50] The most active older women's association is the Italian chapter of OWN-Europe (Older Women's Network), which has played a crucial role in the development of the European association. Following pioneering contacts between Maria Teresa Marziali, an officer of the Equal Opportunities Office of the City of Perugia and a London colleague, a network linking older women's associations across Europe was established in 1993. Their goal is to give older women a voice by developing social and cultural programs to meet their needs, promoting intergenerational communication, and tackling policy issues relating to pensions, housing, and continuing education both locally and in connection with European institutions.[51] A variety of research projects undertaken by the Italian chapter of OWN-Europe in the past decade is well documented on their website and in a number of publications.[52] Two publications in particular, *Generazioni di donne* (2001) and *Older Women Acting* (1997), report the results of cultural initiatives that are, unfortunately, located almost exclusively in the Umbria region. *Generazioni di donne* publishes interviews and reports events and activities involving women of different generations—among them, the organization of local festivals and the teaching of traditional skills to younger women. The association "Generazioni," whose aim is to create intergenerational actions that embrace the point of view of women living in rural areas, has also launched courses on the use of the new communication media, directed specifically at younger and older women.

Older Women Acting illustrates role-playing activities focusing on age identities in drama workshops in various nations. The Italian group involved in this initiative is AIDA (Association of Older Active Women), a cultural association that has promoted, among other things, singing and creative writing workshops.

Italian Feminism and Age Studies

Although older women's interest groups testify to the need to promote cultural resources and policies that take into account women's specific concerns, building a bridge between the experience of feminism and a markedly gendered old-age experience does not seem to be an easy task. The premises for bridging this gap are there, since the women who took part in the 1970s movement are entering the third age today. Also, the dismantling of the patriarchy's dualistic logic by Italian feminist philosophers (in particular, Luisa Muraro and Adriana Cavarero), and their emphasis on female genealogy "as a social and symbolic practice of countermemory and cultural generativity"[53] should undermine the idea of a youth/old-age opposition and, consequently, of older people's "otherness."

A few scattered special issues of feminist journals have been specifically devoted to age issues: a pioneering 1986 issue of *Memoria* titled *L'età e gli anni: Riflessioni sull'invecchiare*, and *L'età inventata*, a less indepth survey in *Leggendaria* in summer 1999. They feature demographic reports, cultural history surveys, philosophical considerations, critiques of paintings and novels, and responses to foreign contributions.

The debate opened by *Memoria* was, in my opinion, the first significant step toward a feminist reflection on aging in Italy. The introductory essay argues that people who were affected by the cultural revolution of the '60s and '70s have a strong generational identity, in that they tend to see the different age classes as separate and in conflict with one another. They cherished the illusion that they could remain in a young adult phase, devoid of the dependencies of both childhood and old age. Life passages seemed to "threaten the political optimism which in the movement was sustained by the feeling of an adolescence that, it was discovered, could be prolonged."[54] This delusion has had a profound impact on the Italian feminist movement, which exploded alongside the 1968 protest movement and therefore prized youth, which came to symbolize change.[55] In the collective formative journey these women undertook, "older women and young girls were always left by the roadside"[56] and intergenerational continuity was rejected. Antonella Pinnelli's conclusion to her demographic survey on women's longevity is that the most profound effect of failing to establish a continuity of values and relationships among generations is the lack of continuity among the different phases of one's own life.[57]

Simonetta Piccone Stella calls women's fifties "a decade without citizenship," during which they lose their visibility: on the outside, their presence is no longer acknowledged by the male gaze; on the inside, they find it difficult to come to terms with "the process, the partiality, the hybrid, the gradualness of change."[58] This "difficulty in aging" results from a number of factors: changes in social norms, changes in cosmetic and medical practices, as well as the impact of feminism. Emancipation from roles has also been an "emancipation from time," whose "liberating effects could be seen right away in faces, bodies, behavior."[59] A particularly significant factor in Italy is the fact that today women in their fifties are still daughters. It has been estimated that, while in 1951 only one out of ten women in their fifties had their mother still living, at the beginning of the 1990s, seven out of ten were daughters of living mothers, and more than three out of ten were at sixty.[60] As daughters in a culture where family authority roles and caregiving expectations are strong, they are "authorized, on some levels, not to be mature"[61] and encouraged to maintain strong emotional and practical connections with their parents. Since their mothers' social responsibilities were limited, public life, career, and full development of potential are only partially mapped terrains in which social control has not yet consolidated. "How much do I earn at my age? Where am I? As long as a less emancipated female witness is still alive," Piccone Stella writes, "we are not forced to take stock."[62] The rejection of the female models handed down by their mothers and grandmothers and the partly arrogant, partly naïve exaltation that derives from exploring uncharted territories, have reinforced the notion of being *donne senza precedenti* (women without a past, as well as without precursors), a definition used by Paola Masi in a 1997 article in *donnawomanfemme* to define the generation affected by feminism.[63]

Conflictual though it may be, the interest in women's aging is, for feminist criticism, primarily an interest in generations and genealogies. Genealogy proves to be not only the main age-related interest of feminism, but also—as a landmark in women's construction and/or rejection of their gender lineage—one of its most complex and contradictory issues. As Rosi Braidotti states in *Nomadic Subjects* (1994), a feminist genealogy is "a discursive and political exercise in cross-generational female bonding," whose "political urgency" she underlines.[64]

Whereas Anglo-American proponents of feminist age studies, in particular Kathleen Woodward, are starting to focus on three-stage models of generational continuity that involve grandmothers as well as mothers and daughters, in the European feminist debate the most common configuration of the need to formulate a theoretical female genealogy and a feminine symbolic system is still the "mother-daughter" metaphor.[65] A significant Italian contribution in this area is the notion of *affidamento* (fostering, entrustment). Arising from the need to reassess traditionally static and oppressive mother-daughter relationships as more dynamic and open-ended ones, the practice of *affidamento*, discussed in publications of the Milan Women's Bookshop Collective, involves the establishment of a preferential, formative support relationship between more powerful, informed, and experienced women and younger and less established ones.[66] However, as Carol Lazzaro-Weis remarks, critics of *affidamento* argue that this theory "not only reproposes old structures and schemata but avoids dealing with women's inherited problems" and that "[t]he figure of the older mentor woman who replaces the Omnipotent Goddess that feminists deconstructed also reiterates the standard good mother (me) versus bad mother (them) categories."[67]

As a consequence of the difficulties that women scholars have encountered in their struggle to gain authority and resources, the conciliation of mothers' empowerment and daughters' growth and visibility inside the Italian academy is one of the most burning issues of the intergenerational debate. As observed earlier, the theme of intergenerational relationships was ignored in the first phase of the 1970s women's movement. When, in the late eighties, the theme of *le giovani* (younger feminists) emerged in the Italian debate, it was approached as "an accessory to the (double) theme of transmission-tradition."[68] In the late 1990s, a number of feminist students and younger scholars started a network called "30something." Between 1999 and 2000, they organized gender studies conferences at the major Italian universities, with the intent of creating opportunities for visibility and intergenerational exchange. Invited to participate as interlocutors in projects that they had not "authorized," older feminist scholars have been called to discuss and negotiate established mentor-disciple roles and fund-allocation practices that younger scholars consider stifling and unfair. According to feminist historian Paola Pallavicini, national coordinator of "30something," the debate launched by the network is a vital space for the growth of younger women scholars—who have been treated quite condescendingly by older feminist colleagues—and, ultimately, for fruitful cultural transmission and regeneration. She laments that the relational modes older Italian feminists establish with younger women "are based on a principle of reproduction of what is already given (their own experience) aiming at identity mimesis rather than open to a shareable present."[69] She argues that "'old' Italian feminists easily dismiss 'new' feminists, and are so deaf to their presence that they prefer theorizing a generational relation with an indefinite younger Other that is always to come (an entity so abstract and selfless that it cannot generate contradictions, not even imaginative ones), rather than interrogating themselves seriously on the reasons why young feminists are excluded (though certainly not absent) from their present political spaces."[70]

Demographics

The remaining sections of this chapter aim to organize information and expert opinions into a faithful picture of demographic presence, life conditions, social roles, and cultural expectations of older women in present-day Italy.

When considered from a developmental perspective ranging over the last century, the data on Italian women's life expectancy are impressive. Italy had the highest change in female life expectancy at birth (232 percent) during the secular shift (1880s–1980s): from 33.9 years in 1880 (the lowest figure among developed countries) to 78.6 in the 1980s.[71] In the 1880s, only in Italy, Greece and Bulgaria, among western countries, did over-60 men outnumber over-60 women. In Italy the ratio was only slightly in favor of men: 9.0 vs. 8.9 percent. By the 1950s, the whole of Europe was demographically fairly uniform in having a larger number of women in the higher and highest age groups. In Italy, the balance was 2 percentage points in favor of women (13.1 vs. 11.3), whereas today, for every 100 males that reach age 65, there are 144 females; this becomes 176 per hundred males past age 75.[72] As for the younger/older women ratio, while 15 percent of Italian women are under fifteen years of age, over-sixty women represent 24 percent of the Italian female population.[73]

In 2002, life expectancy in Italy was calculated to be 76 years for men and 82.6 for women. Female life-expectancy figures were slightly higher only in Japan (84.2) and France (83.1).[74] European women's higher longevity, which has increased since the 1930s, owing to fewer deaths in childbirth and lower fertility, can be explained on the basis of several factors, among them harder work conditions for males in the past and the impact of the two World Wars on male population numbers.[75] One must remember, however, that female longevity records are held by women who were born at the beginning of the twentieth century and had different lifestyles than younger female age cohorts: they drank little, did not smoke, and did not suffer from career pressures.

Comparing recent male and female figures regarding marital status also bears some relevance to the study of the living conditions of age cohorts in a gender perspective.[76] As a result of a number of factors—

women's longevity, a relatively large number of women in Europe who never married,[77] and a greater tendency to remarry among men—61.4 percent of men vs. 14.8 percent of women are married among the 80+ population. In the northwest of Italy, where we find a higher concentration of older people and less traditional family patterns, the percentage of over-70 widows is higher than that of married women.[78] As a result of high female widowhood rates, older women are much more likely to live alone than men. In Italy, a country where there are fewer singles than in northern Europe, and young adult people tend to live with their parents longer, half of the single population is made up of older women.[79] According to 2000 figures, over 80 percent of the older people who live alone in Italy are women.[80] An impressive female old-age record in the northwest of Italy is the fact that since the 1980s approximately 80 percent of single households in Turin have consisted of older women living alone.[81]

Life Quality and Patterns

Longevity does not mean high life quality; for one thing, older women are likely to suffer from health problems more persistently than men. Living alone, on the other hand, does not necessarily imply isolation. As discussed earlier, older Italian people are at the center of an often-dense web of exchange and support based on family relations, especially with their children.[82] In most cases, it is the family that takes responsibility for the care of the disabled older people.

Although a discussion of health issues or of present and projected forms of elderly care and institutionalization is beyond the scope of this study, two gender-related facts should be pointed out: approximately 70 percent of older people receiving care in public residential facilities are women (corresponding to almost 2 percent of the older population),[83] and 70 percent of the assistance to the disabled older people is handled by women.[84] As proved by earlier-mentioned studies, the caregiver—typically a female in her fifties, sometimes in her sixties—is quite often afflicted by serious physical and psychological health problems and needs special assistance herself, from such services as professional and voluntary caregivers, daily centers, and counselors.

Older women's economic status is generally worse than older men's. Women's pensions are lower than men's in most cases: their benefits derive from shorter and less remunerative careers or consist of survivorship annuities. As with the United Kingdom, Greece, Portugal, and Belgium, Italy has different minimum pensionable ages for men and women (65 vs. 60). According to the most recent pension reform laws,

Italian women will retire at 65 years of age starting in 2016.[85] Their incidence of post-retirement work income is much lower than in the case of men (3.1 percent vs. 13.2 percent).[86]

Italian studies on women's occupations from a cohort perspective identify at least three successive generations: the generation of full-time housewives (born between 1900 and 1929), that of women who went back to work after childrearing (born between 1930 and 1944), and that of double presence—women who work both at home and outside the home (born between 1940 and 1964).[87] Therefore, most Italian women who are over 65–70 at the turn of this century had housewife careers or left their jobs at a young age. An interesting case is that of never-married mature women, among whom the percentage that are economically active is not as high as one would expect because in the past single women seldom left their families of origin. According to a 1990 study, among western countries, in Italy, Belgium, and Greece, only about one-third of never-married women aged 50–64 were employed.[88]

With the generation born between 1948 and 1953—the transitional aging cohort to which a case study is devoted in the second part of this book—housewife careers significantly decrease; still, in this age bracket nonworking women are nearly half (48 percent) of the female population. While in the total female population 36.7 percent of women are employed, in this age group, 45 percent of women are still active and 7 percent are retired.[89] Though the rate of 45- to 49-year-olds among the total population of employed women in Italy is higher than in any other female age cohort, it is one of the lowest in Europe.[90]

Italian women are less educated than men, and the gap increases in the south and the islands. As discussed earlier, the education level decreases with age for both sexes in all parts of the nation. Very few older people earned a high school or a college degree, but the number of women who did is definitely lower than the number of men (8 percent vs. 14.2 percent).[91]

Older Women's Relationships to Time and Space

When looking at older Italian women's relationship to concepts of time and space, one should keep in mind that, as discussed in the historical introduction, male and female socialization models have traditionally been very different. Another important consideration is that 60- to 65-year-old women's behavior tends to be more similar to that of the preceding age bracket than to that of the succeeding group.[92] Due to the transitional status of Italian old-age culture, recent studies on male and female use of time and space may quite easily contradict one another, as a consequence not only of geographic and sociological variables, but also of the fact that some studies may emphasize changed old-age lifestyles, and others focus on the legacy of ingrained gender biases. While many recent articles on Italian old-age culture tell us that older women's daily routines no longer differ from those of men and that they attend lectures and courses, go to the cinema, visit museums and exhibits in larger numbers than men,[93] other studies reveal persisting areas of gender-differentiated use of both private and public time and space. One of them is the 1997 publication *Anziani in Italia*, which reports the results of a comprehensive ISTAT (National Institute of Statistics) survey on Italian older people. Most of the data in this section are drawn from the 1997 ISTAT survey.

The house is the primary location of the older person's day. If older people spend approximately 19 hours at home, in highly urban areas women stay at home a couple of hours longer than men.[94] When not at home, women tend to visit other people's houses, whereas men spend more time outdoors. There is no hour of the day when the majority of women are outdoors; the highest percentage is on Sunday mornings (46.7 percent), which is still much lower than the percentage of men outdoors at that time (73.5 percent).[95] Sunday morning outings are usually motivated by the obligation to attend Catholic Mass. Interestingly, religious practice undergoes a reversal in old age. Whereas more women attend church at least once a week in the overall population (58.6 percent vs. 37.6 men),[96] after age 75 women go to church less often, and men's involvement in religious activities increases.[97]

While female domesticity increases with age, men's orientation outside remains. In most cases, women have not had the opportunity to establish friendships at the workplace. Most older Italians do not belong to any associations (80 percent), but women's participation rates are even lower (87 percent non participating), with the exception of religious groups, such as parish associations.[98] The ethics of service and the desire to feel useful continue to inspire women's social lives (support of their working children through child care and small household chores, assistance to parents and in-laws or to other non-cohabitant older people, volunteer work). In general, women maintain regular connections with relatives (1–2 visits a week)[99] and—more frequently in smaller communities than in urban areas—with neighbors.

The notion of "spare time" has little relevance among women who were raised to conform their lives to other people's needs. If free time is in second place, after sleep, in retired men's daily routines, women's priorities are house and family care. Interviews with today's older people show that although retired men devote more time to household chores, their average daily contribution—which is lower than that of female teenagers—is 1.5 hours, vs. 5 hours for women aged 65–74.[100] According to the earlier-mentioned Democratic Left Women's survey of older women's conditions and needs, 78 percent of women over age 75 are still involved in some form of caregiving activity for their families, while more than one-third of older women do not receive any household help, either from relatives or from the outside.[101] The need to complete demanding household chores under less-than-optimum physical conditions often forces women to limit the time for physical activities, not only for leisure.

Women's participation in recreational events (public lectures, exhibits, cinema, travel, sports) is, however, dramatically on the rise. For example, women have higher attendance rates than men at universities of the third age. The attendance percentages in "general culture" courses offered by these universities are 70.3 percent for women and 65.5 percent for men.[102] We can predict, moreover, that, owing to the dramatic changes in women's lifestyles during the last century, the cultural revolution projected for older people born after World War II will have a much greater impact on women's use of free time and public space than on men's. In particular, older women's reading indexes are likely to increase, given the fact that there are more female than male readers among the young and adult population. This projection must be seriously considered when investigating the rising interest in old-age scenarios in contemporary women's fiction.

LOW-PROFILE OLD-AGE IDENTITIES

In past representations of female old age, the notion of women's "superiority" appeared to be a fairly widespread topos. Psychological profiles of the older Italian woman reveal that she faces illness and death better than men and that she maintains a more consistent commitment to family relationships and obligations. We have also noted that much of the positiveness of older women's behavior could be traced to the formative years of their young adult and adult lives, for example to their education in service, self-abnegation, and propriety. In addition to, and in contrast with ingrained patterns, an important reality should be considered: for most women aging corresponds to a "forced emancipation" once lifelong family references are lost. Single status has hardly ever been considered a woman's choice in the Italian tradition. Aging is often experienced as a challenge in relation to the quality of life that must be maintained "at the cost of a hidden vulnerability due to the psychological discomfort"[103] that women suffer as frail, often ailing individuals living alone.

Interviews with older Italian women in the 1990s reveal that they are far less satisfied with their lives than men: they complain more about the lack of friends and of a fulfilling social life[104] and are, in general, more prone to depression. Depression is usually related to bad health, solitude, and mourning.[105] Most importantly, women are less satisfied than men with their past. In a 1992 survey, 31 percent declared they had accomplished only few or none of the goals they had in life. Several women emphasized the hardships and the lack of opportunities in their lives. Many expressed their regret for being forced to quit school due to family financial restraints or to the moral obligation of foster-mothering younger siblings.[106] A less recent survey (1984) of "regrets and projects" of older Romans pointed out a combination of vitality and frustration in older women's perspectives on their lives.[107] This reveals, in my opinion, older women's greater difficulty in reconciling different time dimensions in their lives: on the one hand they are better adjusted than men to their present old-age conditions; on the other, their life reviews are less satisfactory.[108] In their recollections, extra-domestic work, usually confined to their younger years, appears as a financial necessity, hardly ever a liberating choice or a form of social participation. More women than men regret having married, feeling that they had to renounce their personality and sacrifice to family well-being. They have fond memories of childrearing but are also aware that they had to sacrifice for their children. On the other hand, unmarried women are even more dissatisfied: they complain about lack of financial comfort as well as missing study and career opportunities.

One of the most comprehensive samples of interviews with older Italian women is the previously mentioned collection of interviews with 65+ women living alone in Milan, *Vediamo passare le stelle*. It is a gold mine of reflections on female old-age identity that deserves a closer examination because of its focus on a circumscribed but growing segment of the Italian population: older—in particular fourth-age—females living alone in an urban setting, most often in northern Italy. The results of these interviews were published in 1992 in a book.

A feature that emerges from these interviews is the fact that the education in self-effacement and the pressure to please motivate many older women to "rationalize" their predicament. Their declarations of self-sufficiency, for example, often mask a stronger desire not to cause inconvenience to their children.[109] These interviews reveal other forms of rationalization and attempts to control and make sense of a reality from which they feel estranged or that they find too demanding. Self-sufficiency is often projected beyond the limits of one's existence: many women express their intent to provide for all funeral and burial expenses. As a result of hypochondria, surges of self-centeredness conflict with and must be managed within a generally low self-profile. The interviewees' high investment in their families' well-being leads them to demand a high return. Not being used to voicing their needs and desires openly, however, they often find consolation in guilt-inducing behavior. Complacency with one's self-sufficiency often becomes a "theorization of self-segregation,"[110] and is complemented by political conservatism, social prejudice, and a general bad disposition toward their community. Their impertinent quarrelsomeness is often the reflection of deep frustration and bitter pride in their solitude.

Another interesting angle is the interviewees' relation to time, to their pasts, presents, and futures. In their reminiscences, references to their subordinate female condition are almost always internalized in terms of value: this condition is seldom condemned or criticized.[111] No matter how short or long their work experiences outside the house have been, these experiences usually occupy a large space in the subjects' recollections of the past. As for their perceptions of the present and of the future, those are inspired by a dreary realism, in which dailiness and detail swell to exaggerated proportions.[112] Older women who live alone seem to be obsessed by their relationship with "things," and tend to overcome their anguish through a sterile hyperactivity. In the present, they usually identify with a standardized old-age condition marked by unavoidable daily chores and deadlines.[113] Their view of the future usually lacks not only a perspective on the continuity of their existences, but also concrete positive projections onto new generations and their values, ethics, and ideas. Young people often display, in the subjects' opinions, criminal behavior: they can be disrespectful, violent, addicted to drugs, a real threat to a weak old woman who lives alone. In the best cases, they see the young as spoiled by affluence and by an overly permissive education.[114] As observed before, death is viewed more as a stage in the life cycle than as a transition to a new state: it is planned down to the last detail, and discussion of it is seldom accompanied by religious reflection, even in women who profess themselves believers and observant. They fear institutionalization because it involves the loss of independence and forces women into an extra-familiar community life to which they are not accustomed.[115]

Particularly if they are in the lower and lower-middle classes, older Italian women seldom complain about their economic status, even when their only source of income is a social pension. Accustomed in their young adult lives to making the best of their husbands' modest salaries and to sacrificing for their family's well-being, and perceiving themselves as socially marginal in the present, they don't appear to feel deserving of any extras and they don't strive for higher income.[116] Some complain that they will not be able to leave anything to their children.

The most frequent targets of their criticism are public institutions: local government, home assistance agencies, health care. The difficulty of keeping their apartments properly clean and maintained is a source of great frustration.[117] Some feel they are not "up to" the cultural initiatives that the city offers to older people because of their limited education.[118] They also do not feel welcome in traditional male-oriented senior hangouts like neighborhood cafés and bocce clubs.

Many aspects of women's old-age culture are reflected in these low-key profiles, in the defeatist, sometimes desperate "survivalism" that emerges from this set of interviews with women who are single not of their choice, after leading publicly marginal lives in their younger adult years. However, when our perspective on old-age culture embraces the entire composite picture revealed by the wide-ranging yet far-from-exhaustive overview conducted in this chapter, we must conclude that old-age identities are also, and more interestingly, reflected in the transitional, often hybrid roles with which contemporary Italian women are experimenting. The elements that make up this hybrid older Italian woman figure are varied and contradictory. She is single, divorced, widowed, childless, a grandmother, a late-age mother. She may be a feminist, a caregiver for older parents, a depressed ex-rebel, a sister, friend or life companion of an older woman of her own age, a role model to a younger female friend, an African immigrant's housemate. She is a person who does not spend as much time at home as her female age peers did in the past, a person who reads a lot, a young man's lover. The analysis of coexisting traditional and transitional models of female old age in turn-of-the-millennium Italian literature will, in fact, be the object of the second part of this study.

Part II
Texts

4
Female Lines in Family Narratives

Introduction

THE THREE NOVELS IN THIS CHAPTER ARE FAMILY HISTORIES THAT feature a female protagonist in her late seventies or eighties. They are fictional autobiographies in which a first-person narration spans more than a century of Italian family history. The internal focalization is fixed in the first two narratives and dual in the third novel, *Di buona famiglia*, which features two narratives of the same family history by sisters with differing perspectives. The narrative mode is confessional, and the structure is that of the life review. In *Di buona famiglia*, the life review is motivated by the need to justify and authorize one life version over the other. *Il catino di zinco* is a review of the deceased protagonist's life by her granddaughter; it is thus conceived as a memorial narrative, though in all three novels the narrator is deeply concerned with the testimonial value of the protagonist's memory.

From a life-review perspective, the protagonists' life courses are far from satisfactory. Whether they have actively pursued self-realization or just unconsciously longed for it, they have been thwarted by external restraints. Although none of these novels engages in a serious critical analysis of the protagonists' roles and choices, it is not difficult to identify the sexual and class politics that have inspired them. The protagonists' lives have been conditioned by some of the most widespread expressions of the Italian patriarchal discourse: confinement of the Mediterranean matriarch to overbearing domestic power roles, emphasis on family respectability and virtuous femininity as a marker of family decorum, Catholic condemnation of transgressive female behavior. The geographic and social contexts of the first and third novel are quite similar. *Va' dove ti porta il cuore* and *Di buona famiglia* are set in the northeastern border regions and focus on the negative impact on female development of upper-middle-class formal concerns. The protagonist of *Il catino di zinco*, born of a schoolteacher and an impoverished aristocrat's daughter, is a Roman lower-middle-class housewife. In her resentful, self-abnegating industriousness we can also read how Fascism's celebration of frugal and sacrificial wifehood and motherhood impacts the individual.

The protagonists' old age allows a broad chronological perspective. It is also emblematic of the endurance of female life models handed down from the past and of their incompatibility with present-day needs. Their alienated, postmodern old-age condition is rooted in their historical ignorance. Having led lives that were quite marginal to twentieth-century historical developments, and unaware of their causes and effects, they are indifferent to or confused by present issues and trends. Their social contacts are very limited, and their daily existences in houses they have inhabited for most of their lifetimes are absorbed by female domestic tasks and crowded with household junk and misplaced memorabilia. Although these protagonists are deeply concerned with cultural transmission, their legacy is often in conflict with the worldviews, lifestyles, and needs of their heirs. Even when their grandchildren and other descendants deem heirlooms valuable, the significance they had for the protagonists and for their ancestors may be lost in the transmission.

Confined to domestic settings and conditioned by family hierarchical roles, relationships are often stifled, predictable, and reflexive. Both inter- and intragenerational family relationships are generally dissatisfactory and polluted by petty revenge or by forms of betrayal and concealment that can have tragic consequences on other family members and on their offspring. Parental and conjugal roles are quite defective; to change or rebel against family mandates earns punishment or disapproval. The protagonists' parents are generally negative figures, presented as distant, repressive, or overbearing. More remote ancestors are often haunting or eccentrically vicious presences. In their mother roles, the protagonists have definitely failed; they may even have inflicted irreparable traumas on their children. As wives, they have not established meaningful, fruitful communication with their generally distant, weak-willed husbands.

The protagonists are placed at the center of a genealogy and represent the pivot of a female cultural legacy that may be generically associated with a burdensome past. As grandmothers and great-aunts, these older women are the bearers of their families' vindictive "wounded Feminine." In her analysis of the three ages of woman as three aspects of the goddess—Maiden, Mother, Crone—Jungian psychoanalyst Naomi Ruth Lowinsky claims that "on the darker side, many grandmothers are a source of the wounded Feminine in a family; they carry a history of suffering and transmit it, consciously or not, to later generations."[1] Possibly to repair a disrupted family past and to purify thwarted female legacies, the protagonists of the first two novels reinvest in their granddaughters and turn to them as recipients of their final messages. In both cases (even in the more intense and productive grandmother-granddaughter bond and transmission presented in *Il catino di zinco*), the relationship with the representative of the younger generation is problematic. In fact, although the relationship is reparatory and projected toward an emancipated future, past misconceptions and abuses remain an integral and necessary part of the descendants' existential baggage.

As Lowinsky points out, a grandmother may stir a granddaughter's consciousness of her female ancestors as well as of her "potential development" throughout the entire life span.[2] In addition to providing both a retrospective and a prospective view, the grandmother figure embodies another paradox: she may unify the maternal line by separating mother and daughter, thus depolarizing their relationship. In the tragic female lines of our novels, however, this potentially healing function is pursued through the real or symbolic suppression of the intermediate genealogical link—the granddaughters' parents—and the appropriation of their roles. In *Va' dove ti porta il cuore*, the granddaughter's father is unknown, and her mother has been driven to mental imbalance and accidental death by the grandmother's faults; *Il catino di zinco* vividly presents an episode of maternal abuse of the granddaughter's father. The childless narrator of the first monologue of *Di buona famiglia* does not establish any emotional bond with her sister's children and grandchildren, but she tries hard and succeeds in stealing their affection away from her sister.

In *Di buona famiglia* the theme of suppressing and appropriating a family member's identity is complicated by the "sister plot." This novel's treatment of intragenerational family relationships from a life-course perspective deserves a separate theoretical introduction. The specific position of the horizontal sisterly bond in ascendant/descendent female genealogies will be discussed in the section devoted to the analysis of Bossi Fedrigotti's novel.

A few final remarks about the authors may be of interest to readers who are not familiar with Italian literature. Susanna Tamaro, born in Trieste in 1957, started her literary career as a writer of children's books. *Va' dove ti porta il cuore*, a best-selling phenomenon in the Italian literary market, is the book that made her famous. She lives on a farm and practices Zen Buddhism and martial arts. *Il catino di zinco* marks the beginning of Margaret Mazzantini's literary career. Mazzantini, a theater actress, was born in Ireland in 1961, and lives in Rome. With *Il catino di zinco* Mazzantini won two literary prizes: Campiello and Rapallo-Carige.[3] Isabella Bossi Fedrigotti, born in 1948 at Rovereto, near Trent, of an Austrian mother and an Italian father, is a writer and a journalist. She won the Campiello prize with *Di buona famiglia*.[4] The three authors, who were in their mid-thirties or forties when the novels discussed in this chapter were published, are much younger than their protagonists and have acknowledged the family models that inspired their characterization in interviews that followed the novels' publication. They are, in reality and symbolically, their protagonists' granddaughters or grandnieces. Although far from explicitly autobiographical, the novels express these young adult writers' interest in their past and attempt to identify the sources of their female identity and creativity in their own family histories.

Susanna Tamaro's *Va' dove ti porta il cuore*

Va' dove ti porta il cuore—the title of the English edition is *Follow Your Heart*—has been a best-selling phenomenon in twentieth-century Italian fiction. Five hundred thousand copies were sold in one year only. Two comparable titles in the Italian literary market of the last twenty years are Elsa Morante's *La storia* (1974) and Umberto Eco's *Il nome della rosa* (1980), sales of which reached 600,000 copies; but the success of both was due to more substantial cultural contents, more complex plots, and the authors' established reputations. The success of Tamaro's novel was immediate: 100,000 copies were snapped up in the first two months, before the publisher decided to invest in marketing. In fact, after reading it, people were going back to bookstores to buy copies to give as presents to their mothers, grandchildren, or friends.

The fact that the book has been a popular gift confirms its strong testimonial value. It is, in fact, a letter-diary that a grandmother bequeaths to her distant granddaughter, who is studying in the United States, as the elderly woman feels her death approaching. While we learn the names of all the other characters as the narration progresses, the name of the addressee of these pages is not revealed, as if the reader herself could be "a hypothetical grandchild of Grandma Olga's, thus a legitimate heir of her inner richness."[5] We anticipate that the granddaughter will find her grandmother's confession after her death, when she cleans out the house. Since it is an unsent letter, it is a free legacy, meant to relieve a burdensome generational heritage of guilt and suffering by means of a redeeming message: the invitation to follow one's heart.

The novel's protagonist and narrator is a woman in her late seventies. After suffering a stroke, she refuses not only to be hospitalized but also to inform her granddaughter in America. Deeply attached to the country mansion that has been her home for nearly half a century, she lives alone, visited daily by compassionate neighbors. She lives in contact with nature, taking care of roses, blackbirds that have fallen from the nest, her granddaughter's dog; she dreams that she will die falling "face-down among the zucchini"[6] in her vegetable garden. The domesticated nature of the garden is the terrain both of her memories of the idyllic symbiosis between grandmother and child granddaughter and of the spiritual energy on which the grandmother's legacy is founded.[7]

The grandmother's neat and sententious discourse seems to reflect "the propriety an old lady's clothes and thoughts."[8] The lady belongs to a respected upper-middle-class family of a borderland, the area near Trieste, in the northeast of Italy. This region, which became Italian only at the end of World War I, after the fall of the Austro-Hungarian Empire, is culturally closer to central Europe than to Italy. At the beginning of the twentieth century, women there enjoyed more freedom than in the rest of Italy: the Austrian code allowed women, for example, to own and manage property outside marital wardship.[9] When talking about the person who inspired his daughter in an interview, Tamaro's father said that Susanna's grandmother had a strong personality: she was the niece of a female tycoon and a relative of Svevo's. Although she was one of three women who obtained a *liceo classico* degree in Trieste in 1920, Tamaro's grandmother, faithful to tradition, had preferred a good marriage and had not pursued university studies.[10]

The protagonist's discourse reflects not only her social status but also her senility. Her enveloping and self-pitying sentimentalism is the result of the "senile bouts of sentiment"[11] of a mind that, according to another older character in Tamaro's narrative, is agitated by "very small, mediocre thoughts."[12] Sentences are often fragmented, rhetorical questions betray anxiety, thoughts are sometimes digressive, and transitions are marked by such phrases as "people say," "I have read," "I have found written." Hers is "a prehensile mind, one, though, that tires easily, can't hold a line of reasoning, loses the thread of an argument then finds it again, piles up readings, memories, experiences, ideologies."[13] Aware of the decline of her mental functions, Olga clings to the cornerstones of her world knowledge: the kitchen, old teachers, pop psychology, and end-of-millennium New Age spirituality. Here are some examples of the reflections and concerns that occupy her long, solitary days:

> You are right, I digress a lot, often enough I deliberately leave the main road and turn off into some narrow lane. I give the impression that I'm lost, and maybe it's not just an impression—I really am lost.[14]

> These pages I've written today seem like a cake put together from several different recipes, all sorts of disparate ingredients all mixed up. . . . Maybe

I've made a huge mess. If a philosopher were to read this, I imagine he wouldn't be able to restrain himself from marking up everything with his red pencil the way my old teachers used to do. "Inconsistent," he'd write. "Not to the point. Lacking logical support." Suppose a psychologist got hold of it! He could write a long essay on my failed relationship with my daughter, on everything I'm repressing.[15]

Olga's senility is a limiting physical condition and also the metaphor for contemporary humanity's fragility in the face of the barrage of information from popular mass-media culture. Older people are the main victims of this culture and of its indifferent multiplication and contamination of points of reference. Their free time, solitary and unproductive, is often devoted to TV, tabloid magazines, and talk shows; their fear of death is heavily exploited by the millenarian spirituality market. "You know," Olga writes, "the TV and newspapers are always talking about the proliferation of religious gurus.... It scares me to think about these self-appointed masters."[16]

Olga's discourse on present times is much more uncertain and vague than her recollections of the past. This could reflect the fact that an old woman's relationship to her present context is one of passive exposure to a barrage of information unfiltered by experience or dialogue with the community and unaffected by the need to make significant choices. In accordance with Butler's life-review theory, recent-memory impairment can also be attributed to the older person's full immersion in the reminiscence process.[17]

In her recollections, Olga surveys her entire life span: a solitary repressed childhood; marriage to a methodical, unemotional man; her passionate secret affair with a married man, by whom she has a daughter; her lover's death and her last years with her husband. Her only child, Ilaria, dies in a car accident, after learning about her illegitimate birth from her mother. She dies after an unhappy and muddled life, leaving a daughter born of a fleeting liaison. The little girl is adopted by her grandmother, who nurtures and supports her as if to compensate for her failures in Ilaria's upbringing. The intimate, magical rapport that bonded grandmother to granddaughter when the latter was a child has, however, deteriorated by the present time of the narrative. We learn that the twenty-year-old granddaughter is restless and sullen, unable to understand herself, in covert and aimless rebellion against her grandmother, who has consented to and financed her plan to spend a year studying abroad.

"... *unhappiness is generally transmitted through the female line* ..."

The "germ" of *Va' dove ti porta il cuore* is found in the title short story of the collection *Per voce sola*, published in 1991 and translated as *For*

Solo Voice, which foreshadows the structure and themes of the novel. In it, an older Jewish lady recounts her tragic life to her granddaughter: marriage to a husband who committed suicide after escaping from a Nazi concentration camp, and an unhappy, maladjusted daughter who also killed herself. The protagonists of this short-story collection—whose central theme is the evil inherent in life—are children and old people. The stories depict abuse and violence but are also karmic tragedies, in that "the horror gets into your very being, it's transmitted to your children and then your children's children . . . it goes on from generation to generation, very gradually it fades until it disappears altogether. It disappears exactly at the time another horror lies in wait."[18] Susanna Tamaro, who started her literary career as a writer of children's books, seems to search for a common ground between children's and adults' literature by representing life passages and the violation of the boundaries between childhood and adulthood that occurs when children are abused, neglected, or ignored, or when their imaginations are stifled. Being more fragile and sensitive, older people and children are the targets of human and cosmic injustice. On the other hand, childhood and old age are also the most romantically "transgressive" ages of life, according to Tamaro.[19] The Wordsworthian awareness of the child, whose eyes look "ancient, distant, wise,"[20] is later stifled by "an invisible shell . . . [that] continues to thicken throughout our adult life."[21] The deterioration of this armor in old age permits the recovery of one's inner voice. It motivates the grandmother in the novel to lift the veil of hypocrisy that had marred her life and to urge her adult granddaughter toward her childhood self, the letter's addressee: "The memories that surround me are memories of you as a child, so ingenuous and vulnerable and confused. It's her I'm writing to, to that child, not to the arrogant, defensive person of later years."[22]

The cosmic-genetic view of human tragedies and the final promise of a spiritual catharsis may distract the reader's critical eye from the sociopolitical roots of "evil." The most tragic developments in Olga's family are in fact ascribable to the impact of bourgeois education, founded on the respect of form and responsible for the distortion of emotions, life rhythms, and paths. Olga's reticence is, according to Tamaro, a metaphor for the silence of the European bourgeoisie when facing various forms of power abuse perpetrated in the twentieth century, from Fascism to ethnic conflicts in former Yugoslavia.[23]

The gendered connotation of a destructive middle-class legacy also needs to be emphasized. The grandmother's discourse reveals that evil is the result of the sexual politics that has marked the lives of middle-class women of different ages and generations throughout nearly a century of Italian social history. It is a *colpa* (fault) deriving from the limitations of bourgeois female education, masked as original sin and karmic tragedy. As such, it cannot be either grasped or atoned for by any woman in Olga's family.

Va' dove ti porta il cuore is not only a fictional autobiography, a narrative recollection spanning over eighty years of history, but also, and foremost, a study of generational conflicts. Generational ties are hereditary defects transmitted along the female line, which the book seeks to eradicate through its final message, the enticing call to listen to one's heart. "Unhappiness is generally transmitted through the female line," the grandmother writes, "passing from mother to daughter the way some genetic abnormalities do. And instead of diminishing as it passes, it steadily grows more intense, more ineradicable and profound."[24] In the genealogy presented in this novel, male characters are little more than walk-ons, necessary for reproduction and the transmission of "the destiny that environment and heredity impose on you."[25] Men have had "their professions, their politics, their wars"; their energy has been able to expand beyond "the bedroom, the kitchen, and the bathroom,"[26] to which women have confined their dissatisfaction. In contrast, female existences are characterized by a sort of "horizontal implosiveness," illustrated by the metaphor of the fireworks unable to soar up into the sky. At one point, Olga's rambling thoughts about feminism and unhappiness along the female line lead to a summer recollection: "Do you remember how every August we used to go out on the promontory to watch the fireworks over the ocean during *Ferragosto*? Every now and then we saw one that exploded before it got very high. Well, whenever I think about my mother's life, or my grandmother's, or the lives of so many people I know, that's the image that comes to mind—fireworks that fizzled down in the lower altitudes instead of climbing up to the sky."[27]

"*. . . my thoughts were focused on the most practical way of ending my life . . .*"

As we trace back the female genealogy of the novel, we learn that the great-grandmother, who "was rich and coveted a noble title, even though she was a Jewess and converted to boot,"[28] married an older man at sixteen, a baron who had been charmed by her talents as an opera singer. After producing the heir that the family's good name required, they lived together to the end of their days vexing and spiting each other, "the notion that some of the fault might lie within her"[29] never crossing the great-grandmother's mind.

As for Olga, her education was marked by a respect for appearances and the repression of emotions. Her growth is presented as a passage from childhood to old age, in which the spontaneity of growth is replaced by the predictability of death. The insistence on appearances and strict manners produces an association between deception and death that will influence Olga's destiny and that of her offspring. When she had to sit up straight at the table with her elbows against her sides, Olga recalls, "my thoughts were focused on the most practical way of ending my life."[30] Her first experience of death was one of emotional repression. One day she could not see her old dog anymore, and the only explanation given to her was that her dog had left because he was tired of her teasing. Afterward the dog became "a little dead thing"[31] that she has carried around inside for her whole life.

When Olga finished high school, her father opposed her intention to go to college, and she realized that her "supposed intelligence" was not taking her anywhere. She wasn't capable "of setting out on a long trip, of studying anything in depth."[32] At twenty-eight, she suddenly felt old and understood what direction her life was taking. Her parents would soon die, and she would be "left alone in a big house filled with books"; she would "take up embroidery to pass the time, or painting watercolors, and the years would fly away, one after the other."[33]

Religion seems to have been the only acceptable escape from a horizontal movement toward death. Through it, Olga could experience the verticality of the fall into sin and of mystical ecstasy. At the boarding school she attended as a child, the nuns kept a nativity scene set up year round. Each sheep stood for a pupil and, depending on the girl's behavior during the day, the little sheep was moved closer to or farther from Jesus's manger. On the opposite side of the hut there was a very deep chasm, over which the bad pupils' sheep dangled. Among them was Olga's, "always on the verge of falling."[34] Later, when she was around thirty, Olga turned back to religion for a period while trying to overcome depression. Her spiritual experience is not presented as ascent, but as "falling slowly . . . into mystical delirium," as the madness that strikes "all old maids and widows."[35]

When she experienced her first major depressive episode, Olga had been married for just a few years and had followed her husband to central Italy: her wifely duties were limited to planning meals and to weekly meetings with the wives of Augusto's colleagues at a downtown café. She had to give up her long, solitary walks, the limited autonomy that women of her social class were allowed in Trieste. In the meantime, the tragic events of the thirties and forties (Fascism, racial laws, the outbreak of World War II) barely touched her existence: Olga was occupied with the "microscopic movements"[36] of her spirit. Her encounter with love during a three-week stay at the hot springs to cure depression took her by surprise, in that she "had already foreseen [her] entire life, right up into old age."[37] One night, toward the end of her stay, she wanted to tell Ernesto, the resort doctor, that she wished to die; she said instead that she wanted a child with him.

". . . the young vine scented my guilt like a bloodhound . . ."

Olga's relationship with her only daughter was marked from the start by the sin of adultery (Olga hid the truth from her husband, Augusto, and made him believe the child was his) and her grief over Ernesto's tragic death. The growing emotional unbalance in Olga's daughter, Ilaria, is ascribed to her unconscious intuition of her position in family history: "[t]he young vine," Olga recalls, "scented my guilt like a bloodhound."[38] Actually, Ilaria's position is much more complex. Genealogical guilt is interwoven with the generational one: the daughter figure exemplifies the seventies youth's acritical participation in student revolt, feminism, psychoanalysis. When listening to Ilaria's rare reports of university sit-ins, Olga felt that "[e]verything was frenetic, elusive, there were too many ideas, too many absolutes."[39] In feminist debates and claims, she found things she agreed with, but also "many forced conclusions and distorted, unhealthy ideas."[40] As a result of sexual liberation, "erotic activity was considered a normal bodily function, to be indulged in whenever you felt like it."[41] The psychoanalyst Ilaria sees regularly is presented as a fraud who has also convinced her to sign the guaranty for a business of his that goes bankrupt. "[Y]our mother . . . wasn't intelligent at all," Olga writes to her granddaughter, "a slave to a new dependency, first politics and then the relationship with that man."[42]

The novel's ideological relentlessness against the daughter's generation is much stronger than that shown toward the paths of other generations: so strong that Ilaria's lot is not only spiritual death but a tragic physical death in a car accident in which many critics have seen the irrevocable liquidation of the political and sexual revolution of an entire generation of women. As it is transmitted from mother to daughter, the guilt yields an ideological and genealogical trial that calls for a generational purge. "From the way she looked at me sometimes," Olga writes, "I was certain that if there had been a people's tribunal with her presiding, she would have sentenced me to death."[43] Instead, it is Ilaria who is sentenced to death. At the time when Ilaria is most unbalanced, Olga considers suing her psychoanalyst for undue influence and declaring her mentally incompetent. Ilaria reacts with a fit of hysteria, crying that it is a scheme to take her child away. Although the threat is not carried out, we may say that, on the symbolic level, the grandmother bypasses a link in the genealogical chain: she takes her granddaughter away from her daughter, expropriates from the latter her maternal function, and appropriates both the mother and the grandmother roles. By forging the "father's name"—both the daughter's and the granddaughter's—Olga is also responsible for violating the paternal genealogy. This will have destructive consequences for both daughter and granddaughter. Upset by her mother's tardy confession that Augusto is not her real father, Ilaria runs away from her mother's house and her car crashes into a tree. Her little girl survives the accident and is raised by Olga, who tells her granddaughter—conceived during a vacation to Turkey—that her father is a "prince of the Crescent Moon."[44] The genealogical fairytale that unites granddaughter and grandmother during the childhood idyll[45] turns the little girl into the laughingstock of her schoolmates. One day, at ten, she comes back home in tears. "Liar!" she shouts, then locks herself in her room. The granddaughter's accusation strikes home. This is how Olga comments about the incident: *"Liar could be the title of my autobiography. In all my life I have told only one lie. With that lie I destroyed three lives."*[46]

". . . if I put that on, I'll have to wear curlers and slippers, too . . ."

Olga's letter is an attempt to erase deceit and guilt through a sacramental act—a confession—and to redeem a failure by giving meaning to an existence. It also represents the attempt to purify a genealogical line. The letter is addressed to the narrator's granddaughter, but the real addressee is her daughter: "I should have written this letter to your mother, but I'm writing it to you instead. If I hadn't written at all, then my existence really would have been a failure. Everybody makes mistakes, but if you die without ever having understood them you've lived your life in vain."[47]

The genealogical purification is not accomplished, however. The objects the grandmother invites her granddaughter to look for in the attic after her death—some she has already brought downstairs for her—are charged with allusions to the humble domesticity and the Catholic education in self-loathing to which the roots of the family women's malaise can be traced. The objects are the nativity scene sheep used by nuns to instill the notion of sin in the little girls, the apron, the slippers and, above all, the great-great-grandmother's cake pan that Olga hopes her granddaughter will use and will bequeath to her own daughters "because the history of this humble object sums up and reflects the history of our family's generations."[48]

Giancarlo Lombardi astutely observes that *stampo*—the Italian word for cake pan—refers to the imposition of a model—"a paternalistic discourse which demanded their [women's] confinement to the *oikos*"[49]— that the granddaughter significantly resists. In one of the last rare moments of complicity, the episode in which Olga teaches her granddaughter how to make a cake, the latter refuses to put on the apron. "If I put that on," she says, "I'll have to wear curlers and slippers, too. *Heinous*!"[50]

If the heirlooms become cultural texts aimed at directing the granddaughter's future, one should not forget that the grandmother's testament intends to neutralize a legacy of objects and places and point toward a universal spirituality (the invitation to listen to one's heart) that should guide the ethical and political choices of the new generations. The essential nature of the spirit is identified as the instrument for facing and fighting the abuses of technological society and overcoming conditioning and prejudice. However, in Tamaro's juxtaposition of oriental mysticism to leftist ideology, of feeling to reason, of the private garden to the public arena, many critics have read a reactionary message, aligned with the rhetoric of the political class that was emerging from the end of the First Republic in 1993 and from the reorganization of the political parties that were born from the Resistance.

This reading of the ideological content of the novel is confirmed by Tamaro's narrative choices. Olga's spiritual testament is affected by her senility, which, as discussed previously, defines the narrator figure and, consequently, the narrative technique. Olga's discourse is as fragile as an old person, and its simplicity conceals the need to simplify a world that appears to her complicated, in that it is new and different. "When I think about the span of nearly a century I've lived through, the basic impression I've got is that time has somehow started accelerating,"[51] Grandma Olga writes. At the end of nearly a century of personal and collective life that has been marked by rapid and radical transformations, old age criticizes, accuses, and dismisses what it can no longer understand or accommodate in a mind and a heart that are overwhelmed and tired. Vital relationships with one's offspring are no longer possible:

> Young people always think that serious matters must be discussed in serious, resounding tones. A short while before you left, I found that letter you put under my pillow, the one where you tried to explain to me why you were so unhappy. Now that you're far away I can tell you that what you wrote made it clear you were indeed unhappy, but aside from that I didn't understand a thing. It was all so convoluted and obscure. I'm a simple person; I belong to an era different from the one you belong to: if something's white, I say it's white; if it's black, I say black. The ability to resolve problems comes from everyday experience, from seeing things as they really are and not the way someone else says they should be. . . . Many a time I've had the impression that the books you read confuse you instead of helping you in any way.[52]

4: FEMALE LINES IN FAMILY NARRATIVES

The generation-gap issue—with the stereotype of the old person wagging a finger at the young and pouring edifying presumptuousness over them—takes us back to the political reading of this novel. In Goffredo Fofi's caustic review, the novel's protagonist becomes, in a political present that likes to define itself as postideological, the vehicle of involutional phenomena and attitudes. The so-called *riflusso* (backlash) of the eighties and nineties that *Va' dove ti porta il cuore* champions is characterized by an ageism oriented against youth, in particular the condemnation of the '68ers' youthful idealism and a distrust of the potentiality of new generations:

> The old women of *Va' dove ti porta il cuore* seem to agree in ascribing all this [political and social decay] to the transitory episode of an intermediate generation, that has tried, mistakenly, to "climb up to the sky," and to build a new ethic, certainly less bourgeois and selfish than the one the grandmother advises her granddaughter to follow.... Let an old 1968er—to be a precise a pre-68er—be suspicious of this order, and deeply. Today there are a lot of old geezers and old hags who delight in giving advice to young people. They are a literary genre. Tamaro ... deserves to be embraced by the good grandmothers and mothers of this self-satisfied, vulgar, imperfect Italy.[53]

Fofi's gerontophobia reveals, on the other hand, that the 1968 experience (as with, perhaps, all cultural revolutions) is intrinsically ageist in juxtaposing generational values and outlooks. At the very least, revolutions are conducive to ageist ideologies. This thorny implication, which is rooted in the conflict between progress and "the static nature of old age" discussed by the Lefkovitzes in their study of the modern imagination, will be further explored in the chapter dedicated to the aging of the 1968 generation.

MARGARET MAZZANTINI'S *IL CATINO DI ZINCO*

The grandmother in the novel *Il catino di zinco* [The Zinc Basin], Antenora, appears to us in a more positive light than Olga. If the character of Olga embodies the faults of bourgeois female education, and if the meaning of her existence, marred by deceit, can be recovered only on the spiritual level by means of the final message, the life of Margaret Mazzantini's grandmother protagonist, a Roman lower-middle-class woman whose vigorous temper flared especially in the dramatic war and postwar times, "rough-hewn but made of good olive tree wood,"[54] seems to have made sense in itself; it represents a model for the granddaughter and, through her, for readers. Most critics—who have inevitably compared the two novels, which were published in the same year—seem to agree on this point.⁵⁵ The physical and heroic ways in which Mazzantini's grandmother faces Italian history have been contrasted with the absence from history of Tamaro's central European bourgeois grandmother.

The novel's events take place over three generations and, if Antenora is placed at the center of this genealogy, they are divided into three parts. The first part presents Antenora's ancestors; the second her existence as a wife, mother, and widow; the third focuses on the relationship with her granddaughter in the last stage of her old age and physical decline. The long trip into memory starts in the second chapter; the function of the first is to define the narrator. After a few pages dedicated to the funeral, which introduce the young adult granddaughter, who stands by as her grandmother dies and vividly recalls her laid-out corpse, the first chapter presents a series of flashbacks of visual and olfactory sensations connected with the granddaughter's childhood visits to her grandmother's house. They establish and justify both the granddaughter's viewpoint "from below" of her grandmother's daily actions and moods and the sources from which her story is reconstructed (the granddaughter's personal memories as well as the reminiscences the grandmother has narrated to her).

Il catino di zinco begins and ends with the grandmother's death, which the granddaughter witnesses. Antenora's death is therefore known and expected; it is a past that has been present in the imagination of the narrator, who, by evoking it, pays a love debt and at the same time averts the impact of the years and of oblivion. The grandmother's death generates the granddaughter's writing and motivates her to narrate Antenora's whole life in a flashback that is almost the entire novel, by tracing back her genealogy. *Il catino di zinco* is a memory- and a memorial novel: doleful, poignant, and sweetly melancholy. In Mazzantini's book, the emphasis on the physical and material dimension of old age reflects the need to focus the reader's attention on human decay, but it also has a strong iconic value consistent with the novel's ethos, in that it signifies the intensity of memory, which is as hauntingly present in the book as sensory perception.

The unifying object of family memory is the zinc basin of the title. As with the kitchen utensils passed on by Olga, it denotes a tradition of female housework. The zinc basin also symbolizes a stoic, archaic civilization, and it is a place of purification. "I didn't like the title at first," the author maintains. "But I defended it. The basin delineates Antenora's entire existence, a journey from the Middle Ages to virtual reality."⁵⁶ The basin is present during the crucial transitions of Antenora's life and witnesses the actions that characterize her personality. In the first chapter, the basin, a simple object of her household inventory, joins child granddaughter and grandmother who, "wet with steam, hair uncombed, bustled around me with a hard sponge, sodden with hot water."[57] It is the place where Antenora washes away the traces of her alienated intimacy with her husband. In the basin she does her last washing and, with the leftover soapy water, also scrubs the grease from the balconies. "Only then the task will look completed to her,"[58] and she will be able to surrender, exhausted, to her terminal illness.

". . . a boisterous family waltz . . ."

The reconstruction of Antenora's genealogy, especially in the first part, is like a whirling "family waltz,"[59] at which great-great-grandparents, great-grandparents, fathers, mothers, sisters, cousins, friends, and servants appear in a vivid web of people, moments, places, objects, feelings, and faded dreams. The analysis focuses on the desires, hopes, and delusions of two emblematic female figures, Antenora and her mother, Monda. As in Tamaro's novel, male characters are developed for the purpose of narrating, understanding, and resolving a transmission along the female line. The patriarchal economy in which the novel locates itself juxtaposes cruel, self-centered matriarchs to gentle, dull, often abused men. Although they take part in the role-play that confines women to the home and catalyze their violent frustrations, they are feminized on the narrative level by their auxiliary status.

Antenora's story starts, in the second chapter, with the only precise reference to setting in time in the novel and a shot of father and daughter walking in the street, the father humbly following a tenderly tyrannical child Antenora:

Rome, nineteen-three.
"Pa, I can't go out with you wearing that cape, you look like a bird of ill omen!"
"I feel comfortable with it, my child! If you are ashamed of it, walk on, pretend you don't know me, I'll follow you like a faithful servant, I don't mind, you know."[60]

Antenora's father is a *liceo* teacher, "modest and bashful."[61] At the end of the month, he hands his salary over to his wife and tries to mediate the difficult relationship between Monda and her children: "he always stands up for her, especially in front of their daughters who—like nobody else in the family—are subject to their mother's impositions."[62] When he is an old widower, the father takes up visiting regularly Antenora's house, content, "like an old pet,"[63] to find refuge near his favorite daughter and to help her as much as he can, keeping the kids away from her and "shelling peas like a woman."[64]

Despotic and eccentric Monda, who, when upset, "goes out in her bright creased clothes wearing her Sunday hat, on whose brim a whole bird is ready to take flight,"[65] is a woman embittered by renouncing her true love. In her turn, she is the victim of the arrogant ineptitude of her father Sauro, an aristocrat who wasted all the family property and enjoyed sitting alone at a sumptuously laid table, served by his seven daughters. His daughters, aware that in the meantime "their youth was fading,"[66] had to learn to manage their resources by themselves. Monda, who at this point "had taken stock, at home in front of the mirror," planned "[a] rather clumsy, unromantic elopement"[67] with the teacher her family opposed because he came from a peasant family. As for Monda's eldest sister, Restituta, she was by then beyond childbearing age. Since the eldest daughter had to be married first, they had to forge her birth certificate, so it was "trimmed of about ten years."[68] When the widower warrant officer who married her found out that he had been cheated—Restituta herself confessed, laughing her head off—the wedding had already been celebrated, and he had to keep her.

Restituta became tyrannical with her husband; one of her cruelest gestures was killing the singing blackbird her husband consoled himself with. Like the memory of the dog Tamaro's grandmother carries inside since her childhood, this animal death signals an irreparable break of family ties. Restituta's act, which ends the chapter devoted to Antenora's ancestors, is "the twin in the narration to another murder performed by female hands,"[69] Antenora's slaughter of her son Vittorio's pet rabbit that significantly closes the third chapter, which focuses on her marriage and childrearing years. Vittorio, Antenora's third son, "a delicate child, whose golden curls were parted on the side, and held with a hairpin because his mother combed him like a girl,"[70] is the narrator's father, and the rabbit episode is, as we shall see later, a link in the genealogical transmission of guilt and in the impetus toward the resolution of that guilt.

"*. . . they clung to her as to a secular tree . . .*"

Antenora marries a kind man, whose "desire [is] subdued and body indulgent, like an aged putto's,"[71] and has three sons. During her adult life, Antenora constantly struggles and rushes between shopping bags and black-market bargains. If she has a relationship with history, it is charitable and defeatist. Antenora's adult life spans two wars. Having married during World War I, "out of respect for her country . . . she renounced the white dress."[72] She paid Fascism and World War II the tribute of her sons, who were first enchanted by Fascist iconography, then enlisted. During the war she worked for a homeless and orphan shelter. She spoke with Fascist officers and with priests; she collected used clothes, consoled the other mothers, who "clung to her as to a secular tree."[73] After Mussolini's fall, she tried in vain to rescue her youngest son, Vittorio, from the Republic of Salò. The episode in which Antenora tracks down her son on the train leaving for northern Italy, "together with a raked-up bunch of sixteen-year-olds,"[74] is one of the most intensely dramatic moments of the novel, in which the mixture of pity and repugnance Vittorio feels for his mother's body is conveyed through a just-as-intensely contradictory perception of her age:

> How could she hope that he would follow her, that he would hold her hand, blindly, as he did when a child. . . . He wanted to kick her in her bulky ass, and throw her off the train. . . .
> . . . She has dragged her body odors this far, her bad breath, the smell sent out from where her hair is parted. How well he knew her smells! Poor Ma, poor little girl. . . . Get away from this filth, from this male rankness. You have aged so much, Ma . . . What happened?[75]

This episode also contains the only religious leap of Antenora, an old woman as earthy as her counterpart Olga in *Va' dove ti porta il cuore* is receptive to both traditional and tainted forms of spirituality. Nevertheless, Antenora, too, is influenced by popular religious practices widespread among Italian women of her generation. Like Alfonsina, the protagonist of a novel analyzed in the next chapter, she invokes and demands the Virgin Mary's intervention, flatters her and claims her favor as if it were a credit, a sort of feminine score to be settled with God; like Olga, she juxtaposes religious verticality to the horizontality of her female existence. This happens after she has to dash off the moving train, failing to talk Vittorio out of joining Mussolini's army. It is the only time that Antenora, who has always fought her way through life, but has never "got off her track," experiences conscious suffering and resistance:

> Grandma has fallen into the ditch next to the track. . . . On all fours in the weeds, she looks ahead at the point where the tracks join. . . .
> . . . She'd better keep her eyes down on the steel-gray glare of the rails. Then she invents an extreme game: the lunar reflection stretching along the track before her feet becomes her finishing line, impossible to reach because illuminated by the moon that moves forward with her, almost like a fluorescent balloon tied to a child's wrist. . . .
> . . . She mumbles words, talks to herself about her pain, the ordeal of the war, and her children. . . . Her eyes tear hungrily at the sky above her: "To-

night you must come down to earth beside me. You must visit me, Mother of all Mothers!" She has never felt so close, so inside the sky. Her trunk bent upwards, her arms like two mendicant branches, as if she wanted to embrace the whole firmament.[76]

At the end of the war Antenora's children return. She has become more indulgent and enjoys seeing them around again. Expecting them to become adults and fly off soon, she tries to linger in this sort of temporal limbo: "she loved having them lying idly in bed. . . . half naked in rumpled sheets, and they looked like gigantic babies to her."[77]

The children's departure from home marks the beginning of Antenora's maturity and the last stage of her life with her husband, Gioacchino, who dies many years before her. For Antenora aging implies the gradual disappearance of gender distinctions. Therefore physical decline is experienced both as the mature body taking over the young adult one and as a cleansing process of draining, thus of achieving a form of unsexed essentiality. "Men and women look alike when they age," Antenora believes, "the rod withers and does not rise anymore, everything inside the uterus dries up. All her female attributes had fallen a prey to her old flesh, that had filled up every curve."[78] As a consequence of her liberation from the sex she had endured during the reproductive phase, Antenora discovers an intimacy she had never experienced before with her husband, with whom she has a sweet and melancholy idyll in the years preceding his death. The older body's drying up paves the way to the fluidity of feelings. Where young bride Antenora was "as dry as salt," and penetrating her was like "hoeing up a clod,"[79] in her maturity she accommodates her husband's desire for the sea. At first she follows him unwillingly in their Sunday outings to Fiumicino; after his death she takes care of the "big four-family house"[80] Gioacchino had talked her into building near the sea at Lavinio, hoping to gather there children, daughters-in-law, and grandchildren in the summer.

The beginning of the fourth stage of Antenora's life coincides with her sale of the summer house and with the resolution of her relationship to her husband, who becomes a man in an old photograph and an idealized landmark; it is a phase when Antenora frees herself emotionally from family obligations. Disengagement is perceived as "depopulation." Although as an unreflexive character she usually "rushed to evict from her heart"[81] the few doubts she may have had, and did not linger over life review and assessment, Antenora starts to develop a retrospective view of her life span and of the stages that marked it:

> When she thought about her life, she divided it into four parts. First childhood and youth at her parents' house; right after that, married life and child-

bearing; then that fragment, brief but intense, of being alone with her husband; and finally, her widowhood. It had been a slow process toward depopulation. Yet, this fourth and last slice of life, which on paper was supposed to be the saddest, enveloped Grandma in its big airy arms and lifted her into the sky of lightness.[82]

The freedom and lightness Antenora experiences during the active phase of her fourth age, the one preceding her stroke, manifest themselves in her defense of living alone and in her late-discovered passion for traveling. Like Grandma Olga, Antenora rejects relatives' and neighbors' compassion and assistance: although "still strong and vital," she appears "disoriented, her corset untied under her clothes, the grater in one hand, a pair of socks in the other"[83] to the graying children dropping by to pay her a visit. Both on the strenuous organized tours she takes and during the visits to her son Vittorio, who has transferred to Tangeri, she seems to move horizontally, her eyes fixed on the nearest objects, the way she did when her horizon was confined to the kitchen. Charmed by Arab markets, where she finds "a bit of her Middle Ages,"[84] she "jumped in at the deep end. . . . detested geography, museums, monuments and everything that had been buried. She kept her eyes man-high. That was where she pinned her curiosity."[85] The horizontal perspective reflects Antenora's tendency to avoid confronting depth, reflection, questions on existence and afterlife, but it is also the sign of her humanity. Her man-high gaze is receptive to Arab women's hips as well as to the "small army of dark-skinned children . . . that followed her wherever she went."[86]

In Antenora's fourth age her family ties loosen, even though she keeps exercising her old matriarch's power when she visits her children, by "sticking her big dirty hands into every intimacy,"[87] into the chest of drawers with their clothes to be ironed as well as into the glances sons and daughters-in-law exchange. Her last bond is with Vittorio's daughter, who accompanies her to death in a more and more exclusive relationship. Significantly, an absence of other familiar presences, more likely symbolic than real, highlights the fact that the granddaughter has an exclusive testimonial role as her grandmother's caregiver, both at the hospital and at the nursing home where Antenora is taken after she has a stroke.

"... *granddaughter, don't let me die, you can't escape from my eyes' investiture* ..."

In *Il catino di zinco* the saving intervention is reversed from that in Tamaro's novel: this novel is written by a grand*daughter* to save her grand*mother*. Just as Tamaro's grandmother-narrator never named her granddaughter, assimilating her to the implied reader, in the discourse of Mazzantini's granddaughter, the grandmother is named only in the last line. The choice to give the grandmother a name at the end of the novel—incidentally, the etymology of Antenora is "she who fights"— emphasizes both her iconic power and the strength of her legacy. On the stylistic level, if the grandmother's discourse in *Va' dove ti porta il cuore* is diluted by the reassuring sententiousness of a respectable tradition and dulled by senility, *Il catino di zinco* baffles the reader through unusually effective forcing of the language, in which "expressionistic distortions, family jargon, neologisms, morphological audacities, vernacular, earthly and bodily terms mix with . . . elevated and archaic vocabulary"[88] that echoes grandparents' tales.

"My earliest recollection of her is olfactory,"[89] writes the granddaughter, who, frightened by the darkness and mystery of her grandmother's bedroom, recognized her house from the smell of the old age it was saturated with: "I was afraid of the crack under that door, of what was beyond it in the inaccessible, forbidden room. I only recognized the bad smell of the house, where her old body lived, and the floors breathed her naked thing under her nightgown, when in the night she slid out of bed to piss."[90] The same pitiless child perspective is used in the granddaughter's description of Antenora's older friends, whose bodies—grotesquely deformed both by age and by the view from below—were observed by the little girl from under the table where they sat sipping coffee: "I looked at Grandma's friends. The impudent glare of the sun lit up the porosity of their skin, under the blotches of badly spread face powder, and the lipstick channeled up along the wrinkles around their lips. I threw my napkin on the floor, and disappeared to pick it up. Down below, together with the rusty table legs, there were old-fashioned mink coats, oxidized ankles inside support hose, and the smell of old cunt."[91]

A common feature of infant and elderly perspective is the importance of nearby objects. As children discover the world by exploring objects within reach, likewise the aged surround themselves with objects, both because a quantity of objects reflects the quantity of life and because doing so averts the final separation from worldly things. In her granddaughter's recollections, Antenora's world appears as a magical emporium. Objects pile up as the years go by, and the physical and mental energy and motivation needed for ordering, selecting, and directing one's own resources fail in old age. Since we are dealing with objects preserved by a frugal woman, constantly busy with household chores and business, disorder implies the fragmentation of tasks, chores, and activities performed out of daily necessity, without long-term goals.

The first chapter of the novel takes us to a corner of the Quartiere Africano in Rome, on a path choked with weeds, where grandmother and granddaughter used to walk uphill, up to a "clearing where an empty café stood, sad and rotten,"[92] a pile of chairs stacked up against its plaster, next to the rusty plate of the faded ice cream sign. From there one could reach the house where Antenora spent her last years before she was hospitalized, a place characterized by both resigned senile shabbiness and childish wonder. When the little girl went to look for a candy inside the old pewter vase, she found there "only dust, an old nail and a rubber band."[93] Then she sat on a stool looking at the cuckoo clock, which had been silent for quite some time because one day it had broken and Grandma had never had it repaired. For years she had waited spellbound "at every hour for the exit of that black cuckoo,"[94] just as she had curled up on the floor to play with Grandma's buttons: buttons of the most varied kinds, "in cloth, printed fabric, bone, plastic, mother-of-pearl, dome-shaped, golden, silvery."[95]

The interior of the house was an "emporium of old trunks, tomato jars, plastic bags, screws, bolts, faucets, strings, newspapers, basil pots, and the beloved slippers,"[96] that every day Antenora threw away, only to change her mind later and go retrieve in the street at dawn, before the street sweeper came. In her dining room, in a conglomeration of times and fashions, of attachment to memories and surrender to mass-media modernity, "the intermittent glimmer of the icy light" of the TV set, Antenora's reading glasses and the illustrated magazines featuring the memoirs of Mussolini's wife, Donna Rachele, in installments stood out among "a crowd of furniture, remnants of various family moves."[97] In the end, in the delirium foretelling the stroke, kitchen objects seem to turn against Antenora, who struggles to grab them and move them around so as to clear her mind. "[T]he mysteries amassed through the years ... assault her"[98] and projects, marked as they are by daily domestic deadlines, turn into persecuting memos.

In an interview in which she referred to the autobiographical nature of the novel, Margaret Mazzantini also clarified the purpose of her writing:

> This book was born out of a sense of rebellion. I had recollections of my grandmother as a strong, almost virile woman, one of those who in the past used to hold together ... blood ties. Then, all of a sudden, I saw her reduced to a nothing, a human shred in the hospital where she had been taken following a stroke. The book was prompted by the will to give her back dignity by telling her great story. Of this story I remember really everything: her immense surge of affections and her cruelty, deriving from the fact that she found it difficult to accept her role as a woman in that she had been limited

by her mother, who preferred her sons. She has attacks of anxiety because she feels trapped by social conventions to spend all her time inside the house. Today she would be a single, career woman. Writing has been an attempt to tear her from the past in order to project her into the future.[99]

The function of the granddaughter's testimony is to solve the paradoxical relation of past and future that the grandmother's archetype, according to Lowinsky, embodies. *Il catino di zinco* has been called an apprentice novel, an initiation to writing (it marks the debut of a theater actress as a writer) more than to life.[100] It is a merciless apprenticeship, a school of cruelty, that the granddaughter faces armed with a crudely expressionistic and visionary style, so as to guarantee a future generative—and regenerated—space to her existence as a woman and to her family history.

In a dream she had when Antenora was ill, the granddaughter, while walking up "a never-ending stairway," sees her grandmother's body tumble down like a bundle that dissolves into "a black liquid sewage stain."[101] Above her, she sees a blazing, deflated sky that has nothing but eyes: "the docked-tail dog's red frowning eyes, Grandma's eyes, holding me like conscience, like the keen-eyed God that peeps threateningly out of the glowing clouds in Sunday school film strips."[102] A cry rises from the sky: "Granddaughter, don't let me die, you can't escape from my eyes' investiture."[103] The granddaughter reads an unavoidable investiture in the eyes of her grandmother, who cannot talk anymore because of her facial paralysis. Through those eyes, which embody the gazes of former generations that the granddaughter has been called to "take in again," the eyes of other family members are recalled, and thus their thoughts, dreams, memories—the eyes that Antenora's father "rested on his arm at the balcony banisters," the eyes that her little son, killed by typhoid fever, closed "before the Virgin's reclined face," the smile of her husband Gioacchino slicing bread, Great-Grandma Monda's "predatory eyes."[104]

If in this family "evil" is carried through the eyes of fathers and mothers, sons and great-grandmothers, its roots—and the reasons for the investiture—are to be found in the female bodies that grandmother and granddaughter inhabit. Antenora's last trip, which marks the end of the chapter on her active fourth age, is a visit to a friend in Sicily; she drags along her unwilling thirteen-year-old granddaughter. This trip coincides with the girl's menarche and with her gruesome perception of the manipulation of life passages. We see her reaction to the decline of the female body in the sketchy portrayal of the lady companion of Antenora's friend:

4: FEMALE LINES IN FAMILY NARRATIVES 109

It was hot. We couldn't even breathe at night. The lady companion, a skinny eagle-faced spinster, was insane. She turned on the radio, and let her hair down with a feline gesture: a lot of blond hair, falling all over her. "Look, seen from behind I am like a fifteen-year-old child, am I not?" she said, inspired, dancing in the room, to the rhythm of a samba on the radio. I answered yes. But her young hair and that bony paw stretching out of her black skirt, like an eroticized antenna, horrified me because I knew that the concealed half of her appearance was decrepit.[105]

Tamaro's grandmother hands down to her granddaughter the memory of a female sexuality associated with deceit and silence; the transmission of sexual guilt by Antenora, in contrast, is more openly crude and linguistically menacing. Her tales about "raped little girls, thrown into a well,"[106] and the images of blood and dirt in news reports, meant to teach her granddaughter to be mistrustful and reserved, prefigure the girl's perception of her grandmother's body, from her "recollection" of young Antenora's sexually hostile body to the markedly sexed transfiguration of Antenora's corpse in the vision the granddaughter has under the shower after the funeral. In this vision, Antenora appears "isolated in a cone of light. . . . naked, lying . . . on a bed of rotting lichen and moss . . . a puff of white hair around her sex, lonesome and gaping like an abandoned quarry."[107]

The representation of a woman's life as punishment is founded on sexual guilt. The female legacy passed on by the grandmother is profoundly sacrificial in nature. Most book reviews of *Il catino di zinco* and interviews with the author have stressed the ethical value of the "intense sacrificial natural morals" of Antenora, "which held together a fragile family fabric haunted by a thousand adversities."[108] An interviewer also observes that Antenora's life is absolutely typical "in the sense that sacrifice and self-effacement were the norm for women of that sociocultural condition."[109] This novel emphasizes the punitive power of female sacrifice. Besides representing the strength and virtue of a premodern, stoic culture, the notion of life as punishment, as a "sentence to-stay-in-this-world-to-suffer" triggers the explosive energy of revenge. Female revenge expresses itself in minute gestures of daily cruelty and in the denial of male pleasure. The genealogical mechanism of revenge is illustrated in a particularly clear and powerful way in the episode when Antenora kills Vittorio's pet rabbit:

The mother rises powerful, strong with virile vigor and determination, entrapped in those female boundaries that are so narrow for her. . . . "[T]oday I'm going to undo it." She means the house, devouring it with her hands. . . . The nasty rabbit, scared by the hubbub. . . . [h]as left traces everywhere. . . . At first she can't see it. She promptly heads for the window. . . .

... Come on! at it! to tackle it on the carpet, without even letting go of the broom, dragging it along, hurting herself. Anger grows with pain; it finds a motive. Woman and rabbit are on the floor, their hearts throbbing, the broom in between them. ...

What happens on the table, in the kitchen, I don't know. I don't want to know. There is only a jerk of her shoulders. ...

... Then her fury subsides and she sets the marble table without the least remorse. ...

This thing of offing the animal, it was a rapture that seized her suddenly. She was not so pitiless as to consciously want to deprive her son of his only friend. ... She was simply annoyed by the hours of clandestine diversion the rabbit offered to her child. Through those games, it seemed to her that he evaded the life-punishment she had consigned him to. He could not escape, he himself among her children, the most imaginative one ... the sentence to-be-in-this-world-to-suffer, that had been inflicted on her by nature itself, because of that mute cicada she had between her thighs.[110]

Vittorio, who from that day severs all bonds of affection with his mother, is the narrator's father. As in *Va' dove ti porta il cuore*, the children's generation is a missing link in the genealogical chain. The granddaughter narrator attempts to eradicate the legacy of guilt by avenging the punishments sustained within the genealogy at whose center Antenora stands, as well as those inflicted within that genealogy. To this end, she appropriates the grandmother's discourse in her declining phase in a more and more violent and invasive way by becoming the driving power of the paralyzed grandmother's actions and gestures, and the interpreter of her nonverbal, illogical discourse. She writes the delirium preceding Antenora's stroke in the form of a Joycean interior monologue; at the onset of paralysis, she uses an increasingly expressionistic language and turns her grandmother's character into a grotesque caricature. The granddaughter's manipulation of the grandmother's helpless body during her visits at the hospital and at the nursing home are among the most dramatic acts in the novel; in them, desire for revenge mixes with compassion. While pushing Antenora's wheelchair around the hospital halls and into the nursing home garden, the granddaughter falls prey to homicidal fantasies and engages in accusatory soliloquies with her physically and mentally impaired grandmother, as in the two following scenes:

I wrap her up well and lift her into her wheelchair. In a less crowded hospital wing I push her along the deserted halls. ... We rush out. I take my hands off the wheelchair: for an instant only. I catch hold of her again immediately and run, run and push her again faster. ... I follow Grandma through the altered gaze of a vision: she is far enough already, her crocheted shawl flutters, the mad wheels creak on the floor, she waves her living hand,

and goes. She goes alone, toward the large window at the end. She crashes. I can hear the glass explosion, the crash of fragments falling inside, while Grandma is already flying with her wheelchair, out of the livid neon light. Forever. One more second, and my hallucination would become reality. Instead, I rush to grab her again in time. She trembles: these moments of terror are the only moments when she feels alive.[111]

At the back of the hospital, there is a path that leads into a field. . . . The field swarms with cats looking for food, meowing in the hospital garbage. . . . I pick a few up and drop them into her lap. . . . She laughs, for the pleasure of feeling those warm things on her. I'd like to tell her: "Here, nana, I'll hand you a nice rabbit, one of those you can eat cacciatore. You know how to make rabbit cacciatore, right?" Would she start? Who knows. She smiles, that slanting smile (the way the villains smile in cartoons) that only partially responds to nervous impulses. A frightening sneer, beneath drooping eyes looking for support. . . .

. . . I could keep her there all night. She's mine. She looks for me with whatever life she still has in her body. Now I could make her pay for everything, and finish her off like my father's rabbit, strangling her with my purse strap. She would turn purple and I would cry: "Why? Why did you kill his rabbit, bitch?!" Or, alternately, slaughter her to the rhythm of a macabre nursery rhyme: "You dirty little slut, lonely young boys shouldn't be emasculated, their little pet rabbits shouldn't be eliminated. . . ." But it wouldn't make sense anymore . . . Poor soul, she has had more than her share of troubles! On her face there is no more trace of her ancient crimes. When one turns old, one is so dull-witted, so forgetful of the evil one has done.[112]

What finally prevails is compassion, toward the grandmother's body as well as her own, which bends under Antenora's weight while she helps her to get up from her wheelchair to clutch the bar in the dance room at the hospital. Along with her compassion, we see the granddaughter's self-affirmation as she rebels against the investiture, against the invitation to the "boisterous family waltz in which all relatives are twirling."[113] "My dance card is crammed!" the granddaughter cries. "What makes you think that I resemble you all?"[114]

ISABELLA BOSSI FEDRIGOTTI'S *DI BUONA FAMIGLIA*

Di buona famiglia [From a Good Family] narrates the life courses of two sisters from a Trentine upper-class family. Isabella Bossi Fedrigotti reconstructs in her novel an Italian borderland microcosm, deeply affected by the events that shook central Europe in the first half of the twentieth century, in particular World War I.

The *Bildung* of the two protagonists of *Di buona famiglia*, who were born at the beginning of the twentieth century and are both in their eighties in the narrative present, is characterized by an emphasis on formal concerns and social privilege, by the will to preserve a world and the awareness of its decline. The sisters' defensive resistance in response to decline underscores the anachronism of this world. They ignore changing times and new borders because these belong to a newly constituted national culture, that of Italy, which is perceived as foreign. Deception and hypocrisy, distortion and concealment are rooted in this historical ignorance, which in the novel has a destructive effect both on individual lives and on entire genealogies. The incisive comment of the author's father—"This book is a fake because two real old women of our family would never have talked"[115]—brings to light a further level of deception, manifested in the protagonists themselves and their confessions. In addition to this, the author practices a "linguistic fiction": had they "talked," the two sisters would have spoken German, not Italian. According to Ferdinando Camon, aristocratic Isabella would have come into conflict with her origins through the act of narrating and would have felt compelled to "kill the language" that expressed a privileged culture and social condition.[116]

Di buona famiglia is a diptych novel, consisting of two confessional monologues similar in length, in which two old sisters remember the same family history, each from her own point of view. It is a sort of trial, in that Clara and Virginia, the witnesses/accused, live separate non-communicating old-age experiences in their ancient family mansion. The discourses of the two protagonists are rigorously separated in the novel. The narrative, devoid of dialogue, is affected stylistically by the absence of direct verbal exchange and in the second part— Virginia's monologue—by the repetition of facts and events that the reader knows already. Virginia narrates her version in the first person; Clara uses a curious "you" that becomes in some cases "we," thereby incorporating the points of view of the mother and of the housemaid. This narrative point of view connotes her as the "good family's" spokesperson, as the character that will win in the long run and is thus authorized to seek the reader's complicity.

Clara is the younger sister, reserved and plain, the obedient guardian of tradition. After the disappointment of an engagement twice broken by the same man, she has resigned herself to living as an old maid, the daughter who never became independent of the family. This role allows her, however, to maintain a solid relationship with the house and with family property, which she restores after the wars. Her connection with family property reinforces her power over her sister in old age, when they both end up living under the same roof. Envious of and scandalized by her sister's sexual boldness since their adolescence, Clara blames Virginia for her own love failures. She is convinced that Virginia seduced the two men of her life, first her fiancé, then her lover in maturity, a partisan doctor whom Clara met during wartime evacuation.

Virginia is beautiful and lively, charmed by all things modern. She had several romances, among them marriage with an "Italian" from Venice, followed by a second marriage with a Fascist party official, whose death Clara may have commissioned to her Partisan lover. Her two marriages allow her to leave home and have children, but it is to her parental home that she returns after each separation; and, in the end, she returns there to face maturity and old age in solitude. Anguished by physical decline, she envies the ordinary existences of those around her, regrets her past, and must learn Clara's ways: self-control and concealment of strong emotions.

Bossi Fedrigotti's minimalist novel depends more on atmosphere than on events, revealing "an almost Proustian taste for colors and smells"[117] that can "narrate the imperceptible traces of time in our lives."[118] *Di buona famiglia* has been described as a "typically female novel for its language, sensibility, content, particularly in dealing with the delicate theme of old age."[119] It has also been called a "showcase novel"[120] that exhibits the entire inventory of family goods (and evils) to be preserved under glass. From this perspective, the two protagonist sisters' old-age conditions, although different from each other, represent a waning historical moment and its sociopolitical conservatism, as well as a conservative geographic space, the Trentine landscape, "with its austere mountains at the horizon and a countryside bound to tenaciously defended traditions."[121] In this landscape, nature, represented by a patrician house and a garden that resist fashions and war ravages, seems to always get the better of history.

References to historical events focus on the impact of two world wars on a small borderland mountain community. Wars impact the good family by devastating surrounding villages and lands and destroying old power landmarks. As Clara notes upon returning home at the end of World War I, "one did not know anymore who to turn to, who to ask for protection, where authority was": the fact of becoming Italian "was a minor detail after all."[122] The isolation from history, which intensifies with World War II, is a form of "preservation." It is emblematically rendered by the fact that the men in the family are either too young or too old to fight, and by the consequent absence of casualties. Clara writes:

The war came, the second one, and it was the one that freed you. You were preserved again, like the first time, when Dad had returned from Poland after four years fighting behind the lines, between a tea party and an afternoon snack with ladies without husbands. The second time there were no more men who could die in the family, no brothers, no sons, Virginia's eldest son just a bit too young, and her husband, Tullio, too old.[123]

Wars had a liberating effect on the two women's development. The "disorder of evacuation"[124] during World War I gave the adolescent sisters the opportunity to go out unchaperoned and explore sexuality. Later, during the Partisan resistance in the mountains, Clara established a bond with a Communist doctor that would have been quite improbable under any other circumstances. For the rest, the family experienced evacuation in the mountains as a sort of holiday, and their survival largely depended on donations of food and clothing from relatives and acquaintances, particularly from their housemaid Beppina.

In the daily domestic routines of their narrative present, the sisters have developed a reciprocal intolerance, the result of two long parallel lives of blackmail, wickedness, loneliness, and envy. Although their upbringing, emphasizing self-control and the preservation of class identity and family patrimony, has had antithetical effects on them, the antithesis of conservatism and rebelliousness is more apparent than real. The prisons of appearance, judgment, and reticence have played significant roles in both sisters' developments and have prevented both from learning how to construct autonomous life zones in harmony with life passages. Clara's unhappiness derives from her submission to family rules, Virginia's from her impatience with them, but unhappiness is an ineluctable state for both. Time has consolidated the effects of their repressive education, whose power derives from the roles that divided them.

"... *Clara, Virginia, and I* ..."

The juxtaposition of sister characters, often paired in the premarriage competition, is a widespread topos in classical literature and in myth. The "sister plot" is a narrative trend in nineteenth-century fictions by British women writers, and one as fertile for "generating plot" as the theme of adultery. The setup reverses the traditional pattern of the struggle of two males over the same love object: here, two women compete for a single man. In this triangle, "[l]ike an adulterous woman, a significant sister subverts the social order by creating an excess, a duplication for which there is no place."[125] The theme of sister rivalry is the product of a patriarchal vision that classifies women according to juxtaposed stereotypes. Some studies of sisterhood and of women's friendship have related the general phenomenon of women's bonds to the mother-daughter paradigm and have pointed out that competition among women is the language both of separation and of the nostalgia for the primary fusion with the maternal.[126]

Quantitative research on sibling relationships in a life-course perspective reveals that, among the three possible gender combinations of the dyad, the sister-sister bond is the strongest and the most significant, and the one that tends to strengthen in old age.[127] Sharing a long common history—in particular, character-forming childhood and adolescent experiences—can deeply affect life-review processes and the use of reminiscences for validating and clarifying earlier events and relationships from a mature perspective, and may prove crucial to the resolution of deeply ingrained conflicts.[128] Comparing reflections on the significance of one's position at a given stage of a given genealogy with same age-group siblings who have shared that stage can be fundamental in the search for "a sense of integrity," of having lived "one's life in harmony with one's own values and with those of one's family."[129]

In *Di buona famiglia*, the sisters' parallel life reviews do not result in any form of reconciliation either with self or with sibling. The life reviews are kept rigorously separate by the narrative structure, and there is no evidence that sources or versions may have been at any time compared. On the basis of their confessions of voyeuristically violating each other's privacy in several past episodes, all we may expect of the sisters is a return to adolescent secret diary reading in their old age. An analysis of the two monologues reveals how the positions of victim and victimizer, prosecution and defense that are taken by the sibling narrators have evolved and solidified over the course of time.

After a few opening pages describing eighty-year-old Clara, recollection is triggered by the family picture album. The sisters' dual identity ("the two of us") is introduced: it is also underscored by their mother's photo caption that reads "Clara, Virginia, and I."[130] If their father gets them mixed up with each other when he is very old and his eyesight is failing, "his unfairness, his preferences"[131] for the firstborn daughter do not escape Clara's notice. In Clara's retrospective gaze she and her sister are already different in their early childhood: Virginia "chubby and laughing with outstretched arms" and she stern and "bony in . . . her Sunday dress."[132] Nonetheless, the two sisters are "always mentioned together, paired, dressed the same way, sleeping in the same room, same toys and presents for both, same piano and drawing lessons, dance lessons later."[133] Their education is typical for girls of a good family, based on the transmission of a traditional model rather than on the development of individual talents and preferences. No consideration is given to the fact that "you loved drawing, she did dance, neither liked the piano, you liked comfortable clothes and she liked tight ones, you chose milk chocolate, she preferred it plain."[134] Difference in their life destinies is affected not by the pursuit of individual skills and attitudes, but by physical appearance: "above all," Clara adds to the list of their differences, "Virginia was a beauty."[135]

Because the age gap is minimal, the two young women go through the rites of passage to female adulthood—sexual initiation and the search for a suitable husband—together. In the courtship stage, Clara's "potential fiancés"[136] often met with Virginia's admirers. Clara's suitors were "more rustic . . . and out-of-fashion," but it also happened that someone "missed his target and fell in love with Virginia, who did not bother to make things clear," just "for the sake of weaning him . . . [and] ridding him of that nice-boy look."[137] It is at this point in life that the rift between the two women becomes irreparable. The male gaze—direct or internalized as a cultural construct—separates them by introducing, inside the carefree microcosm of infant and adolescent sisterhood, the knowledge that they are rivals. After recalling childhood laughing fits shared with Virginia and Beppina, Clara notes that her sister had changed later: "she had started to be interested in boys, and she had not laughed much any more, not with you at least."[138] While dividing them, however, the awareness of the male gaze also reinforces their dual identity. Significantly, after learning about the death of Clara's first fiancé, Virginia wonders if the three wives he had "might have been better than us."[139]

Clara's sexual initiation comes when she sees her fifteen-year-old sister naked under a young man's eyes. Caught by a soldier during the evacuation while she is taking off her bathing suit after swimming in the lake, Virginia lingers in dressing, gratified and disturbed that her sister is watching. This scene, which "haunted" Clara for many years, making her "taciturn and distracted during the day" and keeping her "awake in bed in the night,"[140] triggered her envious voyeurism. Later she would read her sister's diaries and listen through her bedroom wall to the conversations between Virginia and her husband, when they visited their parents' house.

This scene from adolescence highlights the dependence of the sisters' growth and differentiation on the mirror-gaze: one as a spectator of life, the other intrigued by the narcissism of seduction. Affected as the sisters' existences are by their reflexive representations, however, these roles are less fixed than they appear. In fact, Virginia's sexual initiation had taken place under similar circumstances to Clara's: she had played the role of spectator when she secretly witnessed scenes of paternal adultery, which Clara seems not to know about. When she returns, in her maturity, to her girlhood room, it is her turn to be "awake at night . . . hearing the wood creaking"[141] during the visits of Clara's friend. During her own visit to the doctor's apartment in Milan, where her sister is considering moving, Virginia opens closets, touches clothes, finds Clara's perfumes and jams. However, having internalized her role of the sexually connoted half in the double-identity frame, she denies her sister's erotic intimacy. Lying on the bed where Clara sleeps with the doctor, "to better imagine I am my sister,"[142] Virginia cannot free herself from the image of Clara as "wooden and monastic."[143] In a home that is not their family house (the doctor's apartment), Virginia finds "tenuous but eloquent traces" that upset her by suggesting that "Clara was just like this shadow of hers . . . thoughtful, kind, discreet, loving, and everything else was but a figment of her imagination."[144] When faced with Clara's amiable public image, Virginia admits that she too would have liked to be able to love her, be close to her and win her favor,[145] and Clara, after reading Virginia's diary, admits that she would have liked Virginia, had she not been her sister.

The sisters' development is marked by the irreconcilable roles that the judging gaze has assigned to them. (It is worthwhile to observe that the pressure of this gaze is particularly felt in a context in which the function of words is to politely cover silences more than to signify or communicate). An age-conscious reading will focus on the fact that both women's condemnation of inappropriate actions and behavior in the other follows criteria of appropriateness that are age- and gender-based. "Age roles" have limited both sisters' self-fulfillment by preventing them from pursuing—or at least from pursuing with serenity and conviction—what their destinies or their inner maturation clocks disposed them to experience at a given age. The result is a different yet shared maladjustment in relation to both life-span time and historical time. The opening words of both confessions respectively, "You are a survivor"[146] and, "Something went wrong at some point in my life,"[147] suggest the two sisters' different but equally problematic relation to time: on one side, the failure to enter the course of time; on the other a defeat *en route*.

"*. . . something went wrong at some point in my life . . .*"

As observed earlier, the relationship between Virginia and Clara is marked primarily by sexual rivalry, and their roles are constructed on the juxtaposition of their bodies. At the base of this construction we find a stereotypical equation of western culture, the association of female seduction and youth, which has been often used as point of comparison and division. The novel analyzes two aspects of this equation: the dependence of women's youthful image on the male gaze, and the dependence of women's ability to have an emotionally and sexually fulfilled life on youth. The first aspect is well illustrated by Virginia's description of how the doctor's frequent visits to the small community of mature women who were left alone in the house after the war (the two sisters, their old mother, and the housemaid Beppina) affected them. While wondering what the Partisan doctor and her sister "might have talked about, what they might have had in common" (he being "more interested in stories of the present and in the future to come" and she being an expert "in stories of the past, of better times, in the cultivation of vines"),[148] Virginia uses the young/old antithesis to delineate their incompatibility. She was, in fact, "silent, melancholy, unimpressive, already almost more old than young," while he was "noisy, talkative, young—so he seemed, at least—and also conspicuous, with a large mouth and a large body."[149] Thanks to the doctor, Virginia declares, "all four of us were back to being women again, not just sisters, daughters, mother, or housemaid."[150] Virginia also remembers the "still-fresh complexion, the long, thick brown hair, rolled up in a handsome plait"[151] of the maid, whom she had previously described as being "slovenly . . . young but plain and with a big nose."[152] In Virginia's recollection of the doctor's visits, age imposes powerful limits on female sexuality; it is definitely taboo for a mature female to engage in sexual seduction. She recalls, for example, her mother's earrings, which the elderly woman took to wearing again every day, "her too-purple lipstick,"[153] and her too-powdered face. Conscious of no longer being the protagonist of the family's love games, Virginia feels old and wonders, critical of herself as well as of the other women, if older women have a right to adorn themselves to please: "Why should older women wear makeup, I asked myself? Is this supposed to make them look better? What about earrings? And perfume? Do older women believe they can still be liked?"[154]

In the case of the beautiful Virginia, the consciousness of decline is the direct consequence of narcissism, and the seduction-youth association has a personal significance: seduction is a behavior of her past, and she cannot admit to it as a tendency in her maturity. When she returns to the paternal house as a widow and a mother, she confines herself to the role of spectator of her sister's relationships, both with the doctor and with her own children. Moreover, if the conservative Clara is a woman of the past, Virginia bears the label of "woman with a past,"[155] "still a flirt in spite of her age."[156] Having felt ridiculous when, "in her full womanhood already,"[157] she fell in love with Clara's first fiancé, she continues to suffer the consequences of the negative judgment toward her seductive, youthful image. This image is now doubly condemned, in that the attractiveness that facilitated her sexual transgression and violation of propriety codes as a young woman is made more inappropriate by old age. In old age, her body awareness becomes obsessive neurosis. Frozen in an unchangeable image of the past, her old body is paralyzed in its movements and thoughts, and prevented from interacting with memory:

> It is not easy because they look at me whenever I go out; I still like to dress nicely, style my hair, wear good shoes. Street paving is at times disconnected, and I must concentrate on walking straight, without staggering. . . . If I only let my thoughts go once, if I yielded to a recollection, I would stumble immediately, I would slow down like someone who is not in her right senses.[158]

The time of the paternal house, of traditions and festivities, of furniture and gardening and of family property management, becomes for Virginia an exclusively retrospective time, which virtually "takes revenge" on those who tried to project themselves into modernity. The punishment for her youthful flight away from the paternal house and her hasty dismissal of tradition is her being frozen now in an out-of-time and out-of-place image, "stuffed, with fixed glass eyes like a fox."[159] Virginia writes, "Do the people I meet perceive that my life stopped an imprecise number of years ago? . . . Perhaps they pity me, they say: 'Poor woman, just think that in her time. . . .'"[160] Excluded from Clara and Beppina's daily chattering and spared from all household chores, Virginia is, in her old age, an unwelcome distinguished guest, alienated from the places of her childhood and from the memories of her youth. More importantly, in spite of her compliance with female biological life stages, she is alienated from her offspring, who seem to have "passed to their aunt's side":

> I don't know what to do with myself. I could go into the garden; at least she has not put her furniture, her objects, her photographs there to mark off her territory. I go down to this no-man's-land when my grandchildren visit me, although they don't spend much time with me, a few courtesy phrases before passing to their aunt's side. I have wished sometimes that I could start some conversation, learn about their lives, get to know them better, but I see they are inattentive; they can't wait to pass to the other territory. . . .
>
> . . . I go . . . to the window to watch people walking by, sometimes for hours. I have nothing to do, anyhow. Someone looks up. . . . They see an old woman, her hair not so in order as she would like, a bewildered face against the large façade of the house. Not happy, not sad, nothing, just an old woman looking down, with nobody to really think about.[161]

> I no longer keep photos of my children when they were little—they have changed too much in the years—nor do I keep those of other people who were dear to me. I don't want to recall any beautiful memories; otherwise in my present situation I would succumb to nostalgia.[162]

The punishment Virginia suffers for her rejection of family possessions in youth is her attachment to and regret for those objects in old age. In the past, when she came home for the holidays, she not only ignored tradition by going to the movies on Christmas day, "as if it were a day like any other,"[163] but was also accustomed to giving fashionable presents that would never be used, "sponge rests for the shower they did not have in the house, radios and record players, electric food warmers, automatic cigarette lighters."[164] She advised her sister to leave home, "not to sit there rotting . . . [in] a dead world."[165] Annoyed when, on her first visit to a cousin in Venice, she was looked down upon as a mountain village girl, she took that opportunity to eagerly observe "every detail to learn as much as she could about how to dress."[166] She swore to herself that she would never again be criticized for her attire. Because of her love for things that represented Italian modernity, her family associated her with the "new millionaires,"[167] whose dissolution contrasted with the sobriety of the decayed aristocracy. In the old-age present, the absence of earlier possessions—which she threw away to feel "free, modern, positive"—prevents her from finding the "continuity . . . [of her] existence."[168] She is unprepared to face death because of the absence of keepsakes for herself and of heirlooms to bequeath to her descendants. Over the years she has sold most of her property to Clara and has delegated to Clara the management of house, garden, and relationships with the village community; thus Virginia loses herself in maniacal automatisms. She occupies herself "in finding something wrong inside the closet or the chest of drawers,"[169] always careful not to make a false move, to "live slowly . . . the days."[170] She has learned to let festivities go by "ignoring them, from morning to night, as if they were like any other day,"[171] and to hide herself on anniversaries.

Virginia's problem, the "something [that] went wrong" at a certain time in her life, is the presumption that she could defy the anachronism of the house in her youth, and then return to it in her maturity. In the unequal struggle between the precariousness of living in one's time and the solidity of a world that resists history, emancipation has been punished with the "demotion" to that accord with the old that her heritage had decreed for her. The accord with the old is a form of knowledge that dates back to "the beginning of childhood," to a time before the child could see monsters in the old furniture; a time, then, that precedes history and ignores it:

> It is as if I had been demoted to the beginning of childhood, before the age of discretion, when everything around me seemed right, normal, perfectly in place, irreplaceable. When all I knew about was the old, to be more precise the ancient, and had not yet seen anything modern. It is as if the insecu-

rity of all these years, the many changes that my life has seen, had pushed me back, making me believe that the only certainty is my house as it was in the past. And now, all of a sudden, the lion legs that appeared from under the chest of drawers, the eagle talon feet of some small tables don't bother me anymore, they seem to me the only possible ones. . . . I feel again a prisoner of the old that has chased after me for my whole life, that I have fled for years; it has reached me, has besieged me, has killed my desire for the new.

It is a slow perversion that has seized me, has made me deny the good rebellious seasons. It is in fact perverse that I should miss that dark big bed. . . . It was absolutely right, instead, that in my childhood nights the furniture in my room should appear to me as monsters.[172]

The house is like a fortress that protects only those who have been faithful to it. Virginia, afraid of possible raids on the house by thieves and criminals, avoids the poorly lit attic and constantly checks whether the French doors are locked. She feels hostile forces threatening and often associates them with the disasters and tragedies she reads about in the papers.

"... *you are a survivor* ..."

Unlike Virginia, Clara has always been faithful to the order of the house. Clara's unbroken relationship with the paternal house causes her to adopt a circular notion of time that guarantees her preservation. Circularity is evident both in nature and in the repetition of models and patterns that were already obsolete when the sisters were young. This concept of time defines Clara's relationship with the garden, her involvement in domestic rituals, and her consciousness of her parents' physical and chronological old age. The nature of the garden is domesticated, untouched by new trends, like the house and the family. Clara in fact detests "flowerbeds and paths, fashionable flowers and decorative trees."[173] In the present Beppina reconstructs for Clara the ceremonies her mother "desperately" repeated "in the same exact way as the year before, same food, same songs, same table,"[174] the Christmases she "copied from the real Christmases of the times when the world was different."[175] Without needing to be told what to do, Beppina knows family traditions to the last detail. At night, after turning off the light, old Clara enjoys the creakings and smells of the house, that, in the perceptions of her visiting nephews, are "the smells of staleness, skirts, and slippers."[176] Smells activate memories and enable recognition across time. The smell of the house is the same "smell of old and wax, of wood and garden, of a touch of mold on the stairs, a touch of camphor in the carpeted drawing room"[177] that Clara deeply inhaled whenever she returned from the visits to her lover in Milan.

Clara's faithfulness to her ancestors' time, which has made it problematic for the young adult character to connect with both twentieth-century transformations in female lives and with the rites of passage and emancipation from the family of origin, turns her old age into a victory over her sister and over history. So compelled has she been throughout her life to submit to her genealogy that she has failed to establish her own descent. However, although she has not participated biologically in the evolution of the family genealogy, Clara has succeeded better than Virginia at carrying out the transmission inside this genealogy because she has complied with the preservation mandate the good family has assigned to its offspring. In her old age Clara is "a survivor" who, "not . . . too unhappy"[178] with herself, shows off her outdatedness. Neither anagraphic old age nor physical deterioration in the narrative present is relevant for this character. Old age is the emblematic condition of her anachronism, which has made her antiquated throughout her entire existence. In old age, outdatedness turns Clara into a figure that is simultaneously ridiculous and unique; it protects her from vain and fleeting fashions and reinforces her identity and integrity. Her clothes and her shoes are "leftovers from another world": she always chooses them "in an outdated model, similar to the ones she bought before, which in their turn resemble those that came before them."[179] Her wavy hairstyle, the narrator observes, "was out-of-fashion even before you started wearing it."[180] Crime in the news, a source of anxiety for Virginia, leaves her indifferent. The newspapers she reads are three days old, and she turns on her black and white TV three or four times a year. She is not interested in books because they "are seldom about your world."[181] If Virginia as an older woman suffers from anxiety and depression, Clara has become harder, more calculating and suspicious. The solitude of old age, consolidated throughout an entire existence, "is the condition in which you find yourself most at ease."[182] Her ties with family property have been consolidated too, thanks to her purchase of some of improvident Virginia's inheritance. Although the two sisters' old-age experiences under the same roof are quite similar and equally desolating, Clara's maniacal relation to house objects is not dictated by the pain of loss but by her will to reaffirm her territorial control.

We can infer from the text that Clara the survivor is destined to survive her sister, in that she tells us that, "as the only one . . . left in the family,"[183] she had to provide for a distant relative's burial. Virginia also predicts, in the last page of her monologue, that she will be the first one to die. Clara's lot as a survivor is less solitary than one would imagine.

The subordinate and devout presence of the third old woman of the house, Beppina, grants Clara not only discreet and obliging company and support from which Virginia is excluded but also a continuous and aproblematic connection with the previous phases of her existence, all of which have included the maid. This figure embodies a female double that is unthreatening in that it is subjected, always a mirror and confirmation of Clara's image, never antagonistic or complementary. Almost as old as Clara, Beppina is "the last one" who really knows her, "who knows how things should be done, how you want the table to be set, the bread toasted, the potatoes sautéed."[184]

Following a model that was quite common among aristocratic and upper-middle-class families, Beppina is the housemaid employed when she was little more than a girl, who has been raised in the patriarchal house and has herself raised the girls of the family. Typically, this figure is considered part of the family and does not establish a family of her own. Her domestication is made possible by the financial and emotional dependency of a work and cohabitation relationship that started when she was very young and has not been very open to contacts outside the family's realm. Like Clara, Beppina also skipped the rites of passage of female adulthood out of loyalty to the good family's mandate, but she is destined to survive Clara, so as to be able to assist her also in her death. If Virginia belongs to a new class of spendthrift millionaires, Beppina, a small saver who insists on turning down her nephews' suggestion that she should quit working, knows how to preserve herself by living a sheltered existence devoid of consumption and of personal investments. She has also carved for herself quite a strong domestic power. Treated by the old mother like a more reliable daughter than Clara and Virginia, Beppina supplies the family during the war and continues, in the present, to insist on getting presents for Clara. In her turn Clara, having recognized that Beppina now has more money than she, has bequeathed to the servant in her will the pieces of junk that Beppina admires. Beppina is gratified by her domestic power, limited in her old age to her relationship with Clara, an ambiguously unequal servant-mistress relationship in which the servant is jealous of her mistress's relatives because her caregiving is exclusive to the mistress. Since Beppina is denied both a retro- and a prospective imaginary of her own, her past coincides with Clara's, whom she "loves for her past," for the way she used to be. As for her future, it consists of waiting for Clara's death.

Strengthened by her survivor role, frugal and wise Clara indulges in new whims in her old age, such as the cigarette and the glass of grappa when her grandnephews, Virginia's grandchildren, take her to the restaurant. With them she takes the lion's share, after creating an emotional void around her sister by alienating Virginia's children, grandchildren, and great-grandchildren. "Leave your great-grandmother alone, don't tire her," Clara says to the children, and runs with them in the garden, "like a girl, cheerful the way she usually is not," inventing for them "more beautiful tales, more stunning surprises"[185] than her sister can think up. Even if her nephews' visits upset the quiet and order of the house, Clara conceals her impatience and carefully manages their interest in the property under her control. She sparingly gives away items to the children—whom the parents "send forward,"[186] encouraging them to ask their great-aunt for spoons, vases, and ashtrays—and reaffirms the power of the tradition she represents over modernity. In fact, though her nephews would like to sell everything and "with the proceeds purchase something at the seaside, or in the mountains, or in a more elegant countryside," their wives have instead discovered "a passion for antiques"[187] in advertisements or in interior decorating magazines. If old curiosities are promoted as "antiques," the good family's class consciousness is reaffirmed and transmitted. The nephews' wives don't like the "junk" Beppina is fond of, but the "good pieces."[188] They would even consider coming to live there, "so as to be able to play chatelaines, to show their friends that they have a past, with the ancestors' portraits in the stairwell."[189]

Having argued with Virginia in the past over the ownership of furniture "as if the pieces of furniture were her children,"[190] Clara makes furniture the pivot of a family transmission that has been emotionally sterile and thwarted by masks and role-playing. Their sterile legacy is the result of a badly addressed exchange of gifts and resources in the past—an example of this is the clothes that Virginia used to give to her mother and sister, that the two other women either never wore or donated to the parish needy. Paradoxically, while pieces of furniture are viewed as children, the grandchildren and grandnephews, unreliable and unpromising heirs of a historically and socially bankrupt genealogy, completely modern in their propensity to divorce and job loss, are "Martians, foreigners with other customs":

> Those who come to you now, paying a visit to their aunt in the old house they hope to inherit, are your nephews' children, with their wives and children. At first sight they seem better than their parents, but it is probably because of their age. They bear no traces of your family, anyway, neither of you nor perhaps of Virginia, and not because of their physical appearance. You recall again your hopes. What has disappointed you is neither their scant success nor the number of marriages nor the wives they have chosen, but the absence of memory in them. Even Beppina looks at them as if they were Martians, foreigners with other customs.[191]

Disillusioned by her family's thoughtlessness yet aware of the need to make a will and order her legacy, Clara directs her final arrangements toward settling scores and the concealment of revealing clues both of family memory and of whatever would associate her memory with Virginia's:

> You must remember to tidy everything up, to settle everything before leaving: burn letters, remove photos, leaf through books for notes you forgot among the pages. Order your file, the account books, the linen closets and also your clothes. . . . You don't want them to discover life fragments that you have never told about, don't want to leave behind traces that may reveal something about you. So that what happened to Virginia will not happen to you.[192]

Identifying Clara as the long-run winner is, however, drawing an inaccurate conclusion. If one examines Clara's condition from a wider chronological perspective than that of her old-age present, one observes that her resistance to change and passages—which tips the scales in her favor in the final confrontation—has in the past caused infinitely greater frustration than her adventurous sister ever experienced. The consequences of her past lifestyle in the present are dissatisfaction and the inconsolable regret for unlived experiences and choices she did not make.

Clara has lived in a sort of temporal limbo "in the warm, at home with Mom and Dad . . . forever underage."[193] Significantly, the first and only reference to her anagraphic age—from which we infer the approximate age of her elder sister Virginia—establishes an identity association with her childhood—"eighty years ago you used to eat the same things"[194]—and underscores the fact that Clara's growth and aging have not substantially changed her childhood habits.

Naturally, it is during young adulthood that the "aged child's"[195] identity is least adequate to Clara's needs. If one considers again the seduction-youth association, one notices that Clara has been the victim of cultural stereotypes that traditionally associate only with female youth both the right to a certain degree of emotional experimentation and the right to the investment of time and family resources in a woman's initiation to relational life. The same stereotypes identify young adulthood as the time of a woman's emancipation from the daughter role through marriage and procreation.

Young Clara's fiancé leaves her at the altar twice. Clara's second man is "[a]n Italian from Milan, one who was involved in politics,"[196] who arrives at the village where the two sisters, their mother and Beppina have evacuated to contact the Partisans and organize the Liberation Committee. The mother is ill-disposed toward him at first because he is a Communist and, although he "[l]ooks decent, is polite, and even better off than us," comes from "another social class."[197] The evening when she finds him playing cards with Clara, Beppina, and Beppina's cousin, the mother rebukes Clara "as if she were a child."[198] In spite of this, Clara cultivates her friendship with the doctor and, after a period of short visits to his apartment in Milan, contemplates the possibility of moving in with him. This relationship is experienced as a transgression of age roles, in relation to both the childhood role in which her parents have cast her and that of a maiden woman who is too mature for love. Conscious of the tardiness of her initiation into adult sexuality, Clara keeps her eyes closed when she undresses for the first time in front of a man "so as not to see a 'no-longer-young maid.'"[199] The fact that she still has "her girlish figure, not spoiled by anything or anyone"[200] pleases her, and the estrangement she experiences in the doctor's city apartment is counterbalanced by the pleasure of making love with him in the paternal house. This gratification represents her revenge over Virginia's visits to that house with husband and children, a violation of her chaste domestic roles, and a profanation of the territory of the house. On the other hand, Clara associates her most intimate moments with the doctor with the loss of her identity: "to prolong to infinity that oblivion," she writes, "allowed her to be like the other women, like Virginia."[201]

". . . how well preserved your sister is . . ."

The dramatic climax of the rivalry with her sister is what allows Clara to preserve her old order and to recover her accord with her mandate and with her anagraphic age. Leaving home would have been possible and fruitful twenty years earlier, not in her middle age.

On the verge of breaking the circular spires of survivorship, Clara is tempted to turn back because she cannot recognize herself in "that other woman dressed in city clothes who timidly climbed the stairs of the doctor's house under the caretaker's inquisitive eyes."[202] This retreating urban alter ego prefigures the event that will precipitate her back to her lot: Virginia's visit to the doctor while she is in Milan to complete some paperwork. This is a short visit that proves to be crucial for its dramatic effects on the sisters' conflict; it adds a suspenseful note to the novel. While rummaging in the closets in search of some traces of Clara, Virginia finds her late husband Tullio's Fascist party membership card and senses that Clara might be responsible, through her association with the doctor, for Tullio's execution. In the same closets Clara finds, some time after Virginia's visit, her sister's robe and slippers; these clues of Virginia's umpteenth betrayal convince Clara to break off her relationship with the doctor without explanations.

"You were not forced to choose between the doctor and your old habits, between the doctor and your mother," Clara reminds herself, "you were granted the privilege of remaining at peace, faithful to yourself, in order."[203] If older Clara's peace is the reward for her delayed choices, choosing her parents and the old order does not however redeem her from genealogical arbitrariness. The fact that in their advanced old age both parents seem not to be able to recognize their daughters—the father could not tell Virginia from Clara, and the mother Clara from Beppina—emphasizes their distance from their offspring and an absence of memory that will be inherited by their grandchildren and great-grandchildren. More importantly, the blurring of the daughters' identities illustrates the interchangeability of roles that had been established in their childhood. Virginia bitterly observes that the result of her and Clara's existences has been "to see their roles exchanged":[204] from her life-review perspective, the sister who has established contacts with the world outside and has procreated does not own anything anymore, and the sister who has never left home has acquired solidity and control over their descent.

We may be tempted, as remarked earlier, to take Virginia's life review as final and see Clara, the survivor's, long-run victory as a sociopolitical commentary that is confirmed by narrative choices. In terms of narrative technique, in fact, Virginia's words are made conclusive by her second-narrator position, and Clara's point of view is made stronger by her incorporation of the mother's and the housemaid's points of view. Ultimate victory in a dual-identity perspective, however, is so tied up with the loss of whatever each took away from the other that the two sisters' life reviews cannot but reflect the mocking paradox of a self-punishing contest.

Interestingly, references to some of the most mockingly arbitrary age-related cultural constructions are employed in the final paragraphs of the sisters' monologues to both bring closure to their rivalry and to leave it ambiguously open-ended. Clara concludes her section with a comment on mistaken age: in the villagers' eyes, Virginia is younger than Clara. "How good your sister looks!" people say when they meet Clara in the street, "[h]ow well preserved she is! Yet, she must be only a couple of years younger than you."[205] Virginia, as the second narrator, closes the novel with the same age-competition motif. In wishing that she will die first "out of revenge," under the illusion that, "if I leave her alone she is forced to pity herself, pity me, love me a little, in her memory," Virginia claims her firstborn primacy. She wants to die first "according to the correct accounting of the dead, because I am the elder."[206] By doing this, she projects an unresolved rivalry—and an equally unresolved desire to be loved by her sister—beyond the boundaries of two interlaced lives and perspectives.

5
Ripening and Completion in Women's Old-Age Novels

INTRODUCTION

THE TWO NOVELS IN THIS CHAPTER ARE MORE DIRECTLY CONCERNED with exploring the realm of old age. The main characters are people who are well into their eighties and struggling with the reality of senescence (Alfonsina in *Ultima luna* and Doris's father in *Apri le porte all'alba*), and people in their fifties and early sixties who must come to terms with their own aging and with their caregiving responsibilities (Silvana and Bruno in *Ultima luna* and Doris in *Apri le porte all'alba*).

The experiences of the protagonists are interwoven with those of other members of old-age communities, and in the course of the narratives the communities are dissected and their inner workings are critically analyzed. The single thematic focus and the critical approach to old-age issues and politics allow the authors to explore diversity in old-age scenarios, in both experiential and institutional terms. The novels narrate the life stories of major and minor characters, different stages of their aging consciousness and senescence, and their individual and collective responses to physical and social impairments. While family relations are just as important for character development as in the first set of novels, the interest in the characters' "age citizenship," i.e., in their relation, as older people, to institutions, from the retirement home network of *Ultima luna* to the municipal interest groups of *Apri le porte all'alba*, places their genealogical concerns in a new perspective. As a social being, the older person is seen in her daily interactions with friends, neighbors, surrogate children, as well as with public officials or strangers she meets or observes in the street. As an older person, she often experiences socialization in terms of fatigue and frustration, as forced exposure to the unfamiliar, as substitute for meaningful contacts or antidote to isolation.

The fact that both novels end with convivial dinner scenes alludes to another common statement they make about socialization. In the final pages of *Ultima luna*, Bruno and Silvana dine with a Japanese ex-Communist friend of Bruno's during the couple's visit to Tokyo; the last dinner in *Apri le porte all'alba*, which takes place at the home of Doris's father, brings together most of the characters with whom the protagonist has interacted in the course of the novel. These communal dinners, in which newly formed couples and singles, friends and parents, children and foster children take part, reveal some optimism regarding intergenerational communication. Both endings celebrate the willingness to integrate complementary drives toward socialization within a vision of old age that is communitarian without being institutionalized. The characters, in fact, seem to be opening to new relationships as well as to be consolidating, under new terms, ties woven into the course of their long existences.

Issues of legacy and continuity are forcefully addressed in the two novels, yet the characters seem to be more open to relationships that question the primacy of biological ties than were the characters of the novels in the first chapter. Flashbacks are quite frequently employed, but they are more fragmented, and interspersed with the narrative present; moreover, the reconstruction of family histories does not extend back in time to distant ancestors. The protagonists are occupied with recollections and life reviews, but are also more realistically situated in present-day Italian contexts. They are also projected toward the future and highly interested in the exploration of their old-age imaginary and in carving their own old-age scenarios out of the options offered by a variety of contemporary sociocultural discourses of aging. Within their single thematic focus, these novels tackle the most relevant and controversial contemporary old-age issues, i.e., older people's institutionalization, urbanization, and socialization patterns, entrustment of caregiving functions to women and to immigrants, impact of feminism on older women's aging consciousness and experiences, and age-role reversal in love relationships. The characters' professional identities, both in the present and in the past, are also explored and play an important role in their development.

The interest in experiences and issues that reach beyond individual and family stories affects narrative technique. *Ultima luna* features a third-person narrator. The first-person narrator of *Apri le porte all'alba* is the protagonist, Doris; since she is a very active and social young-old woman, her account of a maturity crisis is more a social testimony than a personal confession. While focusing on the perspectives and experiences of one or several major characters, the narrators delineate— sometimes merely sketch—a host of minor characters and voice their individual concerns and responses to old age. Although walk-ons abound, often functioning as case studies of eccentric and unpleasant old-age behavior, the narrators' equanimous sympathy for older people keeps them from lapsing into stereotype.

Another result of the interest in multiple perspectives on aging is the experimentation with old-age genres. Although there appears to be no conscious attempt on the part of the authors to situate the novels in existing old-age genres or to launch new old-age genres, many features of these genres are variously employed here. Like many "novels of senescence," *Ultima luna* deals with the "indecencies" of extreme old age; it rejects sentimentalized or idealized notions and focuses instead on food consumption and waste, physical deterioration, and sexual impulses, the latter often presented in their most aberrant forms as manifestation of the will to live. The setting is, as in other novels of senescence, the community or the institution, and the point of view alternates among a number of characters. Like the protagonists of *Vollendungsromane*, the eighty-eight-year-old protagonist of *Ultima luna* is involved in an elaborate process of preparation for her death, entailing not only the life review but also material, practical considerations such as setting up her son with her gerontologist, whom she has decided is the right match for him, and leaving directions for her own funeral and for the allocation of her finances and personal belongings. While disengaging from her life, she also re-engages at different levels and in a different realm: she settles her score with the religious intermediaries—the Virgin Mary in particular—with whom she has maintained a lifelong discourse and sets out in a tragicomic journey through the world of geriatric institutionalization. This and many other narratives of completion are characterized by an ironic or humorous tone born of the awareness of precariousness and loss, and of the arbitrariness of closure.

Reflecting on decline, senility, and death—their own and those of their dear ones—exposes the young-old characters of both novels to psychic growth and allows them to discover new values and life choices. Like the protagonists of *Reifungsromane*, Silvana and Bruno in *Ultima luna* and Doris in *Apri le porte all'alba* experience the awareness of decline and death as a ripening process. Although this process is not necessarily presented as a journey—a typical scheme of *Reifungsromane*—the ripening young old of these novels do travel and, in the process, expand both their self-knowledge and their knowledge of other realms. Bruno and Silvana's most animated discussions on old age and Doris's reflections on companionship and death take place during long car rides across the Roman countryside. Bruno and Silvana's trip to Japan after Alfonsina's death adds a new cross-cultural perspective to their exploration of old age. More importantly, aging awareness engages young-old characters in experimentation with new modes of sexuality and of couple relationship.

The interests of both authors reach far beyond literary creation. They are *engagé* writers and essayists who previously dealt with a number of pressing contemporary issues in quite controversial terms in other writings.

Luce D'Eramo died quite recently, on March 6, 2001, at age 76. Her biography is so exceptional that it is well worth noting its high points. In 1943, at age eighteen, she gave up her comfortable upper-middle-class family life—both parents held offices in the Fascist government—to run away to Germany and enlist as a volunteer worker for the Third Reich. Her aim was to verify the truth of what she had heard about concentration camps. Her odyssey is narrated in the novel *Deviazione* (1979): the internment in a lager, the escape from Dachau, the bombardment that left her paralyzed in her legs while she was helping excavate the ruins of a building and confined her to a wheelchair at age nineteen. The themes of all her subsequent novels, including *Ultima luna*, are "deviations," experiences of otherness, extreme scenarios that speak of marginalization. In *Nucleo zero* (1981), for example, she analyzes an imaginary group of terrorists who work undercover; *Partiranno* (1986) is the story of some extraterrestrials who live on Earth among humans.

Besides writing fiction, Elena Gianini Belotti, who was born in 1929, has been a pedagogist and a freelance journalist. She directed the Montessori Birth Center in Rome from 1960 to 1980 and authored the essay *Dalla parte delle bambine*, a landmark in Italian post-1968 feminism that has had forty-one editions since its first publication in 1973. The book, whose English title is *What are Little Girls Made of? The Roots of Feminine Stereotypes*, is a study of the nature and impact of gender-based cultural conditioning in the formation of female roles during the early years of life. At the other end of the spectrum, Gianini Belotti has also demonstrated a long-standing commitment to denouncing cultural constructions of female old age that restrict women's freedoms. Before *Apri le porte all'alba*, she published the short-story collection *Adagio un poco mosso* (1993) on the same topic. Another age- and gender-related concern of Gianini Belotti's is age-role reversal. In addition to the essay discussed in the first part of this study, *Amore e pregiudizio*, she also wrote *Il fiore dell'ibisco* (1985), a novel on the eye-opening encounter of a young man with the middle-aged woman who had been his nanny when he was a child.

Both authors published their novels when they were in their late sixties. Their closeness in age to their protagonists and their direct experience of old age explain their familiarity with the realm of old age and its articulations, as well as with the diversity of human types that people it. D'Eramo's personal history of disability also contributes to her insight into the experiences of old age as frailty and of physical limitation as conducive to reification in both physical and social terms.[1]

Luce D'Eramo's *Ultima luna*

Ultima luna [Waning Moon] is an extensive work, packed with themes and probing questions. It is divided into five parts and twenty-seven chapters, and contains three narrative threads set in the present and one set in the past. One of the narrative threads chronicles the last days in the life of Alfonsina, an eighty-eight-year-old resident of Villa Felice, a luxury retirement home in the Roman hillside. Alfonsina is visited by her sixty-year-old son, Bruno, a writer and journalist who lives in Japan, where he sought a new start twenty-six years earlier, after a disappointing militancy in the Italian Communist party. Alfonsina engineers the plot of the entire novel. Before dying, she wants to realize her long-nourished dream of setting up Bruno with Silvana, a very caring fifty-year-old gerontologist who works at Villa Felice. Since Alfonsina has often mentioned Silvana in her letters to Bruno and has read many of Bruno's letters to Silvana, Alfonsina's son and the gerontologist — who already know a lot about each other — develop a strong, almost conjugal bond in the few days of Bruno's visit. The second thread in *Ultima luna* concerns the growth and consolidation of Bruno and Silvana's couple relationship, both in Italy and in Japan. After Alfonsina's funeral, in fact, Bruno and Silvana leave on a trip to Tokyo. This is another wish of Alfonsina's, who had even set some money aside for two return tickets, to make it possible for the two to meet after her death. During the trip, Bruno shows Silvana his tiny apartment and takes her on a comprehensive visit of the city. They visit buildings, streets, and communities that are in poorer, older neighborhoods of Tokyo; these communities are marginalized and usually escape the eye of the tourist. The chronicle of the visit to Japan, which is intertwined with the second narrative thread, is the third and concluding story of *Ultima luna*. The novel closes on an open-ended dinner scene at a Tokyo restaurant, during which Bruno introduces Silvana to a Japanese friend, and future professional goals and plans for rendezvous across Italy, Russia, and Japan are discussed.

Ultima luna also features a novel within a novel, Bruno's autobiographical manuscript, regarding which he intends to make editorial contacts in Milan during his Italian visit. While in Milan, Bruno leaves a copy of the manuscript with Silvana; Bruno's autobiography fills his short absence and gives Silvana the opportunity to become acquainted with his past. While the narrative present in which the other three stories are set is a relatively short yet highly eventful time span—Bruno spends little more than a week at Frascati, a couple of days in Milan, then he and Silvana leave for Tokyo—the autobiographical manuscript covers thirty years of a life. It narrates in third person the childhood of a man abandoned by his father and raised by a mother who bravely fought against financial restraints and familial hostility and sacrificed her own life to give him a good education. It also describes his unhappy and naïve youth, during which he enthusiastically embraced the Communist cause; the story ends with his expulsion from the party and escape to Japan.

Ultima luna is a conglomerate of life-course genres—novel of senescence, *Reifungsroman*, *Vollendungsroman*, *Bildungsroman*, and travel narrative—as well as of styles and themes. Filippo La Porta points out that "the novel presents itself . . . as a capacious container in which ethical-philosophical reflections, minute descriptions of in-patients, treatise-like discussions of old-age issues are quite comfortably crammed with expositions of various theories . . . observations on very prosaic daily facts, numerous quotes by other authors . . . and even . . . with an internal novel."[2] *Ultima luna* is ambitious and unusual in many ways, in its setting as well as in its treatment of major narrative themes (love, death, corporeality, money). Yet, it is a mainstream novel at its core: the great-saga rhythm, the compact and explicative dialogue, the minimalist touches, the employment of linguistic commonplaces and stereotypes, and the rejection of ideologies reflect, in fact, widespread contemporary narrative practices.

Ultima luna is, at the same time, a postideological and a paradigmatic novel: although characters are markedly ideological—the narrator seldom misses the opportunity to comment on the sociopolitical implications of individual actions and conditions—D'Eramo's mistrust for every ideology or pseudo-ideology is underscored to the utmost. As with other turn-of-the-millennium Italian novels—for example, the best-seller *Va' dove ti porta il cuore*—old age is associated with a sensitivity to the core of one's humaneness and with the dismantling of ideological delusions. All that is not "human"—political or geriatric institutions, scientific progress, economic and intellectual productivity—ends up backfiring on humanity itself. In this novel, old age is an opportunity for the characters to take stock not only of their existential choices but also of the cultural trends of their time. Having weeded out what was least essential in their lives, older people become "prisms reflecting mentalities and ideas of their time."[3] As we shall see through concrete examples taken from the text, the "almost indecent morality"[4] with which the novel highlights both the prosaic nature of physical decay and the relation between this aspect of physicality and desire, turns old age into the metaphor of a process of "unveiling"[5] and of cultural deconstruction.

As a novel of senescence, *Ultima luna* presents perhaps the most complete picture in Italian literature of the old-age planet and of its inner relations: relations between active and marginalized or institutionalized old age and between different old-age and aging classes. One may argue that in *Ultima luna* the novel of senescence contains the *Reifungsroman* — Bruno and Silvana's love story. Chiara Maucci maintains, in fact, that "by discussing the senile realm the well-tuned minds of the two 'contestants' begin to confront and, ultimately, understand each other."[6] My study investigates, within the complex structure of *Ultima luna*, the novel of senescence, the *Vollendungsroman*, and the *Reifungsroman* and takes into account their intersection as well as the variety of themes they include. References to the two other novels in the novel — Bruno's *Bildungsroman* and the travel narrative set in Japan[7] — are cursory and functional to the analysis of the three protagonists' development.

". . . let me tell you once and for all that I'm not your grandma . . ."

The novel of senescence presents a wide-angle view of the geriatric care market. When leaving Rome on the Tuscolana to head for Villa Felice at Frascati, Silvana sees an endless row of billboards for private residences with inviting names: Happy Villa, Joyful Hotel, Placid Villa, Rebirth Hotel, House of Life, Spring Oasis, Immaculate Conception Home, Sweet Refuge.[8]

In public hospices, house rules are stricter than in private residences — "couples are separated . . . husbands and wives live in different pavilions, divided also during meals" — and a hospitalized resident "loses her bed"[9] to the next person in the hospice waiting list. However, one of the consequences of the need to manage the imbalance between high demand and limited facilities is the creation of model communities selected according to distributive-equity criteria, real examples of Socialist ghettos for older people. Signorina Proietti, a cheerful and active resident of the public retirement home at Pineta Sacchetti, describes her stay there in such positive terms as to convince Alfonsina that this would be the ideal solution for her, in that it would allow her to cease being a financial burden on her son Bruno. At the Pineta Sacchetti there are "no differences between the rich and the poor" since every older person contributes half of her retirement pension and they are all treated the same way; they all have "an identical single room."[10] Furthermore, since personnel turnover is compulsory, "there can be no favoritism, you can't buy any special assistance from the attendants with tips."[11]

5: RIPENING AND COMPLETION IN WOMEN'S OLD-AGE NOVELS 135

Another option is home assistance. Silvana regularly pays home visits to a few patients who, taking advantage of a willingness they rarely find in their relatives, vent all their resentment on her:

> At first, following a reflex of her profession, she had tried to understand to what degree the older woman was affected by senile regression and where play-acting began. Impossible to disentangle: the old maid and the little girl had blended in the spires of her brain, so that an adult cunning sharpened her childish whims. "You are evil," Signorina Cubini's voice screeched on the phone, "you pretend you love old people yet do not cure my intestines." Or she would welcome her at the door by saying: "Bad Doctor Lanzi, bad, bad, have you repented abandoning me?"[12]

The stereotype of the "old child," of the return to a childish natural state freed from the complications of adult life is fairly widespread. Even Silvana, who deeply respects and loves her patients, is accused by Bruno of treating them like children. When organizing a wake and a memorial party in honor of Alfonsina, Silvana tries to shake up the geriatric institution by allowing all the residents to express and share their responses to Alfonsina's death. The institution inclines instead toward sheltering the residents from the reality of death—for example by moving the dying to the hospital by ambulance, "possibly in the middle of the night when there are no witnesses."[13] In the exhilaration of a challenge by which she knows she is liquidating her career (she resigns from Villa Felice after this episode), Silvana adopts a protection strategy similar to those employed by the geriatric institution to conceal the truth from the old. She pretends that the refreshment and the funeral wreath were paid for by Bruno, not with the money Alfonsina had set aside for this purpose. She does this because older people wish to believe and to make others believe that their children take on financial and social responsibilities in their stead and on their behalf. After the funeral, she instructs the drivers of the shuttle buses that carried the Villa Felice residents to the cemetery and warns them in a businesslike manner: "Drive all the residents back to Villa Felice. Heaven forbid you leave anyone behind! Ask Signor Oliviero Zanchi to help you assemble and count them."[14]

Assembling and counting the elderly, opening their purses and paying for them, as a male nurse does with the taxi driver who transported Alfonsina, physically tried by her visit to the public hospice, back to Villa Felice, is not really an imposition. The older person's psychophysical decline necessitates social and medical care. Like the child, the older person, at the other end of existence, must be protected and taken care of. The problem of senile weakness and regression is, however, complemented by the need of the active community to control old age and to exorcize it by simplifying it. A way of simplifying is the habit — particularly common among the personnel of hospitals and geriatric institutions — to address the residents informally and call them "granny" or "grandpa," thus placing them in one of the most reassuring roles of our cultural imaginary. "My dear little grannies and grandpas, dinner is ready!"[15] a nurse shouts to the mass of old people heading for the public hospice cafeteria. "Let me tell you once and for all that I'm not you grandma,"[16] Alfonsina would like to say to the taxi driver who took her to Pineta Sacchetti. But she chooses to take no notice because she feels so exhausted. The domestication of old age is thus accomplished through the familiarization of the older person, who is no longer Mister, Miss, or Doctor, but whom we turn into our grandfather, or even our son. Thus the private nurse of centenarian Professor Gabetti, a "medical luminary . . . who still reads Catullus in Latin," brags to Villa Felice residents and visitors about the fact that, if she is gone for five minutes, the professor "starts crying, he calls me Mama, you know, he's like a three-year-old child."[17]

A great man's humiliating decline illustrates the transformative power of old age over the adult personality, over styles and behaviors that required "a long exercise of courtesy,"[18] over values and convictions founded on lifelong reflections and choices. At the level of identity, old age is both an unknown realm and a revelation. The notion that "one ages the way one has lived"[19] is clearly not true. A person who has devoted her life to the cultivation, search for, and construction of the self may become a model of proper bearing, like Professor Maria, or a source of wisdom, to whom people turn for advice, like Oliviero Zanchi, but she or he may also fail to become either, as in the case of Professor Gabetti.

Certainly old age, particularly when it involves adjusting to a new, totalitarian microsociety such as a geriatric institution, demands a redefinition of the self, a work of deconstruction with respect to the roles and the power relations one has exercised or to which one has been subjected in one's life outside the institution; it also demands a reconstruction of one's persona within the new community. The psychophysical decline and the implosiveness of a claustrophobic, repetitive, and unproductive lifestyle may transform the new persona into a grotesque caricature of herself. Alfonsina's case is different and will be discussed later: her successful adjustment and a good public image within the Villa Felice community represent for her an opportunity for personal refinement and social redemption.

The retirement home residents redefine their identity in relation to both the institutional microcosm and the outside world. This is a community that, even in its internal relationships, lives in the reflected light of the "real" society, by which the residents measure themselves, particularly when someone's relatives enter, either physically, as visitors, or conceptually, as heroes of individual narratives that become part of the collective imaginary in the closed discourse of the community. The relationship with the outside society may be one of imitation or of antagonism: the elderly in the novel seem to model themselves "for play"—the play of old age, that distorts features and turns characters into tragicomic masks—or "out of spite" toward the outside world—the same spite that animates and motivates the existences of Gianini Belotti's older women. No matter how open and gratifying socialization within the geriatric institution may be, in terms of identity, the relationship with the other elderly is exclusively one of antagonism because each of them is horrified to see herself reflected in the other members of the community. Silvana describes to Bruno the community's reaction to a new member's arrival as a process of redefining territories and hierarchies, a process founded on a dynamics of investment in and resentment of their active relatives. Retirement home residents, in fact, perceive their relatives as their representatives in the productive society, as if they had delegated their younger family members to fill, in their place and on their behalf, the social roles that older people can no longer play:

> Try to put yourself in the shoes of an older person who enters a retirement home knowing that she has to settle there. This older person has crossed the threshold. She knows that, from now on, she'll live side-by-side with old people. The thought wrings her heart. She mirrors herself in the contemporaries she sees around. . . . "No," she rebels; "I'm not like them." And she cannot but prove to herself, to her peers, to the home personnel, that she is different. She is not an outcast. She is not a wreck. . . . But also the longtime residents feel cut to the quick when they are looked at as wrecks by the newcomer. . . . They go up to her cautiously, in small knots; they stop nearby, all singing the praises of one another too loudly. The new resident introduces herself. They start to up the ante. . . . In the hall, in the living room, when they meet each other in the corridors, veterans and newcomer try to outdo each other, dropping names of relatives, friends, first-rate acquaintances who are very, very attached to them. . . . But the more they brag about their dear ones, the more they reproach in their hearts the people they have mentioned, for sending them away. Resentment activates memories; the turmoil of grudges and regrets stirs up their minds. It is an insidious phase for the hypertensive. Some break down. But they are few. Resentment is such a source of energy! It gives them purpose.[20]

When the older person recollects and shares her memories with the other residents, "the turmoil of grudges and regrets" produces composite narratives. In these narratives, the personal recollection transfigures the old-age present; it also intertwines, at the same time, with the present experience of institutionalization. In the Villa Felice living room the residents tell each other dreams in which late-lamented uncles and grandmothers invite them to join them in death. This is a resident's dream:

> Yes, Signora Alfonsina, they had come out of the door to welcome me. "Wait before you come in," they say, "we have a surprise for you." As you know, yesterday was my seventy-ninth birthday and I realize that they are preparing a party for me in the room behind that door. I'm no longer afraid and I suddenly feel very happy. I was looking good, wearing my best outfit; I had the figure I used to have once. And just when I was feeling so happy, a door is flung open. My father and Uncle Angelo line up on either side of me. And what do I see?. . . .
> . . . I see a dining room with square tables like the ones we have in our cafeteria. And who was sitting at the tables? . . . My maternal grandmother, my paternal grandmother, Aunt Umberta whom I could never stand, Aunt Caterina, Aunt Sandra, my mother-in-law, all deceased, you understand? Wearing black veils on their heads, they were saying: "Come, come and join us."[21]

Because the ghettoized older people do not participate in political events and decisions, some of them tend to obstinately dig in their heels in their opinions and keep "their eyes fixed on the outside world that reaches them through television."[22] In the presence of a visitor like Bruno, whom the Villa Felice residents consider a qualified interlocutor, they try to outdo one another in capturing his attention and to involve him in debates. Their obsessive demands for his opinions regarding their often-categorical stances (which are made absurd by the absence of real cultural exchange with a rapidly transforming society and by forms of senile delirium), are paralleled by a just-as-categorical deafness of the external interlocutor. The visitor in most cases turns them out either because she thinks that an older person's words carry no weight or because she is afraid to see herself mirrored in the politically informed older person. This is, understandably, one of Bruno's major concerns: *"politics as the last resort* [my italics] darted across Bruno's mind; his hair stood on end; in a flash he had a vision of himself wizened and furrowed by sclerosis, repeating over and over the outdated convictions of his youth."[23]

". . . she implored the Virgin Mary to help her begin all over again . . ."

Alfonsina's case is different: her retirement to a luxury geriatric institution represents the opportunity to disengage from a dissatisfactory adult persona, that of a humiliated and resentful woman of the people, abandoned by her husband and rapaciously attached to her son. Her old-age persona, instead, is that of an older widow who is respected and loved by the Villa Felice community because of her urbanity and human availability. Alfonsina's *Vollendungsroman* has an interesting development, the phases of which require a close analysis. The fact that her personality, social status, and power over people and events grow through an experience of institutionalized old age is the basis for her heroine stature in the novel. Moreover, this peculiar direction of her old-age development is the true reason for the incongruence between the character of Alfonsina in Bruno's *Bildungsroman* and the same character in her own *Vollendungsroman*. There is in fact a noticeable age-identity gap in Alfonsina's development across the two narrative levels, a gap that some reviewers have identified as a narrative limitation of *Ultima luna*.[24]

Alfonsina, born at the beginning of the twentieth century, a single mother in Fascist Rome and a hard-working trouser maker constantly struggling against economic restraints in postwar times, has not had an easy life. After her husband left for America and started a new family there, Alfonsina became very attached to her son. Her exclusive love for him "fed on a three-headed hate: hate for the Fascist rich and the priests, disguised with smiles, entreaties, and propitiating thanks; arrogant and, at the same time, oblique hate for her 'dirt-poor' neighbors; finally, unconditional hate for her 'home enemies,' that is her relatives."[25] At thirty, her son, disillusioned with the Communist party and eager to leave behind a painful past that he associated with his mother, left for Japan. Alfonsina "was 62 at the time, and at 70 she realized she could no longer keep house. She wrote to her son that she would retire to an old-age hospice."[26] At the beginning of the novel we find her at Villa Felice, where she has lived for eighteen years, eager and proud to show her son Bruno to the community. She has not seen him for twenty-six years, and he has shouldered the expenses of his mother's residence at Villa Felice all these years. Alfonsina hopes that this visit will allow her to realize the dream of setting her son up with gerontologist Silvana Lanzi, for whom she feels strong esteem and affection. It is more plot than dream: she has been weaving this plot for a long time, in her correspondence with Bruno and in her conversations with Silvana. On the eve of her nineties, she is finally a fulfilled woman—fulfilled by her son's presence and success, a patrimony she can show off to the other residents by introducing him with "a whole hierarchy of tones": sometimes "haughty, other times confidential, or even careless."[27] Within the warily managed limits of her modest existence, Alfonsina has become a powerful woman. Her character is a very realistic example of the particular power an older person may exercise at the end of her existence, of the way one can play all the available cards in one's last game. The novel aims to highlight, through the study of old age, the ethical and economic conditionings of this type of power, first of all by openly addressing the relation people are likely to establish with money in the final, economically unproductive phase of their lives.

Alfonsina's stake is high for an eighty-eight-year-old woman, for whom the emotion of seeing her son has just caused a heart failure. She wants to make Bruno return to Italy, to find him a suitable old-age companion, and to bequeath some money to him. Grounded in the petit-bourgeois culture of saving, Alfonsina carefully calculates the costs of both her own old age and Bruno's, as well as the costs of her death. Personal dignity in this culture is founded in no small part on the ability to anticipate and autonomously provide for the expenses of funeral service and burial: a gesture of financial independence that redeems the humiliations of an existence of sacrifice and economic dependency. Alfonsina includes two unnecessary expenses in the costs of death: a sumptuous reception for the Villa Felice residents and a solemn, sung mass. She knows that the shrewdest way of managing family resources is to rigorously avoid extras (she has never had a coffee at the Villa Felice café), so as to set aside part of the sum that each month Bruno sends for her boarding charge. In addition to covering funeral and burial expenses, her postal book savings are intended for the purchase of plane tickets to Japan for both Bruno and Silvana. She has carefully calculated the cost of the one-way and return flights necessary to join them after her death. Alfonsina's will is like the directions for a treasure hunt: meticulously laid out in her room, in old boxes whose keys she keeps fastened to her underwear with a safety pin, are letters and receipts that instruct Bruno how to proceed. The directions are complicated by the fact that Alfonsina cannot know exactly when she will die; thus it is impossible to say when the commands in her missives will be put into effect. The letters are numerous, and the gradualness with which Bruno and Silvana retrieve them creates a dramatic crescendo in the rhythm of the long wake sequence.

Alfonsina's most challenging final scheme is the decision to move to the public hospice. This absurd plan is presented as "the revolution that was about to take place in her life."[28] Although such revolution may rejuvenate the character, who devises escape plans like a boarding-school girl and is "thrilled" by the prospect of "new acquaintances, new habits, a new world,"[29] her preparation for a new life phase is not functional to a life passage. It is a prelude and, in some ways, an attempt to carry out, through a last and supreme waste of her life energies, the only real possibility of an existential passage, that from old age to death.

5: RIPENING AND COMPLETION IN WOMEN'S OLD-AGE NOVELS 141

For a believer like Alfonsina, the preparation for this new phase is, first of all, of a religious kind. The most interesting aspect of this passage is the combination of spiritual and economic rationales, the disclosure, through Alfonsina's delirium, of how the mixture of self-interest and superstition typical of popular religiosity between the two world wars[30] may become foundational to the exercise of power *in extremis*.

Alfonsina has been able to enjoy a comfortable old age, thanks to her son's earnings in Japan. Through her final decision to move to the public hospice, whose boarding charge she could pay on her own, she intends to take a further step toward overcoming a past of misery and humiliations, that of total financial independence:

> She was no longer a dependent old woman, who rests on someone else's will. She was making decisions, undertaking things. Against winds and tides.
> She pushed away her blanket and set her feet on the ground. She knew what she was looking for.
> She pulled a small box out of the wall closet, locked with a key that she constantly kept on, fastened to her underwear with a safety pin. She unlocked the box and took out the postal savings book, which she slipped into her purse.
> "If only they had told me," she chuckled under her breath, "when I was working as a maid, then as a trouser maker, and even as a seamstress, and I had to economize on everything, that one day I would become a millionaire! This too I owe the Virgin Mary, the satisfaction of dying as a lady, without feeling ashamed."[31]

Alfonsina's declaration of independence is not merely an invocation; it is a sign of decisiveness and initiative, which translates into definite acts, such as moving away the blanket, getting off the bed, taking the savings book out of the box. However, the satisfaction of dying as a lady is not perceived as her own achievement; it is rather a supernatural gift. Her interlocutor is the Virgin Mary, also a woman, more accessible than the Almighty, therefore endowed with a positive power that can be influenced; with her, one can enter "into negotiation."[32] When leaving her room to set out on her secret journey to Pineta Sacchetti, and "[f]eeling that she was on the verge of collapsing, [Alfonsina] implored the Virgin Mary to help her begin all over."[33] Alfonsina's "last wish"[34] is presented as an outstanding account: as such, it cannot be denied. Conversely, the received favor turns into a "credit"[35] that the Virgin Mary has with her. When Alfonsina happens to overhear a resident of the public hospice talking about that place in very positive terms, she interprets this coincidence as a manifestation of the divine will: it is in God's plans that she should move there. Rather than trusting in the signs of the divine Providence, however, Alfonsina appropriates these signs by transforming them from mysteries into revelations of certainties, and from certainties into commodities:

> Our Lady of the Divine Love was thus granting the two greatest wishes of her life: that her son get married and that he come back to live in Italy. At the incredible thought of what her little prayer had set in motion—all was fulfilled at once—Alfonsina felt as if she were melting like water. . . .
>
> When she was alone, she crossed herself: "Virgin and Mother Mary, how can I thank You? You have even allowed me to catch a glimpse of Your designs. Queen of Heaven, I know, you have never left things half-done. . . ."
>
> She also understood that she must repay the Virgin for the immense favor she had granted her of seeing Bruno with her own eyes, for the new request she put forward to Her, and for the two-birds-with-a-stone deal the Virgin had sent flashing through her mind.[36]

In the intense religious discourse that pervades the pages devoted to her visit to the public hospice, Alfonsina not only invokes and flatters the divinity, as is natural; in the urgency of the last prayer, she also adopts authoritarian tones by "speaking resolutely to God Almighty's face" and trying to corner Him so that "He could not sneak off."[37] She "pockets" divine favors, "repays" and "returns" them, or "throws them in the Providence's face," renegotiates pacts and discusses expenses. By doing so, she also casts light on some far-from-spiritual aspects of the "death market":[38]

> So I implore You [Divine Providence], suggest to me quickly something to lay at the feet of the Virgin of the Divine Love. I will never be able to repay Her, but let Her at least take pity on me in light of my good will. . . .
>
> . . . I have pocketed this third favor as if it were already granted. To the point of even throwing it in the Providence's face! . . .
>
> . . . I return Your third favor to You now, unused until such time as I am able to renew my vow.[39]

But the Virgin Mary also ought to remember that she had never wasted a penny: "The remainder of my boarding charge, You know that, I deposit it in my postal savings book every month, together with most of my retirement pension. And I have saved so much money that, after buying my coffin and paying for the funeral, a tidy sum of money will be left for Bruno. I only want a two-horse carriage to take me to the Verano. Is it too much? Consider, though, that I don't want any waste of flowers. I have seen them, you know, all those wreaths thrown into a pile behind the mortuary to rot like garbage. I'll have only a pillow of seasonal flowers prepared." A flash of light crossed her face: "Why on earth should we leave this flower pillow to waste in the cemetery. Don't you agree? I'll ask Bruno to pick it up, after accompanying me to my tomb, and to take it to Your Sanctuary on my behalf."[40]

In her feverish attempts at settling scores and making life-changing decisions before dying, Alfonsina reveals a strong final determination to steer the course of her life. Although ultimately forced to implosion by the lack of vital energies, her almost-frantic determination to supervise her own death guarantees the execution of her will and strongly affects the process of image de- and re-construction after her death.

Alfonsina not only manages to deliver letters, receipts, savings books, and gifts, which are unfailingly retrieved and handed out to their addressees, but she also manages to upset the structure and the rules of the geriatric institute by becoming the first case of "authorized" death — with a proper funeral wake, celebrated and decorously ritualized—in the history of Villa Felice.

The problem of what image and legacy Alfonsina may leave to Bruno, her primary heir, is more complex, because Alfonsina's image is tainted by her association with a burdensome past. In Bruno's eyes, his mother embodies the hauntingly vindictive "wounded Feminine" that is associated with older female family members in the novels discussed in the previous chapter.

During the funeral wake, to which the novel devotes two chapters, Bruno witnesses various stages of transfiguration of his mother's face. At first, the dead woman's face appears to him dispossessed of her traits and attitudes by a "Buddha smile impersonating the quiet of the 'mu.'"[41] Later in the vigil, it appears rejuvenated by another expression he "did not know, one of profound indulgence."[42] Ultimately, it goes back to its usual look, regaining its "yellowed . . . old-woman color," "her stubborn expression,"[43] after her jaw has given way and Bruno has had to bandage it.

Although Alfonsina succeeded, on her deathbed, in making Silvana promise that she and Bruno would grow old together, the conflict inherent in the relationship between Bruno and Silvana reaches its peak at Alfonsina's funeral. On this occasion, Bruno is confronted with a new aggressiveness on Silvana's part. By acting as the zealous executrix of Alfonsina's last provisions and dispossessing Bruno of all responsibilities and decision-making power in the organization of the funeral service, Silvana turns into an authoritarian mother figure. In this last hand-to-hand struggle against maternal transfigurations, Bruno seizes the only power left to him: he modifies the epitaph his mother wrote by censuring the information about her identity and keeping only the anagraphic data. Thus Alfonsina's epitaph—which she intended to read, "she lived happily sewing clothes / grew old under the protection of her son Bruno / died in God's faith"[44]—is edited by Bruno into a much drier, standard inscription: "ALFONSINA VINCI widow GORDINI / born in Rome on 13 March 1904 / died at Frascati on 10 September 1992."[45] As expected, this gesture deeply disappoints Silvana and estranges her from Bruno.

Bruno's final act of disobedience to both Silvana and Alfonsina is, however, a deeply liberating stance, which allows him to become reconciled with the maternal figure and, ultimately, to acknowledge her strength. This reconciliation takes place through an emotionally and intellectually powerful associative process, whose central metaphor is the "Lorenz butterfly." The image of the butterfly, whose fluttering of wings in Tokyo may cause a tornado in Arizona a year later, symbolizes the powerful effects of imponderable concatenations. This image, which Bruno has always found very suggestive, represents the inscrutable connections among the most profound issues and emotions in his existence, with regard to his political militancy, his activity as a writer, and his personal ties.

Bruno's experiences as a young man taught him to transcend a linear, consequential interpretive approach, based on cause-effect relations. His personal experiences in fact taught him that "as a boy he was respected by his classmates when he no longer cared about them, and that he was good at school when his heart turned to the Party," and when "he devoted soul and body to Communist militancy, the Party expelled him."[46] Following his departure from Italy and from the places of his youth, he underwent a process of emotional disinvestment. This process was influenced by his contact with ancient Japanese philosophies and with a modern practice, word processing. The ups and downs of his integration in a foreign country made him discover the "incredible permeability" of things: he learned to observe them without getting too involved personally, to pursue "the dream of impassibility that Soseki praised."[47] The exercise in the production of "unstable texts" through word processing also taught him to sharpen his "mental guard" and his immediate awareness of "the incidence of the minutest details."[48] The human ideal that Bruno, a science fiction writer, has gradually developed for himself is an attitude of "docile and neutral permeability,"[49] which can be learned from computers. The docile permeability Bruno pursues is a postmodern, postideological conglomerate of orientalisms and technologisms.

This existential approach was practicable "until the void of old age had gaped before him"[50] and had drawn him back to Italy to visit his

5: RIPENING AND COMPLETION IN WOMEN'S OLD-AGE NOVELS 145

mother after a twenty-six-year absence. Nevertheless, the discipline of permeability is what allows Bruno to finally resolve his conflict with the maternal. Permeability is compatible if not synonymous with obedience: obedience to both the voice of his heart and the will of his mother, who, like a butterfly wing fluttering, has set in motion Bruno's and Silvana's futures. "You are my butterfly wing," Bruno mentally addresses his mother at the end of his second and last visit to the cemetery, "because you have set this story in motion."[51] In the symbolic conclusive act of his relationship with Alfonsina, the cleaning of the tomb after the funeral ceremony, we see Bruno run to the water fountain, then head back for the wall of burial vaults, holding the jar filled to rim in his hands and thinking: "If I don't lose a single drop, Alfonsina will be at peace."[52] Bruno demonstrates propitiatory concerns and gestures that are at once childish and maternal and are, in any case, very distant from his adult lifestyle. This exercise in permeability signals his reconciliation with the maternal figure. It also represents, in more general terms, his acceptance of difference, in terms of both gender and age, that is, his willingness to make room within for the maternal as well as for the childish self.

". . . if you love me, you'll have to love my old age . . ."

The second visit to the cemetery marks the fall of the defensive wall between Bruno and Silvana and opens the way to their constructive acceptance of their relationship. In Bruno's case, this is the first time he accepts a woman as a partner: Bruno "had never lived with a woman longer than two days"[53] before then. Given the characters' ages, this choice signals their maturity and prospective orientation toward old age.

As previously observed, the novel of senescence and the *Reifungsroman* are connected by a reciprocally generative relation in *Ultima luna*. Bruno and Silvana meet first in Alfonsina's heart and mind, then in the setting of the retirement home. On the other hand, the novel's theoretical debate on old age develops for the most part through the numerous heated encounters between Bruno and Silvana on this topic.

Bruno's Marxist training steers him toward a political interpretation of old-age issues, which Silvana finds abstract and ineffective. This perspective, however, allows Bruno to grasp the complicity of Marxism— "which, by praising the centrality of work, makes older people's isolation inevitable"[54]—with certain mechanisms of exclusion and discrimination. With "a singsong intonation in his voice" that betrays, according to Silvana, his "conceptual matrix," Bruno claims that "a society based on the myth of productivity cannot but discredit unproductive old age, at a time when . . . precisely because of its sanitary *productivism*, this same society *produces* many elderly."⁵⁵

While Bruno suggests dealing with aging issues "at the cultural level,"⁵⁶ Silvana firmly supports practical, grassroots intervention. Her stance is first of all motivated by the missionary zeal Silvana brings to her professional duties. Her professional crisis—which has its epilog in the face-off with the director of the retirement home on the occasion of Alfonsina's funeral and which results in her resignation—and the crescendo of the ideological and emotional tension between her and Bruno lead Silvana to radicalize her stance. According to Silvana, "we live in the era of euphemism," which forbids us "to say 'old'": our inability to name old age is only a sign of our "repression of the decay of the body, of the physicality of death."⁵⁷ It is through the language of the aging body and through the purest form of this language—for example, the absolute perfection (absolute in its freedom from reason) of the digestive process of "vegetating" older people—that Silvana tries to interpret reality. This is also the language by which animals communicate; this is how Silvana's beloved cats greet her, by going to their litter box as soon as she comes back home, because "shitting near her was the greatest sign of their friendship."⁵⁸ This is also, and most significantly, the language of sexuality. Only by acknowledging the physical contiguity between the sexual act and physiological functions, the impossibility to disassociate "fecundation . . . [from] the intestines," can one learn not to "separate sex from lived intimacy."⁵⁹

This is the direction in which sexual intimacy between Silvana and Bruno develops. When Silvana and Bruno go to bed together for the first time, at the end of an evening of endless conversations in which only their minds, not their bodies, have communicated, it is difficult for them to initiate sexual contact. Only after Silvana's liberating laugh in response to the noise of the toilet flush pushed by the older man living in the next-door apartment can Bruno relax and be aroused. Sexual desire becomes rooted in the body, and death itself turns into physical desire. "If a dead person smells bad," Silvana shouts at the point of greatest conflict with Bruno and with geriatric institutions for their way of interpreting the funeral rite, "I breathe it in like the future smell of my corpse."⁶⁰ At the time of her difficult parting from her old patients, Silvana declares her love: "I like to be with them because I love them. . . . I live in them. And I also live their death."⁶¹ In the love covenant between Silvana and Bruno, this pronouncement translates into the request to love each other's old age and death: "'If you love me,' she uttered the word they had never said before, 'you'll have to love my old age, you'll have to love my death.'"⁶²

Ultima luna presents a "paradoxically unusual" version of the love-death theme. "The paradox," writes Adele Cambria, "lies in the fact that the story. . . . of two people who love each other while looking old age and death in the face. . . . is unusual in the narrative fiction of a society like ours, which is growing older and older every day"[63] and for which Eros and Thanatos are highly improbable mythological representations. Traditional associations of Eros and Thanatos are in fact more functional to "a society of people in the prime of their youth, to whom death appears, in moments of amorous passion, as desirable as it is unlikely."[64] *Ultima luna*, instead, shifts the emphasis from unlikelihood to dynamic awareness: in the author's words, "the characters who move around this novel are people who know that they are aging."[65]

These two elements, awareness and movement, are central to the protagonists of the *Reifungsroman*. They are, in fact, highly ratiocinating characters, inclined to criticism of the self and of the other; the most appropriate description of them is provided by the title of Bruno's autobiographical manuscript, "The Ruminators." At the same time, they are also extremely active, mobile, and pragmatic. The challenge of mature love consists in reaching a balance that allows them to meet each other *in medias res*. It is a balance of contemplation, action, and emotion, between the adjustment to a consolidated existential course and the dialectic participation in a process of simultaneous disinvestment and reinvestment. The success of Silvana and Bruno's relationship depends on a careful management of times and resources. During the time Bruno has planned for his visit to his mother—approximately a week, broken off by a professional trip to Milan and further shortened by an early return—Silvana and Bruno have to know each other, evaluate their compatibility, and make plans for a commuter relationship. The construction of the amorous discourse of maturity is a complex narrative and strategic plot that will be analyzed in the final pages of the section devoted to *Ultima luna*. The process of getting to know and assessing one another is a self-narrative and self-dramatization that employs three main forms—debate, autobiography, and "rumination"—that develop the love discourse in the presence and in the absence of the other.

The debate—over the terrain of their encounter, old age—takes place, obviously, when the two are together: during the car drives from and to Villa Felice, at Silvana's apartment late at night, in the trattoria at Frascati or the Japanese restaurant where the two eat at the end of Silvana's work day. Bruno's autobiography is interpolated in three installments in the second part of the novel. The reading of the manuscript, to which Silvana devotes odd moments while Bruno is in Milan, sets in motion an analogous memory narrative on Silvana's part. It is an interior narrative, a fragmentary text that, although generated by her interrogation of and response to Bruno's narrative, perceives the other narrative as quite alien. Silvana's recollections—which, unlike Bruno's, are not entrusted to the written page—are composed of reflections on her recent past, thus on her relationship with Bruno, as well as flashbacks about the breakup of her marriage and the relationship with her children after divorce, as exemplified by the following excerpt:

> Now she didn't know why she was so eager to go read the last pages by Bruno, whom she had left at age sixteen in distant 1949. An old story she couldn't really relate to, yet which seemed to ask her permission to come in and take part in her life. A past that was not her own was settling in her thoughts of today. But also in her thoughts about yesterday! How, from the forties of Bruno's writing, has my brain dived into my own issues of the sixties, as if it could not move away from there? The faces of Luisa and Fabio as children have become superimposed on that of little Bruno....
> Yet, something was to be gained from this: from the way Bruno had looked at himself, she could understand more about that nearly sixty-year-old man with a self-concealing soul, who had grown intimate with her in a few hours.[66]

The juxtaposition of the three main forms of love discourse generates interesting textual contaminations. Since ruminations occupy the period of the other's absence, but also of the other's presence, the interior monologue frequently interferes with the dialogue. The considerable length of verbal exchanges affects the impact of dialogue and turns cues into treatises. The two characters' treatise-like speeches, based on the extensive sample of case histories provided by visiting Villa Felice, alternate with reciprocal interviews.

During their interviews, Bruno and Silvana, pressured by the need to make the best use of the little time they have—both because Bruno's visit is short and because the amorous play does not suit mature adults—"peel each other away"[67] in a way that is not one "of kids, but of older people who take the cue from the slightest remark to question the whole universe, and not in an easygoing way: they do it warily, testing the lie of the land with their foot before setting the foot down."[68]

The urgency of knowing and assessing the other's compatibility generates a nervous, aggressive, often prevaricating discourse. Within the same paragraph, the reader may find miscellaneous extratextual references—quite often elicited by Bruno's readings in Japanese literature—as well as self-contradicting stances and assessments, sometimes resulting in discrepancies among dialogue, interior monologue, parenthetical clarification, or asides. As for narrative technique, swift transitions between Silvana's and Bruno's points of view, first- and third-person narration, internal and external focalization are frequently

5: RIPENING AND COMPLETION IN WOMEN'S OLD-AGE NOVELS 149

employed. A few examples will demonstrate the rhetorical strategies employed in Bruno and Silvana's love discourse, the effect of which is to reflect the tension between criticism and self-criticism, between the strain of probing and that of neutralizing the other. The first excerpt is a rumination over dinner at a Frascati trattoria on the day the two have been introduced. They have been talking about Japanese novels that deal with old age, in particular about *Narayama* by Shichiro Fukusawa, in which an older woman, accompanied by her son, leaves her village for a mountainous retreat when she knows she is about to die:

> Bruno stared, as if he were still seeing the old woman and her son on the mountain. Silvana poured him some more wine. She sketched a little speech on the sense of the sacred in tradition and immediately felt scholarly. The man looked at her impenetrably: "Do you want contemporary older people?" and, before she could answer, introduced her into a brothel for impotent old men, "in today's cosmopolitan Tokyo" he said.[69]

The second passage is a brisk exchange in the car, on the way to dinner at a Japanese restaurant. Bruno and Silvana, who will make love for the first time that same night, have been talking about older people's sexuality, and Silvana has mentioned some examples from her experience at Villa Felice:

> "Much better now," Bruno answered. "They can fall in love without being laughed at." He didn't like Silvana's entomologist tone.
> "Of course," she said, then added in a suddenly lively voice: "Bruno, you haven't told me about your mother yet."
> She changes the subject, must have something against sex matters, Bruno thought, and answered: "Alfonsina likes to assert her independence."[70]

Two representative examples of rumination-conversation take place the morning of the next day. After they have spent their first night together, Silvana drives Bruno to the airport, where he will catch his plane to Milan:

> She goes against the tide, but without coming out of her shell. Her compassion for the elderly is existential (rich or poor, it doesn't matter), it is a substantially irreparable pain (I know that pain), which she, however, is able to keep at bay—one must grant her that. In her attitude to men (to me) she is inclined to the maternal, with feminist overtones. She suffers from the myth of youthfulness, which she fights. Not only does she ignore older people's eroticism (without her knowing, the very thought of it fills her with disgust), she also can't rid herself of the consciousness of being fifty. She is passionate but she doesn't want to be. She drowns herself in work. The solvent of her inner tangles is Christian.

Bruno smiled, all of a sudden his harshness softened at the thought: and this original, haphazardly mixed cocktail is the only woman with whom I have ever conjectured I could live long-term (the formula is: till death us do part).[71]

"You are the one who is judging me with your words." While saying this, the light suit he was wearing seemed shaded on the shoulder to her and she brushed it with her fingers. Wife's gesture she thought and said: "Bruno, I have no designs on the long-term."

"I have them for the two of us."

He retraced his steps.

When I am back I'll ask her to introduce me to her parents. Also to her daughter and her son-in-law. I wonder how they will look at me: that dope who wants to get hitched to their mother. It's premature. Silvana will never leave her work, her grandson, her parents, especially her cats that would suffocate in my Ginza closet.[72]

The discourse of the "ruminator" is influenced by a long consuetude with solitude, with judgmental introspection, with fictitious interlocutors—for example, the cats to whom Silvana talks every night. In relation to their present times, Silvana and Bruno are two *vetero*,[73] who must dismantle a consolidated wall of impediments to create a free flow of emotions and new ideas. They hide behind ideological masks and struggle against personal emotional phantasms that they also tend to project onto each other. The following two quotes are complementary examples of the couple's ideological soul-searching, whose purpose is both to interrogate their own choices and scrutinize those of the other. In the first—an imaginary conversation with Mauro, a friend of his Communist youth who died shortly after he left for Japan—Bruno draws Silvana into his ideological self-assessment. In the second excerpt, Silvana's attempt at a psycho-ideological explanation of Bruno's hang-ups betrays a typically feminine insecurity:

He smiled: you would have liked her, precisely because she is a pain in the neck with her fixation on old people. She still believes in the power of resentment! Can you imagine that? . . . At that thought he suddenly burst out into loud laughter: she is mature enough to take on the revolt of the united older people. She is a *vetero*! While laughing, he had stopped walking. A well-tried anti-Marxist who nurses a *vetero* inside . . .

He resumed his walking. How young she is compared to us.[74]

Why has he been living in Tokyo for the last 30 years? she was wondering. . . . The effort to find something that would make sense to all (Communism) and the delusion of being rejected were such that he fell back to the mental condition (estrangement) of his childhood and early boyhood. This could be an (unconscious) explanation of those displays of iciness of his part. . . .

Now I understand why I become excessive with him, as if I had to counterbalance his spasmodic self-control. But the mistake is his: he has committed himself to working for the people believing that he could achieve a result here below![75]

If the amorous discourse of maturity is aged by experience and burdened with layers of interpretive schemata, the mature lovers' advantages, on the other hand, are the terrains of daily practice in the present and that of planning for the future. This is a realm of the couple, characterized by rapid changes of location and by a mental and physical elasticity that set the mature adult protagonists apart from the background of the novel of senescence. Within this realm they establish an immediate, highly efficient conjugality, the naturalness of which compensates, on the behavioral level, for their emotional and intellectual rigidity. The morning after their first meeting, Silvana already knows what she should put in Bruno's suitcase for his trip to Milan; after his argument with Silvana, Bruno knows that the right thing to do is go into her kitchen and feed her cats. The words with which Bruno wakes Silvana up the morning after their arrival in Tokyo are an example of how his solipsistic propensity for planning—like his mother, Bruno also shows his concern for old age by calculating expenses and negotiating options—may prove to be constructive in a mature relationship:

"Good morning Silvana." Dressed impeccably in his gray suit, Bruno was kneeling in front of her: "It's 6:34, get up, I am coming back at 8. I have two days to spend with you, because on Thursday I go back to work. Today we are visiting Tokyo clockwise, so that you may have a general view of the city. While I'm out, call your parents. You called at the last minute to tell them that you were leaving for Tokyo, instead of Paris! They must be worried. Call your children too. You can find the area codes for Italy and for Germany on that piece of paper on the table. See you soon," he kissed her forehead and went out.[76]

Bruno and Silvana's rapport reveals that the success of a connection established later in life should ideally be based on the awareness that personalities are sufficiently established as not to resent normative remarks, and lives are so regulated by work and family investments that precede the meeting with the new partner as to benefit from acquiescence to the adjustments the partner has accomplished at the end of a long process of self-construction. The acceptance of one's own maturity becomes the foundation of an instinctive agreement with the needs and habits that accompany the practices and world views of the other, of a conjugality that is the finishing line of a long life as a self. An example of such agreement is Silvana's reaction to Bruno's change of professional course at the end of the novel—a stay in Russia as a foreign correspondent for his newspaper, which will result in a one-year postponement of his retirement and his reunion with Silvana. Her positive response is the sign of a calm confidence and assurance that has nothing to do with lack of interest or passive compliance.

The affective pragmatism of the two characters proves to be the strength of both the individuals and the couple, particularly with respect to their preparation for old age. It is in this direction that the confused and anguished individual imaginary can turn into a constructive project. Bruno is an emigrant who is unwilling to face the phantasms of the youth that he left behind in Italy twenty-six years before and is, at the same time, eager to spend his old age in his own country. Silvana is a gerontologist who tries to escape from the daily misery of institutionalized old age by envisioning a homeless old age for herself. She even explores this possibility concretely in her night visits to the railway station and conversations with the older people who take shelter there. Together, the two project, in the visions of a shared old age that they express toward the end of the novel, a solid, luminous, and open space, in which apartment sales, life under the same roof, and arrangements for parents and for children can be easily negotiated:

> "Now listen to the plans I have in mind for us: we could 1) buy the apartment where you live with your cats; 2) open a place for old people. I would like to continue to write and would also like to translate novels from Japanese. You'll have your work. If you accept me, I'll help you. . . .
> . . . We are going to ask your parents to come and live with us; we will renovate their apartment, so your son can live there with his partner. If we also buy the apartment where your daughter, son-in-law, and their Giorgio live, we are all settled and that's that. When I come for a few days at Christmas, it would be good if you introduced me to your family."[77]

> Silvana . . . was thinking: we care for each other, we know we will not be alone when we are old, and that we can still enjoy some freedom. On the other hand, she needed time, to understand well what kind of work she would do with the elderly in the future: no longer *about* them, but *with* them (this was clear to her now).[78]

This imaginary space is the foundation not only of personal and couple identity, but also of the social identity of old age. This perspective is, in my opinion, the key to a correct reading of D'Eramo's open-ended conclusion, of the way in which a long and ambitious novel ends, "as if suspended, almost casually, in the middle of a dinner, in the company of a Japanese ex-Communist friend."[79] The last page is the page of invitations. Silvana invites a person whom she has just met and who lives in a profoundly different culture from hers to join her and Bruno in Italy: "You will be happy," she says to Osamu, "I swear it, and we are not going to live far from each other; we'll be able to see each other often, right Bruno?"[80] Bruno invites Osamu to Moscow and, while doing this, he indirectly proposes to Silvana. "You'll visit me in Moscow, won't you?" Bruno asks his friend, then adds: "But first I would like Silvana to consent to marrying me."[81] The final message of *Ultima luna* is articulated at an imaginary crossroads of Japan, Russia, and Italy, maturity and old age, singleness, conjugality, and friendship.

Elena Gianini Belotti's *Apri le porte all'alba*

The age-class focus of *Apri le porte all'alba* [Open Your Door to the Dawn] is female young-old age. The protagonist, Doris, is a sixty-four-year-old woman who undergoes an experience of awakening.

At the beginning of the novel, Doris is presented as a woman who has been a little hardened by life, or at least anaesthetized in her feelings. She lives alone in an apartment building inhabited mainly by older people. She has not gotten over her unsuccessful marriage completely. Her father is still living; he lives alone, too, in their old family house, located in a degraded suburban area. Doris loves him in an awkward and guilty way. Doris has two close women friends: Irene and Marta. Irene lives in the same building; although they see each other daily, are very supportive of each other, and share similar worldviews, Doris has some reservations about Irene's unquestioning militant feminism. Marta is also coping with a marriage breakup and with a difficult relationship with her pregnant daughter.

Although retired, Doris has a modest and quite unstructured freelance occupation—the compilation of alternative tourist guides to Lazio, the value of which she has doubts about. During one of her long car drives across the Roman countryside in search of unspoiled places, Doris witnesses the "suicide" of a crow that hurls itself against a moving car in despair over the death of its female mate. Doris's distress following this accident—onto which she projects the notion of a lost dream of male-female union and strong subsequent feelings—paves the way to a slow awakening that unwinds across places and events of her present daily life and, to some degree, also across her memory.

That the novel is about an awakening process is clearly announced by the title, an invitation to reconsider the dawn metaphor and its traditional associations with the beginning of a new course. The inspiration for the title is a poem by Emily Dickinson, whose opening lines are: "Not knowing when the dawn will come / I open every door."[82] These lines are recited by the protagonist when, burdened by both bad memories of and nostalgia for her married life, she discovers the pleasure of leaving the French window in her bedroom open and letting the morning light wake her. In this novel the dawn belongs to older people and connotes unrestful senile vitality; older people, in fact, "sleep little, are restless, and wake up at dawn."[83] The dawn also belongs to African immigrants who, as will be seen later, play a very important part in older people's new support systems. When waking up at five to contemplate the dawn in her father's house, Doris finds Margarida on the doorstep. Margarida, a very positive African immigrant character who ends up taking care of Doris's father, is "standing there, in her nightgown, contemplating her vegetable garden with an eager smile"; she turns to Doris and says, "Me like watch sun rise."[84] The dawn also marks the insurmountable barrier dividing Doris and men. As in the case of her ex-husband Pietro, the presence of her new lover, Ernesto, is also an obstacle that prevents Doris from enjoying the energy of the dawn: Ernesto expects the blinds to be rolled down when he sleeps at her place.

Although she lives alone, Doris is at the center of a fairly strong support system and community network. She can count on a small circle of just-as-active women friends, is sensitive to community issues, open to meeting new people, and genuinely interested in cultural diversity. The protagonist's social nature makes her experience of awakening contagious; as the novel proceeds, a larger and larger segment of humanity, which encompasses various age, social, and ethnic identities (excluding white males), seems to be opening up to new realms of consciousness and communication. The "reawakened" community, white male friend and elderly father included, is symbolically united around the same dinner table in the final pages.

Doris and her friends live in a typical postindustrial urban setting of 1990s Italy, characterized by the deterioration of the environment, the standardization of interests and consumption patterns, institutional paralysis, and the demographic increase of two social components: older people and non-European immigrants. There are four main settings in the novel: a large apartment building, the streets, parks, and public offices of a large city, routes in the Roman countryside, and the modest suburban house where Doris's father lives.

In the apartment building, feuds and tragedies are played out. One older woman in particular, Signora Sebastiani, shows evident signs of derangement: she plays music and screams in the middle of the night and, out of spite toward the neighbors who want to have her committed, insults them and leaves garbage on their doorsteps. These are blocks of

5: RIPENING AND COMPLETION IN WOMEN'S OLD-AGE NOVELS 155

flats inhabited mostly by older people. Human isolation and daily exposure to small crime have turned some of the residents into loonies or have, at the least, fed their excessive concerns with their safety and the respectability of the building. Others, like Doris and her friend Irene, are searching for new ways of living their third age.

While older men in the novel seem to have very limited resources and flexibility, the active older women try to interact with the world outside their apartments. When they go out, however, they find chaotic traffic and environmental deterioration. They turn to public institutions for assistance and reparation: police stations, mental health centers, humane societies, and municipal offices. Their reports and claims are either half-listened-to condescendingly or dismissed without ceremony. When they go out, older women also meet other women and social misfits, particularly immigrants. These meetings lead them back to their apartments, where they offer tea or cognac to people in trouble, participate in condominium and feminist consciousness-raising meetings, and test new forms of cohabitation and family arrangements. White western men, as observed earlier, are admitted with suspicion and kept at a distance; it is up to young immigrants to renew outworn relationships and take the places that the biological children have left vacant. An Egyptian waiter who works at the café down the street and delivers coffee and newspapers at home takes the place of Signora Sebastiani's dead son in her heart; an extremely vital young Cape-Verdean woman settles into Doris's father's house and starts to take care of him. This house—a sort of farmhouse miraculously still standing on the outskirts of the city—is the place where the novel ends, with a dinner among the members of the new, heterogenous community built over the course of the novel.

The novel has no chapter divisions, as if to emphasize the continuum of life, the accumulation of casual, assorted experiences and encounters within a cross section of bustling daily urban existence. Transitions from one setting or episode to another, or between narration of external events and interior mental activity, are marked only by space breaks.

The novel has been cautiously placed in the *Bildungsroman* category by some reviewers. This definition is, according to Laura Lilli, "bold," in that the heroine of the novel is "an older woman who lives alone performing the customary tasks of a lifetime, writing a guide of Lazio for a very limited audience and taking care of her elderly father and of women friends surviving unsuccessful marriages."[85] A more precise approach to life-course genres places *Apri le porte all'alba* more appropriately among *Reifungsromane*. Like most *Reifungsromane*, the novel follows a woman's process of reinvestment in the face of experiences with mortality and spiritual loss. The "boldness" women display in this particular novel—their capability and willingness to reinvest in their lives under new terms—is proportional to the degree of creative resistance they exhibit in attempting to implement new forms of survival and coexistence within their everyday reality. The search for fulfillment in spite of age-based social constraints is a defiant affirmation, and the newly discovered freedoms are nothing but scraps of self-assertion, carved-out niches within a wearying yet intensely *lived* urban texture. Significantly, because of the characters' involvement in their humble present-day routines, recollections from the remote past are less frequent than in most Italian old-age novels. Yet the realm of memory is neither absent nor secondary, as will be discussed later.

Later-life awakening manifests itself in rebellious acts and in day-by-day invention of zones of freedom and joy within and in spite of—more precisely, "out of spite" for—a sclerotic social system. As such, it takes the form of a "second, more knowledgeable and conscious adolescence built on the extreme margin of life."[86] A distinctive trait of Gianini Belotti's, revealed in another old-age fiction, the short-story collection *Adagio un poco mosso*, is the interest in representing active old age more as a second adolescence than as maturity, as a stage when women attain new forms of knowledge by experiencing new forms of freedom rather than refining their capability to take stock of and review their past.

Written a few years earlier, in 1993, and more popular than *Apri le porte all'alba*, *Adagio un poco mosso* more explicitly reveals the author's ideological reading of women's old age. As victims of multiple forms of oppression and abuse, perpetrated by guilt-ridden children, suffocating husbands, and insensitive public authorities, the protagonists of the seven stories, mostly women in their eighties, become "avengers," committed to settling long-standing scores and doing justice. A woman takes revenge on the son who has banished her to a retirement home by pretending that she is demented and cannot recognize him. A very frail-looking shoplifter decides to charge the police officer that held her for hours in the supermarket with kidnapping. Two women friends take a terminally ill woman away from her husband's smothering care for a one-day outing and decide to let her enjoy good food, wine, and songs one last time, even though they are aware that these excesses will kill her. In the story endings, Gianini Belotti uses the technique of reversal: she upsets the readers' "reasonable expectations" and directs them toward "an ending that is often open and takes them by surprise."[87]

What needs to be pointed out, however, is the fact that in both old-age fictions by Gianini Belotti, the disruption of expected age-appropriate behavior is framed within a rigorous, predictable "thesis narrative." Characters are so heavily ideological as to lack subtlety, and therefore credibility. Although this aspect of *Apri le porte all'alba* may be perceived as a limitation and even annoy the reader, the author sees it as a feminist narrative program. While discussing the novel *Il fiore dell'ibisco* in a 1986 interview, she maintains in fact that "women have inaugurated a new literary genre in which autobiography, narrative, militancy, and nonfiction blend harmoniously."[88]

"*... love and death, a pattern for primitives ...*"

Doris's awakening is set in motion by her reflection on love and death experiences that she observes in others and that make her aware of her own spiritual death. One of the main causes of Doris's spiritual death is her inability to establish a symbiotic relationship with a man after her divorce; it is a case of inner withering, of the loss of strong passions. A similar sense of estrangement from the masculine inside and outside herself is experienced by the protagonist of *La fontana della giovinezza* at the beginning of her aging narrative. The protagonist of Passerini's novel conducts a deeper investigation of her aging consciousness than Doris ventures into; she realizes that this estrangement results when the discourse between the masculine and the feminine becomes uncertain, loose, almost irrelevant in a mature woman's psychological makeup as her gender identity undergoes a redefinition.

Apri le porte all'alba opens in a springtime landscape in the Roman countryside. The protagonist's first observation—"natural rebirth at the right season is one of the few certainties we are left with"[89]—is a declaration of her grounding in nature and naturalness. It is also an ironic hint that season-appropriate expectations are soon to be subverted in the age-conscious discourse of the novel. The protagonist's initial predicament is to redefine what is natural for her, since natural laws—those that regulate the environmental balance as well as those governing the relationships between the sexes—have been upset and irretrievably altered. She soon learns that ecosystems can be rebalanced through sociocultural critique conducted at various levels, not just those of the personal life review or of a romanticized environmental consciousness.

Doris is headed for Bomarzo, one of several places she visits because she wants to test whether they should be included in the Lazio guide for an "audience . . . of educated and exacting travelers"[90] that she is writing with her friend Ernesto. A road accident—a crow is run over by a car and its male mate, in apparent distress, "commits suicide" by flying into a running car—rouses "a disproportionate anguish"[91] in her. This is an intensely epiphanic event for Doris, who comments:

> It was the power of that love, its supreme fidelity that upset me, almost as if a zoological melodrama had suddenly routed the skepticism that I believed to be firmly ruling my existence. So, without my knowing it, a nostalgia for

extreme feelings and passions was smoldering in the deep of my heart. Love and death, a pattern for primitives.[92]

The projection of an emotional discomfort onto a couple of anthropomorphized birds is a motif that reappears, in different forms, in the novel. *Apri le porte all'alba* is in fact peopled by very diverse couples that Doris observes as spectator of a large sample of affective and social role plays. She is a single woman who cannot recognize herself within a couple identity. "The price one pays for skepticism is to stay on the threshold and watch what happens inside," Doris comments on her lack of emotional involvement with Ernesto and adds: "[t]he price I paid for stepping beyond the threshold had been much higher."[93] Doris feels divided between conflicting drives—for fusion with man in a dream of all-encompassing love and for the redefinition of her own space as a woman—and between complementary primary yearnings. The conjunction in love and death of the crows, which Doris identifies as male and female though they are "perfectly identical in color, shape, and size,"[94] recalls the harmony of an "elderly couple of rosy Nordic tourists,"[95] whose perfect agreement of gestures and movements reveals the naturalness of an ancient consuetude. In its turn, the image of the older couple is associated with the "perfect fusion"[96] of a beautiful young couple whose uninhibited behavior triggers, by contrast, Doris's "regret for a richness" that a repressive sexual education had "snatched from the hands"[97] of her generation. Places appear charged with signs: two names inscribed on a stone seat, the memorial monument Vicino Orsini dedicated to his young wife Giulia Farnese, the two swans Doris and her friend Marta find dead in the Villa Borghese park, near the Aesculapius shrine. Split between contrasting notions of love, Doris on one hand romantically observes that she has never been the object of such love and that she is old for love; on the other, she is aware that memorial monuments are, in reality, forms of self-celebration and that animals do not commit suicide but obey mysterious natural laws dictated by species survival.

Unlike *Ultima luna*, this novel does not open up to or investigate new levels and forms of love discourse between mature adults. The next section will discuss in greater depth the author's view of gender roles and relationships, which does not allow for the discovery of new terrains of communication and new alliances between the sexes. However, closure with the pernicious dualism of the dream of fusion can be attained, and the fruit of Doris's gradual disinvestment after experiencing an emotional breakdown on her way to Bomarzo is the joyous discovery of her body and of an unattached yet reciprocally respectful sexual intimacy

5: RIPENING AND COMPLETION IN WOMEN'S OLD-AGE NOVELS 159

with her friend Ernesto, one that does not entail the condivision of emotions, ideas, interests, or values.

The representations and self-representations of young-old women's bodies, as reflected in mirrors, dreams, men's physical and verbal responses, are generally positive. Doris, in particular, perceives her body as both desirable and entitled to feel and express desires. Some of her dreams are explosions of youthful narcissism, as when she dreams she is doing a partial striptease in front of a stranger in a large crowded room:

> I was issuing an insolent challenge, I don't know to whom and why. I was possessed by a boundless, cheerful sense of release, as if I had relieved myself of other laces, zippers, and tangles. I unfastened the second button of my blouse, loosened the neckline and blew inside it, a vigorous blow that gave me goose bumps. My neck-opening gave off a tenuous mandarin fragrance, so I stuck my nose into it and sniffed myself again and again with greedy pleasure. Under my blouse, my skin glowed with the brightness of a corolla....
> ... [I]n that aura of childish joy, conspiratory play and exultancy, that man and I had kept on clutching at each other and rubbing against each other until a deafening applause exploded.[98]

Although she is aware that excesses and romance are not appropriate to her age, Doris is flattered by Ernesto's devotion to her body and his disregard of physical marks of aging. The effects of her lover's gaze are so corroborating for Doris's self-image that she prolongs them after he has left by looking at her body in the mirror and taking note of the good state of legs, thighs, and breasts:

> I have understood ... that I am not at the age for excesses, nor do I want to throw myself heart and soul into cultivating useless sentimentality instead of a healthy detachment. I told him, because I want to be honest with him; he laughed and replied that he doesn't give a damn. The joy of having me from time to time, whenever I feel like it, is enough. And I do believe I will want to. Not only because of his fervent dedication to cultivating every surface of my body ... but because I haven't felt at all ashamed of my worn-out body. On the contrary, I felt so proud of it that I saw it beautiful, slim, and solid like when I was a girl. After he left, and if was daytime by then, I looked at myself naked in the mirror. Legs have always been my strong point.... My thighs have grown thinner, as if time had drained them. I always disliked my small breasts when I was young.... But as an older woman ... mine have remained almost intact in their place.[99]

The awareness of the gaze and of one's body image as a precarious reflection of the subjective gaze of the other also guarantees the continuity of the self-image in quite a paradoxical way. In fact, the failing vision of old age puts age marks out of focus, and the general weakening of the senses turns out to be a blessing:

> Older bodies, I had sometimes thought, must exhale degenerated and decomposed odors because time corrupts humors. I smelled myself and I could tell no difference. Perhaps Ernesto was still too young to be old, or perhaps smell, like the other senses, eventually loses some of its sharpness. Irene claims, for example, that wrinkles are a false problem; luckily, eyesight deteriorates with age, so we can no longer see them.[100]

The point that a feminist writer like Gianini Belotti wants to make by emphasizing the positive effects of Ernesto's admiration is not that women need the male gaze in order to appreciate their bodies. Ernesto, who is seven years younger than Doris, is the embodiment of a thesis that is dear to Gianini Belotti and that she has developed in previous writings, that of the positiveness of age-role reversal. The reversal of the traditional mature man-younger woman model, more and more common today, has made women aware of a new form of power: the attraction that many younger men feel for "aged women."[101] As discussed in the first part of this study, Gianini Belotti made a significant contribution to the Italian debate on age and gender with the essay *Amore e pregiudizio* and the novel *Il fiore dell'ibisco*. According to her, the younger man-older woman relationship represents both a desirable complementarity of masculinity and femininity and a social critique of fertility and reproduction myths associated with the female body. The author's critique is also a generational one: the men Doris and her friends chose as life partners in their young adulthood represent in fact patriarchal discourses and practices against which the women of Doris's generation have fought and that they may have finally outgrown.

The fact that the education of younger men may have been less influenced by manifest forms of gender-based prejudice perpetrated in the past does not, however, turn them into allies, partners, or soul mates. In spite of his devotion, Ernesto does not play a leading role in Doris's awakening, simply because he cannot understand it. The women characters of *Apri le porte all'alba* can neither establish deep and reciprocally constructive communication with men nor share life passages with them. A man like Ernesto "is perfect for carnal dealings," Doris admits quite frankly, "but for a conversation I prefer my women friends."[102] Things are not different among young people because, whereas young women today have "clear ideas in mind . . . study, prepare themselves . . . are curious, interested, lively, and vital," their male contemporaries are "narrow-minded boors who are only interested in soccer."[103]

That women are superior to men in all respects—intellectual, moral, social—is a point the novel makes very clearly and incontrovertibly. The author's representation of the "battle of the sexes" is at times so militantly biased as to produce humorously improbable developments in the story. This is the case with the unusual campaign in which Irene's feminist group tries to involve the municipal authorities, a campaign based on a survey of the "social costs of men." The survey documents that most criminal offences, acts of vandalism, and traffic violations are committed by men; it also documents the costs of such actions to the community. Irene and her friends demand that this gender-based social injustice be repaired by cutting women's taxes. They argue that women, who cost much less than men to the community, are forced to contribute more than their share to public expenses.

". . . an anthropological mutation in progress . . ."

A young woman speaking during a feminist meeting at Irene's refers to the increasing gap between young women's and young men's ambitions and expectations as "an anthropological mutation in progress," one in which "females advance, [and] males fall behind"; these are, she claims, "the signs of the end of patriarchy."[104] This study's objects of investigation are not so much the implications or correctness of this rather simplistically expressed assessment but the representations of female superiority in old age.

To use a term that was quite in vogue some years ago, Doris and her friends are Italian "gray panthers." In a novel that has been called "the latest Italian fictional representation of the vitality of the female subject,"[105] the vitality of older women characters is based on their capability to see an old world with new eyes and to be defiantly young while everything around them undergoes gradual deterioration. Rosa Cutrufelli writes that this novel is "new in its women protagonists."[106] Another previously mentioned review maintains that Gianini Belotti's old-age narratives are about a "second adolescence." In their countercurrent stances, as well as in their choice of younger men as lovers, these older women characters express the scandalous vitality of "anachronism" that Mary Russo celebrates. "Untimeliness" is, according to Russo, a "risk" for women, "given the common placement of women's lives within the symbolic confines of birth, reproduction, and death,"[107] but it is also a powerful tool of social critique in that it disrupts a consecrated developmental model.

The celebration of anachronism in women's lives leads, ideally, to an intergenerational view of women's relationships. While observing the faces of the women taking part in a feminist meeting at Irene's, Doris is particularly aware of the "age rainbow" they represent. "Snow-white leonine manes" blend with "carrot-color hair"; "beautiful ironic faces stitched with wrinkles" stand out next to "round, suntanned faces."[108] When Signora Sebastiani, the emotionally disturbed neighbor, arrives, Irene carves for her "a space between a skinny girl with a ponytail and a fifty-year-old with a radiant smile and a mass of gray curls on her small, elegant head."[109] Examples abound in the novel of older women trusting in younger women's capability to bring about "the end of patriarchy." The most vivid of them is the image with which the novel ends: "a colorful group of young women with wind in their hair and backpacks on their shoulders,"[110] for whom Doris is planning to write her next guidebook.

In practice, however, Doris can share her aging process only with her contemporaries. There are historical reasons, discussed at a greater depth in the first part of this study and in the next chapter, behind their exclusive communication on the terrain of aging. Having shared, as young adults, engaging experiences of political and personal growth in the feminist movement of the late sixties and seventies—a movement that was marked by a metaphysics of youth—they can find understanding and possible answers only in one another. Since they have accepted the challenge of anachronism, their awareness of aging raises a host of contradictory emotions and experiences in them in terms of both physical and social identity:

> We had aged and from time to time we were surprised at it, as if it were a curse; every one of us still felt like the girl she used to be. Of that girl we had retained the voice that still rang like in our youth, clear, sharp and deceptive. "When will the definitive change take place?" we sometimes wondered. "When will the idea we have of ourselves come to coincide with our external appearance; when will we finally feel really old inside and outside?" "Never," Irene replied defiantly. "We will remain girls until we die."[111]

Although younger women, whose strength derives from their less restricted education, are likely to dismantle patriarchal models completely, the novel lacks for fully developed young women figures. The only exception is Margarida, who represents, however, the immigrant woman caregiver rather than the ideal heir of Doris's feminist generation. The fact that younger women are nothing but walk-ons in this novel is consistent with its celebration of women's old age as a second adolescence. The real young women in *Apri le porte all'alba* are Doris and her friends, and the author's assumption is that transformations are more likely to take place in later life than at earlier stages of women's existences. The reason is that in later life women may be freed from the pressure to comply with the demands of married life and with the behavioral models they acquired in their youth. Although external circumstances (divorce or death of a parent) may bring about major life changes, older women's openness to change is ideally the result of a long and consolidated process of personal maturation.

While projecting women like Doris toward open old-age scenarios, the novel also investigates to some degree the models these women were handed down from the past—that is, the expectations regarding the way their young and adult lives should have been and the way their old age should be. These models are analyzed at two levels of the narration: in flashbacks of Doris's life with her parents—some of which are examined in the next section in relation to the new foster-daughter figure of Margarida—and in her observation of both older and younger people in the street.

As pointed out in the introduction to this chapter, Elena Gianini Belotti is an expert in the study of how female cultural roles are formed, a subject to which she devoted her best-known work, *Dalla parte delle bambine*. Furthermore, older characters in life-course genres are quite often engaged in both the assessment of the models that have molded their life choices and in the transmission of those models, and/or of new ones, to future generations. The approach of this novel to the models of the past reflects its orientation toward the "anthropological mutation." Doris and her women friends are both projected toward their future and attentively involved in the observation of their present context. They review their memories so as not to re-enact them: the legacy they wish to leave to the generations to come is not their past but the willingness to let the younger women alter it. At the level of family genealogies, for example, they do not look for continuity; they open up instead to new relational plots and new ways of transmitting their cultural and affective legacies. They pursue this aim mainly by disinvesting from their biological children and reinvesting in new figures that, in two cases, belong to emergent cultures in European societies.

Doris did not have children because her husband did not want any. She is at peace with her childlessness; she remarks, while following with her eyes a young pregnant woman crossing the street with a child, that "she could be my daughter . . . and I find myself smiling with pacified tenderness at the arched back of the young woman who disappears in the crowd."[112] The child she might have had appears to her as "an insubstantial possibility, lost in a past so remote as to be unreal."[113] As observed earlier, the novel closes on the image of a colorful group of young women tourists, for whom Doris intends to write a guide of Venice—a sort of legacy to which she is committing herself, since she is a tour guide writer. She envisions them as they step onto the trestle bridge to board a ferry, "rowdy and gentle, laughing and tender,"[114] waving their arms to greet Doris on the retreating bank. Doris's friend Marta would like to find an emotional compensation for her separation from her husband in a grandmother role. "I'll be a grandma," she says, "I'll let myself age, it is about time. This child will have a strange mother . . . let at least its grandma, the only one it will have, resemble a real grandmother."[115] She must, however, redirect her natural impulse to take care of her pregnant daughter toward a group of former students who have remained close to her. Marta's daughter wants to manage on her own, just as Marta did not let her mother and mother-in-law, "two women from the nineteenth century,"[116] help her. Traditional genealogies break down because "youth is always ruthless."[117] As demonstrated, however, by the relationship Marta has established with her former students, and by the intergenerational feminist meetings at Irene's, it is possible to find terrains of communication with younger women—natural mistresses of a mental and physical freedom that older women are gradually conquering—and embrace the "anthropological mutation" that will bring about the end of patriarchy side by side.

This announced end is far from tangible, however. As in *Ultima luna*, this novel presents a disturbing panorama of old-age case studies, people with whom Doris comes into contact in her apartment building or through chance encounters in the streets. As is to be expected, while older single women seem to be groping for some form of freedom, older married women and elderly men are presented as either the victims or the unwitting perpetrators of consolidated patriarchal views of old age.

In their daily errands and interactions, Doris and her friends see figures who are helpless scapegoats when urban stress escalates into violence; some of them are portrayed as greedy bloodsuckers or sour and unreasonable sadists. Most of these figures, which are scattered throughout the book, are nothing but grotesquely diminutive character sketches. They are: "the imploring. . . . little man, his hands clawed to the steering wheel, his face pale-white,"[118] who blocks the traffic on the Salaria; the "cross-faced lanky little old man who moved forward in small shuffling steps, supported by a robust young black man";[119] the "grim old woman with a slave-driver's soul,"[120] for whom Margarida works; the woman who steps out of her front door "avidly clutching"[121] her husband's arm. There are also a few group portraits, like those of the "tablefuls of older people"[122] that feast rowdily during organized excursions, and Doris's "catatonic" co-tenants who sign a petition to have Signora Sebastiani committed; they are "a platoon of delegates of the third age . . . well-kept, well-dressed, and well-fed, their expressions half-pathetic and half-bellicose."[123]

A few more developed figures stand out in this tracking shot of human types. One of them is Signora Sebastiani, whose mental balance has been altered by a personal drama and who nevertheless reveals uncommon intellectual resources. Another such figure is her antagonist, Signora Ruggeri, a proper old woman "with blue-tinted white hair, three strings of pearls around her neck"[124] and a past as a Partisan courier. She is portrayed as the pitiless organizer of the building-association campaign to expel Signora Sebastiani but also as a victim: the target of the latter's daily vendettas and an older woman whose complaints are met with the indifference of public justice.

Doris sometimes compares faces and gestures of the older people she observes. She contrasts, for example, the disoriented expression of the woman in her sixties who clings to her husband's arm—whose "gloomy lost face . . . avidly groping arm . . . tiny tottering steps" appear to Doris as "the degenerate fruit of captivity"[125]—with the persistence of a much older woman struggling with the electronic system at a bank entrance. Doris elects this "little old lady" who does not surrender, so similar to some protagonists of the stories in *Adagio un poco mosso*, as her model:

> I felt a rush of affection for the older lady who did not abdicate her freedom. Her existence heartened me regarding my future of analogous, inevitable decline. I hope I'll be as fearless as she is, at her age. I will be. . . . I must be, I know I can only count on myself, on women friends in case of emergency. But they will be as old as I am, by that time.[126]

One of the issues with which *Apri le porte all'alba* is most concerned is how to repeal trite traditional genealogies and what to replace them with. Horizontal gender and generational alliances based on ideal rather than blood ties are definitely an answer, and this answer is discussed in greater depth in the next chapter. Doris's remark that her women friends "will be as old as I am, by that time" underscores, however, the need to cultivate vertical intergenerational lines as well. These may no longer be biological-family lines; they should definitely be elective lines, engendered in creative and regenerative ways.

"*. . . as in the time of slavery, it is blacks again who preside over the white man's birth and death . . .*"

Apri le porte all'alba deals with another "anthropological mutation in progress," that effected by the rising immigration wave from non-European countries. Like women's takeover, this anthropological mutation also undermines western models of caregiving, transmission of legacy, and aggregation. Young immigrants take on roles that have traditionally been filled by biological children and pump new blood into moribund relationships. Mohammed, the Egyptian waiter who delivers coffee and the newspaper to Signora Sebastiani, proves to be the only therapy that can heal her after the breakdown she suffered when her son died. With her irresistible vitality, Margarida manages to fill places that were or should have been Doris's in the older woman protagonist's past, present, and future family history.

Margarida is a twenty-two-year-old woman from Cape Verde, whom Doris meets at a bus stop. The first time they meet, Margarida is very upset because she has just missed the last bus and is terrified at the thought of her abusive employer's reaction. Doris invites her to her apartment to console her and gives her a ride home; then she starts seeing Margarida and her friends, who also work as domestic helpers. Later Margarida decides to leave her employer and take care of Doris's father. She moves into his house and settles in the room Doris occupied as a girl; she is presumably going to take care of Doris's father more efficiently than Doris, and without the constraints of negative family memories and obligations. As for the old man, he transfers his fatherly love and concern onto a new daughter figure quite naturally:

> He was waiting for Margarida's return. He would also wait for me, in the good season, sitting in the same place, when I was a girl and came home by bus at night. He had found a daughter, in his old age, and it wasn't me; it was a lively and affectionate young black woman who comforted his solitary old age better than me. I was grateful to Margarida and, at the same time, experienced an excruciating sense of failure. I must learn from her, because she knows more than I do, I thought.[127]

Because western societies have destroyed the naturalness of primary relationships, "it is blacks again who preside over the white man's birth and death."[128] Caregiving, "a virtue we have irreparably lost," seems to be "an innate, spontaneous talent"[129] among them. In this novel caregiving is not approached as a socioeconomic issue. Beyond representing a thriving job market created by a demographic imbalance and the demands of a postcolonial society, caregiving appears as the magic potion that heals first- and third-world wounds. In *Apri le porte all'alba*, older parents and adoptive children seem to be equally yearning after the reestablishment of new families. They are brought together by marginalization and need. Other things they have in common are missing their families, growing up in rural societies where they learned "the art of getting the best out of minimal resources,"[130] and an orientation toward values of a past that is extinct in the West and threatened with extinction in the Third World.

Among contemporary Italian old-age narratives, *Apri le porte all'alba* is one of the few fictions that analyze the relationship of older people and immigrants within a postcolonial society. Another example is a short story by Susanna Tamaro titled "Chissene. . . ." In this story, entrusting older people to the care of foreign domestic helpers becomes the metaphor for a widespread indifference and moral deterioration that affects the new ethnic groups as well. The story ends with a young woman caregiver and her friend abandoning the moribund older protagonist on a smashed couch by the roadside; they can neither find help nor directions to a hospital on a hot mid-August day when the man's children are on vacation and the city is deserted.

Gianini Belotti's non-European immigrants, in contrast, are idealized figures: any limitations they have may be traced to the patriarchal discourses of their cultures—that of Islamic fundamentalism, in Mohammed's case. The young-old women of the novel believe in fact that they cannot renounce forms of behavioral freedom they have arduously attained just "to please a Moslem boy."[131] As for immigrant women, both the group of domestic helpers with whom Margarida spends her free time and the prostitutes that Doris befriends in her neighborhood are people the protagonist instinctively likes and finds interesting.

The novel expresses the awareness that the "reverse invasion" has the inevitability of a "historical nemesis."[132] "Will we be changed, transformed by them?"[133] Doris wonders. Her personal experience seems to point in that direction: she realizes in fact that "by declaring how much she needed Dad, [Margarida] suddenly overturned my way of looking at things."[134] This process leads Doris to not only accept a failure that transcends her family history but also to search for and consolidate alternative ties. The result of a disinvestment-reinvestment process prompted by an external—foreign, in this case—presence is enlightenment because, "when someone comes from the outside to weave new textures of love, one is compelled to step back and, all of a sudden, the scenery is inundated with light."[135] Thanks to Margarida's overthrow of her family landmarks and heirlooms, Doris can reconcile herself with a family legacy that is manifested in markedly gendered objects—like the "pile of cloth sanitary pads lurking in the chest," which seems to hint at an "idea of life they could not force into me."[136] From a more detached perspective, she can thus assert the overall value of the direction she chose for her life, namely of "thinking with her head instead of theirs, in the good and the bad."[137]

Doris recounts a few visits to her father in the course of the narration. These visits precipitate memories of her childhood and adolescence that are charged with strong and mixed feelings: compassion, a sense of guilt and of failure, inexpressible longing to nurture her father and be nurtured by him.

Until Margarida enters the older man's life and revitalizes him, his house, and his farmyard, he spends long, solitary days "in the livid semi-darkness"[138] of the TV-lit living room. His life, Doris observes, "little by little . . . has shrunk, weakened, lost autonomy";[139] he has even given up fighting the weeds in the garden he once was very proud of. Doris suggests that he come to live with her; she even considers moving back to her family house to take care of him when he falls ill with bronchitis. Neither plan is carried out because father and daughter are strangers to each other's territory. Doris knows that her father would feel like a "guest, lost and disconsolate"[140] at her place and he concurs: "Here I have all my things."[141] As for Doris, although she is aware that she could "do the same things, except for the noisiest ones" at her father's, she knows that she would be "provisional, [t]here, a mere necessity."[142]

The feeling of sadness permeating the sections devoted to this father-daughter relationship derives to some extent from the man's extreme old-age condition; but it is also pervasively ingrained in the nature of this family's legacy. During the first visit, in the early part of the narration, Doris's father breaks his reserve and engages in a long soliloquy of memory that recalls the moods and objects of his past. His has been a "narrow" life of "infinitesimal, obsessive, and perfectly useless saving" and of "chronic fear of a grim future rooted in a past of destitution and sacrifice."[143] The objects that figure in the bare-bones paternal narration are worn-out shoes, uncomfortable bicycles, and charcoal flatirons. He recollects that, when shoes became too short, "one would cut the tip so that the toes could get out, though they would freeze in the cold."[144] In his daughter's eyes, his bike was "lugubrious like a hearse, clattering like a tractor,"[145] and the charcoal iron her mother, grandmother, and great-grandmother used "would spit ashes from of its holes and stain the laundry."[146] When Doris offers grudgingly to drive her father to the cemetery, she remembers scenes of her mother's last hours. She recalls that ten years earlier, when her mother had to be taken to the hospital urgently, she was more concerned—despite her life-threatening predicament—with keeping up a proper appearance than with anything else. Much like Alfonsina in *Ultima luna*, Doris's mother wanted to leave directions for a decorous death and, since her main preoccupation was having new underwear so as not to make a bad impression at the hospital, she had entrusted her daughter with the execution of her will. Doris remembers that her own effort to comply with her mother's concern for propriety in such an emergency exasperated the incredulous male nurses:

> I could hardly curb my anger when, with the gestures and tone of a sacrificial victim, she had led me into her bedroom, had opened a drawer and had

showed me a tidy stack of brand-new undergarments. "If I fall ill," she had said, "and have to go to the hospital, you must put the new underwear on me, I don't want to make a bad impression." We didn't have the time, she had felt bad suddenly, Dad had called me, stammering incoherent words, I had run there, had called the doctor who had ordered emergency hospitalization. . . . She was wearing an old worn and patched flannel nightgown. . . . I must change her, I thought, I must do it, she asked me to. . . . Dad stood in a corner staring, silent, scared, biting his lip. Then the ambulance had arrived, two rough and brusque male nurses had carried her on the stretcher, dressed as she was. There is no time, she is seriously ill, they replied to my request, and one of them said: "What on earth is in your mind? It's urgent, can't you see she's in very bad condition?" Then, turning to his colleague: "I can't believe what's in people's minds!"

During the journey I kept talking to her, I caressed her, I laid my hand on her cold forehead. She moaned and did not answer, perhaps could not even hear me. But all of a sudden she whispered: "My underwear." "Relax," I lied to her, "I put it on you."[147]

Doris recalls that in this predicament her father was paralyzed with fear and totally incapable of helping his wife; in addition to taking care of her mother, she had to relieve him from the pain and the fatigue of assisting his dying wife because he was "as frightened as a child."[148] Doris is protective with her father also in the present. She cannot tolerate it if those who treat the ailments of his worn-out body humiliate him. When she notices that the two young assistants at the chiropodist's stare, horrified, at his tumefied feet, covered in sores, she "stiffen[s], her claws unsheathed, ready to defend him at the slightest offense."[149]

The fact that Doris's father is presented as helpless, useless, at a total loss in the tragic circumstance of his wife's terminal attack, reflects the traditional Italian pattern of delegating caregiving almost entirely to women. Moreover, *Apri le porte all'alba* presents a caregiving relationship uncommon in Italian women's old-age fiction, one involving a father and a daughter. Women writers have typically been more interested in the complex mother-daughter paradigm, and are inclined to produce caregiving narratives that feature older mothers and middle-aged daughters.[150] In Gianini Belotti's novel, the care of an older father seems to require a painful involvement and a just-as-painful review of one's family legacy. Unlike caregiving scenarios that bring into question the mother-daughter paradigm, it does not, however, enter the realm of female identity. This caregiving relationship is charged with guilty melancholy, a vague regret for unexpressed emotions, and an embarrassment at breaking the taboo of handling the father's body. Although this relationship is not burdened with the identification/separation issues raised by contact with the maternal body, Doris is aware that her father's past is also hers and that the father figure is an inescapable component of her old-age imaginary. The "explicit marks of descent,"[151] both physical and behavioral, are associated with strong feelings of guilt and shame:

> I recognized the same red swollen knot on my left big toe. . . . As a girl . . . I was ashamed to wear sandals and, resentful, I would secretly hold Dad responsible for passing that physical flaw on to me.[152]

> I too collect, one by one, the breadcrumbs from the tablecloth, and put them in my mouth, just like I turn off the light every time I leave a room, and every time I detest myself for that.[153]

Experiencing the sadness of an incommunicable or clumsily expressed devotion to her father, Doris also has dreams in which their roles are reversed. In one such dream, she is a little girl at first, clinging to her old father's hand; then she turns into a young woman walking by a young stranger who irritably pulls his hand away from hers and leaves her behind. On waking up from this dream, Doris reminds herself severely that she is sixty-four and that, if she does not rescue herself, nobody will.

These are, in conclusion, the lessons that the older women of *Apri le porte all'alba* learn as a result of their awakening at the threshold of old age. Their fourth age will be profoundly different from that of the previous generation. They must detach themselves from the delusion of depending on their families. They must acknowledge the defeat of the old-age models handed down within western cultures. After reflecting on Marta's remark that today, as in the time of slavery, white people delegate blacks to assist them at the beginning and at the end of their lives, Doris concludes:

> We have failed; we pile up claims, expectations, and misunderstandings for entire existences and thus become incapable of the simplest and most natural things. We have managed to push older people away to the margins and make them disappear into nothing without hampering or bothering us and without leaving a trace. As a consequence of this, their memory, instead of soothing our spirit, causes us to feel only remorse and guilt.[154]

These women also learn that they have to prepare new terrains of socialization, bonding, and nurturing by following uncharted horizontal and vertical (both ascendant and descendent) bonding and caregiving patterns. An example of these new relational webs is the community that meets for dinner at the end of the novel. All the significant old and new presences in Doris's awakening journey are there: her long-time friends, Irene and Marta; her lover, Ernesto; the two young immigrants, Margarida and Mohammed; Doris's neighbor Signora Sebastiani, who has recovered her wits; and Doris's father, who has recovered his health and will to live a few more serene years. In the symbolic gesture of sharing foods from different cultures, many existences are tied together. Margarida and Mohammed fall in love, and Doris defines her project of writing a guide of Venice for women. Most significantly, the dinner guests recognize that a young-old age accompanied by the presence of a parent who has not been expropriated of freedom and dignity is a value, indeed a "privilege," to be shared and treasured. In line with the ecological orientation of the novel, this final message also implies that the elderly father's preservation guarantees the preservation of his habitat—which perhaps suggests the answer to Doris's fruitless search for uncontaminated places for her Lazio guide:

"We have to come back and visit your father often," Marta said. "Why did you keep him hidden from us all this time? None of us has a father any longer, it is a privilege you must share with us. An old age like his is an encouragement for our future that is coming on apace. It comforts me to think that he is here, and welcomes us in his shy yet benevolent way. Besides, a place like this, that has remained intact, encapsulated like an islet in the sea of high-rise buildings, with the vegetable garden, the roses, the oleanders, where in the world can one be found anymore?"[155]

6
A Case Study: The 1968 Generation

Introduction

THE BOOK DISCUSSED IN THIS CHAPTER IS RICH AND COMPLEX, BOTH structurally and thematically. *La fontana della giovinezza* combines the short novel, autobiography, and essay genres, while developing a narrative thread that features a woman protagonist in her fifties and integrating into that narrative the languages of the visual arts and of anthropology. Luisa Passerini defines her book as "a hybrid, between apologue and narration, cultural-history survey and observation of the present."[1]

As a cultural-history survey, this book is about the defeat of a generation.[2] In a newspaper interview, Passerini said that the protagonist of *La fontana della giovinezza* is the symbol of the generation that was young in the seventies and that believed their youth would last forever. Having somehow burned themselves out, today they suddenly find themselves face-to-face with old age—which is particularly difficult for them to accept.[3] The problem lies in the fact that those who took active part in the 1968 protest movement have often failed to establish a proper relation to time. They have been accused of self-referentiality, of always addressing one another, of being scarcely interested in relationships with both younger and older people. When they were young, they cast their minds into a utopian future and felt nostalgic for a golden age, striving to "recapture places like old taverns and their sensations."[4] Today they are trapped in ambiguous categories, such as *vetero* (concerned with the conservation of leftist ideals) or *rinnegati* (those who have become conservatives shifting to the right). The youths molded by the 1968 movement have, as they aged, turned a stage of life into an ideological anachronism. Having defined the generation of the anti-Fascist Resistance as old, they keep turning their heads whenever the youth are mentioned, as if people were referring to *them*. They resent the ideological backlash and the postmodern indifference that characterize their present territory; this generation is burdened by the political defeat of the ideals they fought for, the historical defeat of the Italian left over the last forty years, and the end of Eurocentric modernity. The reflection on aging becomes a must for them in that "an entire world of thoughts and hopes has clamorously aged with them."[5]

In addition to approaching contemporary Italian aging discourses from a political-history perspective and tracing the cultural roots of the old-age imaginary of the western world in a variety of visual, mythological, and philosophical sources, Passerini also responds to the debate in feminist age studies that has flourished outside Italy. In the endnotes to her book, she explicitly refers to Margaret Morganroth Gullette's studies of midlife progress and decline discourses, to the autobiography of the leader of the Gray Panther movement, Maggie Kuhn, to the old-age journals and memoirs of Doris Grumbach, May Sarton, and Carolyn Heilbrun, and to Barbara Walker's study of the archetypal representation of older women as crones. She is also intrigued by the comprehensive research on aging accomplished by key figures in feminist history, such as Simone De Beauvoir, Betty Friedan, and Germaine Greer.[6]

In terms of genre, *La fontana della giovinezza* can be described as a "midlife progress narrative," in that the author learns to recast an incipient decline narrative, inspired by her first awareness of aging at midlife, into a story of progress. This definition is tentative, however, because Passerini is critical of the propensity in American feminist age discourses to repress the bereavement involved in aging.

Another genre-related issue raised by this book regards its classification as autobiography. In spite of the fact that *La fontana della giovinezza* is the result of a complex and comprehensive reflection conducted by a leading feminist scholar on the basis of her own aging experience, the book is not comparable to any of the aging journals or autobiographical essays by American feminists. It is, indeed, the most autobiographical of the six narratives examined in this study, and the one in which author and protagonist are closest in age (the protagonist is fifty-five and the author, born in 1941, was also in her mid-fifties at the time of composition). Apart from their different marital status (the author has never been married and her protagonist is coping with a marriage breakup) and the fact that Passerini, as a university professor, holds a higher position in a professional field similar to that of her narrative alter ego — who works for an educational research center — the cultural experiences and ideological orientation of the protagonist reflect those of the author quite closely. That her education, political stance, and generational cultural experiences are analogous to the author's affirm that the book is fundamentally autobiographical. The perspective is generational, however. Although no programmatic advice on how to deal with aging is offered, the fact that the protagonist remains nameless and recounts a variety of significant personal and interpersonal journeys that are culturally representative, makes her, in many ways, exemplary. Since the choice of this perspective is clearly a political statement, the particular autobiographical nature of this book, the sources that have inspired it, and the author's conclusions regarding individual and collective responses to decline and death should be clarified before engaging in a close reading of the text.

Following Passerini's first narrative endeavor, *Autoritratto di gruppo*, published in 1988 and translated as *Autobiography of a Generation: Italy, 1968*, *La fontana della giovinezza* is the fruit of her reflection on collective experiences and her generation's sense of identity. Both works reflect her historical research interests and methodology. Passerini has been a pioneer in the study of the history of subjectivity. A leading contributor to methodological discussions in oral history, she has examined the sources and uses of memory for historical analysis and has studied the relationship between politics and the imagination.

Although the individual prevails in *La fontana della giovinezza* and the thematic core is located in one's relationship with one's ultimate destination,[7] the genesis of Passerini's two narratives is essentially similar. Both consist of chronologically arranged blocks of materials based on personal and collective testimonies. We know from interviews with the author that *La fontana della giovinezza* is based on fragments written in the years after 1994, notes she jotted down in third person rather than first in order to gain some distance. We also know that she relied on female friends' stories when writing about an experience she did not have, the loss of a partner who turned to a younger woman and had a child with her.[8] The choice of using "the life stories some women have told me on several occasions in an informal practice of oral history"[9] as narrative source is grounded on feminist theories that evaluate the narrative discourse of "an exposed and relational self": in other words, rather than tell one's own life story, the narrative is related "from" and "to" another woman.[10]

For the protagonist of *La fontana della giovinezza*, the experiences of betrayal by and separation from the man with whom she shared political struggles and convictions is the starting point for an "awareness journey" into old age, a journey that raises a number of questions and suggests several solutions. What makes this book especially relevant to age studies is the author's perspective on the protagonist's predicament, which is represented as an "old-age attack"[11]—that is to say, the sudden intrusion of age consciousness upon the ideological and emotional makeup of a woman whose cultural identity is markedly generational. The function of the narrator-essayist is to channel this malaise into a process that will promote personal as well as political growth.

6: A CASE STUDY: THE 1968 GENERATION

In the early stage of her journey toward old age, the protagonist finds herself off balance in her perception of space and time: she cannot coordinate as effectively the choices, actions, and rhythms of her existence. Motivated by this deterioration, and the resulting imbalance, to confront individual and collective aging processes, she finally manages to pull out of her predicament, not because she has found ideal or functional solutions but because she has conducted an intensive cultural revision in light of the cognitive categories she acquires as she discovers that she also has an "age identity." It is a radical, complex endeavor. Natural reasons and historical reasons for aging intersect and interact constantly; the impairment affects various levels and directions, both linear and circular, of the spatial-temporal order. The search for a new order, balance, and commitment involves questioning generational and gender identities as well as cultural genealogies (but also biological genealogies, which had been dismissed) in a context so wide as to include—and connect—activities of private and microcommunitarian daily existence, European historical processes, and myths of various cultural origins.

As the narrative parallels the protagonist's growing age awareness, the analysis of the transition from crisis to recovery of meaning, from disinvestment to reinvestment, is conducted on the level of various temporal patterns and involves their disruption and their subsequent reconfiguration. The disruption of life chronology manifests itself, as previously observed, in various directional patterns. It involves both circular-biological and linear-historical time, which overlap in the intersection of past, present, and future realms. Significant events and places of the past—which often consolidated into choices, habits, lifestyles, and rhythms—are recollected and assessed. While acknowledging their end and/or loss in the present, the protagonist also tries to lay the foundations of a constructive old-age discourse. The chronological disruption also involves, in linear time, the crisis of horizontal-generational alliances and the necessity of reviewing genealogies to acknowledge the intergenerational verticality of human relationships and of cultural transmission, particularly through the female line. The gender perspective calls into question the relation between time and gaze, and the possibility of giving meaning to one's female body in the absence of recognition by the gaze-mirror. The book addresses the question of whether, and to what degree, gender identity interacts with generational identity and, within a generation marked by a particularly difficult relationship with time, what aging modes recur among men and women—and which of these are most adequate.

The attention to both gender and generational components of aging provides a means to achieve a wider political perspective on the issue;

but *La fontana della giovinezza* is ultimately and most importantly a secular journey toward coherent and dignified death and reconciled fulfillment. The last part of the book suggests possible syntheses in response to the multifaceted disruption caused by the protagonist's sudden awareness of physical and emotional aging. Although the author sees a way to overcome cultural prejudice and achieve a new, more suitable existential balance in the detachment from passion and the acceptance of more introverted scenarios, she does not close with an ideal picture of sheltered, wiser, and triumphant disengagement. A final assessment of the cultural archetypes underlying the narrative discourse shows that the reconciliation is as problematic as the disruption, since while an older individual might find solace in inner peace as opposed to political action, she ages within a community and a civilization.

Luisa Passerini's *La fontana della giovinezza*

La fontana della giovinezza [The Fountain of Youth] is divided into four parts that are similar in structure and length. The narrative sections, approximately twenty pages long, are titled after the seasons of the year and introduced by five to six-page descriptions of paintings (reproduced in the text) that are related thematically to old age. In the introductions to the narrative sections, the myths on which the pictorial discourse is grounded are explored, the focus being feminine archetypes of aging.

The paintings range in date from the mid-sixteenth century to the early twentieth, and they are not ordered chronologically. The first painting, *The Fountain of Youth* (1546), by Cranach, refers to a widespread legend of medieval and early modern Europe. Such fountains were believed to restore female bodies to youth and, through them, men's bodies as well, by the means of regenerating love. The second painting, *The Defense of the Sampo* (1896), by the Finnish painter Gallen-Kallela, deals with the defeat of a Nordic Great Mother in an episode from the Finnish epic poem Kalevala. The third is a 1934 painting by Ernest Blumenschein, *The Old Storyteller*, in which a Native American girl, embraced by a handsome old woman, listens to her tales pensively. The fourth is a painting by Rubens representing Baucis and Philemon, a seventeenth-century version of a classical myth well known in Europe and variously rendered in the art and literature of the modern age. It is a singular myth, in which rebirth is not effected by a child announcing a new order, but by an old couple who act as intermediaries between the gods and the regenerated world.

The narrative thread of *La fontana della giovinezza*, in the third person, focuses on the internal experiences and transformations of the protagonist. The protagonist of the narrative is a fifty-five-year-old woman who, in the past, has been passionately involved in politics and feminism. She has traveled, been sexually active, and participated in consciousness-raising groups and alternative cultures. As to her present condition, the reader learns that she lives alone, has no children, works for an educational research center and, on Saturday mornings, she buys groceries, does the laundry, has a snack, takes a walk. The acute experience of failure and of loss of meaning at this particular stage of her life is undoubtedly prompted by external events: her separation from a husband who, having strayed from their shared generational roots, enjoys a late paternity with a younger woman, and the subsequent loss of common friends and interests as well as of a common home. These new circumstances force the protagonist to review her existence. She must reassess her lifestyle, adjust her pace, reorganize her social life, clean out her belongings when moving to a smaller apartment, and visit places that were crucial in her *Bildung*. She also explores bodily sensations related to sexuality as well as to physical decline, meets old acquaintants in homes, in trattorias, and on walks, and observes strangers in the street and on the subway. As she investigates and debates aging-related issues, her theoretical reflections are stimulated by her readings—especially of foreign feminist literature—as well as by the commercial exploitation of women's fears of aging.

The protagonist's quest starts in autumn and ends in spring. This deviation from a more traditional sequence, from winter-death to spring-rebirth, locates the balance of death and maturity in the summer. The epigraph, from a poem by Louise Glück, refers to this capability to establish a mature, full relationship with death: "summer has returned to me, this time not as a lover but a messenger of death, yet it is still summer, it is meant tenderly."[12] In the fall—that is, at the end of the summer preceding the onset of time consciousness—and as a consequence of the greater exposure of the body in the summer, the woman notices signs of psychophysical deterioration: hand freckles and wrinkles, hot flashes, sleep disorders, teariness, forgetfulness. Mirrors and domestic objects, clothes and habits reflect a cracked self-image; they do not fit the body anymore and, if they do, as in the repetition of daily gestures, they produce "ferocious boredom."[13] Although waking up in the morning is neither desirable nor meaningful, the protagonist unconsciously perceives that she must not give in "until the worst is over."[14] She reports several dreams: one of the dreams in the first part of the novel makes her recall the town where she was born, and provokes a recollection of what things were like before life's decisions were made and its course was determined. In that town she could have made different choices, but she did not. In winter the protagonist begins to analyze her unease: she investigates the discourse of aging, the lexicon and the cultural representations of the deterioration of the individuals, models, and objects of the European modernity in which she was formed. Her move to a new place forces her to devote time and energy to sorting out what is alive and what no longer is. While recovering from a bad flu, she plans a trip to the places of her youth. In spring she visits those places: Paris, New York, California, and the city where she had lived in the seventies (references to streets and hangouts indicate it is Turin). She notes changes in the appearance of people and places, and meets old friends. After her return she reorders notes and impressions and reevaluates ideas, inspired by the feminist essays she bought in the United States. In the fourth part she goes back to her former routine, with a few innovative projects. They are "little things,"[15] such as meeting with students or organizing film series and debates on middle and old age. In a transformation involving not so much the choice of lifestyles and spaces as her interior disposition, the protagonist seems to emerge constructively and joyously—fortunately not giving in to sententiousness or triumphalism—from what she consciously identifies as her first "old-age attack" to find a conciliation among the stages of human life.

". . . she could no longer control the boundaries of transitions . . ."

A close reading of the text will illustrate and clarify the complexity of Passerini's discourse on aging. The old-age attack that the protagonist of *La fontana della giovinezza* experiences is not so much an epiphany as an alteration. It is the first emergence of the symptoms of an "illness" that is nothing less than our creatural finitude. This warning of the approaching end can grow into "awareness pervading the body,"[16] and this awareness can foster intellectual commitment, possibly "a new militancy"[17] for the protagonist's generation. It is important that this generation arrive at a secular approach to death, consistent with the materialism to which it has committed itself. The sacredness of final purposes cannot but be "lay sacredness"[18] that disregards the illusion of transcendence. Aging awareness is ultimately the awareness of the temporal and spatial coordinates of human contingency.

The seasonal organization of the book and the recurrence of cyclical time markers (days of the week, parts of the day) underscore the loss of meaning in the intimacy with oneself in daily existence, and recall the circularity of the journey from birth to death. The effects of the seasons on the protagonist's body are noticed, as is the absurdity of opposing to them the idea of surviving her body. Night and day invade each other: nights are disturbed by "resurgences of minor events [that went] unnoticed during the day, but all of a sudden took defined contours and . . . claimed revenge or reparation . . . forced her to call the next day to change plans"[19] or inhabited by dreams that are analyzed the next day. The crisis also affects her life rhythms. After years of "hard work, always rushing,"[20] she experiences "a slowness in realizing many things, as if there were a diaphragm between her and reality."[21] Natural processes slow down, too, as the protagonist undergoes a lengthy convalescence from a flu.

In linear time, memory divides into two painful feelings: nostalgia (for what has been lost) and regret (for what has not been lived), while planning and fear replace desire and utopia in the imagined future. The nostalgia for the past turns out to be a generational attitude, and is intensified by the technological progress that renders things obsolete much more rapidly than in the past. In the realm of regret, too, memory has both an individual dimension—particularly intense in relation to unconsummated loves—and a collective-generational one—since ideological critique has involved, especially for women, the rejection of more traditional life patterns. In collective memory, linear and circular time overlap, in that ideas and actions have (or have not) become life choices; choices, made in opposition to tradition, have themselves become elective customs and rituals, and as such have often been reassessed and shared with other people of the same generation:

> Going back and again to the same places produced successive stratifications: how many times had she been to Paris, from the early sixties on, so full of hope of meeting and communicating.[22]

> Then she returned to Europe and stopped for a few days in the city where she had lived in the sixties. Among those days there was a May day and, after some hesitation . . . she walked through the square where the political rallies were ending. She slipped among the small groups that were lingering . . . remembering bits and pieces of other May days. . . . Now those May days got all confused, in a mix of images of her memory to which photos taken on various occasions were superimposed.[23]

As to the future, the immediate one is obsessively "sliced up."[24] The protagonist expends a lot of energy consulting calendars and appointment books and trying to forestall unforeseen occurrences. When she travels, she can no longer arrive at the station or at the airport at the last minute: "she could no longer control the boundaries of transitions."[25] She is aware that her planning strategies are tricks to delude herself into believing she can control the succession of time—fixations that, in her relation to space, manifest themselves as collecting, accumulating, and preserving manias, particularly within the domestic geography of feminine time:

> A piece of furniture that she hardly noticed anymore appeared repulsive to her because of its worn uselessness and, had she been younger, she would have got rid of it.[26]

> It was somewhat painful for her to look at those old pieces of furniture and household appliances, awkward and not hidden anymore in the recesses of the house that had hosted them for a long time. Others, arranged in her new freshly painted apartment, showed their age at last. People can go on without us, she thought, things can't: if nobody takes care of them constantly, they deteriorate and disappear.[27]

The pain of losing objects masks the fear of the final loss. One must decide, with respect both to commitments and possessions, what to retain and what to eliminate. Certain objects, just like certain kinds of fabrics, age as well, and have, as we shall see later, a generational identity. In the most time-resistant, like the teapot, the protagonist likes to recognize "aspects of her body."[28] Even the most perishable and replaceable items, like the soap bar, turn into anthropomorphic traveling companions: "if she and the soap had lasted until the summer, the end of the soap would have coincided with the end of that difficult period and the beginning of vacation."[29] As a consequence of this strongly projective attitude toward objects, the move to a new apartment is experienced as "a dress rehearsal for death."[30] The fear of the "small deaths"[31] that, in the present, forecast death—the decease of loved ones, especially contemporaries, the loss of passions, or the wear and tear on objects—colors the protagonist's vision of the future. In the projections of the next life phase—which is no longer what follows, but rather what comes last—she foresees the loss of her living space, as well as the decrease in financial resources and physical energy:

> The film had presented to her what she obscurely feared, not the present state which, although miserable, still contained autonomy and self-sufficiency, but the state before extreme decrepitude, old age in specialized institutions, ghettos at the margins of daily life. . . .
> For the time being she felt grateful she was in a bed at night, in a protected room; she could not take that for granted, and was afraid that this relative security might end.[32]

> She went to visit some very elderly women, overcoming the fear she had of extreme old age, which struck her from time to time in the form of anxiety about the future. After retiring, she found herself thinking, she couldn't

have afforded taking a taxi, buying expensive face creams—and she had not saved, she had lived like a grasshopper in every way.[33]

The identification of the fear of aging and dying with the fear of losing places and objects is the result of maintaining a materialistic orientation toward old age and death. It is an extremely difficult, offbeat choice, yet a crucial ideological test. When facing old age and death, many yield to the illusion or hope of transcending their end. The determination to find meaning in human finitude makes the perception of passing time material, and it is in the territory of human finitude (body, house, travels, but also interiority and history) that the awareness of time materializes.

This awareness is initially, and paradoxically, perceived as heedlessness. A typical symptom of senility, forgetfulness, is the result of a "distraction," of a forced shift out of the track of the illusion of being eternal, significantly conveyed through the metaphor of the train:

> While driving to her office she found herself thinking that aging was like when a train enters a tunnel in daylight and comes out of it at twilight, and the hilltops stand out against a nearly white background, but just above them the blue of the sky has darkened under the transparent moon of the last quarter. It had happened suddenly, as if she had ceased paying attention for a moment.[34]

The shock of losing control, "of having been trapped in a consciousness blank,"[35] generates a sense of foreignness to one's own life territory. Why must the journey, the protagonist wonders, take its metaphors from an unfamiliar landscape? Why must it be like traveling through a wasteland and not, for example, like the confusion of a pedestrian walking on a rainy night on an equally threatening highway crossed by speeding trucks, or pushed by a rowdy crowd inside a dirty tunnel between the station and the market? She finds a "spatial answer" to the eternal riddle of what being young and aging may mean:

> Those who were born in a similar order to the one that surrounds them, those who automatically recognize their environment can be called young. What causes the sense of aging is the experience of not recognizing, of being a stranger to one's present habitat, compared to that of one's childhood and adolescence.[36]

The spatial perception of one's aging is linked to the consciousness of personal decline within that of a civilization, civilization meaning a symbolic space of shared ideas, choices, and movements. Old age is a relative notion: one is old, of course, in relation to a temporal otherness.

It is the foreignness to one's own age that Jean Améry refers to, "the awareness of one's outdatedness,"[37] particularly upsetting for those who were once culturally at the forefront. When we grow old we ignore "entire worlds":[38] new ideas and new books, certain kinds of music and TV shows. We ignore them because they do not interest us; they do not interest us because we do not partake in the cultural territory of "up-to-dateness." The protagonist acknowledges "the end of places";[39] revisiting significant locations during the trip in the third part of the book, she either cannot find them (for example, the bars she used to go to regularly), or finds them changed (the same streets are populated by new ethnic groups). One feels "out of place"[40] and the problem is "where to place one's old age."[41]

One of the most common ways of remaining contemporary is through fashion. Significantly, what is not of the present time is defined as "out of fashion." If outdatedness becomes more manifest in clothing and its accessories, particularly in women's clothes—"silk and ivory once were the symbols of the positive value of old age, because their value increased in time . . . but perhaps today, when novelty always prevailed, this was no longer the case"[42]—household items also have a generational identity: the iron, the hair-dryer, the citrus-fruit squeezer belong to a "new, lighter, and more carefree generation."[43] The speed of technological transformations makes the notion of one's own transformation in time more complex. Changes in domestic routines, in the house, and in the way we treat our bodies have been so radical as to alienate us both from the old-age models of former generations and, within our own life history, from the past (some practices and objects from our childhood and adolescence, like doing the washing in the tub and cloth sanitary pads, do not exist anymore) and from the vision of the future, in that "also in relation to the aging process there had been modernization and technologization, which included household appliances and vitamins, plastic surgery and bright-colored clothes."[44]

It is true that certain phenomena of popular culture make a comeback. However, the comeback is often a result of cultural globalization, of its standardizing indifference, rather than of the revival or rediscovery of neglected aspects of past phenomena and of possible connections among them. Therefore, if the "village festival atmosphere"[45] noticed in a gay pride celebration in the Latin Quarter during her visit to Paris reminds the protagonist of old Communist Party festivals, her friend points out that it is not much different from Berlin on similar occasions: "it is a global tendency towards the fair," he says, "in which we gay people revel."[46]

". . . the by now uncertain discourse between male and female . . ."

As to the different ways men and women '68ers deal with aging, it is a well-known fact that women are, more than men, wooed by the "market [for] . . . youthfulness":[47] skin-toning creams, plastic surgery, genetic manipulation, advice on how to face menopause. "EMBRACE MENOPAUSE! A FRIGHTENING AGE? A GOLDEN AGE!!!"[48] a notice on the pharmacy counter proclaims in capital letters. Not particularly affected by the crisis of menopause as the end of her reproductive phase, the protagonist wonders instead why it is difficult, even after the experience of feminism, to renounce the "idolatry of femininity." "Self-embellishment, self-ostentation, self-admiration"[49] are the foundations of traditional female sexuality in the western world, at least the heterosexual one. Her new awareness of aging undermines the "triumphant" ignorance of time by a narcissistic eroticism that freezes the body in "an instant of absolute immobility":

> Narcissism had been the hesitant satisfaction with her own body, and sexual desire had been roused and governed by the pleasure of adorning herself with stockings, shoes, jewels and, most of all, bras underwear garters corsets, in all colors and especially in black. . . . There was a moment, when she was perfectly ready, when time would stop on the triumphant image of the body dressed for being admired and admiring itself, and it seemed as if hair and nails did not grow anymore and even could not get dirty, an instant of absolute immobility, under her own gaze and the gaze of others.[50]

Now in the mirror at the café the protagonist recognizes "not her own features but those of her grandmother."[51] While applying the Lacanian notion of "mirror stage" to the representations of old age, Kathleen Woodward claims that at this stage "the narcissistic impulse directs itself *against* the mirror image as it is embodied literally and figuratively in the faces and the bodies—the images—of old people."[52] She identifies a resurgence of the "mirror stage" discrepancy between the perceived inner self and the outer image typical of the mirror stage in infancy, though it is reversed in old age: the mirror image is that of a fragmented and deteriorating body while the inner adult notion of self is that of a unified whole. That discrepancy between self and image often causes psychological disorientation and a sense of loss.

The narcissistic construction of sexuality involves the loss, in old age, both of female identity and of the relation to the masculine, as the definition of female identity through the male mirror-gaze fails us. For this reason the protagonist feels that her husband's absence is actually the "absence . . . of the masculine."[53] In one of her dreams Peter Pan appears as "phal-logos, erotic center of the by now uncertain discourse between male and female,"[54] a discourse that confines her today to a "long permanence in the neuter."[55] Older people are situated in fact in a territory at the border of neutrality and invisibility. Their visibility is the neutral, generic one of stereotypes: gray hair and emotiveness are not individual physical or personality traits but the sign that they belong to a category within which the gaze of the Other/young cannot make distinctions:

> At Santa Cruz she took a bus to the university, convinced it was a campus shuttle. The driver called her back to make her pay for the ticket and she got flustered while looking for some change. The young man was looking at her as if she were senile. . . . She realized she had been classified as older than she was—not only because of her gray hair, but also due to her anxiety and confusion, behavior that would have been interpreted differently in a young person.[56]

The most dramatic confrontation with male responses to aging occurs in relation to the protagonist's husband. When commenting, at the beginning of the narration, on his falling in love with a much younger woman and his late paternity, the protagonist uses expressions like "scandal," "defying time laws," "with impunity," "going away to pursue youth in the form of a young woman."[57] Her main accusation is that of escaping "from the world they have shared,"[58] thus of breaking the generational compact. In his life choices he shows a rootedness in the present that she has lost—he is setting up a media consulting agency with his new partner and a younger colleague—but the water of the fountain of youth has not immunized him from the physical symptoms of aging: he has experienced a slow-down first because of the change of house and habits, then because of the sleepless nights after the birth of his child. He often wakes up in the night with a feeling of estrangement.

The middle-aged women the protagonist identifies with seem to care more about horizontal relationships, which represent a conquest of parity and reciprocity, as opposed to the genealogical verticality—or circularity, if we consider the repetitive models in the female tradition wherein their mothers and grandmothers had situated themselves.

In the absence of the family-related elements typical of women's novels of aging—nursing elderly parents (there is a cursory reference by the ex-husband to his mother's poor health), communicating with children, looking after and educating grandchildren—and because the reconstruction of ancestors' experience is limited and fragmentary, the presence of family genealogies is felt in this book only at the symbolic level. Mothers, grandmothers, great-grandmothers (as well as unborn children) often appear in the protagonist's dreams, and the rupture of female genealogies takes the form of regret. The dream of unconsummated youthful loves activates the regret for not having lived the life prescribed by tradition and her family—a career as a teacher in the small town where she was born and a bourgeois marriage to one of the sons of the local notables. The thought of the children she did not have, too, is situated "among the resurgences of what could have been and had not."[59] The features of the protagonist's grandmother are actually hers as an old woman at the mirror, and she ascribes her own interest in Paris to her grandmother's tales of her travels in the thirties. When she identifies with female models of the past, they are "old women she remembers from her childhood"[60] rather than women of her family. The dream, in the fourth part, of her mother and grandmother who, "in fifteenth-century clothes . . . sumptuous and stately . . . were watching her from the balcony of the old building where they had lived for years . . . not from the fourth floor, as had been the case, but from the first," is interpreted "as an indication of her lesser distance from the dead,"[61] of a symbolic recovery of the collectivity of the dead. The collective memory of the dead "could be recalled by lists of names like the ones on her artist friend's papyrus scroll or even just by a pious attitude to one's own past," as well as by "old and ancient women's serene and aware relation to death."[62]

In the narrative present, the protagonist identifies with the elderly women she observes in the street, with her eighty-year-old friend Marzia, with a college mate's mother, with the portrait depicting an old painter.[63] As a consequence of her adherence to ideal rather than to blood genealogies, intergenerational discourse reaches well beyond family relationships, and also involves the possibility of transmitting a legacy to posterity. As to the transmission of legacy we are most interested in, the transmission along a female line, it is natural that, in the absence of daughters, the protagonist's attention—both her critique and her reflection—go to the young women she observes during her trip, to her young female friends, to her husband's new partner, and that she should confront them more from an intergenerational than from a personal perspective. Following a visit by a nearly thirty-year-old former student, who tells her about experiments with drugs and sexual promiscuousness similar to those of young people in the sixties and seventies, the protagonist remarks that "her relation to these young people was not maternal/filial" and that they belonged to two different "discourse traditions,"[64] in spite of a few common points. Moreover, the distress at being replaced by a younger partner is transferred to the level of intergenerational gender relations: not understanding why young women choose older men, she wonders if it is "a challenge to the feminist mothers' generation."[65] Young women are critical of separatism and of feminist self-consciousness, and seem not to be burdened by the self-referential narcissism of the protagonist's generation. They are less involved in the body mystique, less interested in female identity and more aware of being full subjects, more open to difference, in particular to immigrant women. In the consternation of ascertaining a communication gap between her generation and the new generation of women, the protagonist wonders if she will be able to dispense her jewels and valuables before dying, like the old women of her family had done, to unburden herself of them in order to be well-prepared for death, hoping that her things, although scattered and divided, will be preserved with care.

Transmission to younger men is a less complex issue: relationships with them have more lightness, playfulness—which also reveals the resistance of the narcissism of seduction. The most important legacy is perhaps "the right to feel,"[66] a legacy that the feminism of the protagonist's generation—which had claimed the importance of the private in the political sphere—addressed first of all to the men of the same generation. Always bearing in mind the interweaving of gender and generational identities, the book records numerous encounters of the protagonist with men of the same age, with whom she manages to communicate on contiguous terrains of feelings and experiences of aging, or to discover new forms of reciprocal seduction. A college mate of her husband's experiences "a loss of enthusiasm and curiosity at work . . . and some weakness in his daily struggle,"[67] and is deeply aware of his physical decline. The old gay friend she meets in Paris serenely points to the "fading of passions"[68] and to the hypothesis of surviving after death, through forms of reincarnation. A slightly older friend she meets at the bookstore—certainly the best-sketched example of male old age, in his moderation and irony, his body "bent and wrinkled" but his word "sparkling and paradoxical"[69]—comments briefly on the color of the protagonist's jacket and on the quality of the fabric. Although "a little stiff in receiving his compliment," the woman wonders, "in the play and confusion of the farewell"[70] and in the light, confidential contact between his arm and her armpit, whether this is a new form of eroticism, subtle and unconsummated, more adequate to this age, to the need of unburdening and detaching from passions, of being less relational and more introspective. Word and sexuality appear, in fact, as "the burden of the past": both "had pushed her outside herself, toward others. But now emotions and the relationship with herself prevailed."[71] One of the protagonist's rediscovered friends, a schoolmate who, after his mother's death, is experiencing something similar to what the protagonist's ex-husband is experiencing—a second paternity with a new partner—maintains that "now it came natural to him to see the future through female eyes and, in a certain way, to open up to the feminine."[72] It is a "revolution of sentiment"[73] reaching far beyond the affection, complicity, and respect he has with his first son.

Both in the affinity and in the diversity of responses, aging reduces differences in gender identity. Men become more conscious of the body, more sentimental, more interested in child-rearing. Women—the affirmation of the male gaze failing them—discover a new form of self-referentiality, quite different from erotic narcissism, which opens up the possibility of a deeper self-centeredness. It is no coincidence that the protagonist sees her "feminist phase" as the only phase of her generational militancy that was free from the nostalgic projection into the past. It is in fact starting from her reflection on gender identity that she can initiate a process of reintegration and reinvestment, a "re-generation" that reaches beyond both gender and generational identities.

Contemporary feminist criticism has opened to the reflection on ageism, which the protagonist investigates in her new readings after her trip. The debate on this issue has been particularly active in the United States, following the entry into the third age—sometimes into the fourth, as in the case of Maggie Kuhn, May Sarton, Doris Grumbach—of important figures for the women's movement of the sixties and seventies. The notion of age prejudice concerns all age classes (young people are often the object of negative generalization) and represents an expansion of the constructive study and critique of stereotypes. Some feminists, for instance Germaine Greer and Betty Friedan, point to the critical and regenerative potential of the emancipation from the male gaze that is confirmed by the opening-up of older women to bisexuality and homosexuality. As the protagonist's American friend Linda points out, at the threshold of old age, in contemporary western society, as well as in ancient tribal societies, women can afford the option of actively discovering their bisexuality and of having, like men with their new partners, "a second life."[74] Linda can think of several women friends who, after raising their children in fairly traditional marriages, entered into lesbian love relationships and were transformed by them. The entry of older women into the category of the neuter on one hand shifts the attention from female and age identities to the variety of women's experiences in different aging stages, and opens the way to cultural androgyny on the other.

Accustomed by the political engagement of their youth "to weigh the possibilities for revolution, as if by a conditioned reflex," the women of the protagonist's generation can become "the subjects of change"[75] again, and in new ways. The enormous possibilities for social critique inherent in age awareness involve refashioning the power structure by which culture is transmitted. Critical work on female genealogies may lead to both the dismantling of the daughter-servant and mother-mistress roles suggested by Félix Vallotton's painting reproduced on the book cover—"where a young woman, firm, confident and cheerful, helps an older woman enter the water"[76]—and to the transformation of traditional familiar presences into internal ones:

> While walking home, she thought for a moment that a presence was waiting for her, but she remembered all of a sudden that this was not the case, and called that sensation back, from the house to herself. The presence, which had appeared almost as if an automatic habit had arisen after years, had a vague profile: her mother? her grandmother? a man?. . . . Whereas now that presence was internal—like a feeling of reconciliation—it was almost becoming a daily consuetude.[77]

The power derived from the condition and awareness of old age is aging consciousness, that is the consciousness of both chronological age and the human aging process. It is not—as the celebration of the crone's magical powers by Barbara Walker would suggest—a new version of matriarchy, but "a power that would result from the knowledge of many things."[78]

The contributions of feminist research on ageism are important to the protagonist's reflections. Still, she has veiled reservations about American women's aging discourses, which we can understand in light of the different sensibility and ideological foundations of Italian and American feminism. The protagonist notes "a certain futility"[79] in Carolyn Heilbrun's discourse on aging, in reference to the decision to commit suicide at seventy, and "an excess of confidence"[80] in the triumphant conclusions—"I had never felt freer"[81]—of Betty Friedan's ambitious study. Her young psychologist friend's critique of the "insufficient acknowledgement of the bereavement involved in aging"[82] by some American feminists is particularly perceptive. The protagonist appreciates, conversely, the critical pessimism of Simone De Beauvoir. She notes the extent of De Beauvoir's research and the absence of illusions in her comments on the refusal to acknowledge older people's subjectivity and on their consequent marginalization from world history.

". . . a sense of completion like getting to close a circle . . ."

Having conducted a profound, honest search for a possible answer to the question of whether the women of her generation may access their own fountain of youth, the protagonist seems able to explore realms that reach beyond the gender- and generation-related aspects of aging. On the level of spatial-temporal balance, aging consciousness leads to a wider notion of self, of one's own roots and destiny. In the journey from egoistic narcissism to the search for the self, the fruits of the disinvestment from the ego are detachment, relief, and rediscovery of the joy of living:

> What had changed? On the face of it she could see no relevant changes. She experienced a sense of relief, as if she had relaxed her grip—on what? Perhaps regrets—she still had some, but she saw them detached from her. She had given up on some ambitions—accomplishing at all costs, questioning and protesting or promoting and being promoted, enough! If losing all this was the price of aging, she seemed to see also some small gains: recovering crumbs of pleasure in living.[83]

The recovery of the joys of living also means the recovery of childhood and pre-adolescence, of "specks of girlish cheerfulness."[84] This is not regression to a childlike state but the deconstruction of the adult ego. The discovery of the garden as an alternative to the fray of the city-worldliness,[85] celebrated in Sarton's and Grumbach's old-age diaries, has enabled the mother of one of the protagonist's schoolmates to follow desires that date back to childhood and to realize an ideal "equanimous detachment."[86]

The assessment of the past and the projections of the future—the protagonist's trip as return to certain places, the meeting of old friends, memory, the reflection on unmade choices, the construction of a vision of old age—should be read as integration of linear and circular time, of detachment and return, and of regenerative transformation and reassessment utilizing a more far-sighted perspective than the self-referential one of the adult present, as well as that of memory. The fullness "of the last or of the penultimate phase of life" is "a sense of completion like getting to close a circle, a higher or more preferable satisfaction than that deriving from reaching a set goal at the end of a linear or ascending path, like the top of a mountain, from which one must in any case descend."[87] If it is true that the past does not come back and "the linear dimension of time is the one that has the better in the end—with death," it is also true that "there is another dimension, another form of time where things come and go and return in a spiral pattern."[88] The awareness that "there are various old ages"[89] that come and go, invade a period of life, then disappear deceptively only to reappear as more severe forms of decline, is the foundation of the only acceptable hypothesis, from a secular standpoint, of the relationship to time, that of the "self-government of seasons,"[90] which is in its turn based on a revolution of interior times and spaces. A good management of time, desirable in every phase of life, becomes, for an older person, a necessity that cannot be ignored.

This revolution is interior yet extremely complex. The transition from disinvestment to reinvestment is a comprehensive repositioning, which involves choosing alternative modes of behavior in all areas of life. For example, the choice of dyeing one's hair or having a facelift not at fifty but perhaps at sixty, indicates a repositioning from fashion consciousness to the consciousness of life passages. In fact, coming to terms with one's first gray hair and wrinkles is a crucial mid-life rite of passage. Women prefer white to gray hair because they are more often willing to "move from maturity to old age in a night" than to "walk with their eyes open."[91]

Repositioning oneself, through deceleration, from the hectic pace of young adult life to the slower one of old age prepares us for the immobility of death, but may also "enable us to discover something."[92] Being aware of the seasons-phases, listening to the rain, paying attention to the blossoming of trees are modes of thought that are naturally regenerating. We can return to our bodies with a new dedication, moving from "body staging" to "various forms of body work,"[93] both therapeutic and expressive. We need to reconfigure memory and, with it, the future space in which we can locate our old age. For the protagonist, refiguring takes place through the sorting of books, photos, and objects during her move and after her trip, which becomes an opportunity for taking stock and resetting priorities. Refiguring means reorienting her anxious collecting toward the preparation of a space for her old self:[94] "a small home for herself and her things,"[95] or perhaps a project of communal life with her friend Olga. From this perspective, the choice of not disposing of objects is a form of donation of/detachment from a legacy in favor of the "image of a very old woman—not even resembling her present self anymore—who would contemplate those simulacra of a remote past and, thanks to them, would go back to it for a few moments," hoping that "that old woman's eyes would ultimately give a meaning to those garments."[96]

It is necessary to start some form of disinvestment in relation to collective identities, in that aging is a substantially individual experience. As the narrator states, "aging alone seemed to mean giving up all this—the hope, always nurtured in some hidden corner of herself, that that shared world would reappear in some form."[97] This is an important discovery for those who were used, in the experiences of political struggle and of feminist consciousness-raising groups, to situate suffering "in the context of a mass in motion."[98] The relationship with the collectivity is reconstructed in far wider connections than those of the blood or ideal communities—a connection with the humankind of the past, a vaster humankind than the one the protagonist is rebuilding in her friendships or meets at work—in the direction of discovering, perhaps, "a lay sacredness" in which both the living and the dead may partake. In fact, if the reflection on ageism represents a new stage of awareness of prejudice, the highest form of union and reconciliation is the awareness of death and its subversion of class, gender, and age differences.

". . . remaining faithful to change . . ."

The narrator-essayist attempts, in the final page of the book, to synthesize the formative influence on the protagonist's journey of the four founding myths. This effort at synthesis underscores the unity of *La fontana della giovinezza* and suggests the extent to which its mythical-figurative level, the narrator's reflections, and her narration are integrated in a more or less explicit way in all four parts.

In the first part, the narrator intervenes in the painting-analysis section, juxtaposing her voice to that of the author-essayist. She maintains that the legend of the fountain seems true to the protagonist even today, with respect to her husband's procreative love for a younger woman. Her final purpose in writing is ascribed to the need to "understand what water to plunge into,"[99] to discover if an analogous regenerative fount exists for the women of her generation.

The goddess Louhi in the second painting and myth, "strong and still fearsome, although at the end of her resources,"[100] represents the defeat of the heroic age and combines the two characters of creator and ancestor. She is associated with the winter phase of strenuous struggle, resistance and confrontation with ideological defeat, and with the creative possibilities of female old age. Like the weakened goddess-witch Louhi, the protagonist can no longer use her charms: the weapons of seduction, clothing, and make-up can no longer make her body last forever.

The importance of cultural transmission through the female line, represented by the older narrator in the third painting, recalls the protagonist's encounters with younger women and her need to entrust more than a merely nostalgic legacy to posterity. In fact, the elderly narrator in the painting does not appear inspired by a feeling of nostalgia, but seems instead projected toward the future in her relation to the young, pensive girl. The protagonist seeks to overcome the genealogical power roles of tradition, beginning with the negative view of older women's educational function associated with the Christian notion of older women as witches with demonic powers. Other female archetypes that are taken into consideration in the section on Native American legends are figures of old women offering help and advice to young people, establishing conditions that the young, in their carelessness, do not respect. The failure to heed the lessons of old age, to consider the "four directions... of humankind's journey on the earth"[101] is what may prevent the twins of a tale, and the protagonist's generation, from accepting their destiny and learning to "rule" the stages of life wisely. Among these figures of wise but unheeded old women there is also Grandma Spider who, deaf to the arrogant shouts of others, sets out on a journey and finds her way back home by following the thread she has woven during her outward journey. Similarly, the protagonist sets out on a conscious journey into her past.

The last painting and myth, representing Baucis and Philemon, is announced in the third part, when the narrator explains the paradox of its irreducibility to the personal experience of the protagonist—who was, in the set up of her marriage, distant from traditional choices of conjugal fidelity and is, in the present, free from marriage ties and from the illusion of old age shared as a couple. We are thus warned that this myth must have a deeper significance for the protagonist. Baucis and Philemon represent conjugal old age as balance and moderation: they are a model of primeval society, of primigenial salvageable unity of the masculine and the feminine. *"Tota domus duo sunt,"* writes Ovid, who also underlines their equality, both in age and in roles.[102] Their essentiality is no doubt a reference to the detachment from passions and regrets the protagonist is pursuing. The two are a model of regenerative yet not procreative old age, destined to tell a prodigious story to the youth who flock to the hut-temple of which they have become guardians; Baucis is not presented "as mother, but as partner."[103] The story of the old married couple contains the paradox of a transformation that is a rooting—Baucis and Philemon turn into trees—and of a regeneration that, while it has a pedagogical impact (they tell their story to the young people visiting them), is not procreative.

The issue of procreation is not significant for the protagonist. It is on a more deeply symbolic level that the myth has a value for her, as inspiration for the "reconciliation with oneself and with the destiny of being old"[104] and for fidelity. The fourth narrative section, in fact, abounds in images and experiences of union and reconciliation: with the community of rediscovered friends and of dead people lost along the way, with unconsummated loves (the man for whom she was about to lapse into the throes of passion), with her shadow (a coeval woman with whom she had rivaled in youth), and with her blood genealogy (the mothers, grandmothers, and great-grandmothers of her last dream). The action and imagery in this last section advance the harmonious synthesis of phases, styles, and rhythms of life: the exchange of glances with a young tabla player, the gestural dance of an old man, a child and a young boy at a water fountain, the hypothesis of a future partnership binding her journey from middle to old age with that of her new friend Olga. The myth of Baucis and Philemon is "redeemed" from the reversal of the modern period (in particular, Goethe's version, in which Faustian "colonialism" condemns to destruction the little world rescued by the old couple from the Flood, has been crucial for modern versions). This redemption occurs through a postmodern image—significantly inserted in the mythical-figurative discourse of the fourth part—of an old couple from Southeast Asia met on the New York subway, whose "suntanned farmers' faces"[105] resemble the faces of Philemon and Baucis. It is an image that implies the acceptance, on a historical-political level, of the transition from a Eurocentric past to a postcolonial contemporaneity, and at the same time clarifies the significance of the fidelity symbolism embodied in the fourth myth. *La fontana della giovinezza* is a book on metamorphosis as a premise of fidelity, about "remaining faithful. . . . to change."[106] Just as Baucis and Philemon must turn into trees in order to stay united and not witness each other's death, likewise the fifty- and sixty-year-old ex-'68ers, marked by a horizontal investment on the level of alliances and by a self-referential temporal identity, must allow themselves to grow older, "so as not to risk transmitting only veterans' tales and nostalgic stories."[107] The conciliation of metamorphosis and fidelity Passerini recommends to her own aging generation entails acknowledging rather than dismissing conflicts and placing utopia in a different perspective. Far from encouraging nostalgia and resignation, old age and aging discourses can engage us in a process of "relocation," in terms of both political practice and cultural conception and definition. By highlighting the limitations of our western productivity-oriented model, age awareness can partake in the plurality of the counterdiscourses that increasingly multicultural communities oppose to such a model. By articulating their estrangement from present times and values to a higher degree, the aged can make more visible the inadequacy of contemporary society to the needs of many individuals and groups. Furthermore, as approaching death forces us to disinvest from existential identities, age awareness can be a powerful critique of the cultural stereotypes implemented by the "politics of identities," by reminding us of their transitory nature. Finally, as the diversity of the approaches to the issue of aging in this book suggests, there is a wealth of knowledge to be recovered and reflected upon, both in the individual and in the collective past, that can help us make some sense of decline and loss.

Conclusion

As I remarked in the introduction, serious and comprehensive research on the origins and diffusion of present-day constructions of women's life courses and on their future prospects is of the utmost relevance in light of Italian demographic records and of the rapidly changing status of women's old-age culture. Since the aim of this book is to encourage research in these areas and its scope is clearly bifocal, encompassing cultural studies and narrative analysis, a few concluding observations on the status of and prospects for Italian cultural and literary age studies, along with suggestions for future research, seem to be the most appropriate and productive way of ending this book and paving the way for more contributions. I have become aware, while writing this manuscript, of directions I have not had the opportunity to address here. One suggestion for future research is in the area of literary studies of age and gender; two others reach beyond the gender focus of my research, toward the "large interdisciplinary zone" that, according to Gullette's definition of age studies, should become the meeting ground of practitioners in various disciplines.

A neglected and potentially fertile sub-field of literary age studies is the investigation of late-life creativity issues. As mentioned in the chapter "Aging in Italy Today," the few and scattered signs of interest in this area are exclusively devoted to the study and appreciation of the late works of men. Rita Levi Montalcini examines some male champions of late-life intellectual creativity as an appendix to her study of the "neuronal plasticity" of the brain, *L'asso nella manica a brandelli*. Some attempts at cultural sensitization in this direction have taken the forms of conferences, art exhibits, and catalogs: e.g., the art catalog series *Dipingere in tarda età* and *I grandi vecchi* distributed by the Associazione De Banfield in Trieste, and the conference sponsored in Milan in 1993 by Fondazione Mudima and Pratica Freudiana, titled "La vecchiaia come opera d'arte," which was accompanied by an exhibit of eighty-year-old Picasso's engravings. Two of the conference papers discussed Michelangelo's and Ariosto's late-life styles.[1]

While the investigation of male artists' and writers' late-life creativity is beyond the scope of this book, let me mention a few Italian women writers whose production might be fruitfully studied from a life-course perspective.

A possible approach is to examine the stylistic and thematic development of long-lived women writers who were creative from youth to advanced old age, and whose last publications were either their most critically acclaimed works or were, at least, quite significant in relation to their entire production. Sibilla Aleramo (1876–1960) wrote her first and most famous novel, *Una donna* (1906), when she was in her mid-twenties and dedicated herself to her last and most comprehensive work, her literary diaries, from age sixty-four until a few days before her death, twenty years later.[2] Another long-lived writer, Fausta Cialente (1898–1993), who started her literary career in her early thirties, published the autobiographical fiction *Le quattro ragazze Wieselberger* (1976), her most renowned work, at age seventy-eight. Gianna Manzini (1896–1974) published her best novel, *Ritratto in piedi*, in 1971, when she was seventy-five, three years before her death. Her last work, the short-story collection *Sulla soglia*, was published two years later. Manzini enjoyed a prolific and prestigious career, publishing numerous novels, stories, and essays, right up to the end of her life, despite a serious chronic illness that forced her to write her last few novels while breathing with the aid of an oxygen tank.

The case of writers who started their literary careers later in life is even more intriguing for an age-studies critic. Anna Banti (1895–1985) started writing novels in her early forties. Her last novel, *Un grido lacerante* (1981), published when she was eighty-six, sheds light on certain aspects of Banti's midlife, widowhood, and old age, particularly on the fact that the transition from her career as art critic to fiction writer was an act of emancipation from the intellectual authority of her husband and mentor, art historian Roberto Longhi, after his death. Like Anna Banti, Lalla Romano (1906–2001) had literary as well as artistic interests and made her debut as a fiction writer in midlife. She published her best-selling novel, *Le parole tra noi leggere* (1969), when she was sixty-three, and was a prolific and acclaimed writer until the end. Her last work, *Dall'ombra*, was published in 1999, two years before her death at age ninety-five. In most cases, however, a woman's mature literary debut is the result of a long apprenticeship that started quite early in life in the form of notes, diaries, and letters. A representative case is that of Dolores Prato (1892–1983), who published her first novel, *Giù la piazza non c'è nessuno* (1980), a monumental and stylistically impeccable childhood memoir, in 1980. As revealed by the impressive amount of archival material that was retrieved in Prato's apartment after her death, the novel, although composed in a relatively short time (it was dictated to a typist by the eighty-eight-year-old writer), is the fruit of a seventy-years-long preparation.

I hope that this book will add a new perspective, that of age studies, to the vital international debates in Italian cultural studies. A number of sociocultural studies discovered in the course of my research on contemporary representations of women's age cultures demonstrate that the examination of generational cultures is the prevailing age-related interest of Italian cultural scholars. These studies—some of which have been only cursorily mentioned in the first part of this book because they are beyond its gender focus—are relevant to my research in that they share the same concern with intergenerational communication that connects women's age discourses.

The most interesting publications in Italian age studies, quite often based on interviews with target groups of older people and on children's responses, aim at analyzing the significance of old-age cultures for younger generations. Some may be considered pioneering discourses in the direction of developing a "pedagogy of aging." Fulvio Scaparro's *Storie del mese azzurro: La vecchiaia narrata ai giovani* (1998) is based on a radio program whose purpose was to explain what old age is in a format that would be captivating to younger audiences. In the essay collection *I bambini e la vecchiaia: Quadri di un immaginario* (1998), children's representations of old age are analyzed.[3] The school projects presented in the book were carried out in the Abruzzi region. The Associazione Goffredo De Banfield, an organization committed to the protection and assistance of non-self-sufficient elderly, has promoted essay contests in the Trieste area schools on age-related themes for three consecutive years: "I nonni" in 1993, "I vecchi" in 1994, and "Io da vecchio" in 1995.[4] Children's drawings of their grandparents in Brescia elementary schools are discussed in a chapter of Tamanza's essay on the representations and transitions of the last age of life.[5] Some of the above-mentioned school projects were closely analyzed in chapter 3, "Older Italian Women: Between Tradition and Transition."

A similar pedagogical intent can be found in the most recent essay collection on Italian generational cultures, *Vivencia: Conoscere la vita da una generazione all'altra* (2003). The authors of these essays pursue and promote a generational- and gender-conscious perspective, focusing on the transmission of *saperi* and *vissuti* (knowledge and experience) of 1968-generation scholars and educators to younger—and possibly *irriconoscenti* (ungrateful)—"heirs."

Prevailing cultural discourses, as well as the novels analyzed in the second part of this study, show that generational transmission is one of the major concerns of Italian age studies. This theme should be further investigated, particularly in light of the major transformations that parenting and grandparenting roles are undergoing in a country with such a dramatically low birth rate. The analysis of contemporary women's fictions confirms that the most significant development in the Italian old-age imaginary involves the new questioning of biological ties and legacies and the frequent privileging of ideal, elective ones. In spite of the inevitable contradictions and losses that this shift entails, the fact that the newly developing age-class alliances are both inter- and intragenerational is a sign of cultural growth in a traditionally family-oriented nation.

A further possible development of Italian age studies is suggested by an acclaimed 1993 publication, *Vecchi* (1994), by Sandra Petrignani, the result of six months of meetings and conversations with older people. The short essay contains life narratives and confessions collected in nursing homes and public parks. A similar publication is *Vediamo passare le stelle: Storie di vita di donne anziane sole*, the collection of interviews with women over sixty who live alone in Milan that I analyzed in chapter 3. These texts belong to genres that Wyatt-Brown discusses in her overview of the sub-fields of literary gerontology under the heading "narrative studies and guided autobiography."[6] Since the characteristics and potential of life narratives have only been marginally acknowledged in this book, I would like to emphasize their value for the age-conscious critic. I believe that retrieving, studying, and encouraging the production of such texts is of primary importance for Italian age studies, since life narratives represent the terrain on which the research interests and methodologies of the humanities and the health sciences may meet. Both gerontological theory and the tools of literary and cultural criticism can be fruitfully applied in analyzing the life review, reminiscence, or autobiography.

Life reviews and reminiscences can be very interesting texts for the literary critic, who may approach them via canonical theories about the life review, Robert Butler's in particular—which focus on individual narratives as self-healing, integrity-building processes and on coherence and closure as features and goals of the ultimate life narrative—or from a postmodernist perspective critical of the Aristotelian idea that lives form a coherent whole. The latter approach holds that "the final picture is only more valid by virtue of being last" and that "the end of life . . . is given shape and value and tone by both the facts of life and the imagination (cultural, historical, personal) by which those facts are perceived and interpreted."[7] Older people's narratives can be constructed as reminiscences, more fragmentary discourses than the life review, often framed by two people—the nursing home resident and the interviewer/therapist—under specialized dialogic circumstances. Another interesting interactive experience is the production of guided autobiographies in life-writing workshops. As composite texts that are negotiated with the listeners and the environment,[8] these life narratives often present dual or multiple authorship issues. As shown by my own use of the interviews of *Vediamo passare le stelle* in the first part of this book, personal narratives can also provide valuable insights into old-age cultures.

Finally, I would like to make a methodological remark about the conclusion of this book. Borrowing once more Woodward's description of the imagination as "prospective as well as retrospective," I admit that although I had originally planned to write a retrospective conclusion, drawing together the multiple threads of my study, finally I have opted instead for a prospective conclusion. This choice reflects my reluctance to say anything too conclusive about a dramatically transitional and proteiform object of study and indicates a strong orientation toward what has not yet been said and written in age and aging discourses. I want to finish on a note as open-ended as the Italian age imaginary appears to be today.

Notes

Abbreviations

The following abbreviations are used in the endnotes to chapters 4, 5, and 6:

APA   Elena Gianini Belotti, *Apri le porte all'alba* (Milan: Feltrinelli, 1999)
BF   Isabella Bossi Fedrigotti, *Di buona famiglia* (Milan: Longanesi, 1991)
CZ   Margaret Mazzantini, *Il catino di zinco* (Venezia: Marsilio, 1994)
FG   Luisa Passerini, *La fontana della giovinezza* (Firenze: Giunti, 1999)
FYH   Susanna Tamaro, *Follow Your Heart*, English translation of *Va' dove ti porta il cuore*, by John Cullen (New York: Dell Publishing Group, 1996)
UL   Luce D'Eramo, *Ultima luna* (Milan: Mondadori, 1993)
VPC   Susanna Tamaro, *Va' dove ti porta il cuore* (Milan: Rizzoli, 2000)

Introduction

1. I have borrowed this term from Mary Russo's essay "Aging and the Scandal of Anachronism." What Russo defends in this essay is "randomness as a way of understanding and assuming the risks of aging" (21). She is particularly interested in "texts which disrupt the developmental model of a woman's life and emphasize an untimeliness in relations between women" (ibid., 24). I consider Russo's identification of women's "anachronism" a powerful tool for detecting and encouraging creativity in women's age imaginary.

2. Gullette, *Declining to Decline*, 91.

3. Gullette, *Aged by Culture*, 33.

4. Ibid.

5. See Cavigioli, *La fatica di iniziare il libro*. Aleramo started writing her diary when she was 64. The last entry was written a few days before her death, at age 84. Conceived as a temporary diversion from literary writing, as a compensation for a lack of inspiration, and resulting in an archive of her published and unpublished writings, this diary is an all-encompassing record of the aging consciousness of a woman and of a literary persona.

6. Critical gerontologist Harry Moody suggests that "there are a variety of 'languages,' 'metaphors,' or 'world hypotheses' that constitute a plurality of conceptual paradigms for looking at the meaning of life through autobiographical consciousness" ("The Meaning of Life and the Meaning of Old Age," 27). The re-integrative aspects of the life review are discussed by Robert Butler in "The Life Review." According to Butler's definition, the "life review" is "[a] naturally occurring, universal mental proc-

ess characterized by the progressive return to consciousness of past experience, and particularly, the resurgence of unresolved conflicts; simultaneously, and normally, these revived experiences and conflicts can be surveyed and reintegrated . . . prompted by the realization of approaching dissolution and death, and the inability to maintain one's sense of personal invulnerability" (66).

7. Rooke, "Old Age in Contemporary Fiction," 252. The attempt to construct an "authorized" life version is presented as a characteristic of the discourse of the *Vollendungsroman*, an old-age genre that will be discussed later in this introduction.

8. Gadow, "Subjectivity," 133.

9. Moody, "Overview: What is Critical Gerontology," xxxviii. Concerned with the critique of ideologies that hinder older people's possibilities for emancipatory social change, "critical gerontology" is inspired by critical theorists of the Frankfurt School (Adorno, Horkheimer, Marcuse, and, more recently, Habermas).

10. Weiland, "Criticism Between Literature and Gerontology," 77.

11. Prince, *Narratology*, 1.

12. Woodward, "Reminiscence and the Life Review," 161.

13. Gullette, "Creativity, Aging, Gender," 45.

14. According to Rosi Braidotti, one of the "ethical aims" of psychoanalysis is "to lead the subject to accept [the] inscription into time, the passing of generations and the dissymmetries it entails, so as to accept the radical otherness of the self" ("The Politics of Ontological Difference," 98).

15. Woodward, introduction to *Figuring Age*, x.

16. Gullette, "Age Studies as Cultural Studies," 223–24.

17. Woodward, introduction to *Figuring Age*, x. For a discussion of gender-based prejudice, see Sontag, "The Double Standard of Aging."

18. Russo writes that "acting one's age . . . can be understood as a caution against risk-taking, with higher and higher stakes associated with advanced chronological age until finally, acting one's age means to die" ("The Scandal of Anachronism," 27). The imperative of "acting one's age" is at the basis of "age-appropriateness" codes.

19. In the first edition of the *Handbook of the Humanities and Aging*, Wyatt-Brown surveys a research zone at the intersection of literary criticism and gerontology that she names "literary gerontology" (see Wyatt-Brown, "Literary Gerontology Comes of Age," 331–51). She provides an overview of recent publications in the field, an introduction to the most common critical frameworks used by scholars, as well as suggestions for future developments. In the second edition of the *Handbook*, she re-examines how status, trends, and prospects of literary studies in gerontology have developed in the decade after the first edition was released (see Wyatt-Brown, "The Future of Literary Gerontology," 41–61). A less specialized overview of aims and directions of literary studies is: Achenbaum, "Foreword: Literature's Value in Gerontological Research."

20. Lefkowitz and Lefkovitz, "Old Age and the Modern Literary Imagination," 131.

21. Ibid., 132.

22. Ibid., 148.

23. Sokoloff, *The Margin that Remains*, 2. In this essay Sokoloff examines novels by W. Defoe, J. Austen, C. Brontë, G. Eliot, H. James, and V. Woolf. Her study of *Moll Flanders* first appeared in *The Gerontologist*.

24. Sokoloff, "Character and Aging in *Moll Flanders*," 681.

25. See Mangum, "The Aging Female Character in Nineteenth-Century British Children's Literature."

26. See Gullette, "Creativity, Aging, Gender."

27. Gullette, *Declining to Decline*, 4–5.

28. See Gullette, "Age Studies as Cultural Studies." In this essay Gullette examines three cases of ageism: gerontophobia, middle-ageism, and representations of "youth in crisis." For a detailed definition of "feminist age studies," see Gullette's entry "Age Studies and Gender" in the *Encyclopedia of Feminist Theories*.

29. Gullette, *Safe at Last in the Middle Years*, xxxi.

30. Gullette writes that "a close reader of the structure of these novels will learn strategies for constructing life stories as ameliorative sequences" (*Safe at Last in the Middle Years*, xiv). Unfortunately, the pillars of canonical education are "philosophical" and "literary pessimists" who told "decline narratives" (ibid., 147, 149). Interestingly, in *Aged by Culture*, Gullette revises her 1980s' stance. "Exhilarated by the novelty of 'midlife progress novels,'" she writes in her 2004 essay, "and by my own ability to 'grow,' I was convinced that the proliferation of positive representations signaled a new paradigm" (28). She adds that, by the time of *Declining to Decline* in 1997, she had learnt that decline was an ideology, not a philosophy and an aesthetic genre.

31. Waxman, *From the Hearth to the Open Road*, 188. Waxman claims that *Reifungsromane* "may well serve as precursors to some major sociopolitical revolution exalting old age for women, subverting traditional myths of senescence by presenting plausible social and psychological frameworks for proud, intense, active old women" (ibid., 187–88).

32. For a critique of this perspective, see Freedman, "Sufficiently Decayed," 50. While the "Editors' Foreword" to the essay collection in which Freedman's essay appears, *Aging and the Elderly*, underlines the commitment of the humanities to "the spiritual values of freedom, dignity, and beauty, and the critical values of openness, toleration, and a measured skepticism of all dogmas" (vii), Freedman identifies the limitations of such perspective. In his study of gerontophobia in English literature, Freedman points out the "inhumanity" of literary handling of old age (gerontophobia), and argues against the assumption that the humanities are expected to provide some sort of magic balm for the pains of old age. He writes: "The intention here is not to buttress or even countenance western society's hostile treatment of the aged, but perhaps to confront that treatment—as The Enemy—in some of its more eloquent and enduring literary manifestations. The hope is to demonstrate that great literature neither takes sides nor necessarily promotes what we think of as social good; that its true greatness, perhaps, lies precisely in its ability to face unflinchingly the lowest, least "humane" instincts of human beings, and that to see literature—or any of the "humanities"—as necessarily benign and affirmative is to make a great mistake about its provenance, basic assumptions, and ultimate value" ("Sufficiently Decayed," 50). On the semantic level, he also warns against the confusion between the words "human," "humane," "humanist," and "humanities."

33. As remarked by Wyatt-Brown in her 1992 survey of literary gerontology, the first group of humanists to enter the field was concerned with negative stereotyping, in particular in fictions for children and adolescents. These studies, mostly published in *The Gerontologist*, tend to be less interpretive and more statistical. Since their main goal is to determine whether books present balanced or distorted views of aging, they are of particular interest to teacher trainers, classroom teachers, and librarians. For examples of this approach, see Wyatt-Brown, "Literary Gerontology Comes of Age," 332–33.

34. American library catalogues feature an impressive number of fictional series and individual publications for children, adolescents, or adults that focus on aging issues. As a consequence of a growing interest in education on the part of academic programs and associations of gerontology, excellent bibliographies and guided anthologies have been published recently. The Association for Gerontology in Higher Education has sponsored the publication of critical bibliographies for course planning, e.g.: Wyatt-

Brown and Waxman, *Aging in Literature: Brief Bibliography*. Extensive bibliographies arrange critical abstracts or plot summaries according to a genre or thematic perspective. Two titles of bibliographies, both prepared by Yahnke and Eastman, are: *Aging in Literature: A Reader's Guide*, and *Literature and Gerontology: A Research Guide*. In addition to numerous handbooks in various areas of the humanities and social sciences, a few anthologies have been published, in which excerpts may be organized following a thematic or life-stage sequence or may be followed by questionnaires for readers, among them: *The Oxford Book of Aging*, eds. Cole and Winkler; and *Women in Literature: Life Stages*, ed. Eagleton. For a complete list of anthologies published from the eighties to the early nineties, see Yahnke, *Literature and Gerontology*, 73–78. Finally, suggestions for syllabi based on courses offered by literary gerontology scholars may sometimes be mentioned in their studies, e.g.: Woodward, *Aging and Its Discontents*, 168; and Gullette, *Safe at Last in the Middle Years*, xiii.

35. Wyatt-Brown, "Literary Gerontology Comes of Age," 333.
36. Ibid.
37. Weiland, "Criticism Between Literature and Gerontology," 77.
38. Moody, "Overview: What is Critical Gerontology," xxiv.
39. See Erikson, *Identity and the Life Cycle* and *The Life Cycle Completed*; Levinson et al., *The Seasons of a Man's Life*. For an application of Erikson's theory on identity and the life cycle to the analysis of a cinematic text, Bergman's *Wild Strawberries*, see: Erikson, "Reflections on Dr. Borg's Life Cycle."
40. Wyatt-Brown, "Literary Gerontology Comes of Age," 336.
41. See Gutmann, *Reclaimed Powers*. See, in particular, chapters 6 and 7: "The Inner Liberation of the Older Woman," 133–54; and "The Virile Older Woman," 155–84.
42. Gutmann, "Beyond Nurture," 228.
43. See Gilligan, "Visions of Maturity." Further insight into the female life cycle is offered by such psychoanalytic feminist theorists as Nancy Chodorow and Jean Baker Miller, who, like Gilligan, maintain that women's identity is based on intimacy and connectedness.
44. See Moretti, *Il romanzo di formazione*.
45. I refer here to a genre that has not been defined in a gendered perspective. The term was used by Celeste Loughman in "Novels of Senescence," to designate a new focus on the process of degeneration and decay in contemporary novels, beginning with the publication of Muriel Spark's *Memento Mori* in 1958. The merit of this genre is to recognize old age as "the great suppressed and censored subject of contemporary society, the one we do not care to face, which we regard as indecent" (79). Other examples of novels of senescence are: Tanizaki's *Diary of a Mad Old Man*, Bellow's *Mr. Sammler's Planet*, and Kingsley's *Ending Up*.
46. Gullette devotes a chapter of *Declining to Decline* to female midlife progress heroes. This new genre, which ignores "both male patterns of success and stereotypical female midlife patterns of decline" (78), is bound to affect the midlife cultural imaginary and to represent "the most effective strategy for antisexist and antiageist resistance" (ibid., 79). Midlife heroines face vicissitudes with "strength they haven't needed or known how to use" (ibid., 82). In these novels "progress" implies the realization that "it feels better to be older than younger" (ibid., 87) and that midlife is "safer" than youth because the heroine is "a site of comparative power, intelligence, understanding, pleasure, expectation, intention" (ibid.). Among the authors of midlife progress novels, Gullette mentions N. Gordimer, D. Lessing, P. Marshall, T. Morrison, M. Sarton, and A. Walker.
47. Waxman, *From the Hearth to the Open Road*, 2. According to Waxman, "new commitments, self-discovery, and a joyful self-affirmation in old age are the new themes

of aging" (ibid., 11). *Reifungsromane* depict "women's rite of passage into senescence thematically as a ripening process" (ibid., 16). The narrative structure is commonly a journey, and the point of view is often internal to the older protagonist. Cultural roots and past experiences are revisited and become an opportunity for self-knowledge and internal growth. Women's *Reifungsromane* are also linguistically and structurally innovative: they "exhibit jumbling of time, space, and conventional meanings of words; challenge the proprieties of *Bildungsromane*; and undermine binary oppositions between youth and old age, logic and fantasy, senility and sanity" (ibid., 186).

48. Waxman, *To Live in the Center of the Moment*, 4. According to Waxman, "autobiographies of aging focus on how elders recast the gender roles enacted by more youthful members of society, particularly those within the family," and explore how "relations among older men and women are renegotiated in non-family contexts" (ibid., 8). While acknowledging that older women may endure fewer gender constraints than young women, Waxman intends to investigate these renegotiated gender roles. She studies autobiographical narratives by P. Roth, M. L'Engle, D. Grumbach, A. Lorde, L. Clifton, M. Angelou, and F. Scott-Maxwell.

49. See Rooke, "Hagar's Old Age." Rooke also discusses the *Vollendungsroman* in "Old Age in Contemporary Fiction." This genre is concerned with the last phase of life, which entails leaving the social stage, deconstructing the ego, and letting go of social power. The most interesting feature of these narratives is the fact that "disengagement" is often paralleled by "reengagement" at a different level and in different realms. Although this process may "actualize previously dormant aspects of the self," as in the case of the *Reifungsroman*, the emphasis here is on the awareness that "this renewal within the quotidian is temporary" (248). The ironic or humorous tone of these narratives may be explained by the awareness of precariousness and loss and of the arbitrariness of closure. The task of the *Vollendungsroman* is to discover "the tension between affirmation and regret" (ibid., 251), "some kind of affirmation in the face of loss" (ibid., 248). In this kind of novel, the act of speech may be imperfect or lost, just when some vital message needs to be delivered and some final authorized version of one's life needs to be written. The life review, one of the most common themes of the *Vollendungsroman*, "is also a common structural device" (ibid., 253). Besides *The Stone Angel*, some of the texts mentioned by Rooke are also listed by Loughman among the "novels of senescence," e.g.: *Ending Up*, *Memento Mori*, and *Mr. Sammler's Planet*. Other novels in her list are: Figes's *Waking*, Gardner's *October Light*, Lessing's *The Diaries of Jane Somers*, Olsen's "Tell Me a Riddle," Pym's *Quartet in Autumn*, and Updike's *The Poorhouse Fair*.

50. Westerwelt, *Beyond Innocence*, xii. The *Altersroman*, or "age novel," is a story of life assessment that features characters "confronting mortality toward the end of middle age" (ibid.). Westerwelt analyzes Cervantes's *Don Quixote*, James's *The Ambassadors*, Cather's *The Professor's House*, Faulkner's *The Mansion*, Stegner's *Angle of Repose*, Didion's *A Book of Common Prayer*, and Morrison's *Jazz*.

51. Woodward, introduction to *Figuring Age*, xi. In another essay from the same collection, Woodward elaborates a three-stage model of generational continuity, which involves grandmothers as well as mothers and daughters. This model—whose implications for relationships and power roles among women of different ages in the academy are also discussed—is presented as an alternative to the Freudian model of Oedipal struggle between generations, with its emphasis on binary oppositions based exclusively on sexual difference. An important point Woodward makes is that generational continuity should be viewed in a prospective as well as a retrospective mode (see Woodward, "Inventing Generational Models"). An illuminating collection of essays on "feminist generations" in the American academy is: *Generations: Academic Feminists in Dialogue*, eds. Looser and Kaplan.

52. Wyatt-Brown, "Introduction: Aging, Gender, and Creativity," 2. Another remarkable study of older women writers' creativity is: Ladimer, *Colette, Beauvoir, and Duras*. Ladimer studies three famous twentieth-century French writers who were not only very productive until advanced age but were also great innovators in French literature. They led quite unconventional lives, during which they challenged traditional definitions of femininity. All three were conscious of their own aging process and made it a central theme of some of their works.

53. George, "Who is the Double Ghost," 135.

54. Heilbrun, *Writing a Woman's Life*, 130.

55. The most sophisticated contributions in this field are the essays in *Memory and Desire*, ed. Woodward and Schwartz, and in Woodward, *Aging and Its Discontents*.

56. See Woodward, "Instant Repulsion."

57. Freedman, "Sufficiently Decayed," 60.

58. Rooke, "Old Age in Contemporary Fiction," 252.

59. Améry, *On Aging*, 86.

60. Gadow remarks that frailty can be experienced as "reification." At the personal level, in fact, "the body becomes an object in opposition to the self when a person experiences physical limitations" ("Subjectivity," 133). Physical frailty becomes a social experience when "the body as object becomes the person as object" (ibid.). Aged and disabled, she claims, "are doubly 'thinged,' objects in both a physical and a social sense" (ibid., 134).

61. Rooke, "Old Age in Contemporary Fiction," 255.

62. Aleramo, *Diario di una donna*, 407: "il peso di tanta vita."

63. Waxman, *From the Hearth to the Open Road*, 184–85.

64. Woodward, "Inventing Generational Models," 163.

65. Moody, "The Collector," 1–2.

66. Ibid., 2.

67. Rooke, "Old Age in Contemporary Fiction," 254–55.

CHAPTER 1. REPRESENTATIONS OF . . . LIFE

1. For an exhaustive critical bibliography of the contributions of social history and cultural history to old-age historiography, see Troyansky, "History of Old Age in the Western World." For a critical analysis of trends and fields of inquiry in western historiography, see Thane, "The History of Aging in the West." Achenbaum's survey of historical gerontology, "Historical Perspective on Aging," identifies three modes of inquiry: descriptive ethnography, sociocultural comparative research, and case studies of individuals and institutions.

2. E.g., two studies on early American history—Abramovitz, *Regulating the Lives of Women*; and Premo, *Winter Friends*—and two investigations of premodern and modern European history—*Poor Women and Children in the European Past*, eds. Henderson and Wall; and *Women and Ageing in British Society*, eds. Botelho and Thane. Banner's *In Full Flower* is an investigation of aging women's power throughout western civilization that is grounded on the author's interest in feminist spirituality and the prepatriarchal goddesses. A comprehensive collection of studies is a 2001 special issue of the *Journal of Women's History*, titled *Ages of Women*, that features social and cultural history surveys, some of which are from a world-historical perspective.

3. E.g., *Handbook on Women and Aging*, ed. Cole. In addition to a number of cultural-history essays on the historiography of older women in America and on the images of aging women in different periods, the book devotes an entire section to essays on

"Racial, Ethnic, and Demographic Issues." For an analysis of how aging Native-American, Spanish-speaking, and Mormon women coped on the frontier, see: *On Their Own*, ed. Scadron.

4. See Saletti, "I seni di Eva." The two versions of Tiziano's painting are at the Prado Museum in Madrid and at the Hermitage in St. Petersburg. Bernardo Strozzi's painting is part of a private collection in Genoa.

5. For a study of the iconography of human lifetime in the western tradition, see Cole, *The Journey of Life*. Cole argues that the origins of "age grading" in our chronologically defined, bureaucratized course of life are to be found in the search for religious and social order in early-modern northern Europe. From the late fifteenth to the seventeenth century, it became increasingly common to view life as a spiritual drama, as a pilgrimage entailing a sequence of stages.

6. Ibid., 5.

7. Ibid., 26. Cole's essay also includes a few illustrations of the woman's and the couple's ideal life cycles, e.g.: two prints by seventeenth-century Dutch engravers (fig. 10, 11), one eighteenth-century British print (fig. 17), and two American *Lebenstreppen* (fig. 19, 21). A late-sixteenth century print representing the "Nine Ages of Woman" designed by an Italian engraver, Christoforo Bertelli from Modena, is reproduced in Chew, *The Pilgrimage of Life*, fig. 102.

8. Cole, *The Journey of Life*, 40.

9. Ibid., 26.

10. Falkner and de Luce, "A View from Antiquity," 30.

11. Herlihy, "Growing Old in the Quattrocento," 106.

12. Minois, *History of Old Age*, 215.

13. Banner, *In Full Flower*, 158.

14. Ibid., 159. Banner points out that it was uncommon for widows to remarry; she also argues that "the homosexuality that foreign travelers to Italy noted in the city-states there may have partly originated from the lack of older women available for young men as sexual and emotional partners" (ibid.).

15. Ibid., 158. See also Riemer, "Women, Dowries, and Capital Investment."

16. Banner, *In Full Flower*, 158. See also Hughes, "Domestic Ideals and Social Behavior."

17. See Trexler, "Une Table Florentine d'Espérance de Vie"; and Müller, "Charitable Institutions."

18. See Trexler, "A Widow's Asylum of the Renaissance."

19. See Herlihy, "Old Women in the Italian Renaissance," qtd. in Banner, *In Full Flower*, 376.

20. Molho, "Deception and Marriage Strategy in Renaissance Florence," 194.

21. Ibid., 212.

22. Kertzer and Karweit, "The Impact of Widowhood in Nineteenth-Century Italy," 238.

23. See Saraceno, *Sociologia della famiglia*, 75–79.

24. Barbagli, "Asymmetry in Intergenerational Family Relationships in Italy," 144.

25. Ibid., 147. Barbagli's data on the present situation in Emilia-Romagna, an economically developed rural region, are confirmed by studies of other regions in central and northern Italy, e.g., Marche (Paci, *Famiglie e mercato del lavoro*, 9–69) and Veneto (La Mendola, "I rapporti di parentela in Veneto"). In eighteenth- and nineteenth-century Sardinia, on the contrary, the dominant system of kinship seems to have been matrilateral (see Oppo, "Madri, figlie e sorelle"). According to another study by Barbagli, *Sotto lo stesso tetto*, it was common practice for many centuries that at least one son (the firstborn) took his wife into his father's house in the rural areas of Piedmont,

Liguria, and Lombardy, while this custom was followed by more than one son in Veneto, Emilia-Romagna, Tuscany, Umbria, and the Marche.

26. Kertzer and Karweit, "The Impact of Widowhood in Nineteenth Century Italy," 231. Kertzer and Karweit also explain why kinship patterns were of primary importance for sharecropping: "A contract bound the entire sharecropping family; emblematic was the fact that landowner consent was required before a family member could marry. Since landowners stood to gain by maximizing the number of adults on each farm, hence maximize their half of the produce, households composed of more than one kin-related family were the rule" (ibid.).

27. Zuccino, "The Three-Generation Rural Family in Italy," 439.

28. Scaraffia, "Essere uomo, essere donna," 208: "Questa conflittualità [tra nuore, cognate e suocere] nascondeva un'importante posta in gioco: è solo attraverso la propria influenza sugli uomini che la donna riusciva ad imporre il proprio potere e questa alleanza non si verificava quasi mai fra moglie e marito, ma piuttosto fra madre e figlio. La madre possedeva un'autorità che le derivava dalla realizzazione della sua potenzialità riproduttrice: questa autorità veniva esercitata attraverso i figli e quindi sulle loro famiglie. L'autorità paterna, infatti, cominciava ad indebolirsi nel momento in cui si formavano i nuovi nuclei familiari—le coppie figlio-nuora—che si fronteggiavano fra di loro e contro l'anziano padre, che stentava ad imporre il suo potere, fondato sul pubblico e sui rapporti maschili, all'interno della famiglia. Egli doveva necessariamente passare attraverso la mediazione della moglie la quale, attraverso l'alleanza con i figli, corrodeva i confini del potere del marito."

29. Dauphin, "Single Women," 433. A comprehensive study of domestic service is: Arru, *I servi e le serve*. See also Arru, "Protezione e legittimazione."

30. E.g., Smith-Rosenberg, "The Female World of Love and Ritual."

31. Knibiehler, "Bodies and Hearts," 355.

32. De Giorgio, *Le italiane dall'Unità a oggi*, 16–17. De Giorgio points out that, besides carrying out anthropometric measurements across most of the national territory, turn-of-the-century anthropologists (Sergi, Niceforo, Vitali, Livi) studied associations between regional types and moral values or limitations. Paolo Mantegazza also remarked that, due to the existence of different regional types (which he calls *subnazionalità*), he could not describe the psychological, moral, and intellectual character of his national sisters (*Le italiane dall'Unità a oggi*, 16, 35). De Giorgio's extensive research on the representations and experiences of Italian women in the second half of the nineteenth century and the early decades of the twentieth century is the main critical and bibliographical source of this section. In addition to her monographic studies of cultural models and social behavior in relation to women's marital status—"Signorine e signore italiane fra Otto e Novecento" and "Raccontare un matrimonio moderno"—a wealth of information on age-based images, roles, and expectations can be found in her comprehensive cultural history survey *Le italiane dall'Unità a oggi*.

33. Baccini, *Il the delle cinque*, 4: "prima c'erano le fanciulle, le ragazze e le ragazzine: ora non ci sono che *Signorine*. La figliuola del mio ortolano è una *signorina* come la figliuola del Marchese di Rudinì" (qtd. in De Giorgio, *Le italiane dall'Unità a oggi*, 41).

34. De Giorgio, *Le italiane dall'Unità a oggi*, 41.

35. Ibid., 44: "tutte le spinose questioni dell'inserimento sociale delle nubili nella società postbellica. 'Signorine d'ufficio' . . . 'signorine dattilografe' . . . in cui si incarnano le illusioni di emancipazione di molte giovinette."

36. In her 1877 book of etiquette, *La gente per bene*, Marchesa Colombi suggests the use of *signora* after a certain age. In 1913, the popular women's magazine *Margherita* launches a campaign for the abolition of this sad reminder of "fatal" family and social mishaps (see De Giorgio, *Le italiane dall'Unità a oggi*, 46–47).

37. This was the case of Italy up to the 1970s; the divorce law was activated through a referendum in 1974.
38. De Giorgio, "Raccontare un matrimonio moderno," 369.
39. Ibid., 360.
40. Ibid., 370.
41. De Giorgio, *Le italiane dall'Unità a oggi*, 325.
42. De Giorgio, "Signore e signorine italiane fra Otto e Novecento," 464: "il limite *prima* e *dopo* il matrimonio interveniva con la forza di un rito di passaggio a derimere questioni riguardanti l'accesso all'esplorazione di più ampie possibilità comportamentali: stili di abbigliamento, tipi di letture, gestione del tempo libero, modalità di rapporto con l'altro sesso."
43. In the 1870s, foreign perspectives were introduced and promoted by a number of important publications: in particular, by Mozzoni's translation of *The Subjection of Women* by Stuart Mill, and by the success of Ferrero's comparative study of gender relations in northern and southern Europe in *L'Europa giovane*.
44. Vertua Gentile, *Come devo comportarmi?*, 384: "rinunci coraggiosamente alle pretese della donna giovane . . . come una vedova" (qtd. in De Giorgio, "Signore e signorine italiane fra Otto e Novecento," 473).
45. De Giorgio, "Signore e signorine italiane fra Otto e Novecento," 476: "obbligato, dimesso, inetto."
46. Bonomi, "Le non maritate": "ambiente della società italiana che all'esplicarsi dell'individualità femminile all'infuori del matrimonio e della famiglia [opponeva] una cerchia ferrea e insormontabile" (qtd. in De Giorgio, *Le italiane dall'Unità a oggi*, 349).
47. "Ancora un concorso" (see De Giorgio, *Le italiane dall'Unità a oggi*, 179).
48. Groppi, *I conservatori della virtù*, 146 (see De Giorgio, "Raccontare un matrimonio moderno," 375).
49. Serao, *Saper vivere*, 312 (see De Giorgio, "Signore e signorine italiane fra Otto e Novecento," 477).
50. De Giorgio, *Le italiane dall'Unità a oggi*, 104.
51. Mantegazza, *Fisiologia della donna*, 314: "la durata della bellezza sarà in ragione della cresciuta robustezza."
52. Ibid.: "Oggi la contadina lombarda è vecchia a trent'anni, la signora italiana è bella anche a quaranta; la donna inglese, che per noi è già innanzi a noi di un secolo, è bella anche a cinquanta, talvolta anche a sessanta. E così dovranno essere tutte le donne dell'avvenire."
53. Drake, *What a Woman of Forty-five Ought to Know*, 32. In the Italian translation, *Quel che la donna di 45 anni deve sapere*, 39, the quote reads: "ripigliare o raggiungere alcuni dei sogni della sua età giovanile"
54. See Napione, *Varcando i quarant'anni*.
55. Another exceptional fictional relationship is that between a twenty-nine-year-old woman and a twenty-year-old man in Tommasina Guidi's *L'età della moglie*. This novel, however, may be seen as a "counter-thesis" to another marriage novel by the same author, *L'amore dei quarant'anni*, in which the age gap is reversed. This is the case of an unhappy love of a forty-year-old uncle for his twenty-year-old niece.
56. Baccini, "Le vinte: Le vecchie" (qtd. in De Giorgio, *Le italiane dall'Unità a oggi*, 180): "immeritata espiazione."
57. Vera, "Per essere belle" (1936), 346: "E infine un consiglio alle meno giovani: cercare di non voler troppo ringiovanire *esteriormente* coi facili comodi ed inutili mezzi che non servono più: un'attitudine mentale spiritualmente giovane, un ambiente, una vita di comprensione e di solidarietà verso i giovani (figli e nipoti che siano) ringiovaniranno più di tutti i trucchi del mondo. La tragedia della bellezza incrollabile non è per

il nostro tempo. Invecchiare è un diritto, invecchiare serenamente è una scienza e se ci si riesce non è più 'invecchiare': è vivere."

58. Vera, "Per essere belle" (1941), 312: "non più schiava come un tempo di pigre abitudini, di pregiudizi, [la donna moderna] ha imparato a mangiare meno perché spesso deve lavorare di cervello, a muoversi di più, a uscire a qualunque ora e con qualsiasi tempo" (no longer enslaved to lazy habits and prejudice, the modern woman has learned to eat less because she must work with her brain, to move more, to go out at any time and in any weather).

59. Scaraffia, "Essere uomo, essere donna," 244.
60. De Grazia, "How Mussolini Ruled Italian Women," 144.
61. Ibid., 131.
62. Ibid., 135.
63. Ros, "La nonna": "la nonnina d'adesso balla ancora, / tinge i capelli, il volto ha imbellettato; / talvolta accade pur che s'innamora! / E per seguir la moda ella ha tagliato la chioma (grande pregio ai dì d'allora!). . . . / Il tempo anche la nonna ha trasformato." Besides summarizing stereotypical expectations, this poem focuses on color as an age-code marker. In Mediterranean countries, older women's dress codes, enforced by strict mourning practices, have traditionally been less tolerant of bright colors than in northern Europe and in the United States. In the Catholic liturgy white is, on the contrary, associated with youth, in that it symbolizes virginal purity.

64. Scaraffia, "Essere uomo, essere donna," 244.
65. In 1928 there were 66,153 *giovani italiane* and 364,300 *piccole italiane*; in 1939, 441,254 and 1,622,766 respectively (see De Giorgio, *Le italiane dall'Unità a oggi*, 72).
66. Ibid., 71.

Chapter 2. Aging in Italy Today

In this chapter, as well as in the next, my criterion for quoting quantitative sources has been their relevance to the overall discussion of turn-of-the-millennium Italian old-age culture. For this reason, I have used information that is mostly drawn from studies variously distributed in the last decade, in particular in the late 1990s. The most updated surveys reported in this chapter and in the next were conducted in 2002. I have also made limited use of 1980s studies that I consider significant and still illustrative of present-day conditions and trends.

1. Fasolino, "Donne italiane sempre più longeve."
2. Crepaldi and Maggi, "Italy," 188.
3. Sansone, *La quarta età*, 173.
4. Fasolino, "E' l'Italia il paese più vecchio del mondo." According to the most recent population estimates (July 2002), the life expectancy at birth is 79.25 years (*Nationbynation.com*).
5. According to 2002 estimates, Spain has the lowest ratio with a birth rate of 1.15. The Italian birth rate of 1.19 children is less than half the 2.1 births per woman required to keep population constant. But it is not just Italy that is experiencing a "birth dearth." Women throughout the developed world are increasingly having fewer children. The Czech Republic, Romania, and Bulgaria all are producing children at a rate of just 1.2 per women. Germany, Japan, Greece, Russia, Portugal, Hungary, and the Ukraine all have similar fertility rates ("Italy: Women's Status").
6. Palma, "Terza età, nuovo record italiano." In the last twenty years the 0–14 population has decreased from 22.6 to 14.4 percent; conversely, the over–74 population has risen from 13.1 to 18.2 percent. In 2002, 14.1 percent of the population was in the

0–14 years age range, and 18.6 percent were 65 years and over. The over 65/under 15 ratio is projected to increase further in favor of older people: in 2010 it will be 146 to 100 (Fasolino, "E' l'Italia il paese più vecchio del mondo").

7. Condorelli, "L'elisir di lunga vita," 65. The expression "demo-psychological" is frequently used by Giuseppe Pitré (1841–1916) in his studies of Sicilian folklore. According to Italian family historians, in the last century we have witnessed deep transformations not only in the approach to life and death issues but also in the definitions of children and of older persons. The older person and the child, "respectively a rare and a frequent entity in the past, have seen their presence in life and society completely reversed" (Golini, "Profilo demografico della famiglia italiana," 329: "entità rispettivamente frequente e rara un tempo, hanno visto ribaltare completamente la loro presenza nella vita e nella società").

8. According to 2000 ISTAT (National Institute of Statistics) data, foreign immigration has positively affected birth rates: 1.25 children per woman vs. 1.2 in 1999. The projected increase in the Italian population up to 2010 is attributable to the recent phenomenon of immigration from non-European countries ("Italiani più longevi e numerosi").

9. Although establishing quite strict work permit quotas, meant to impose a turn of the screw on clandestine immigration, the immigration decree approved in July 2002 (the "Bossi-Fini law") does not set any limit on the number of *badanti* (older and disabled people's caregivers) a family may employ. The visa status of *badanti* remains, however, as precarious as that of other categories of immigrant workers. Their work permits need to be renewed yearly and are terminated upon the assisted person's death. Although illegal immigration makes it difficult to provide exact figures, at the time the law was approved, approximately 200,000–250,000 foreign home-helpers and caregivers, for the most part women, were estimated to be working in Italy (Valentini, "Badanti nella bufera").

10. See Mirabile, "The Politics of Old Age in Italy." Mirabile also provides an overview of the types of noncontributory or partially contributory pensions distributed in Italy (118).

11. "The greatest innovation, stipulated in the 1995 reform, concerns the introduction of the contributory method of calculating pensions, based on the individual's entire working career. It did away with the previous method of calculation based solely on the salary of the last working years because it had created a wide variation in pension benefits, and the state could no longer sustain this level of payment (April 1997). The retirement age was extended to 60 years for women and 65 for men; changes were also introduced for so-called old-age pensions (whereby retirement was allowed after 35 years of work, making it possible to retire at 50 if one had started to work at the age of 15), by increasing the minimum retirement age to 57 and creating incentives to make individuals stay at work. . . . These changes are to come into force in the year 2008" (Mirabile, "The Politics of Old Age in Italy," 116). For further information on the "Dini reform" and for general discussion of Italian pension system and reforms, see also Sansone, *La quarta età*, 86–94; and Scortegagna, *Invecchiare*, 100.

12. The strongest retired people's trade union, Sindacato Pensionati CGIL, celebrated its fiftieth anniversary in 1998, counting approximately 3 million members. The union is the most popular association among Italian older people, who represent a large part of the union's membership. A study undertaken a few years ago estimated that about 20 percent of over-65-year-olds were members of the main unions. There are about 5 million members in the three unions (Mirabile, "The Politics of Old Age in Italy," 111).

13. Following a terminology in use in English-speaking countries, in Italy the over-

60 population is often referred to as belonging to three subgroups: "young old" (age 60–70), "middle old" (age 70–75), and "old old" (over 75).

14. Pedemonte, "La vecchiaia non c'è più," 46: "non è facile accettare di lavorare fino a settant'anni anche per mantenere legioni di anziani che, quarantenni, furono prepensionati dalla vecchia DC (o dai governi di centro-sinistra) per garantire la pace sociale e fare spazio ai giovani del baby boom."

15. Mirabile, "The Politics of Old Age in Italy," 111.

16. Ibid., 113.

17. The European average of people who receive assistance in old-age institutions is never below 7 percent. In Denmark, the best scenario in older people's care, 18 percent of the disabled elderly receive home care and 10 percent live in retirement homes ("Vacanze, dieci milioni di anziani").

18. Amabile, Lepri, and Masci, "Il nonno mantiene una famiglia su quattro."

19. Mirabile, "The Politics of Old Age in Italy," 111.

20. A survey was recently conducted by the EPPA (European Psychoanalytic and Psychodynamic Association) on older people's support of their families. According to 30 percent of the 55- to 75-year-old interviewees, children establish their new families in their parents' homes owing to the difficulty of finding employment and housing. For 18 percent of the interviewees, the cohabitation of children with parents is necessitated by the lack of adequate childcare services ("I nonni italiani sono superattivi"). The percentage of grandparents who live with their children's families is five times higher than in other European countries; on average, the elderly family members contribute 11 percent of their income to the household (SPI-CGIL, "Gli anziani spesso mantengono un' intera famiglia").

21. Life expectancy varies regionally, in relation to latitude: there is a five-year difference between Trentino Alto Adige, in the upper northeast, and Sicily. In 2030 Trentino will hold the longevity record: women will live to be 90.4, men 83.3, while life expectancy in Sicily will be 85.7 years for women and only 79 for men. Other 2030 regional projections across the nation are: Lazio (87.3 for women and 80.5 for men); Sardinia (87/80); Lombardy (89/82.4). Liguria holds the record in the over 65/under 14 ratio: in 2010 there will be only 100 young people to every 254 elderly. The youngest region will be Campania with a birth rate of 1.7 children per woman and 90 elderly for every 100 young people, followed by Sicily (108/100). See Fasolino, "2050: Cinque milioni di italiani in meno."

22. Ricci, "Images of Ageing Around the World."

23. Sansone, *La quarta età*, 126. Real estate represents 94.6 percent of older people's patrimony, while in the overall population the corresponding average is 87.1 percent (ibid., 207).

24. Ibid., 100.

25. Lazzarini, "Analisi sociologica dei risultati della ricerca." Sociologist Guido Lazzarini has authored several studies on elderly urbanization: among them, *Risorse e generazioni* and *Habitat e lavoro nella città in transizione*.

26. According to 1997 national statistics, 16.9 percent of homes with a 65+ person as family head live below the poverty line (the overall rate is 7.5 percent). Older people represent 33.8 percent of the country's poor (see Sansone, *La quarta età*, 118; and ISTAT, *Anziani in Italia*, 61-63).

27. Palma, "Terza età, nuovo record italiano," 19.

28. Mirabile, "The Politics of Old Age in Italy," 113.

29. E.g., Faini, "Dove nasce l'euro-disagio."

30. Dipartimento Politiche Sociali e Salute, "Euro: Occhio alle truffe."

31. In 1962, compulsory education was extended from elementary to middle school.

As a result of late-sixties student protest, access to university, formerly limited to those who had attended a *liceo*, was opened to students from all secondary schools. The liberalization of university access was started in 1961 and completed in 1969.

32. Mirabile, "The Politics of Old Age in Italy," 111.

33. Palma, "Terza età, nuovo record italiano"; Sansone, *La quarta età*, 118.

34. According to data provided by Centrale Media Universal (a McCann Erikson affiliate), older Italian people hold another negative record: on average, they spend more time in front of the TV screen (372 minutes per day) than any other European age peer. See Comune di Roma, "Contro la solitudine."

35. Palma, "Terza età, nuovo record italiano," 19. According to a 2002 survey, in their free time 25 percent of older people prefer to walk in parks, 20 percent watch TV, and 16 percent meet friends in senior centers, cafés and dance halls ("I nonni italiani sono superattivi").

36. The financial resources older Italian people invest in tourism increased 70 percent in the last ten years. This and other data on older people's tourism can be found in the proceedings of the conference-seminar L'anziano protagonista nella città e nella società, sponsored by the city council and the Chamber of Commerce of Turin in May 1999. In spite of a blooming old-age-targeted tourist industry, *ferie* (summer vacations), an institution of Italian popular culture, are still a luxury enjoyed by a limited number of older people: 30 percent of people over 60 and 15 percent of those over 75. Ten million 65+ people spend the entire summer at home ("Vacanze, dieci milioni di anziani").

37. These adult education institutions, which are widespread in many countries, are attended in Italy by an expanding older population (approximately 150,000), for the most part 60- to 70-year-old people with a junior or senior high school education. 15 percent of the people who attend these courses are over 75. Very few people with university degrees attend these courses. Launched in Turin and in Trent more than twenty years ago (in Turin in 1975 and in Trent in 1979), today they flourish all over the nation. There are about 300 *università della terza età* in Italy: this is a high figure, considering that there are 3,000 such institutions worldwide ("Anche gli anziani vanno a scuola"). One of the most thriving universities of the third age in Italy is the "Università popolare della terza età" in Rome (UPTER). Besides featuring its own publishing house, it offers nearly one thousand courses, ranging from foreign languages to criminology, from philosophy to flamenco, mantra meditation and creative writing or drawing. Since out of the 12,000 students enrolled in UPTER, half are over 60, "popular universities" are a great opportunity for intergenerational cultural exchange (De Tomassi, "L'allegra vecchiaia"). UPTER also offers scholarships and European summer exchange programs for older people who are engaged in volunteer work in social, environmental, and cultural initiatives. For an international overview, see: Swindell and Thompson, "An International Perspective on the University of the Third Age."

38. The small percentage of older Internet users is destined to increase. Recent studies on the evolving profiles of Internet users have revealed that a "progressive aging" of Internet users is taking place. By 2005 the number of over-55 web surfers will be three times higher: from 1 out of 10 in 2002 to 3 out of 10 in less than three years from the time the survey was conducted (Parini, "Giovani navigatori crescono"). Quite a few universities of the third age and volunteer associations organize computer-literacy courses that help older people to socialize through the web. Special-interest discussion forums and chat rooms are spreading: among them, "Chat 60!" (sponsored by Eurotre, European Association for the Third Age) and "Internet Point Intrage" of Bologna—a project aimed at fighting older people's digital exclusion and at promoting communication with age peers in other geographical areas. Often using quite imaginative nicknames, older people are in the process of building a solid virtual community.

39. Titles or catch phrases of chapters in gerontological essays and of conferences or workshops quite often reflect these trends and concerns: e.g., the conference I piaceri della vita aiutano ad invecchiare meglio (Life pleasures help us age better), organized by the European school for the Third Age (EUROTRE) in Turin on November 27, 2000; the workshop "L'anziano: Peso o ricchezza economica e culturale della società" (The elderly: Burden or economic and cultural asset in society) at the 1999 conference L'anziano protagonista nella città e nella società; the section "Creatività e curiosità" (Creativity and curiosity) in Scortegagna, *Invecchiare*, 112–14. One of the main concerns of the Conferenza governativa per l'Anno internazionale delle persone anziane organized by the National Department of Social Affairs (Palasport, Rome, May 27–29, 1999) was to make the old-age condition "l'età dell'agio" (the age of ease). Older people were described as "the only global natural resource on the uprise" by gerontologist Alexander Sidorenko, coordinator of the UN program for the 1999 International Year of Older Persons. The third age has even been called "l'età leggera" (the light age). In the March 13, 1998 special issue of *Venerdì di Rupubblica*, titled *La vita comincia a 80 anni*, a photo caption (the photo shows two happy-looking third-age couples eating at a pizzeria after a fitness class) reads: "A little exercise then everybody merrily goes out to eat; after leaving the worries of the past behind, older people have reached the light age."

40. Recent research by the Milan Chamber of Commerce has estimated that the presence and availability of grandparents during their grandchildren's first three years of life discourages children's enrollment in preschool at an 80 percent rate (Tamanza, "Fili d'argento a colori," 49).

41. This results from the research conducted by the European Psychoanalytic and Psychodynamic Association in Italy, Sweden, France, Germany, Spain, and Great Britain on a sample of 4,800 men and women in the 55–75 age bracket. These results applaud Italian grandparents over those of other European countries, who work on average 5–7 hours a day. Italians devote one-and-a-half hours a day to housecleaning, one to grocery shopping, another hour and a half to meal preparation, and two hours to pet care. They devote the remaining four hours to their grandchildren, looking after them at home, picking them up from school, and taking them to extracurricular classes. Most over-60 Italians take on family responsibilities and chores because their children's occupations leave them little time for children and household care. Only a few interviewees (20 percent) complain about their workloads, while 45 percent declare themselves satisfied with their lifestyles ("I nonni italiani sono superattivi").

42. At the 1999 Turin conference L'anziano protagonista nella città e nella società, it was projected that in 2020 there will be 53 over-60 people in Italy for every 100 employment-age persons. This will mean a 13 percent increase in comparison to the present rate, while the European average will be 47, with a 9-percentage-point increase.

43. According to 2001 ISTAT data, out of three million and a half people involved in volunteer work in Italy, 400,000 are in the third-age bracket (Petraglia, "Anziani: il nuovo tempo libero"). The most common forms of social reemployment proposed and practiced today involve supervising school access ways and public parks, museum information and animation services, and assistance to needy children or to families of disabled elderly. An interesting initiative involving people across different ages and social stations is that of the "time bank," by means of which time and resources are exchanged according to individual needs, availability, and skills.

44. Bobbio, *De senectute*, 24–25: "una forma larvata e per altro efficacissima di *captatio benevolentiae* verso eventuali nuovi consumatori." Bobbio died quite recently, on 9 January 2004.

45. For a discussion of recent surveys of older people's consumption trends, see "Il consumatore trascurato," in Sansone, *La quarta età*, 204–9. See also data on finances,

savings, credit, and consumption of older people in Turin in the report of the workshop "L'anziano: Peso o ricchezza economica e culturale della società" at the conference *L'anziano protagonista nella città e nella società*.

46. Masci, "Bravi ragazzi, eterni adolescenti."

47. Ginzburg, "La vecchiaia," 22: "abbiamo invece sempre amato la sete e la febbre, le inquiete ricerche e gli errori."

48. Minois' history of old age documents instances of longevity among religious people from the middle ages to the sixteenth century. A glance at Vasari's *Lives of the Artists* reveals impressive longevity records among Italian painters.

49. In an article on the benefits of longevity published in 1923 in an Italian women's journal, "the happiness of the religious and virtuous old man" is defined in terms of the knowledge of the loftiest aims of life and of the insignificance of human vanities. It also derives from the awareness of the high value of the time employed in the spiritual improvement of oneself and of others (Cravenna Brigola, "L'inestimabile beneficio della longevità": "E' chiaro che io qui ragiono con persone di provata fede nostra, di chi conosce gli alti scopi della vita, e il nulla delle umane vanità; di chi sente la preziosità del tempo impiegato alle più nobili conquiste; al miglioramento proprio e alla elevazione delle anime altrui: di chi insomma sa comprendere tutta la felicità del vecchio religioso e virtuoso").

50. A number of interesting editorials appeared in the January 11, 2000 issue of *La Repubblica*: Bocca, "La carne e lo spirito"; Politi, "La volontà di Woytyla"; and Tarquini, "Un Papa può rinunciare per il bene della Chiesa," an interview with theologian Hans Kung. It is also significant that, while the Pope does not consider "retirement," bishops are expected to retire at age 75.

51. Bocca, "La carne e lo spirito": "[l]a vecchiaia e la malattia del Papa sono un argomento che affascina credenti e agnostici. . . . il fascino delle chiese, delle religioni che durano mentre le istituzioni e le idee del mondo temporale continuano a scomparire."

52. The most notable example is the already-mentioned Bobbio's essay *De senectute*. Some well-known journalists have also recently authored essays on old age: e.g., Ottone, *Il grande gioco*, and Levi, *La vecchiaia può attendere*.

53. Thirty photographs of renowned older people appear on the magazine cover page. Among them, the Italian *grandi vecchi* are: F. Modigliani, M. Antonioni, G. Einaudi, E. Cuccia, E. Bernabei, M. Monicelli, P. Ingrao, E. Calindri, I. Montanelli, N. Bobbio, R. Murolo, C. Bo, L. Di Bella, and A. Bertolucci. The seven women are: Alida Valli, Suso Cecchi D'Amico, Pupella Maggio, Rita Levi Montalcini, Lalla Romano, Irene Galitzine, and the English "Queen Mother." This *Venerdì* issue reports several cultural initiatives for older people: among them, the Compagnia Teatro Instabile, a theater company composed of full-time actors who are aged 70–90. While publicizing an enterprise that features older people as cultural subjects rather than as target audience, the author of the article also praises their young director's (Gianluca Bottoni) "patience" and the willingness of the sponsoring cooperative (Nuova Socialità) to "believe" in these older actors (De Tomassi, "L'allegra vecchiaia," 18).

54. Levi Montalcini's essay argues that awareness and study of brain structure and functions can help us make the best use of the multiple resources that this organ, thanks to its "neuronal plasticity," can grant us even at an advanced age. The champions of later-life intellectual creativity that she discusses in the last section of her book are: Michelangelo, Galilei, Russell, Ben Gurion, and Picasso. Rita Levi Montalcini, born in 1909, received the Nobel prize for medicine in 1986 for her research on cellular growth.

55. Both Nilde Iotti and Rita Levi Montalcini have served in the Italian Parliament. In summer 2002, Montalcini was the target of ageist remarks by another MP. After

ninety-year-old Montalcini had intervened to strongly oppose his bill introducing "legitimate suspicion" among the causes of change of venue, senator Melchiorre Cerami thus commented on her first stand since her election: "Almeno la dotassero di stampelle giuridiche. . . ." (I wish they had at least provided her with legal crutches. . .). To this he added: "Non le hanno offerto neanche il thè e i pasticcini. La colpa è di chi l'ha invitata" (They didn't even offer her tea and cakes. The fault lies with those who invited her.) See "Legittimo sospetto: Ricusazione dei giudici."

CHAPTER 3. OLDER ITALIAN WOMEN

1. An interesting example that does not fall into the stereotypical grandfather-grandchild category is an anti-ageist TV commercial sponsored by Pubblicità Progresso. It represented a company personnel committee turning down Pablo Picasso at a job interview. His work was deemed outdated, and he was advised to submit it to some other company. Interestingly, this commercial—whose slogan was "Chi rifiuta un anziano non sa cosa perde" (Those who turn down an older person don't know what they are missing)—while focusing on a champion of male late-life creativity, was created by an all-female staff (copywriter Grazia Usai, art director Chiara Calvi, and creative director Milka Pogliani).

2. In the late 1990s a Bertolli olive oil TV spot featured a trim and fit over-sixty male soccer team. More than one commercial has portrayed older males gazing at a young woman, among them a 2002 advertisement for Trony electronic appliances chain stores. On older people and the advertising industry, see Di Matteo, "Lo spot ha successo se i nonni si amano." This short article mentions a few examples of Italian commercials featuring older characters: e.g., copywriter Lorenzo Marini's ad for Tuscan brand Rifle (old widow and widower fall in love in a cemetery while visiting their deceased spouses' tombs), and director Joe Pitke's spot for Pepsi-Cola (showing an ultracentenarian living in Abruzzi who says she cannot understand why the young generation drinks Pepsi). The article also reports the results of a market survey conducted by McCann, a multinational of advertising, asking which popular figures older people would like to see in advertising campaigns. While rebel youth-cult singer Vasco Rossi and sexy private-TV journalist Cristina Parodi turned out to be the top choices, the interviewees named older established comic actors Raimondo Vianello and Paolo Villaggio as the figures they least wished to see in commercials for third-age audiences.

3. See the various versions of the Candeggina Ace spot, a long-lasting ad that has updated both the grandmother's and the daughter/granddaughter's looks over time.

4. See Sasso, "La terza età multimediale."

5. In particular, products by Bolognese company Beghelli, which has developed an extremely profitable market by studying and investing in new instruments for disabled older people living at home alone.

6. E.g., the advertisement for Centro Acustico Sonar in *Terza età*, supplement of *La Stampa*, May 28, 2001, 8.

7. It may be worth mentioning here that Italian TV channel Canale 5 launched a markedly ageist program in summer 2003, called "Velone," a parody of the popular showgirl contest "Veline." The aspiring "velone" are over-65 women who sing and dance on the open-air stage of Italian piazzas, and compete for a 250,000 euros final prize. Canale 5 is one of Mediaset TV channels, a private news and media group owned by current Prime Minister Silvio Berlusconi.

8. Some titles of Italian films that deal with old-age themes are: *Amici miei* (Monicelli, 1975), *Amici miei atto II* (Monicelli, 1982), *Amici miei atto III* (Loy, 1985), on male

buddies' fear of aging; *La casa del sorriso* (Ferreri, 1991), dealing with old-age love; *Che ora è?* (Scola, 1989), *Parenti serpenti* (Monicelli, 1991), *Buon Natale Buon Anno* (Comencini, 1989), *Corpo d'amore* (Carpi, 1973), *L'età della pace* (Carpi, 1974), *Gruppo di famiglia in un interno* (Visconti, 1974), focusing on intergenerational family conflicts; *La valle di pietra* (Zaccaro, 1992), about friendship; *Umberto D.* (De Sica, 1952), *Nestore l'ultima corsa* (Sordi, 1994), about loneliness and marginalization from productive society; *I giorni contati* (Petri, 1963), dealing with the fear of approaching death. The best portrayal of an older protagonist is, in my opinion, *Umberto D*. At the Italian debut of his neorealist cinema masterpiece, director Vittorio De Sica commented: "La tragedia degli anziani, esclusi da un mondo che hanno contribuito a costruire, è una tragedia che si nasconde nella rassegnazione o nel silenzio e spinge a paventosi suicidi. La decisione di morire presa da un giovane è certamente grave, ma che dire del suicidio di un vecchio? Di un individuo già naturalmente vicino alla morte? E' una cosa orribile. Una società che permette una cosa simile è una società perduta" (The tragedy of older people, excluded from a world they have helped to build, is a tragedy often concealed by resignation or silence and is the cause of dreadful suicides. A young person's decision to commit suicide is certainly momentous, but what can we say of an older person's suicide? Of the suicide of someone who is already naturally close to death? It is a horrible thing. A society that allows such a thing to happen is a lost society).

9. See Bini, "L'immagine dell'anziano nel cinema d'oggi"; Cecconi, "Vivere alla grande"; and *Vecchiaia, cinema e audiovisivi*, eds. Girardi and Giumelli. The two articles classify old-age movies into thematic categories, e.g.: "the age of peace," "love seasons," "middle-age crisis," "ugly, old, and emarginated," "the family as conflict," "taking stock," etc. The volume *Vecchiaia, cinema e audiovisivi* is intended as a resource for trainees and educators, as a tool for promoting reflection and debate through film viewing. The first part lists both national and foreign feature films distributed in Italy, the second, Italian documentaries. In the first part, seventy-five titles are listed; film synopses, subject keywords, data on production and cast, format and availability, are provided for each movie. The second part provides the same basic information about 103 documentaries. The most interesting documentary is Daniele Segre's *Quella certa età*, in which older people talk about love in a free-hearted and quite impudent fashion. This documentary was produced in 1996 by the Sindacato Pensionati CGIL.

10. The interest in intergenerational family narratives is common to two young women directors, Cristina Comencini and Francesca Archibugi. In Archibugi's *Verso sera* (1990), for example, Marcello Mastroianni is an old professor who adopts his granddaughter and establishes a difficult emotional relationship with her.

11. In a recent Canale 5 soap opera, *Il bello delle donne*, Virna Lisi plays a similar older character, Miranda Spadoni. Miranda is an aristocratic woman whom everybody admires.

12. The titles of some of these articles often reveal the sexism and ageism of their contents: e.g., Boralevi, "Nonne in carriera: Ricerche e storie di vita vissuta dicono che sesso e successo sono per chi sa invecchiare" (Career grandmothers: Scientific research and personal narratives reveal that sex and success are for those who know the art of aging); Schisa, "Ricomincio da 50" (I start all over again at 50); Marcesini, "Questo mezzo secolo ci piace: Concorsi bellezza over 50" (We like this half a century: Over-50 beauty contests). Other significant catchphrases that appear in the texts of some of these articles are: "Il miracolo del raddoppio per le 50enni" (The double-up miracle for 50-year-old women); "Dopo le lolite è il momento delle tardive" (After the nymphet, now it is the old girl's moment).

13. E.g., Pisu, "Vita dura con la bisnonna."

14. This figure was wonderfully characterized by Carla Cerati in the novel *La cattiva figlia*.

15. Spedicato, *Vecchiaia e pregiudizio*, 45.
16. Ibid., 61.
17. De Giorgio, *Le italiane dall'Unità a oggi*, 362.
18. Tamanza, "Fili d'argento a colori," 63: "La prevalente concordanza di genere tra il soggetto rappresentato e l'autore, rafforzata dai diversi elementi della raffigurazione . . . può essere infatti letta come il fatto che il nonno e la nonna rappresentano non soltanto una figura vicariale di accudimento o un interlocutore occasionale delle attività ludiche e ricreative, ma un rilevante riferimento del processo di identificazione attraverso il quale essi procedono nella costruzione della propria personalità."
19. Ibid., 59: "attraverso le attribuzioni degli elementi più tradizionali (ed in parte anche stereotipati) del ruolo e delle azioni, nonché dalla collocazione del nonno e della nonna in ambientazioni differenziate."
20. Alessandro Manzin, Classe II B, Scuola media statale I. Cankar, "Cosa significa per te avere il nonno," in *I nonni secondo i ragazzi*, ed. De Banfield, 61: "Verso sera torniamo a casa. Qui ci aspetta la cena già pronta. Per essere stati a spasso tutto il giorno dobbiamo per penitenza preparare il tavolo e mangiare tutto. Il nonno mi strizza spesso l'occhio. Dopo la cena incominciamo a giocare a poker. Questo è il gioco che io prediligo. E' un gioco che me l'ha insegnato proprio lui. La nonna s'arrabbia spesso quando giochiamo a poker fino a tardi. Poi il nonno mi augura la buona notte ed ambedue andiamo a letto. Penso di avere con il nonno un rapporto diverso che con la nonna. Lui mi capisce, mi asseconda e si comporta con me come un amico e non come un parente. Sento invece molta distanza fra me e la nonna, questo lo noto anche nel suo sguardo. Molte volte mi pare che essa sia gelosa di me e del nonno perché non supporta che io sia più amico di nonno che suo. Penso che in effetti sia così in quanto il nonno si occupa di me e la nonna non si comporta nei miei confronti come lui. Credo comunque di voler bene ad ambedue, questo lo ripeto spesso alla nonna, sebbene lei non ci crede. Lei afferma che io voglio bene solo al nonno e non la considero nemmeno."
21. Jasna Simčic, "I miei nonni," Classe II B, Scuola media statale I. Cankar, in *I nonni secondo i ragazzi*, 91: "Con il nonno gioco spesso a carte. Quand'ero piccola, mi lasciava vincere, però spesso vinceva anche lui. Il nonno è sempre o quasi sempre contento. La nonna ha un carattere diverso è più 'mutevole' e s'arrabbia spesso. La nonna cucina, lava i piatti, fa il bucato e stira. Quando ha tempo pure cuce e si arrabbia con me, poiché io scherzo con lei ma lei non capisce gli scherzi. Se io rido, lei non ride, se io sono seria, ride lei. Sbaglia spesso, se poi glielo dico, mi risponde che ha ragione lei. . . . Il nonno mi raccontava anche delle fiabe ed a me piaceva tanto la fiaba dei gatti ricchi. La sapevo a memoria. La nonna non mi raccontava mai fiabe e dice che io non le voglio bene. Ammetto che il nonno coglie tutta la mia approvazione, voglio però bene ad ambedue. Lei non mi crede, ma che pensi quello che vuole, io voglio bene ad ambedue."
22. Spedicato, "Il 'sapere' dei bambini e la vecchiaia," 180.
23. Lilli, "Una lunga alterna gara": "la donna nasce matura."
24. Ibid.: "[l]o sviluppo mentale della donna si arresta, poi, definitivamente dopo i vent'anni, mentre quello dell'uomo continua fino ai quaranta e oltre."
25. Ibid.: "la diversa natura dell'uomo e della donna. . . . scorie fanciullesche che nell'uomo scompaiono."
26. Ibid.: "[u]n uomo anziano può chiamare 'piccola,' senz'ombra di ridicolo, una donna anziana quanto lui, poniamo, può consentirle capricci, e manifestazioni fanciullesche."
27. Ibid.: "[v]ecchie mogli che sorreggono vecchi mariti costituiscono uno spettacolo, in strada, di tutti i giorni."
28. Ibid.: "[a] questo punto c'è più carica di spirito materno nella donna che carica di spirito paterno nell'uomo, di nuovo."

29. Colombo, "Il mito perduto della giovinezza": "universo giovane maschio-femmina."

30. Ibid.: "Il trionfo della giovinezza, al principio del secolo, è stato un trionfo esclusivamente maschile. 'Il gesto aggressivo, l'insonnia febbrile, il passo atletico, le belle idee che uccidono, il disprezzo per la donna' del manifesto Futurista non va bene per la massa di giovani che sosta in attesa ai confini del mondo adulto, alla fine di questo secolo. . . . Adesso, più della metà della massa di giovani in attesa sono donne. . . . la giovinezza non è più il simbolo febbrile del mondo che deve venire e dell'azione che sta per compiersi, da quando non è più la giovinezza dei maschi."

31. Ibid.: "arte, cultura, visione del mondo, attesa del futuro, tensione, poesia."

32. Ibid.: "una rivoluzione di adulti."

33. Bocolan Parisi, Bosi, and Ghezzi, *Bisogni, opportunità, servizi*, 25: "[f]orse perché sono più forti e meno inficiate da condizionamenti culturali conservano il loro potere, legato ai rapporti familiari più che quelli sociali."

34. Moretti, "Senilità e disimpegno," 15.

35. Colitta and Panier Bagat, "Gli anziani: Rimpianti e progetti," 86–87: "Il non aver svolto un lavoro settoriale, il non immedesimarsi nel ciclo produttivo, le ha portate, attraverso un lungo apprendistato al sacrificio, ad una maggior padronanza delle piccole realtà da vivere e sperimentare."

36. Scortegagna, *Invecchiare*, 65: "diventerebbe un'opportunità e un privilegio (nei confronti dei maschi) nell'età della vecchiaia; la donna cioè sarebbe più attrezzata del maschio, perché più padrona del tempo di vita."

37. Pizzo, "Una nuova scienza per il mondo": "è il pensionamento a fare di un uomo un 'vecchio.' Non esattamente allo stesso modo accade alla donna, per la quale la vecchiaia ha molto a che fare con il proprio aspetto fisico ma anche con la perdita di ruolo in famiglia. Quando viene esautorata dalla cucina, quando non più a lei spetta la gestione del *ménage*, allora una donna invecchia." The newspaper *Il manifesto* has often shown interest in old-age policies. Besides *Senilità*, in which Anna Pizzo's article appeared, other special issues were published: e.g., *L'anziano massa* and *Il vecchio e il male*. Quite a few leftist sympathizers are members of retired workers' trade unions (*sindacati pensionati*), which, as observed in the previous chapter, represent a fairly large and active sector of Italian unionism.

38. Levi, *La vecchiaia può attendere*, 5: "Non che non pensino: accade anche a loro di pensare; ma si affidano più all'istinto che al ragionamento, e raggiungono conclusioni fulminee sulle questioni più complesse. Quel che è peggio è che molte volte hanno anche ragione. Oltre tutto, passano da una stagione all'altra della vita con ammirevole disinvoltura. O forse sanno mentire meglio, agli altri e a se stesse. Decisi che era meglio sentire l'opinione di qualche uomo, di un amico coetaneo o magari più giovane di me."

39. Antonini, "L'età della maturità."

40. Women's public invisibility is not only an Italian issue. Reports on European senior-organization conferences also lament the fact the all speakers on senior-policy issues are men. See, for example, OWN-Europe, *Integrating the European Dimension*, 14.

41. Scortegagna, *Invecchiare*, 66.

42. E.g., "Le differenze sessuali" in Bocolan Parisi, *Bisogni, opportunità, servizi*, 23–26; "Le differenze tra i sessi" in Cesa Bianchi, *Giovani per sempre*, 141–46; and "Invecchiare al femminile" in Lucchetti, *Invecchiare bene*, 80–82.

43. E.g., ISTAT, *Anziani in Italia*; and Sansone, *La quarta età*.

44. See Suardi, *Invecchiare al femminile*; and Romé, *Per una ruga in più*.

45. See Paoletti, "A Half Life: Women Caregivers." Other studies of female caregiving in the Italian family, all stemming from the research carried out by the Ancona Center of social and economic studies of INRCA (National Institute for the Cure and

Care of Older People), are: Paoletti, "Caring Women, Cared-for Women"; and Lamura, Melchiorre, and Mengani, "Caring for the Caregivers."

46. In the same year, an essay on the aging 1968 generation, Lidia Ravera's *Né giovani né vecchi*, was published. I have chosen not to discuss this essay—an ironic confessional collage of anecdotes, character-studies, and epigrams—because it is not relevant to my gender-study perspective. Another *amarcord* essay on the 1968 generation is: Egidi, *Vent'anni appena*.

47. Coord. Naz. DS, "Le età delle donne."

48. Gianini Belotti, *Amore e pregiudizio*, 293: "un gesto sovversivo nei confronti delle norme che le imprigionano."

49. Ibid., 296: "l'alleanza patriarcale per la spartizione e lo scambio tra uomini delle donne giovani e feconde."

50. One of the eight workshops proposed at the Fourth European Feminist Research Conference in Bologna in fall 2000 was "The Controversial Body: Aging in Women's Theories, Literatures, and Cultures." Although focused on Anglo-American feminist age studies, a valuable Italian contribution to this workshop was Vita Fortunati's paper "Controversial Female Body: New Feminist Perspectives on Ageing." Several international conferences have been promoted by OWN-Europe in the past decade (all of them announced and documented on their website, http://www.own-europe.org). Documentary reports on the conditions of older European women have also been published, among them: Coopmans, "How Do Older Women Fare in the European Community," and Nielsen, *Older Women in the European Community*. Massimo Mengani and Cristina Gagliardi prepared the "Italian report" for the publication *Older Women in the European Community*.

51. The principal aims of networks are: "To promote the sharing of knowledge, skills and experience of older women across Europe; to challenge negative stereotypes of age, gender, race, disability and sexuality; to affirm the rights and capacity of older women through self-help, social groups and political activity; to contribute to policy development at local, national and international levels; to work across cultures and generations recognising that age is a lifecourse issue; to work with the European Union and its institutions to ensure the older women's perspective in the development of and activity in, relevant action programmes" (Marziali, "Networking, a way of participating"). OWN chapters from different European nations, including Italy, took part in the Beijing Fourth World Conference on Women in 1995. For the world conference they prepared the Beijing Platform for Action, calling for "the improvement of the status of women of all ages and the end of discrimination against women on the basis of age" (OWN-Europe, *Recognising Older Women's Experience*, 4).

52. OWN-Europe, Italy, has also cooperated to conduct research on women caregivers. In 1998 it launched an action research project, coordinated by Paoletti, which was part of a wider study, "The role of women in the family care of disabled older people," conducted by the earlier-mentioned Ancona Center of Social and Economic Studies of INRCA.

53. Russo, "The Scandal of Anachronism," 23.

54. "Il tema": "insidiano l'ottimismo politico che, nel movimento, era sostenuto dal sentimento di un'adolescenza che si scopriva prolungabile."

55. One of the most common slogans of the 1968 movement was: "Non fidarti di nessuno che abbia più di 34 anni" (Don't trust anyone who is over 34). See Ortoleva, *Saggio sui movimenti del 1968*.

56. "Il tema": "vecchie e bambine sono sempre rimaste sul ciglio della strada."

57. Pinnelli, "La longevità femminile," 59.

58. Piccone Stella, "Un decennio senza cittadinanza," 80: "il processo, la parzialità, l'ibrido, la gradualità della trasformazione."

59. Ibid., 81: "[g]li effetti liberatori si sono visti immediatamente sulle facce, sui corpi, nel comportamento."

60. Coord. Naz. DS, "Le età delle donne."

61. Piccone Stella, "Un decennio senza cittadinanza," 80: "autorizzate, su certi piani, a non essere neppure mature."

62. Ibid.: "Quanto guadagno alla mia età? A che punto sono? Finché è in vita un testimone femminile meno emancipato di noi, non siamo obbligate a tirare le somme."

63. Masi, "Donne senza precedenti."

64. Braidotti, *Nomadic Subjects*, 207, 180.

65. See, in particular, Irigaray, *L'éthique de la différance sexuelle*.

66. This notion and practice was discussed in the essay: Libreria delle donne di Milano, *Non credere di avere dei diritti*.

67. Lazzaro-Weis, *From Margins to Mainstream*, 54. Lazzaro-Weis refers to Laura Grasso's critique in the essay "Madri e figlie nel rapporto fra donne."

68. Pallavicini, "Ritorno al presente": "un accessorio al (doppio) tema della trasmissione-tradizione."

69. Ibid.: "si fondano su un principio di riproduzione del già dato (la propria esperienza) volto alla mimesi identitaria, piuttosto che all'apertura di un presente condivisibile."

70. Ibid.: "le 'vecchie' femministe italiane non sanno che farsene delle 'nuove' femministe, e sono così sorde alla loro presenza da ritenere di molto preferibile il tentare di teorizzare un rapporto di generazione con un altro indefinito, sempre ancora a venire, 'le giovani' appunto, (un ente così estraneo, e privo di sé, da non generare contraddizioni neppure immaginifiche), piuttosto che interrogarsi seriamente sulle ragioni dell'esclusione (non certo della assenza) delle giovani femministe dal presente dei loro luoghi politici."

71. Laslett, "Necessary Knowledge," 10. According to this source, female life expectancy was 50.4 years in the 1920s and 67.9 in the 1950s.

72. Palma, "Terza età, nuovo record italiano," 19; Sansone, *La quarta età*, 57. If we consider male-female ratios within old-age brackets, we learn that the percentage of women among the 60- to 64-year-old population is 52.2 percent; it becomes 56.6 percent between the ages of 65 and 74, and 62.3 percent among 75+ people (Sansone, *La quarta età*, 116).

73. Coord. Naz. DS, "Le età delle donne."

74. 2002 population figures are derived from the website *NationbyNation*. A more culturally interesting perspective than the dry and soon-outdated numerical statistics on life expectancy can be offered by the dynamic and forward-looking identification of the "old-age threshold." Contemporary demography tends to locate the old-age threshold not in absolute terms, from sixty on, but by defining as "old" a person who has a life expectancy below ten years. If we take into consideration 1999—the year when the United Nations summoned national governments to conduct initiatives and surveys on older people, as well as the final year of the decade examined in this essay—the data reported by the then Minister of Social Solidarity, Livia Turco, at the governmental Conference for the International Year of Older Persons, reveal that women have seen their old-age threshold rise much faster than men—from 63 years in 1980 to 79 in 2000—and that 2020 projections are 77 years for men and over 80 for women (Sansone, *La quarta età*, 173).

75. Bocolan Parisi, *Bisogni, opportunità, servizi*, 24. According to Pinnelli and Mancini, significantly higher female mortality rates in the 1860–1920 period are to be attributed not only to child-delivery mortality but also to discrimination in childcare, which accounts for a disadvantage in the first year of life. Girls' breastfeeding was either

shorter or excessively prolonged, food quality during weaning was poorer, and girls were more often put out to nurse under poor hygienic conditions. Only in the 1920s–1940s are equal levels of mortality between boys and girls achieved ("Un indicatore forte dell'ineguaglianza fra i sessi").

76. The document "Le età delle donne" also provides updated age-based marriage rates: 0.4 percent among 15- to 19-year-old women; 10 percent in the 20-24 age bracket; 43.4 percent in the 25–29 age bracket.

77. Coopmans, "How Do Older Women Fare in the European Community," 38. Although, according to this 1990 study, the highest figure is to be found in Ireland—nearly a quarter of women over 55 have never married—"it is not uncommon for over 10 percent of women aged 55 and over to have never been married in the European community" (ibid.).

78. Sansone, *La quarta età*, 116.

79. "Italia 2001, cosa significa la parola famiglia?"

80. Sansone, *La quarta età*, 100.

81. Rutigliano, "Basta con la solita maglia e cucito."

82. Saraceno, *Sociologia della famiglia*, 141.

83. ISTAT, *Anziani in Italia*, 34.

84. Lucchetti, *Invecchiare bene*, 81.

85. "The minimum pensionable age, in the case of pensions paid by compulsory insurance for invalidity, old age, and survivors was increased, by a deputy order of December 1992, to 60 for women and 65 for men, as of January 1, 1993, with a graduality of one year every three years. In 2005 the pensionable age has been established as 65 years for men and 60 for women. Subsequently (from the year 2008), the pensionable age for women will progressively increase, one year every two, to 65. In 2016 women will retire at 65 years of age. The minimum contribution time required for old age pensions has increased from 15 to 20 years, with a progressive application from 1.1.93" (Mengani and Gagliardi, *Older Women in the European Community*, 1-2).

86. Sansone, *La quarta età*, 118; ISTAT, *Anziani in Italia*, 49.

87. See Zanuso, "Lavoro e generazioni."

88. Coopmans, "How Do Older Women Fare in the European Community," 38.

89. Coord. Naz. DS, "Le età delle donne."

90. The rate of employed women decreases to 35.9 percent between ages 50 and 54. 1994 data on women's employment in different age brackets revealed that among working-age women (between the ages of 30 and 59) the unemployment rate was 52.2 percent (12 percent of them with a college degree). This percentage includes both women in search of first occupation and those trying to reenter the work market (see Vitale, "Cinquant'anni senza paura").

91. Palma, "Terza età, nuovo record italiano," 19; Sansone, *La quarta età*, 116; ISTAT, *Anziani in Italia*, 14.

92. ISTAT, *Anziani in Italia*, 78.

93. E.g., Petraglia, "Anziani: Il nuovo tempo libero."

94. ISTAT, *Anziani in Italia*, 75. The daily average for men is 18 hrs. 54 mins.; for women, 19 hrs. 18 mins.

95. Ibid.

96. Ibid., 80.

97. Sansone, *La quarta età*, 120.

98. Bocolan Parisi, *Bisogni, opportunità, servizi*, 24.

99. Lucchetti, *Invecchiare bene*, 81.

100. ISTAT, *Anziani in Italia*, 74.

101. Coord. Naz. DS, "Le età delle donne."

102. "Anche gli anziani vanno a scuola."
103. Lucchetti, *Invecchiare bene*, 80.
104. ISTAT, *Anziani in Italia*, 81–82.
105. Lucchetti, *Invecchiare bene*, 80; ISTAT, *Anziani in Italia*, 82–83.
106. Bocolan Parisi, *Bisogni, opportunità, servizi*, 25; Cesa Bianchi, *Giovani per sempre*, 143.
107. See Colitta and Panier Bagat, "Gli anziani: Rimpianti e progetti."
108. According to the results of these 1984 interviews with older Romans, a reason for women's better adjustment is the fact that they are more likely than men to be living with children or close relatives, possibly because of the services they can still offer in their old age. Living alone seems to be a more widespread condition for older women in northern urban areas in 1990s surveys.
109. Buzzi-Donato, *Vediamo passar le stelle*, XVIII. As remarked earlier in this chapter, the volume features 142 interviews. These interviews are designed to help the interviewee to tell her own life narrative, which may be two to five pages long. In the introduction to the interview collection, the editor discusses recurring themes and concerns under different sections, and quotes several statements from the interviews to illustrate each theme. The section titles are: "Loneliness," "The ideology of residential self-segregation," "Past, present, and future," "Young people," "Economic condition," and "Public assistance."
110. Ibid., XXV.
111. Ibid., XXXI.
112. Ibid., XXXVI.
113. Ibid., XXXIV.
114. Ibid., XXXIX, L, LI.
115. Ibid., XLIII.
116. Ibid., LV.
117. Ibid., LX.
118. Ibid., LXII.

Chapter 4. Female Lines

1. Lowinsky, "Mothers of Mothers," 86.
2. Ibid., 87.
3. Mazzantini's most recent novel, *Non ti muovere*, won the prestigious Strega prize and topped the best-seller list in 2002.
4. The French edition, *De bonne famille*, published in 1998 by Hachette Literature, was a finalist for the Foemina award.
5. Elli, "Letteratura femminile degli anni '90," 96: "ipotetico nipote di nonna Olga e, quindi, legittimo erede della sua ricchezza interiore."
6. Tamaro, *Follow Your Heart*, 16 (hereafter cited as *FYH*). Tamaro, *Va' dove ti porta il cuore*, 16 (hereafter cited as *VPC*): "a faccia in giù tra le zucchine." In addition to the page numbers of the published translation from which the English quotes are taken, I also report the corresponding quotes in the original Italian version and their page numbers. Citations are to the Rizzoli edition of *VPC*.
7. In a critical review of Tamaro's narrative the association of "grandmothers" and "gardens" is thus defined: "Both the grandmother and the garden are symbols and ideological frames: emblematic of rootedness in a tradition (in which the grandmother is the female patriarch). They represent hostility to novelty and modernity in the name of the eternity of 'values'" (Senardi, "Nonne e giardini," 194: "La nonna e il giardino sono

insieme simboli e schemi ideologici: emblemi di radicamento nella tradizione (di cui la nonna è il patriarca al femminile), di ostilità al nuovo e di chiusura verso il mondo moderno in nome dell'eternità dei 'valori'").

8. Mondo, "Nei segreti del cuore": "la proprietà delle vesti e dei pensieri di una vecchia signora."

9. Comm. Naz. Parità e Pari Opportunità, *Quaderni rosa*: "Nel codice austriaco le donne erano 'parificate all'uomo nella facoltà di disporre delle proprie sostanze in ogni contrattazione anche senza tutela maritale nell'esercizio dei diritti di proprietà.' Veniva perciò riconosciuta loro piena capacità giuridica."

10. See Minerva, "Susanna? Non parlava quasi mai."

11. Tamaro, *For Solo Voice*, 94. In the original story, "Per voce sola" (which is also the title of the collection), the quote reads: "intenerimenti senili" (Tamaro, *Per voce sola*, 144).

12. Tamaro, *For Solo Voice*, 99. Tamaro, *Per voce sola*, 150: "pensieri piccoli piccoli."

13. Senardi, "Nonne e giardini," 190: "scandita dai 'si dice,' dagli 'ho letto,' dagli 'avevo trovato scritto' . . . una mente prensile ma che si affatica, non regge il discorso, perde e ritrova il filo, affastella letture, ricordi, esperienze, ideologie."

14. *FYH*, 79. *VPC*, 74–75: "E' vero, nel discorso divago, invece di prendere la via principale spesso e volentieri imbocco umili sentieri. Do l'impressione di essermi persa e forse non è un'impressione: mi sono persa davvero. Ma è questo il cammino che richiede quello che tu tanto cerchi, il centro."

15. *FYH*, 93. *VPC*, 88: "Nelle pagine che ho scritto oggi è un po' come se avessi mescolato diverse ricette. . . . Un pasticcio? Può darsi. Immagino che se le leggesse un filosofo non riuscirebbe a trattenersi dal segnare tutto con la matita rossa come le vecchie maestre. 'Incongruente,' scriverebbe, 'fuori tema, dialetticamente insostenibile.' Figurati se capitasse poi nelle mani di qualche psicologo! Potrebbe scrivere un intero saggio sul rapporto fallito con mia figlia, su tutto ciò che rimuovo."

16. *FYH*, 178. *VPC*, 170: "Sai, adesso dalla televisione, dai giornali, mi capita di vedere, di leggere tutto questo proliferare di santoni. . . . A me fa paura il dilagare di tutti questi maestri."

17. "The oft-stated impression that the aged have relatively greater impairments of recent than remote memory—an impression not substantiated by any experimental data since 'remote memory' is difficult to test—may reflect the older person's avoidance of the present as a consequence of the life review" (Butler, "The Life Review," 73).

18. Tamaro, *For Solo Voice*, 123. Tamaro, *Per voce sola*, 181: "l'orrore si diluisce nelle fibre, si trasmette ai figli, i figli lo trasmettono ai nipoti . . . va avanti di generazione in generazione, va avanti sempre un po' più debole certo, alla fine si estingue. Si estingue nel momento esatto in cui un altro orrore è pronto."

19. Sala, "Romanzi, ricami e karate."

20. *FYH*, 68. *VPC*, 65: "antico, lontanissimo, sapiente."

21. *FYH*, 21. *VPC*, 19: "un'invisibile corazza . . . [che] continua a ispessirsi per tutta l'età adulta."

22. *FYH*, 14. *VPC*, 13–14: "I ricordi che ci sono intorno a me sono i ricordi di te bambina, cucciolo vulnerabile e smarrito. E' a lei che scrivo, non alla persona difesa e arrogante degli ultimi tempi."

23. Gaglianone, *Conversazioni con Susanna Tamaro*, 36.

24. *FYH*, 49. *VPC*, 47: "L'infelicità abitualmente segue la linea femminile. Come certe anomalie genetiche, passa di madre in figlia. Passando, invece di smorzarsi, diviene via via più intensa, più inestirpabile e profonda."

25. *FYH*, 42. *VPC*, 40: "destino che impone l'ambiente di origine . . . ciò che i tuoi avi ti hanno tramandato per via del sangue."

26. *FYH*, 49. *VPC*, 47: "la professione, la politica, la guerra. . . . la stanza da letto, la cucina, il bagno."

27. *FYH*, 50. *VPC*, 48: "Ti ricordi quando la notte di ferragosto andavamo sul promontorio a guardare i fuochi d'artificio che sparavano dal mare? Tra tutti, ogni tanto ce n'era uno che pur esplodendo non riusciva a raggiungere il cielo. Ecco, quando penso alla vita di mia madre, a quella di mia nonna, quando penso a tante vite di persone che conosco, mi viene in mente proprio quest'immagine—fuochi che implodono invece di salire in alto."

28. *FYH*, 42. *VPC*, 40: "ricca ma ebrea e per di più convertita."

29. *FYH*, 42. *VPC*, 41: "[il] dubbio che almeno qualche colpa fosse sua."

30. *FYH*, 45. *VPC*, 43: "dentro di me pensavo soltanto al modo migliore per darmi la morte."

31. *FYH*, 48. *VPC*, 46: "un piccolo morto."

32. *FYH*, 121–22. *VPC*, 116: "supposta intelligenza . . . di partire per un grande viaggio, di studiare in profondità qualcosa."

33. *FYH*, 121. *VPC*, 116: "sarei rimasta da sola in una grande casa piena di libri, per passare il tempo mi sarei messa a ricamare oppure a fare acquerelli e gli anni sarebbero volati via uno dopo l'altro."

34. *FYH*, 70. *VPC*, 67: "sempre in procinto di cadere."

35. *FYH*, 134. *VPC*, 128: "come tutte le zitelle e le vedove . . . sono caduta nel delirio mistico."

36. *FYH*, 125. *VPC*, 120: "millimetrici spostamenti."

37. *FYH*, 149. *VPC*, 142: "da lì alla vecchiaia avevo ormai previsto tutta la mia vita."

38. *FYH*, 170. *VPC*, 161: "la pianta giovane e vitale. . . . [f]iutava i miei sensi di colpa come un segugio."

39. *FYH*, 59. *VPC*, 56: "tutto era convulso, sfuggente, c'erano troppe idee nuove, troppi concetti assoluti."

40. *FYH*, 110. *VPC*, 105: "molte forzature, idee malsane e distorte."

41. *FYH*, 114. *VPC*, 108: "l'attività erotica veniva considerata come una normale funzione del corpo: andava fatta ogni volta che se ne aveva voglia."

42. *FYH*, 85, 101. *VPC*, 80, 97: "schiava di una nuova dipendenza, prima la politica e poi il rapporto con quel signore. . . . tua madre non era per niente intelligente."

43. *FYH*, 58. *VPC*, 56: "Da come mi guardava certe volte ero sicura che se ci fosse stato un tribunale del popolo, e lei ne fosse stata a capo, mi avrebbe condannato a morte."

44. *FYH*, 113. *VPC*, 107: "principe della Mezzaluna."

45. "As fairytales were being collected by the Brothers Grimm . . . women often died during childbirth so that grandmothers who appear as surrogate mothers in the Grimm tales are not uncommon. Nor are the difficulties deriving from an intergenerational (grandmother-granddaughter) relationship uncommon" (Horn, *To Grandmother's House We Go*, 7).

46. *FYH*, 115. *VPC*, 109: "Bugiarda. Potrebbe essere il titolo della mia autobiografia. Da quando sono nata ho detto una sola bugia. Con essa ho distrutto tre vite."

47. *FYH*, 177. *VPC*, 168–69: "Questa lettera avrei dovuto scriverla a tua madre, invece l'ho scritta a te. Se non l'avessi scritta per niente allora sì che la mia esistenza sarebbe stata davvero un fallimento. Fare errori è naturale, andarsene senza averli compresi vanifica il senso di una vita."

48. *FYH*, 199. *VPC*, 187: "perché nella sua storia di oggetto umile riassuma e ricordi la storia delle nostre generazioni."

49. Lombardi, "Thou Shalt Not Break the Mold," 242.

50. *FYH*, 200. *VPC*, 188: "Se me lo metto, poi dovrò mettere anche i bigodini e le ciabatte, che orrore!"

51. *FYH*, 193. *VPC*, 183: "pensando al secolo quasi intero che ho attraversato, ho l'idea che in qualche modo il tempo abbia subito un'accelerazione."

52. *FYH*, 83. *VPC*, 78–79: "Quando si è giovani si è giovani, si pensa sempre che le cose grandi richiedano—per essere descritte—parole ancora più grandi, altisonanti. Poco prima di partire mi hai fatto trovare sotto il cuscino una lettera in cui cercavi di spiegarmi il tuo disagio. Adesso che sei lontana posso dirti che, a parte appunto il senso di disagio, di quella lettera non ho capito proprio niente. Io sono una persona semplice, l'epoca a cui appartengo è diversa da quella a cui appartieni tu: se una cosa è bianca dico che è bianca, se è nera è nera. La risoluzione dei problemi viene dall'esperienza di tutti i giorni, dal guardare le cose come sono realmente e non come, secondo qualcun altro, dovrebbero essere. . . . Tante volte ho l'impressione che le letture che fai, invece di aiutarti ti confondano."

53. Fofi, "Affari di cuore": "Le vecchie di *Va' dove ti porta il cuore* sembrano d'accordo nell'accusare di tutto questo il transitorio e perdente episodio di una generazione intermedia che ha cercato, facendolo certo male, di dare la 'scalata al cielo' e di edificare una nuova morale, certo meno borghese di quella che consiglia alla nipotina la nonna della Tamaro. . . . Ma di questo ordine sia permesso a un vecchio sessantottino, anzi pre-sessantottino, di diffidare, e molto. Sono tanti i vecchioni e le vecchione che in questi anni si dilettano a dar consigli ai giovani, e i loro libri sono best-seller, sono 'un caso,' un genere letterario. Tamaro. . . . merita l'abbraccio di quest'Italia soddisfatta, sguaiata, imperfetta."

54. Marabini, "Mazzantini," 246: "tagliata con l'accetta ma in buon legno d'ulivo."

55. In the same year, another novel with a heroic grandmother as protagonist was published, Laura Facetti's *Passeggiate con la nonna*. This grandmother embodies the values of the valleys where the Partisan guerrilla war was fought. Facetti's character, however, is not as interesting and faceted as Tamaro's or Mazzantini's.

56. Quaranta, "Margaret Mazzantini: Un altare per la nonna": "Il titolo subito non è piaciuto. Ma l'ho difeso. Il catino segna l'intera esistenza di Antenora, un viaggio dal Medioevo alla realtà virtuale."

57. Mazzantini, *Il catino di zinco*, 11 (hereafter cited as *CZ*): "bagnata di vapore, scarmigliata, s'affannava addosso a me con la spugna dura, intrisa d'acqua bollente."

58. *CZ*, 113: "Solo così il lavoro le parrà compiuto."

59. *CZ*, 136: "valzer di famiglia."

60. *CZ*, 23: "Roma, millenovecentotre. 'Babbo, io non esco insieme a voi con quella cappa, sembrate un corvaccio!' 'Ci sto così bene, figlia mia! Se te ne vergogni, tu vai avanti per strada, fai finta di non conoscermi, io ti vengo dietro come un servitorello, non m'offendo sai.'"

61. *CZ*, 26: "modesto e schivo."

62. *CZ*, 25: "la difende sempre, soprattutto davanti alle figlie femmine che—come nessun altro in famiglia—subiscono le angherie della madre."

63. *CZ*, 52: "al pari d'una vecchia bestiola domestica."

64. *CZ*, 51: "sbaccellando piselli come una femmina."

65. *CZ*, 25: "[e]sce con i suoi abiti vivaci e gualciti e col cappello da festa, dove, posato su una falda, c'è un uccello intero intero, pronto ad alzarsi in volo."

66. *CZ*, 36: "andavano sfiorendo."

67. *CZ*, 39: "s'era fatta i suoi conti, in casa davanti allo specchio. . . . [u]na fuga goffa, molto poco romantica."

68. *CZ*, 37: "snellì d'una decina d'anni."

69. *CZ*, 42: "il gemello nella narrazione a un altro ammazzamento commesso per mani femminili."

70. *CZ*, 54: "un bambino gracile [dai] boccoli dorati, spartiti dalla scriminatura, e la molletta di lato sulla testa, perché la madre lo pettinava a femmina."

71. *CZ*, 48: "[dal] desiderio sommesso e [dal] corpo indulgente (da puttino invecchiato)."
72. *CZ*, 47: "per rispetto alla patria . . . lei rinunciò all'abito bianco."
73. *CZ*, 61: "si abbarbicavano a lei come a una pianta secolare."
74. *CZ*, 63: "insieme a un gruppo raccoglitccio di ragazzi, tutti intorno ai sedici anni."
75. *CZ*, 66: "Come poteva sperare che lui la seguisse, che s'affidasse alla sua mano, cieco, come ai tempi dell'infanzia. . . . Avrebbe voluto assestarle un bel calcio nel culo affagottato, e buttarla fuori dal treno. . . . S'è trascinata fin qui i suoi odori, quello del fiato, quello che esala la scriminatura in mezzo ai capelli. Come li sapeva lui quegli odori! Povera mamma, povera bimbetta. . . . Togliti da questo sudiciume, da questa gravezza di maschi. Come ti sei invecchiata, mamma . . . Che è stato?"
76. *CZ*, 68–69: "Nonna è caduta nel fosso accanto ai binari. . . . Carponi nella gramigna, lei guarda davanti a sé il punto dove i binari si congiungono. . . . Lo sguardo è meglio tenerlo basso sul bagliore ferrigno delle rotaie. Allora inventa un gioco estremo: il riflesso selenico che s'allunga sul binario davanti ai suoi piedi diventa il traguardo, impossibile da raggiungere perché irradiato dalla luna che avanza insieme a lei, quasi fosse un palloncino fluorescente legato al polso di un bimbo. . . . Biascica parole, racconta a se stessa la propria pena, il calvario della guerra, e dei figli. . . . Gli occhi sbranano l'alto: 'Stanotte dovrai scendere in terra con me. Dovrai visitarmi, tu, Madre di tutte le Madri!' Mai s'è sentita così vicina, così dentro il cielo. Il torso flesso in su, le braccia come due rami mendichi, per abbracciarlo tutto il firmamento."
77. *CZ*, 80: "le piaceva goderseli inerti nei letti. . . . mezzi scoperti tra le lenzuola raggrinzite, e le parevano giganteschi neonati."
78. *CZ*, 104: "Uomini e donne invecchiando si assomigliano: l'asta rinsecchisce e non s'impertica più, gli interni uterini si prosciugano. Tutti i connotati femminili erano ormai preda della sua carne anziana che aveva riempito ogni curva."
79. *CZ*, 48: "Penetrarla . . . (è scalzare una zolla) asciutta come il sale."
80. *CZ*, 98: "casona quadrifamigliare."
81. *CZ*, 44: "sfrattava in fretta dal cuore."
82. *CZ*, 104: "Quando pensava alla propria vita, la divideva per quattro. Prima l'infanzia e la giovinezza in casa dei genitori; subito dopo, la vita matrimoniale e i figli; poi quel frammento, breve ma intenso, di lei e il marito da soli; e, infine, la vedovanza. Era stato un lento procedere verso lo spopolamento. Eppure, questa quarta e ultima trancia di vita, che sulla carta avrebbe dovuto essere la più triste, avvolse nonna con grandi aeree braccia e la sollevò nel cielo della leggerezza."
83. *CZ*, 13: "ancora forte e piena di vita . . . spaesata, con il busto slacciato sotto i vestiti, la grattugia in una mano, un paio di calze nell'altra."
84. *CZ*, 108: "un poco del suo medioevo."
85. *CZ*, 109: "[s]i buttava allo sbaraglio. . . . detestava geografie, musei, monumenti e tutto ciò che era stato sepolto. Gli occhi li teneva ad altezza d'uomo. Era lì che appuntava la sua curiosità."
86. *CZ*, 108: "piccolo esercito di ragazzini scuri . . . che la seguiva ovunque andasse."
87. *CZ*, 105: "infilava le sue manacce in ogni intimità."
88. Trecca, "Grazie nonna crudele": "deformazioni espressionistiche, gergo familiare, neologismi, audacie morfologiche, termini vernacolari, terragni e corporali arditamente si mescolano . . . a vocaboli aulici."
89. *CZ*, 105: "Il primo ricordo che trattengo di lei è olfattivo."
90. *CZ*, 18: "Avevo paura della fessura sotto quella porta, del suo seguito nella stanza inaccessibile, proibita. Riconoscevo solo il puzzo della casa, dove abitava il corpo

di lei vecchia, e i pavimenti respiravano la sua cosa nuda sotto la sottana, quando di notte scivolava fuori dal letto per pisciare."

91. *CZ*, 15: "Io guardavo le amiche di nonna. Il riverbero impudente del sole illuminava le porosità della pelle, sotto le chiazze di cipria mal stesa, e il rossetto incanalato su per le rughe intorno alle labbra. Buttavo per terra il tovagliolo, e scomparivo a raccoglierlo. In basso, insieme alle zampe arrugginite del tavolo, c'erano visoni dal taglio antiquato, caviglie ossidate dentro calze da riposo, e odore di fica vecchia."

92. *CZ*, 9: "spiazzo dove si ergeva, triste e fradicio, un bar senza avventori."

93. *CZ*, 17: "solo polvere, un vecchio chiodo e un elastico."

94. *CZ*, 17: "ogni ora l'uscita di quel cuculo nero."

95. *CZ*, 18: "di panno, di stoffa stampata, di osso, di plastica, di madreperla, a cupola, dorati, argentati."

96. *CZ*, 11: "emporio di vecchi bauli, di bottiglie di pomodoro, di sacchetti di cellophane, di viti, bulloni, rubinetti, cordicelle, giornali, graste di basilico, e le amate ciabatte."

97. *CZ*, 19: "il chiarore intermittente della luce algida. . . . una ressa di mobili, avanzi dei vari traslochi di famiglia."

98. *CZ*, 114: "i misteri accumulati negli anni . . . l'aggrediscono."

99. Trecca, "Grazie nonna crudele": "Questo libro è nato da un senso di ribellione. Io avevo memoria di mia nonna come di una donna forte, quasi virile, una di quelle che una volta tenevano in piedi . . . i legami del sangue. Improvvisamente, poi, l'ho vista ridotta ad un nulla, ad un brandello umano nel cronicario dove era stata ricoverata per un ictus. Il libro è quindi dettato dalla voglia di ridarle dignità raccontando la sua grande storia. Di questa storia ricordo proprio tutto: gli immensi slanci di affetto e la crudeltà, che nasceva dal fatto che viveva male il suo ruolo di donna perché era stata castrata dalla madre che preferiva i figli maschi. Ha attacchi d'ansia perché si sente costretta dalle convenzioni sociali a vivere sempre dentro casa. Lei oggi sarebbe stata una single, una donna in carriera. Scrivere è stato un tentativo di strappare la nonna al passato per proiettarla nel futuro."

100. See Giovanardi, "Quant'era cattiva nonna Antenora."

101. *CZ*, 135: "una gradinata [che] non finisce mai. . . . una macchia di liquame nero."

102. *CZ*, 135: "cielo afflosciato di vampa [che] non ha che occhi: gli occhiacci rossi del codimozzo, gli occhi di nonna, che mi tengono come la coscienza, come il Dio occhiuto che s'affaccia minaccioso dalle nubi rosseggianti nei filmini delle suore al catechismo."

103. *CZ*, 136: "nipote, non puoi lasciarmi morire, non puoi sfuggire all'investitura che i miei occhi t'hanno dato."

104. *CZ*, 136: "appoggiava al proprio braccio sulla balaustra del balcone . . . di fronte al viso reclinato di una vergine. . . . [gli] occhi predaci."

105. *CZ*, 109–10: "Faceva caldo. Nemmeno la sera si respirava. La dama di compagnia, nubile magrissima e tutta aquilina, era matta. Accendeva la radio, e si scioglieva i capelli con un gesto felino: capelli biondi e tanti che le ricadevano addosso. 'Guarda, vista da dietro sembro una bambina di quindici anni, non è vero?' diceva, ispirata, ballando per la stanza, al ritmo di una samba radiofonica. Le rispondevo di sì. Ma i suoi capelli giovani e quella zampa ossuta che protendeva fuori dalla sottana nera, come un'antenna erotizzata, mi facevano orrore, sapendola decrepita nella metà celata del suo sembiante."

106. *CZ*, 18: "bambine violate, buttate in un pozzo."

107. *CZ*, 8: "isolata in un cono di luce. . . . nuda, distesa . . . su un letto marcescente di licheni e muschi . . . uno sboffo di canizie attorno al sesso, solo e spalancato come una cava abbandonata."

108. Todisco, "Tanto di Campiello," 71: "prorompente morale naturale sacrificale ... che teneva insieme un gracile tessuto familiare incalzato da mille avversità."

109. Scarpa, "Quell'amata nonna-donna": "nel senso che il sacrificio e l'abiura di se stessa erano norma per donne di quella condizione socioculturale."

110. CZ, 56–59: "La madre si sveglia possente, forte di vigore e risolutezza virile, intrappolata in quei confini femminili così angusti per lei.... oggi. 'La disfo.' Parla della casa, divorandosela con le mani.... Il conigliaccio spaventato dal bailamme.... [h]a lasciato tracce dappertutto.... Non lo vede subito. Va spedita verso la finestra.... Via, addosso, per placcarlo sul tappeto, senza nemmeno mollare lo scopettone, portandoselo appresso, facendosi male. Con il dolore la rabbia cresce, trova movente. Donna e coniglio sono a terra, con i cuori pulsanti, e lo scopettone in mezzo.... Quello che succede sul tavolo, in cucina, non lo so. Non lo voglio sapere. Nelle spalle di lei c'è solo un sussulto.... Poi la furia si placa e apparecchia il marmo nudo senza il minimo rimorso. ... Questa d'accoppare l'animale, fu una voluttà che l'assalì improvvisa. Non era così spietata da voler scientemente privare il figlio del suo unico amico.... Semplicemente la infastidivano le ore clandestine di svago che il coniglio regalava al bambino. Attraverso quei giochi, le sembrava che lui si sottraesse alla vita-castigo cui lei lo aveva consegnato. Non poteva sfuggire dei suoi figli, proprio lui, il più fantasioso ... alla condanna dello star-su-questa-terra-a-tribolare, che a lei era stata inferta dalla natura stessa, per quella cicala muta che aveva tra le cosce."

111. CZ, 127–28: "La imbacucco ben benino e me la carico sulla sedia a rotelle. In un'ala meno frequentata dell'ospedale la spingo lungo le corsie deserte.... Via di fretta. Stacco le mani dalla carrozzella: solo per un attimo. Subito la riafferro e corro, corro e la rilancio più forte.... Seguo nonna attraverso lo sguardo alterato di una visione: è già abbastanza lontana, la mantellina da camera all'uncinetto svolazza, le rotelle impazzite scricchiolano sul pavimento, lei agita la mano viva, e va. Va sola, verso la vetrata in fondo. Si schianta. Sento la deflagrazione dei vetri, il rovinio dei frammenti che ricadono all'interno, mentre la nonna è già in volo con la sua sedia a rotelle, fuori dal lividore del neon. Per sempre. Basterebbe soltanto un secondo in più, perché la mia allucinazione fosse realtà. Invece mi precipito a riacciuffarla in tempo. Lei palpita: sono questi attimi di terrore gli unici in cui si sente viva."

112. CZ, 128–29: "Alle spalle dell'ospedale, c'è un sentiero che si perde nel prato.... Il prato pullula di gatti che si nutrono miagolanti tra i rifiuti dell'ospedale.... Ne tiro su qualcuno e glielo mollo in grembo.... Lei ride, per il piacere di sentirsi quegli affari caldi addosso. Vorrei dirle: 'Tieni, nonnina, ti passo un bel coniglio, di quelli che sono buoni alla cacciatora. Tu li sai fare i conigli alla cacciatora, no?' Avrebbe un trasalimento? Chi lo sa. Sorride, con quel sorriso sghembo (lo stesso dei cattivi nei cartoni animati) che risponde solo per metà agli impulsi nervosi. Un ghigno impressionante, sovrastato da occhi abbiosciati in cerca di sostegno.... Potrei tenercela tutta la notte. E' mia. Mi cerca con quello che di vivo le è rimasto in corpo. Ora potrei fargliele pagare tutte, e finirla come il coniglio di mio padre, stringendole intorno al collo la cinghia della mia borsetta. Vederla andare paonazza e gridare: 'Perché? Perché glielo hai ammazzato, porca?!' O, anche, scannarla al ritmo di una macabra filastrocca: 'Porcaccioncella non si castrano i maschietti, non si ammazzano i coniglietti ai bambini soli soletti....' Ma che senso avrebbe ormai ... Poveraccia, quante ne ha passate anche lei! Sul suo viso non c'è più traccia dei crimini antichi. Da vecchi si è così ebeti, così dimentichi del male commesso."

113. CZ, 136: "sgangherato valzer di famiglia nel quale volteggia tutto il parentame."

114. CZ: "Il mio carnet è zeppo!.... Cosa ti fa pensare che io somigli a tutti voi?"

115. Prandin, "Tracce del nostro tempo": "Questo libro è un falso perché due vere vecchie delle nostra famiglia non avrebbero mai parlato."

116. Ibid.

117. Rollo Bancale, "All'ombra di donne non tanto in fiore": "un gusto quasi proustiano per i colori e gli odori del tempo perduto."

118. Prandin, "Tracce del nostro tempo": "narrare le impercettibili tracce del tempo nella nostra vita."

119. Golino, "Troppo rosolio, signora Bossi Fedrigotti," 40: "romanzo tipicamente femminile per scrittura, sensibilità, contenuti soprattutto nel trattare il delicato tema della vecchiaia."

120. Ibid., 41: "romanzo-bacheca."

121. Lagorio, "Addio, famiglia crudele": "con le montagne severe all'orizzonte e la campagna legata a tradizioni difese tenacemente nel tempo."

122. Bossi Fedrigotti, *Di buona famiglia*, 28 (hereafter cited as *BF*): "[n]é si sapeva più a chi rivolgersi, a chi chiedere protezione, dove stesse l'autorità. . . . era in fondo un dettaglio poco importante."

123. *BF*, 66: "Venne la guerra, la seconda, e fu quella che ti liberò. Foste preservati di nuovo, come la prima volta, quando papà era tornato dalla Polonia dopo quattro anni combattuti nelle retrovie, tra un tè e una merenda con signore senza marito. La seconda volta non c'erano più uomini in famiglia che potessero morire, non fratelli, non figli, appena troppo giovane il maggiore di Virginia, troppo vecchio suo marito Tullio."

124. *BF*, 141: "disordine dello sfollamento."

125. Levin, *The Suppressed Sister*, 20.

126. In her psychoanalytic study of sister relationships in literature, Eva Rüschmann observes that "contemporary psychoanalytic feminism is curiously silent on the topic of sisters" (*Those Precious Bonds*, 67). Both French psychoanalytic feminists (such as Irigaray, Kristeva, and Cixous) and American theorists who adopt an object-relations approach (among them, Chodorow, Gilligan, and Baker Miller) focus on the preoedipal relationship between mother and daughter. In this relationship the identification/separation conflict is related to the difficulty women encounter in differentiating themselves from the maternal body, thus in defining the confines of their Ego.

127. A number of miscellaneous quantitative studies of sibling relationships in a lifecourse perspective have appeared in psychology, family studies, and gerontology journals. Some of them analyze and discuss sibling relationships in adulthood and old age, e.g.: Cicirelli, *Sibling Relationships Across the Life Span*; Gold, "Sibling Relationships in Old Age"; Bedford, "A Comparison of Thematic Appercetions of Sibling Affiliation"; and Goetting, "The Developmental Tasks of Siblingship."

128. Goetting, "The Developmental Tasks of Siblingship," 710.

129. Ibid. The uniquely intimate and comprehensive condivision of the same family history is important for the resolution of what Erik Erikson defines the "final psychosocial conflict between Ego integrity and desperation" (*Childhood and Society*, 33).

130. *BF*, 17: "Noi due. . . . Io con Clara e Virginia."

131. *BF*, 20: "le sue ingiustizie, le preferenze."

132. *BF*, 17: "paffuta e ridente con le braccia tese. . . . ossuta nel . . . vestito da festa."

133. *BF*, 21: "sempre nominate insieme, appaiate, vestite uguali, a dormire nella stessa stanza, stessi giochi e regali per l'una e per l'altra, stesse lezioni di pianoforte e disegno, più tardi danza."

134. *BF*, 21: "tu amavi il disegno, lei la danza, nessuna il pianoforte, a te piacevano i vestiti larghi e a lei quelli stretti, tu sceglievi il cioccolato al latte, lei quello amaro."

135. *BF*, 21: "soprattutto . . . Virginia era una bellezza."

136. *BF*, 45: "possibili fidanzati."

137. *BF*, 45: "più rustici . . . e fuori moda. . . . sbagliò mira e s'innamorò di Virginia, che lo lasciò fare. . . . per svezzarlo . . . [e] togliergli quell'aria troppo per bene."

138. *BF*, 75: "ma poi tua sorella era cambiata, si era messa in mente gli uomini e non aveva riso più tanto, non con te almeno."
139. *BF*, 179: "erano forse migliori di noi."
140. *BF*, 25: "perseguitò . . . taciturna e assente di giorno . . . sveglia nel letto di notte."
141. *BF*, 200: "sveglia di notte . . . a spiare lo scricchiolio del legno."
142. *BF*, 201: "per meglio immaginarmi di essere mia sorella."
143. *BF*, 200: "legnosa e monacale."
144. *BF*, 198: "tracce tenui ma eloquenti . . . Clara era proprio come questa sua ombra . . . premurosa, gentile, discreta, amorosa, e che tutto il resto non era che un'invenzione cresciuta sulle mie fantasie."
145. *BF*, 124: "Come potevano non amarla tutti, volerla conquistare, volerla tenere? Sarebbe piaciuto anche a me."
146. *BF*, 9: "Sei una sopravvissuta."
147. *BF*, 113: "Qualcosa è andato storto in qualche punto della mia vita."
148. *BF*, 193–94: "Di cosa potevano parlare, cosa avevano in comune? . . . Di storie passate, di epoche migliori, di coltivazione delle viti? . . . interessato più alle storie del presente, ai tempi futuri."
149. *BF*, 194: "lei silenziosa, malinconica, poco appariscente, già quasi più vecchia che giovane; lui rumoroso, chiacchierone, giovane—almeno sembrava—e anche vistoso, con grande bocca e grande corpo."
150. *BF*, 195: "eravamo tornate a essere donne tutte e quattro, non soltanto sorelle, figlie, madre o cameriera."
151. *BF*, 194: "la pelle rimasta fresca, e i capelli lunghi, folti e castani, arrotolati in una bella treccia."
152. *BF*, 159: "sciatta . . . giovane ma brutta e con un gran naso."
153. *BF*, 195: "un rossetto troppo viola."
154. *BF*, 195: "Le vecchie, mi dicevo, cosa si mettono a fare la cipria? Dovrebbe farle sembrare più belle? E gli orecchini? E il profumo? Credono di piacere le vecchie?"
155. *BF*, 117: "donna con un passato."
156. *BF*, 119: "ancora una civetta, nonostante gli anni."
157. *BF*, 163: "donna già da un pezzo."
158. *BF*, 117: "Non è facile perché mi guardano quando esco, ancora mi piace vestirmi, essere pettinata, portare le scarpe buone. C'è il selciato nelle strade, sconnesso ogni tanto, e devo concentrarmi per camminare dritta, senza traballare. . . . Se una volta lasciassi andare i pensieri, se cedessi a un ricordo, subito inciamperei, rallenterei il passo come una che non è tanto in sé."
159. *BF*, 117: "impagliata, con gli occhi fissi di vetro come le volpi."
160. *BF*, 117: "Sentono forse, quelli che mi incontrano, che la mia vita si è fermata un numero imprecisato di anni fa. . . . Mi compatiscono probabilmente, dicono: 'Povera donna, e pensare che un tempo. . . .'"
161. *BF*, 169: "Non so che fare di me. Di libero ci sarebbe il giardino, almeno lì non ha messo i suoi mobili, i suoi oggetti, le sue fotografie per delimitare il territorio. Scendo qui nella terra di nessuno quando vengono i nipoti a trovarmi, anche se poi con me non stanno molto, giusto quel tanto che serve alle conversazioni prima di passar dalla parte della zia. A volte avrei voluto cominciare qualche discorso con loro, sapere della loro vita, conoscerli meglio, ma vedo che sono distratti, che hanno fretta di passare nell'altro territorio. . . . Guardo . . . dalla finestra per vedere passare gente, anche per ore di seguito, tanto non ho niente da fare. Guarda in su qualcuno. . . . Vedono una vecchia dai capelli non in ordine come vorrebbe, una testa smarrita sulla grande facciata della casa. Non allegra, non triste, niente, una vecchia che guarda giù e basta, senza nessuno a cui pensare veramente."

162. *BF*, 187: "Ormai non tengo più neppure le foto dei figli quando erano piccoli—sono troppo cambiati nel corso degli anni—né quelle di altri che mi furono cari: cose belle non ne voglio ricordare, altrimenti nella situazione presente non sopravviverei alla nostalgia."

163. *BF*, 51: "come se fosse stato un giorno qualunque."

164. *BF*, 64: "poggiaspugna per la doccia che in casa non esisteva, radio e giradischi, scaldavivande a elettricità, accendisigari automatici."

165. *BF*, 53: "non stare ad ammuffire ... [in] un mondo finito."

166. *BF*, 148: "ogni dettaglio per imparare il più possibile su come ci si acconcia."

167. *BF*, 119: "nuovi miliardari."

168. *BF*, 127: "continuità alla mia esistenza. . . . libera, moderna, positiva."

169. *BF*, 119: "a trovare qualcosa che non va, nell'armadio o nel cassettone."

170. *BF*, 115: "vivere piano ... [i] giorni."

171. *BF*, 114: "facendo finta di nulla, dalla mattina alla sera come un altro giorno."

172. *BF*, 191–92: "E' come se fossi retrocessa all'inizio dell'infanzia, prima di ragionare, quando tutto quanto mi stava intorno pareva giusto, normale, perfettamente al suo posto, insostituibile. Quando non conoscevo altro che il vecchio, anzi l'antico, e mai avevo ancora visto qualcosa di moderno. Come se le insicurezze di tutti questi anni, i numerosi cambiamenti che ci sono stati nella mia vita, mi avessero respinto indietro, facendomi credere che l'unica certezza sia la mia casa d'un tempo. Ed ecco che le zampe di leone che spuntavano sotto il comò, ecco che i piedi ad artiglio d'aquila di certi tavolinetti non mi danno più fastidio, mi sembrano anzi gli unici possibili. . . . Sento di essere di nuovo prigioniera del vecchio che mi ha inseguito tutta la vita, che ho fuggito per anni; mi ha raggiunto, mi ha chiusa nell'assedio, ha spento il desiderio del nuovo. E' una lenta perversione che si è impadronita di me, che mi ha fatto rinnegare le stagioni buone e ribelli. Perverso è infatti che io rimpianga quel lettone scuro. . . . Sacrosanto era invece che nelle mie notti di bambina mi sembrassero mostri i mobili della stanza."

173. *BF*, 14: "le aiuole e i vialetti, i fiori che sono di moda e gli alberi piantati per bellezza."

174. *BF*, 50: "disperatamente ... nello stesso identico modo dell'anno prima, stesso cibo, stesse canzoni, stessa tavola."

175. *BF*, 49: "copiati dai veri Natali di quando il mondo era diverso."

176. *BF*, 11: "odor di chiuso, di gonne e ciabatte."

177. *BF*, 88: "sentore di vecchio e di cera, di legno e di giardino, di un poco d'umidità sulle scale, di un poco di canfora nel salotto con i tappeti."

178. *BF*, 9: "una sopravvissuta ... non ... troppo scontenta."

179. *BF*, 9: "Avanzi di un altro mondo ... di modello antiquato simili alle precedenti e alle precedenti delle precedenti."

180. *BF*, 9: "passata di moda prima ancora che te la facessi."

181. *BF*, 61: "è raro che parlino del mondo tuo."

182. *BF*, 13: "è la condizione in cui ti ritrovi meglio."

183. *BF*, 22: "sola ... rimasta della famiglia."

184. *BF*, 14: "l'ultima che sa come devono essere fatte le cose, come vuoi che ti sia apparecchiata la tavola, tostato il pane, saltate le patate."

185. *BF*, 123: "Lasciate stare la bisnonna, non la stancate. . . . come una ragazza, allegra come di solito non è. . . . favole più belle, sorprese più sorprendenti."

186. *BF*, 12: "mandano avanti."

187. *BF*, 53: "con il ricavato comprarsi qualcosa al mare, o in montagna, oppure in una campagna più elegante. . . . l'amore per l'antico."

188. *BF*, 53: "le patacche ... i pezzi buoni."

189. *BF*, 53–54: "per poter fare le castellane, mostrare agli amici di avere un passato, con i quadri degli antenati sulle scale."

190. *BF*, 88: "come fossero stati figli."
191. *BF*, 107–8: "Quelli che ti vengono a trovare adesso, in visita alla zia nella vecchia casa che sperano di ereditare, sono i figli dei nipoti, con le loro mogli e i bambini. A vederli sembrano meglio dei loro genitori, ma probabilmente dipende dall'età. Non portano comunque tracce della tua famiglia, né di te né forse di Virginia, e non per l'aspetto fisico. Di nuovo ti tornano in mente le speranze. Non ti hanno deluso la scarsa riuscita né il numero dei matrimoni o la scelta delle mogli, ma l'assenza della memoria. Perfino Beppina li guarda come marziani, sconosciuti con altri usi."
192. *BF*, 54: "Devi ricordarti di fare ordine, regolare ogni cosa prima di andartene: bruciare le lettere, togliere le fotografie, sfogliare i libri per levarne foglietti e noterelle rimasti tra le pagine. Mettere a posto l'archivio, i libri dei conti, gli armadi della biancheria e anche i tuoi vestiti. . . . Non vuoi che scoprano pezzi della vita che non hai mai raccontato, non vuoi lasciare indietro tracce che parlino di te. Affinché non succeda quello che è successo a te con Virginia."
193. *BF*, 60: "nel tiepido, in casa con mamma e papà . . . per sempre minorenne."
194. *BF*, 16: "ottant'anni fa mangiavi le stesse cose."
195. *BF*, 61: "bambina invecchiata."
196. *BF*, 74: "[u]n italiano, di Milano, uno che si interessava di politica."
197. *BF*, 74: "[s]i presenta bene, è educato, è anche più ricco di noi, ma è uno del popolo."
198. *BF*, 74–75: "come una bambina."
199. *BF*, 77: "per non vedere una 'signorina non più giovane.'"
200. *BF*, 93: "la sua figura di ragazza, non sciupata da niente e da nessuno."
201. *BF*, 94: "prolungare all'infinito quell'oblio che ti permetteva di essere come altre, come Virginia."
202. *BF*, 93: "quell'altra vestita da città che saliva timidamente le scale del dottore sotto lo sguardo curioso della portinaia."
203. *BF*, 100: "Non fosti costretta a scegliere fra il dottore e i tuoi vecchi usi, fra il dottore e la mamma; ti fu dato di rimanere in pace, fedele a te, in ordine."
204. *BF*, 174: "vedere scambiati i ruoli."
205. *BF*, 110: "Come sta bene sua sorella! Come si è mantenuta giovane! E pensare che deve avere solo pochi anni meno di lei."
206. *BF*, 203: "secondo una corretta contabilità dei morti, perché sono la maggiore . . . una vendetta . . . lasciandola sola sia costretta a compatirsi, a compatirmi, ad amarmi un poco, nel ricordo."

Chapter 5. Ripening and Completion

1. See Gadow, "Subjectivity," 133–34.
2. La Porta, "Romanzo morale ma molto impudico": "il romanzo si presenta . . . come un ampio contenitore in cui convivono senza troppo ingombro considerazioni di tipo etico-filosofico, descrizioni minuziose di degenti ospedalieri, riflessioni sulla terza età in forma di trattatello, con esposizione di varie teorie . . . notazioni su fatti molto 'prosaici' e quotidiani, citazioni a non finire di autori . . . perfino . . . un romanzo interno."
3. Scurani, review of *Ultima luna*, 22: "prismi che rispecchiano mentalità e idee del loro tempo."
4. La Porta, "Romanzo morale ma molto impudico": "quasi impudica moralità."
5. D'Eramo, *Ultima luna*, 134 (hereafter cited as *UL*): "disvelamento."
6. Maucci, "L'amore autunnale è colmo di vita": "è discutendo dell'universo senile

che le menti ben affinate dei due 'contendenti' inizieranno a confrontarsi, a scontrarsi, a capirsi."

7. Two interesting studies of the representations of old age in contemporary Japanese society and literature are: Wada, "The Status and Image of the Elderly in Japan"; and Skord, "Withered Blossoms."

8. In the original, the inviting names of retirement homes are: Albergo della Letizia, Villa Placida, Hotel del Risveglio, Casa della Vita, Oasi della Sorgente, Dimora dell'Immacolata, Il Dolce Rifugio.

9. *UL*, 35: "le coppie vengono separate . . . mariti e mogli vivono in padiglioni distinti, divisi anche ai pasti. . . . perde il letto."

10. *UL*, 253: "non c'erano differenze tra ricchi e poveri. . . . un'identica camera singola."

11. *UL*, 252–53: "non ci possono essere favoritismi, non ti puoi comprare nessun'agevolazione delle cameriere con le mance."

12. *UL*, 238: "In un primo tempo, per riflesso medico, lei aveva tentato di capire fin dove quell'anziana fosse affetta da regressione senile e dove cominciasse la simulazione. Indistricabile: la vecchia zitella e la bambina piccola s'erano fuse nelle volute del suo cervello, di modo che un'astuzia adulta argomentava i capricci infantili. 'Lei è cattiva' strideva la voce della signorina Cubini al telefono, 'lei finge d'amare i vecchi e non mi cura gli intestini.' O l'accoglieva sulla porta: 'Cattiva dottoressa Lanzi, cattiva, cattiva, s'è pentita d'avermi abbandonata?'"

13. *UL*, 297: "possibilmente nel cuore della notte senza testimoni."

14. *UL*, 341: "Riaccompagnate tutti gli ospiti a Villa Felice. Guai se ne dimenticate uno. Fatevi aiutare dal signor Oliviero Zanchi a radunarli e contarli."

15. *UL*, 269: "Nonnette e nonnetti, si mangia!"

16. *UL*, 261: "Per sua norma e regola, io non sono la sua nonna."

17. *UL*, 59: "luminare di medicina . . . che legge ancora Catullo in latino. . . . comincia a gridare, mi chiama mamma, sa, è come un bambino di tre anni."

18. *UL*, 134: "un lungo esercizio di cortesia."

19. *UL*, 134: "uno invecchia com'è vissuto."

20. *UL*, 27–28: "Si metta nella pelle d'un anziano che entra a stabilirsi in una casa di riposo. Quest'anziano ha oltrepassato la porta. Sa che d'ora in poi vivrà gomito a gomito in mezzo ai vecchi. Gli si stringe il cuore. Si rispecchia nei coetanei che si vede attorno. . . . 'No' si ribella; 'io non sono come loro.' E non può fare a meno di provare a se stesso, ai suoi simili, al personale della casa, che lui è diverso. Non è un escluso. Non è un rottame. . . . Ma anche i veterani della casa sono punti sul vivo nel sentirsi guardati dal nuovo arrivato come relitti. . . . Gli s'avvicinano con circospezione, in piccoli crocchi, gli sostano nei paraggi, ognuno che decanta a voce troppo alta i meriti dell'altro. Il nuovo ospite si presenta. Comincia il gioco al rialzo. . . . Nella hall, nella sala di soggiorno, quando s'incrociano nei corridoi, veterani e nuovo arrivato fanno a gara a citarsi parenti, amici, conoscenti di qualità che sono loro molto, molto affezionati. . . . Ma più si vantano dei propri affetti, più poi rimproverano in cuor loro alle persone evocate d'averli allontanati. Il risentimento gli riattiva i ricordi, il rimescolio di rancori e rimpianti gli attizza la mente. E' una fase insidiosa per gli ipertesi. Qualcuno crolla. Ma sono pochi. Il risentimento è una tale fonte d'energia! Gli dà uno scopo."

21. *UL*, 66–67: "Sì, signora Alfonsina, erano venuti fuori dalla porta chiusa per accogliermi. 'Aspetta a entrare' mi dicono, 't'abbiamo fatto un'improvvisata.' Come sapete, ieri era il mio settantanovesimo compleanno e capisco che nella stanza dietro quella porta mi stanno preparando una festa. Mi passa la paura e mi viene una grande felicità. Stavo bene, col tailleur, avevo la mia silhouette d'un tempo. E proprio mentre ero così felice, si spalanca la porta. Mio padre e lo zio Angelo mi fanno ala. E che vedo?

... Vedo una sala con tutti i tavolini quadrati come quelli che abbiamo al ristorante. E chi ci sedeva?.... La mia nonna materna, la nonna paterna, la zia Umberta che non ho mai potuto soffrire, la zia Caterina, zia Sandra, mia suocera, tutte morte, capite? Col velo nero in testa, mi facevano: 'Vieni, vieni in mezzo a noi.'"

22. *UL*, 28: "gli occhi aggrappati al mondo esterno che gli giunge per televisione."

23. *UL*, 69: "La politica come ultima sponda sfrecciò nella mente di Bruno, gli si drizzarono i capelli, in un lampo aveva avuto la visione di sé incartapecorito che, rigato dalla sclerosi, ripeteva di continuo le superate convinzioni della giovinezza."

24. E.g., Barberi Squarotti, "Luce D'Eramo pallida luna."

25. *UL*, 129: "nutrito d'un odio a tre facce: quello per i signori fascisti e i preti, fatto di sorrisi, implorazioni e ringraziamenti propizianti; quello arrogante e insieme traverso per i vicini 'morti di fame'; infine l'odio senza esclusione di colpi contro i 'nemici in casa,' cioè i parenti."

26. *UL*, 61: "aveva allora 62 anni, e a 70 s'era accorta che non ce la faceva più a tenere su casa. Aveva scritto al figlio che si sarebbe ritirata in un ricovero per vecchi."

27. *UL*, 60: "tutt'una gerarchia di toni ... altezzoso, altre volte confidenziale, oppure sbadato."

28. *UL*, 270: "la rivoluzione che stava per compiersi nella sua vita."

29. *UL*, 270: "percorsa da un brivido.... nuove conoscenze, nuove abitudini, un nuovo mondo."

30. Scurani, review of *Ultima luna*, 22.

31. *UL*, 258: "Lei non era più una vecchia a carico, che dipende dal volere altrui. Decideva, intraprendeva. Contro venti e maree. Scansò la coperta e pose i piedi a terra. Sapeva quello che doveva cercare. Tirò fuori dal ripiano basso dell'armadio a muro uno scrigno chiuso con una chiave che lei si portava sempre addosso, attaccata alle mutande con una spilla da balia. Aprì lo scrigno e ne prelevò il libretto postale che infilò nella borsetta. 'M'avessero detto' chiocciava a mezza voce, 'quando lavoravo da serva e poi da pantalonaia e pure da sarta e dovevo calcolare il capello, che un giorno sarei diventata arcimilionaria! Anche questa soddisfazione m'ha dato la Madonna, di morire da signora, senza vergogna.'"

32. *UL*, 245: "in trattative."

33. *UL*, 270: "[s]entendosi cedere, implorò la Madonna d'aiutarla a ricominciare tutto da capo."

34. *UL*, 247: "ultimo desiderio."

35. *UL*, 249: "credito."

36. *UL*, 247: "E così la Madonna del Divino Amore le esaudiva insieme i due supremi desideri della sua vita: che il figlio si sposasse e che tornasse a vivere in Italia. Al pensiero incredibile di quello che aveva messo in moto la sua piccola orazione—tutto si compiva in una volta sola—Alfonsina si sentì sciogliere come acqua.... Rimasta sola, si fece un grande segno di croce: 'Maria Vergine e Madre, come posso ringraziarVi? M'avete persino lasciato intravedere i Vostri disegni. Regina del Cielo, lo so, non avete mai fatto le cose a metà....' Intanto però capiva che doveva contraccambiare la Madonna sia dell'immenso favore accordatole di rivedere Bruno coi propri occhi, sia della nuova richiesta che Le aveva avanzato, sia dei due piccioni con una fava che la Madonna le aveva fatto balenare."

37. *UL*, 272: "s'era rivolta a brutto muso al padre Eterno.... [che] non se l'era potuta svignare."

38. For a study of the funeral market, see Wernick, "Selling Funerals, Imaging Death."

39. *UL*, 250–51: "Perciò ti [Divina Provvidenza] supplico, consigliami al più presto qualcosa da deporre ai piedi della Madonna del Divino Amore, non che io mi possa mai

sdebitare con Lei, ma che almeno compatisca alla mia buona volontà. . . . Io ho intascato questa terza grazia come cosa fatta. Al punto che l'ho pure rinfacciata alla Divina Provvidenza! . . . Ti restituisco la Tua terza grazia finché non sarò riuscita a rinnovarTi il mio voto."

40. *UL*, 255: "Però era anche bene che la Madonna ricordasse come lei non aveva sciupato una lira: 'La rimanenza della retta, Tu lo sai, io la verso tutti i mesi sul mio libretto postale assieme al grosso della mia pensione. E ho messo tanto di quel denaro da parte che, comprata la cassa da morto, e pagato il funerale, a Bruno avanzerà un bel gruzzolo. Io voglio soltanto la carrozza con due cavalli per farmi portare al Verano. E' troppo? Ma considera che non voglio sperpero di fiori. Le ho viste, sai, tutte quelle corone gettate in mucchio dietro l'obitorio a marcire come immondezza. Mi farò preparare un unico cuscino di fiori di stagione.' Un lampo le passò sul viso: 'E chi ce lo fa fare di lasciare questo cuscino di fiori sprecato al cimitero. Non ti pare? chiederò a Bruno che, quando m'avrà accompagnata alla tomba, se lo riprenda e Te lo porti al Santuario da parte mia.'"

41. *UL*, 315: "Budda che impersona la quiete del 'mu.'" The character "mu" can be translated as "has not," "is without," "without," "lack of," "absence."

42. *UL*, 324: "lui non le conosceva, di profonda indulgenza."

43. *UL*, 330: "colore ingiallito . . . da vecchia. . . . la sua espressione caparbia."

44. *UL*, 339: "visse felice cucendo abiti / invecchiò protetta dal figlio Bruno / morì nella fede di Dio."

45. *UL*, 342: "ALFONSINA VINCI vedova GORDINI / nata a Roma il 13 marzo 1904 / morta a Frascati il 10 settembre 1992."

46. *UL*, 366: "da ragazzo era stato rispettato dai compagni quando non ci teneva più, andava bene nello studio quando aveva il cuore rivolto al partito. . . . s'era dato anima e corpo all'impegno comunista, il Partito lo aveva espulso."

47. *UL*, 293: "pazzesca permeabilità. . . . il sogno di impassibilità che Soseki decantava." Natsume Soseki (1867–1916) is one of Japan's greatest novelists. He lived during the early decades after the Meiji Restoration (1868) and was critical toward some aspects of the modernization of Japan being implemented under the Meiji regime. For Soseki, alienation is the bane of the Japanese individual torn between modernity and tradition.

48. *UL*, 367: "i primi tempi impazzivo al computer, perché potevo correggere con troppa facilità, non avevo più l'attrito delle parole di quando scrivevo a mano. L'intero testo si fa instabile. Proprio per questo però ti s'affina la sorveglianza mentale, impari a renderti conto all'istante dell'incidenza dei minimi particolari."

49. *UL*, 367: "docilmente permeabili, in modo neutro."

50. *UL*, 293: "sino a quando gli s'era spalancato davanti il vuoto della vecchiaia."

51. *UL*, 367: "Tu sei la mia ala di farfalla . . . perché sei tu che hai messo in moto questa storia."

52. *UL*, 343: "se non perdo un goccio, Alfonsina sarà in pace."

53. *UL*, 309: "non aveva mai convissuto più di due giorni con una donna."

54. *UL*, 320: "che esaltando la centralità del lavoro rende inevitabile l'isolamento dei vecchi."

55. *UL*, 19: "'Una società fondata sul mito della produzione non può che esautorare la vecchiaia improduttiva, nel momento in cui,' (gli venne una voce cadenzata da nenia) 'proprio per il suo *produttivismo* anche sanitario, questa stessa società *produce* molti vecchi. . . . Per me i condizionamenti sociali stanno a monte dell'aspetto morale del problema.' Dovevi pur tradire la tua matrice concettuale, pensò Silvana."

56. *UL*, 37: "sul piano culturale."

57. *UL*, 37–38: "Viviamo nell'era dell'eufemismo. Per carità!, vietato dire vecchi: la

parola è terza età. . . . Tutta una rimozione del decadimento del corpo, della fisicità della morte."

58. *UL*, 199: "cacare vicino a lei era il loro più grande atto d'amicizia."

59. *UL*, 199: "la fecondazione . . . [dagli] intestini. . . . separare il sesso dall'intimità vissuta."

60. *UL*, 340: "[s]e un morto puzza, io lo respiro come il futuro odore del mio cadavere."

61. *UL*, 340: "Sto con loro volentieri perché gli voglio bene. . . . li vivo. E vivo anche la loro morte."

62. *UL*, 421: "'Se mi ami' pronunciò la parola che non s'erano mai detti, 'dovrai amare la mia vecchiaia, dovrai amare la mia morte.'"

63. Cambria, "La vecchiaia, l'amore": "Il paradosso . . . sta nel fatto che la storia. . . . di due persone che si amano guardando in faccia vecchiaia e morte . . . sia insolita nella narrativa di una società come la nostra, che pure diventa ogni giorno più vecchia."

64. Ibid.: "una società di giovani nel fior degli anni, la cui morte appare, nei momenti della passione amorosa, tanto desiderabile quanto inverosimile."

65. Ibid.: "un romanzo in cui si muovono personaggi che sanno di invecchiare."

66. *UL*, 202: "Non sapeva ora perché aveva fretta d'andare a finire di leggere le pagine di Bruno, che aveva lasciato sedicenne nel lontano '49. Una vecchia storia che aveva ben pochi agganci con lei e che sembrava chiederle d'entrare a far parte della sua vita. Un passato non suo che le si stava accasando nei suoi pensieri d'oggi. Ma anche nei suoi pensieri d'ieri! Per quali vie, dagli anni Quaranta dello scritto di Bruno, il mio cervello è andato a ficcarsi nei casi miei degli anni Sessanta come non potesse muoversi da lì? Le facce di Luisa e di Fabio bambini mi si sono sovrapposte a quella del piccolo Bruno. . . . Però un acquisto c'era: da come Bruno aveva guardato se stesso, lei poteva capire qualcosa di più di quel quasi sessantenne dall'animo rimpiattato che le era divenuto intimo in poche ore."

67. *UL*, 50: "si sbucciano a vicenda."

68. *UL*, 54: "di ragazzi, ma di persone anziane, che al minimo spunto si tirano dietro l'universo, e non alla buona: con fare guardingo, tasteggiando il suolo col piede prima di posarlo."

69. *UL*, 21: "Bruno rimase a occhi fissi, come se stesse vedendo la vecchia e il figlio sulla montagna. Silvana gli versò dell'altro vino. Gli imbastì un discorsetto sul senso del sacro nella tradizione e subito si sentì scolastica. L'uomo la guardò ambiguamente: 'Vuole anziani dei nostri giorni?' e, prima che Silvana gli potesse rispondere, la introdusse in una casa di piacere per vecchi impotenti, 'nella cosmopolita Tokio d'oggi' disse."

70. *UL*, 82: "'Molto meglio adesso' rispose Bruno, 'possono innamorarsi senza essere derisi.' Non gli era piaciuto il tono un po' da entomologo di Silvana. 'Certo' disse lei e con voce improvvisamente vivace: 'Bruno, non mi ha parlato ancora di sua madre.' Cambia discorso, deve avercela con le cose del sesso, pensò Bruno, che rispose: 'Alfonsina ci tiene a far valere la sua indipendenza.'"

71. *UL*, 111: "Va controcorrente, ma nel suo guscio. La sua pietà per i vecchi è esistenziale (ricchi o poveri importa poco), è una pena sostanzialmente irreparabile (conosco quel dolore), a cui però—va detto—lei tiene testa. Nel comportamento con gli uomini (con me) tende al materno con spigoli di femminismo. E' affetta dal mito del giovanilismo che combatte: non solo elude l'erotismo dei vecchi (a sua insaputa le ripugna immaginarlo), ma non riesce a spogliarsi della coscienza di avere cinquant'anni. E' passionale ma non vuole. Si annega nel lavoro. Il solvente dei suoi garbugli interni è cristiano. Bruno sorrise, di colpo la durezza gli si spuntò nel pensare: e questo cocktail di prima mano (mescolato alla bene e meglio) è la sola donna con cui io abbia mai congetturato di poter convivere senza termine (la formula è: finché morte non ci separi)."

72. *UL*, 113: "'Sei tu che mi stai giudicando con queste parole.' Così dicendo, l'abito chiaro che lui indossava le parve ombrato sulla spalla e lo spolverò con le dita. Gesto di moglie pensò e disse: 'Bruno, io non ho mire sulla durata.' 'Le ho io per due.' Tornò sui suoi passi. Al ritorno le chiederò di presentarmi ai suoi genitori. Anche alla figlia e al genero. Chissà come mi guarderanno: quel rincitrullito che gli vuole impalmare la madre. E' prematuro. Silvana non lascerà mai il lavoro, il nipotino, i genitori, specialmente le gatte che nella mia capsula di Ginza soffocherebbero."

73. The Italian term *vetero*, derived from the Latin root for "old," is often used to describe people who hang on to the ideologies of the past, particularly Communist sympathizers and first-generation feminists. Interestingly, a different term, *nostalgico*, is applied to someone who looks back to Fascism.

74. *UL*, 51: "Sorrise: ti sarebbe piaciuta, proprio perché è una rompiscatole con la sua fissa dei vecchi. Figurati che crede ancora nella forza del risentimento! . . . A quel pensiero scoppiò di botto in una sonora risata: è matura per fondarci sopra la riscossa degli anziani uniti. E' una vetero! Nel ridere s'era fermato. Un'antimarxista a tutta prova che si cova dentro una vetero . . . Riprese a camminare. Com'è giovane rispetto a noi."

75. *UL*, 353: "Perché vive da 30 anni a Tokio? si diceva. . . . Tale lo sforzo nel cercare un senso comune a tutti (il comunismo) e la delusione dell'esser stato respinto, che è ribaltato nella situazione mentale (estraneità) dell'infanzia e della prima fanciullezza. Questa potrebbe essere una spiegazione (inconscia) di certi suoi geli. . . . Adesso mi rendo conto del perché io con lui divento eccessiva, come se dovessi controbilanciare il suo spasmodico self-control. Ma l'errore è suo: si è impegnato per gli altri credendo di raggiungere un risultato quaggiù!"

76. *UL*, 392: "'Buongiorno Silvana.' Bruno, vestito a puntino in completo grigio, le stava inginocchiato davanti: 'Sono le 6 e 34, alzati, io torno alle 8. Ho due giorni da stare con te, perché giovedì riprendo il lavoro. Oggi giriamo per Tokio in senso orario, in modo che tu abbia una visione d'insieme della città. Mentre sto fuori, chiama i tuoi genitori. Gli hai telefonato all'ultimo minuto che, invece d'andare a Parigi, partivi per Tokio! Staranno in pensiero. Chiama anche i tuoi figli. Trovi i prefissi per l'Italia e per la Germania su quel foglietto sul tavolo. A tra poco,' la baciò in fronte e uscì."

77. *UL*, 377–78: "'Adesso senti i progetti che avrei per noi: potremmo 1) comprare l'appartamento in cui abiti con le gatte; 2) aprire un qualcosa per i vecchi. Io vorrei continuare a scrivere e vorrei anche tradurre romanzi dal giapponese. Tu avrai il tuo lavoro. Se m'accetterai, t'aiuterò. . . . Chiediamo ai tuoi genitori di venire a vivere con noi, gli ripuliamo l'appartamento e tuo figlio ci potrà vivere con la sua compagna. Se poi ricompriamo l'appartamento dove vivono tua figlia tuo genero e il loro Giorgio, siamo tutti a posto e buona notte. Quando verrò per qualche giorno a Natale, sarebbe bene se tu mi presentassi alla tua famiglia.'"

78. *UL*, 421: "Silvana . . . pensava: ci vogliamo bene, sappiamo che non saremo soli da vecchi, possiamo ancora goderci un po' di libertà. Del resto lei aveva bisogno di tempo, per capire bene che genere di lavoro avrebbe svolto in avvenire con gli anziani: non più *su* loro, ma *con* loro (questo l'aveva capito)."

79. La Porta, "Romanzo morale ma molto impudico": "in modo appena sospeso, quasi casuale, nel mezzo di una cena, insieme ad un amico giapponese ex comunista."

80. *UL*, 441: "'Sarà felice, Osamu, glielo giuro, e poi non abiteremo lontani: potremo vederci spesso, vero Bruno?'"

81. *UL*, 441: "'Verrai a trovarmi a Mosca?' gli chiese Bruno e aggiunse: 'Vorrei che prima Silvana accettasse di sposarmi.'"

82. The poem is number LXXXIX in Dickinson's *Complete Poems*.

83. Gianini Belotti, *Apri le porte all'alba*, 148 (hereafter cited as *APA*): "i vecchi dormono poco, sono irrequieti e si alzano all'alba."

84. *APA*, 218: "stava là, in camicia da notte, a contemplare il suo orto con un sorriso trepido. 'Io mi piace guardare sole che nasce.'"
85. Lilli, "Per una vecchia zitella": "audace. . . . una donna anziana e sola, dai doveri scoloriti: scrivere una guida del Lazio per amatori e accudire il vecchio padre e le amiche naufraghe di matrimoni malriusciti."
86. Lilli, "Dalla parte delle nonnine": "una seconda, sapiente e consapevole adolescenza costruita al margine estremo della vita."
87. De Federicis, "Vite a perdere": "il racconto punta sulla tecnica del rovesciamento, catturando le attese del lettore e protraendole fino a una conclusione che è spesso aperta, a sorpresa."
88. Moroli, "Nasce dalla donna un nuovo genere letterario": "Mi sembra che le donne abbiano definitivamente inaugurato un nuovo genere letterario dove autobiografia, narrativa, militanza e saggistica si mescolano in modo armonioso." Gianini Belotti cites Kate Millet's *Flying* as an example of this new and still unestablished genre.
89. *APA*, 11: "Il risveglio della natura alla stagione prevista è una delle poche certezze che ci sono rimaste."
90. *APA*, 16: "'target' . . . di viaggiatori colti ed esigenti."
91. *APA*, 15: "un'angoscia sproporzionata."
92. *APA*, 16: "era la forza di quell'amore, la sua suprema fedeltà che mi sconvolgevano, quasi un melodramma zoologico avesse sbaragliato in un sol colpo lo scetticismo che credevo governasse saldamente la mia esistenza. Dunque, a mia insaputa, covavo nel profondo una nostalgia di sentimenti e passioni estreme. Amore e morte, uno schema da primitivi."
93. *APA*, 232: "Il prezzo che si paga per lo scetticismo è di restare sulla soglia a osservare ciò che accade all'interno. Il prezzo pagato per essere penetrata oltre la soglia era stato ben più alto."
94. *APA*, 15: "perfettamente identici di colore, di forma, di taglia."
95. *APA*, 19: "anziana coppia di rosei turisti nordici."
96. *APA*, 21: "perfetta fusione."
97. *APA*, 21: "rimpianto per una ricchezza che un tempo mi era stata strappata di mano."
98. *APA*, 61, 64: "Lanciavo una sfida insolente, non so a chi e perché, posseduta da uno sconfinato, ilare senso di liberazione, come se di altri lacci, chiusure e viluppi mi fossi alleggerita. Ho slacciato il secondo bottone della camicetta, ho allargato la scollatura e ci ho soffiato dentro, un soffio robusto che mi ha fatto accapponare la pelle. Dall'apertura esalava un tenue vapore dalla fragranza di mandarino, perciò vi ho ficcato il naso e mi sono annusata a più riprese con un piacere ingordo. Sotto la camicetta, la mia pelle irradiava una luminosità di corolla. . . . [I]n quell'aura di fanciullesca letizia, di gioco complice e di esultanza, io e quell'uomo avevamo continuato ad abbrancarci e a strofinarci finché non era esploso un fragoroso battimani."
99. *APA*, 119: "Ho capito . . . che non ho più l'età per gli eccessi, né la voglia di buttarmi a corpo morto a coltivare inutili romanticherie invece che un salutare distacco. Gliel'ho detto, per onestà, lui ha riso e ha ribattuto che non gliene importa un fico secco. Gli basta la gioia di avermi di tanto in tanto, quando vorrò. E credo proprio che vorrò. Non solo per la sua fervorosa devozione a coltivare ogni mia superficie . . . ma perché non ho sofferto la minima vergogna per il mio corpo sciupato. Anzi, me ne sono inorgoglita a tal punto che l'ho visto bello, sottile e solido come quando ero la ragazza che sono stata. Dopo che se n'è andato, ed era ormai giorno, mi sono guardata nuda allo specchio. Le gambe sono sempre state il mio forte. . . . Le cosce sono un po' assottigliate, come se il tempo le avesse prosciugate. Ho sempre deprecato, da giovane, il mio seno piccolo. . . . Ma da anziana . . . il mio si è conservato quasi intatto al suo posto."

100. *APA*, 230: "I corpi anziani, avevo talvolta pensato, devono emanare odori degenerati e decomposti perché il tempo corrompe gli umori. Annusavo me stessa e non notavo differenze. Può darsi che Ernesto fosse ancora troppo giovane per essere vecchio, oppure che l'olfatto, come gli altri sensi, col tempo si faccia meno acuto. Irene, per esempio, sostiene che le rughe sono un falso problema, la vista in vecchiaia fortunatamente si abbassa e perciò non le vediamo più."

101. *APA*, 207: "donne d'età."

102. *APA*, 170: "va benissimo per i commerci carnali, ma per la conversazione preferisco le amiche."

103. *APA*, 189: "idee chiare in testa . . . studiano, si preparano . . . sono curiose, interessate, vivaci, vitali. . . . dei bifolchi dal cervello chiuso che s'interessano solo di calcio."

104. *APA*, 189: "E' una mutazione antropologica in corso, le femmine vanno avanti, i maschi indietro. Sono i segnali della fine del patriarcato."

105. Lilli, "Per una vecchia zitella": "l'ultima declinazione narrativa italiana del vitalismo del soggetto femminile."

106. Cutrufelli, "Doris e le sue amiche": "nuovo nelle sue protagoniste."

107. Russo, "The Scandal of Anachronism," 21.

108. *APA*, 182, 186, 189: "Marta si era scavata una nicchia . . . tra una ragazza giovanissima dai capelli color carota e una sessantenne dalla candida chioma leonina. . . . Fissavo la sua bella faccia ironica ricamata di rughe. . . . una giovanissima dal viso tondo e abbronzato."

109. *APA*, 184: "una tana tra una ragazza mingherlina con la coda di cavallo e una cinquantenne dal sorriso smagliante e una selva di riccioli grigi sulla piccola testa smagliante."

110. *APA*, 252: "un gruppo colorato di giovani donne con i capelli al vento e gli zaini sulle spalle."

111. *APA*, 245: "Eravamo invecchiate e di quando in quando ce ne sorprendevamo come di un maleficio, ognuna di noi si sentiva ancora la ragazza che era stata. Di quella ragazza avevamo conservato la voce che ancora squillava come nella giovinezza, limpida, netta e ingannevole. 'Quando avverrà il cambiamento definitivo?' ci chiedevamo talvolta, 'quando arriverà a coincidere l'idea che abbiamo di noi stesse col nostro aspetto esteriore e ci sentiremo infine davvero vecchie dentro e fuori?' 'Mai,' rispondeva Irene spavalda, 'resteremo ragazze fino alla morte.'"

112. *APA*, 175: "potrebbe essere mia figlia . . . e mi trovo a sorridere con tenerezza pacificata al dorso arcuato della ragazza che scompare in mezzo alla folla."

113. *APA*, 175: "un'eventualità inconsistente, smarrita in un passato remoto fino all'irrealtà."

114. *APA*, 252: "chiassose e gentili, ridenti e tenere."

115. *APA*, 88: "Farò la nonna. . . . Mi lascerò invecchiare, è ora. Già avrà una madre un po' strana, questo bambino, che almeno la nonna, l'unica che gli sarà dato di avere . . . somigli a una vera nonna."

116. *APA*, 148: "due donne dell'Ottocento."

117. *APA*, 148: "la giovinezza è sempre spietata."

118. *APA*, 75: "l'omino. . . . implorante, le mani artigliate allo sterzo, la faccia sbiancata."

119. *APA*, 85: "vecchino segaligno dall'espressione stizzosa che avanzava a passettini strascicati, sostenuto dall'abbraccio robusto di un giovane nero."

120. *APA*, 100: "vecchia arcigna dall'animo schiavista."

121. *APA*, 104: "avvinghiata . . . [con] ingordigia."

122. *APA*, 179: "tavolate di anziani che banchettano."

123. *APA*, 93: "catatonici. . . . un plotone di rappresentanti della terza età . . . ben tenuti, ben vestiti e ben nutriti, dall'aria tra il patetico e il bellicoso."
124. *APA*, 65: "capelli bianchi tinti di azzurro, una collana a tre giri di perle intorno al collo."
125. *APA*, 105: "faccia torbida spaesata . . . avido braccio brancolante . . . passettini traballanti . . . il frutto degenere della cattività."
126. *APA*, 105: "Ho provato un impeto di affetto per la vecchia signora che non abdicava alla sua libertà. La sua esistenza mi ha rincuorato sul mio avvenire di analoga, inevitabile decadenza. Spero di essere impavida come lei, alla sua età. Lo sarò. . . . Devo esserlo, so di non poter contare che su me stessa, sulle amiche solo in casi estremi. Ma loro saranno vecchie quanto me, all'epoca."
127. *APA*, 227: "Aspettava il ritorno di Margarida. Aspettava anche me, nella bella stagione, seduto nello stesso posto, quando ero ragazza e tornavo a casa con l'autobus che era già notte. Aveva ritrovato una figlia, nella sua tarda età, e non ero io, era una ragazza nera vivace e affettuosa che confortava meglio di me la sua vecchiaia solitaria. Ero grata a Margarida e insieme provavo un senso straziante di fallimento. Devo imparare da lei, perché lei ne sa più di me, pensavo."
128. *APA*, 225: "sono ancora i neri, come al tempo della schiavitù, a presiedere alla nascita e alla morte dell'uomo bianco."
129. *APA*, 167: "sembrava in lei un talento nativo, spontaneo . . . virtù irrimediabilmente perduta da noi."
130. *APA*, 165: "l'arte di industriarsi con minime risorse."
131. *APA*, 239: "per fare un piacere a un ragazzo musulmano."
132. *APA*, 23: "l'invasione alla rovescia . . . una nemesi storica."
133. *APA*, 158: "Saremo modificati, trasformati da loro?"
134. *APA*, 244: "dichiarando quanto papà le fosse necessario, [Margarida] rovesciava in un colpo la mia visione delle cose."
135. *APA*, 244: "quando sopraggiunge qualcuno da fuori a intrecciare nuovi fili d'affetto, si è costretti a un passo indietro e di colpo lo scenario è inondato di luce."
136. *APA*, 217: "piramide di pannolini un tempo in agguato nella cassapanca. . . . Non sono riusciti a piegarmi alla loro idea della vita."
137. *APA*, 217–18: "pensato con la mia testa e non con la loro, nel bene come nel male."
138. *APA*, 42: "nella penombra livida."
139. *APA*, 35: "piano piano . . . si è ristretta, immiserita, ha perso autonomia."
140. *APA*, 90: "ospite, sperso e sconsolato."
141. *APA*, 89: "Qui ho tutte le mie cose."
142. *APA*, 203: "fare le stesse cose, salvo quelle più rumorose. . . . Sono provvisoria, qui, per semplice necessità."
143. *APA*, 51: "angustia di un'intera vita . . . risparmi infinitesimali, ossessivi e perfettamente inutili . . . cronica paura di un futuro a tinte fosche radicata in un passato di miseria e ristrettezze."
144. *APA*, 46: "si tagliava la punta, così le dita potevano uscire, ma col freddo gelavano."
145. *APA*, 47: "lugubre come un carro da morto, sferragliante come un trattore."
146. *APA*, 49: "il ferro a carbonella . . . sputava cenere dai buchi e macchiava la biancheria."
147. *APA*, 52: "La furia contenuta a stento quando, con gesti e toni da vittima sacrificale, mi aveva condotto in camera da letto, aveva aperto un cassetto e mi aveva mostrato una pila ordinata di capi di biancheria nuovi di zecca. 'Se mi ammalo,' aveva detto, 'e devo andare all'ospedale, mi devi mettere la biancheria nuova, non voglio fare

brutta figura.' Non ce n'era stato il tempo, si era sentita male all'improvviso, papà mi aveva telefonato, balbettando parole sconnesse, ero corsa là, avevo chiamato il medico che aveva ordinato il ricovero immediato. . . . Indossava una vecchia camicia da notte in flanella lisa e rattoppata. . . . Devo cambiarla, ho pensato, devo farlo, me lo ha chiesto. . . . Papà stava in piedi a fissarci in un angolo, muto, spaventato, mordendosi un labbro. E poi era arrivata l'ambulanza, due infermieri rudi e sbrigativi l'avevano caricata così com'era sulla barella, non c'è tempo, è grave, hanno risposto alla mia richiesta, e uno ha detto: 'Ma cosa le salta in mente? E' urgente, non vede che sta malissimo?' E rivolgendosi al collega: 'Ma tu guarda un po' a che cosa va a pensare la gente.' Durante il percorso le ho parlato di continuo, l'ho accarezzata, le ho tenuto una mano sulla fronte gelata. Lei si lamentava e non rispondeva, forse nemmeno mi sentiva. Ma a un tratto ha mormorato: 'La biancheria.' 'Stai tranquilla,' ho mentito, 'ti ho messo quella nuova.'"

148. *APA*, 53: "spaurito come un bambino."

149. *APA*, 55: "m'irrigidisco, gli artigli sfoderati, pronta a difenderlo alla minima offesa."

150. Two such narratives are the already mentioned *La cattiva figlia* by Cerati, and Sanvitale's *Madre e figlia*.

151. *APA*, 45: "marchio esplicito di discendenza."

152. *APA*, 45: "Ho riconosciuto il mio stesso nodo gonfio e arrossato all'alluce del piede sinistro. . . . Da ragazza . . . mi vergognavo di portare i sandali e, risentita, dentro di me incolpavo papà di avermi trasmesso proprio quel difetto."

153. *APA*, 51: "Raccolgo anch'io a una a una le briciole di pane dalla tovaglia e me le metto in bocca, così come spengo la luce ogni volta che esco da una stanza, e ogni volta mi detesto."

154. *APA*, 225: "Noi abbiamo fallito, accumuliamo pretese, aspettative, fraintendimenti per intere esistenze e così diveniamo incapaci delle cose più semplici e naturali. Abbiamo fatto sì che i vecchi si spostino via via ai margini e svaniscano nel nulla senza procurarci intralci e fastidi e senza lasciare traccia di sé. Così la loro memoria, invece di addolcirci lo spirito, ci procura solo rimorsi e sensi di colpa."

155. *APA*, 247: "'Dobbiamo tornare spesso a trovare tuo padre,' ha detto Marta. 'Perché ce l'hai tenuto nascosto tutto questo tempo? Nessuna di noi ha più un padre, è un privilegio che devi dividere con noi. Una vecchiaia come la sua è un incoraggiamento per il nostro futuro che si avvicina a grandi passi. Mi conforta pensare che lui c'è, è qui, ci accoglie nel suo modo schivo ma pieno di benevolenza, E poi questo posto rimasto intatto, incapsulato come un isolotto nel mare dei palazzoni, l'orto, le rose, gli oleandri, dove mai si trovano più?'"

CHAPTER 6. A CASE STUDY

1. Passerini, *La fontana della giovinezza*, 126 (hereafter cited as *FG*): "un ibrido, tra apologo e narrazione, tra ricognizione di storia culturale e osservazione del presente."

2. For a better understanding of Passerini's notion of generation, see Mannheim's essay "The Problem of Generations." According to Mannheim, a generation is not to be defined chronologically but is constituted of people who "participate in the characteristic social and intellectual currents of their society and period" (304). Since youth is the life stage when "new, formative forces are just coming into being, and basic attitudes in the process of development can take advantage of the moulding power of new situations" (ibid., 296), the passage from youth to adulthood is the time when individuals are most receptive to their socio-political context and most likely to question and break away from the legacy of the previous generation.

3. See Bartolini, "Luisa Passerini e la sua *Fontana della giovinezza*."
4. *FG*, 19: "riacciuffare luoghi come le vecchie osterie e le loro sensazioni."
5. Passerini, presentation, Libreria Campus: "insieme a loro, è invecchiato clamorosamente tutto un mondo di pensieri e di speranze."
6. The American essays and autobiographies concerned with aging- and gender-related issues Passerini mentions in her endnotes are: Kuhn, *No Stone Unturned*; Sarton, *After the Stroke*; Grumbach, *Coming into the End Zone*; Greer, *The Change*; Friedan, *The Fountain of Age*; Heilbrun, *The Last Gift of Time*; Walker, *The Crone*; and Gullette's already mentioned essay *Declining to Decline*. De Beauvoir's pioneering cultural-history essay on old age is *La vieillesse*, published in English with the title *The Coming of Age*.
7. De Federicis, "Generazioni": "il cuore dell'*Autoritratto* stava . . . nel rapporto fra individuale e collettivo, fra il diario privato e il contesto storico che ne legittimava l'impudicizia; nella *Fontana*, invece, l'individuale è prevalso e il cuore tematico è nel rapporto di ciascuno con la propria ultima destinazione."
8. Passerini, presentation, Libreria Campus: "appunti che buttavo giù, scrivendo già sempre alla terza persona, come se avessi bisogno di staccarmi dalle mie esperienze . . . molte erano le cose che mi venivano raccontate nella quotidianeità da amiche che vivevano questa esperienza che io non ho vissuto di vedere il proprio compagno andare verso una donna più giovane e averne un figlio." In the "Ringraziamenti" at the end of the book Passerini also recalls Grazia Cherchi's advice after the publication of *Autoritratto di gruppo*, that next time she wrote about "questo genere di cose," she should do it in the third person.
9. *FG*, 126: "[i] racconti di alcune donne che a più riprese mi hanno narrato parti della loro vita, in una pratica informale della storia orale."
10. See chapter "The Desire for One's Story" in Cavarero, *Relating Narratives*, 32–47.
11. *FG*, 121: "colpo di vecchiaia."
12. *FG*, 120. The quote from Glück's poem is in English. The title of the poem is "Vita Nova"; it appears in *Vita Nova*, 1.
13. *FG*, 18: "feroce noia."
14. *FG*, 33: "finché non finisce il peggio."
15. *FG*, 120: "piccole cose."
16. *FG*, 111: "consapevolezza che intride il corpo."
17. *FG*, 92: "nuova militanza."
18. *FG*, 119: "una sacralità laica."
19. *FG*, 18: "rigurgiti di piccoli eventi inosservati durante il giorno, ma che prendevano improvvisamente contorni definiti e . . . chiamavano vendetta o riparazione . . . esigevano da lei che il giorno dopo telefonasse per cambiare programma."
20. *FG*, 13: "grande lavoro, di corsa."
21. *FG*, 18: "una lentezza a rendersi conto di molte cose, come se ci fosse un diaframma tra lei e la realtà."
22. *FG*, 71: "Tornare ripetutamente agli stessi luoghi dava luogo a stratificazioni successive: quante volte era stata a Parigi, dai primi anni Sessanta in poi, così carica di speranze di incontri e comunicazione."
23. *FG*, 81–82: "Tornò infine in Europa e si fermò per alcuni giorni nella città in cui era vissuta negli anni Settanta. Tra quei giorni c'era un primo maggio e, dopo qualche esitazione . . . passò dalla piazza dove stavano terminando i comizi. Si infilò tra i gruppetti che indugiavano . . . ricordando pezzi sbocconcellati di altri primi maggio. . . . Ora quei primi maggio si confondevano tutti, in un miscuglio di immagini della memoria cui si sovrapponevano le fotografie prese in varie occasioni."
24. *FG*, 18: "diviso a fette."

25. *FG*, 72: "non riusciva più a reggere i contorni degli spostamenti."

26. *FG*, 45: "Un mobile che quasi non vedeva più le appariva ripugnante per la sua consunta logora inutilità e se fosse stata più giovane se ne sarebbe liberata."

27. *FG*, 49: "Lei guardò con leggera pena quei vecchi mobili ed elettrodomestici, goffi e non più nascosti negli anfratti della casa che li aveva ospitati per tanto tempo. Altri, sistemati nella casa nuova e imbiancata di fresco, mostravano finalmente la loro vecchiezza. Le persone possono andare avanti senza di noi, le venne da pensare, le cose no: senza nessuno che si prenda continuamente cura di loro, si deteriorano e scompaiono."

28. *FG*, 14: "aspetti del suo corpo."

29. *FG*, 32: "se lei e il sapone fossero entrambi durati fino all'estate, la fine del sapone sarebbe coincisa con la chiusura di quel periodo difficile e l'apertura delle vacanze."

30. *FG*, 56: "una prova generale della morte."

31. *FG*, 30: "piccole morti."

32. *FG*, 30–31: "Il film le aveva presentato ciò che oscuramente temeva, non lo stato attuale che, fosse pure di deiezione, conteneva ancora autonomia e autosufficienza, ma quello vicino allo stato estremo della decrepitezza, la vecchiaia relegata in istituti specializzati, ghetti ritagliati ai margini della quotidianeità corrente. . . . Per ora provava gratitudine di essere in un letto la notte, in una stanza protetta; non era affatto scontato che fosse così, e temeva che questa relativa sicurezza potesse finire."

33. *FG*, 83: "Andò a trovare alcune donne molto anziane, superando il timore che aveva della vecchiaia estrema, e che si affacciava ogni tanto sotto forma di ansia per il futuro. Quando fosse stata in pensione, si trovava a pensare, non avrebbe più potuto permettersi di prendere taxi, di comprarsi creme costose per la faccia—e lei non aveva risparmiato, era vissuta come una cicala in tutti i sensi."

34. *FG*, 12: "Guidando verso l'ufficio si trovò a pensare che invecchiare era un po' come quando il treno entra in galleria che è ancora chiaro e ne esce che è già crepuscolo, e la cima delle colline si staglia su uno sfondo quasi bianco, ma poco sopra l'azzurro è già cupo sotto la luna trasparente dell'ultimo quarto. Era accaduto improvvisamente, come se si fosse distratta un momento."

35. *FG*, 15: "di essere incappata in un vuoto di coscienza."

36. *FG*, 28: "Giovane è chi è nato in un assetto simile a quello che lo circonda, chi riconosce automaticamente l'ambiente. E' il senso del mancato riconoscimento, di essere straniero al proprio habitat attuale rispetto a quello della propria infanzia e adolescenza, che dà il senso dell'invecchiare."

37. *FG*, 56: "la consapevolezza della propria inattualità."

38. *FG*: "interi mondi."

39. *FG*, 70: "la fine dei luoghi."

40. *FG*, 83: "fuori luogo."

41. *FG*, 50: "dove collocare la propria vecchiaia."

42. *FG*, 48: "seta e avorio un tempo erano stati simboli del valore positivo della vecchiaia, perché col tempo prendevano valore . . . ma forse oggi, quando prevaleva sempre il nuovo, non era più così."

43. *FG*, 14: "una nuova generazione, più leggera e spensierata."

44. *FG*, 44: "anche per l'invecchiamento c'era stata modernizzazione e tecnologizzazione, che comprendeva elettrodomestici e vitamine, chirurgia plastica e vestiti vivaci."

45. *FG*, 70: "atmosfera da strapaese."

46. *FG*, 71: "è una tendenza globale verso la fiera, e figurati se noi gay non ci sguazziamo."

47. *FG*, 89: "mercato [della] . . . giovanilità."
48. *FG*, 20: "MENOPAUSA, CHE PASSIONE! ETA' DI PAURE? ETA' DELL'ORO!!!"
49. *FG*, 26: "idolatria del femminile . . . autodecorazione, autoesibizione, autoammirazione."
50. *FG*, 25: "Narcisismo era stato il compiacimento tremebondo per il proprio corpo, e il desiderio sessuale era stato indotto e governato dal piacere di adornarsi con calze, scarpe, gioielli e innanzitutto reggiseni reggicalze mutandine giarrettiere guépières, di tutti i colori e specialmente neri. . . . C'era un istante, quando era perfettamente pronta, che il tempo si fermava sull'immagine trionfante del corpo allestito per essere ammirato e ammirarsi, e pareva che i capelli i peli e le unghie non crescessero più e addirittura non potessero sporcarsi, un istante di immobilità assoluta, sotto lo sguardo proprio e altrui."
51. *FG*, 12: "non le proprie fattezze ma quelle di sua nonna."
52. Woodward, *Aging and Its Discontents*, 68.
53. *FG*, 32: "mancanza . . . del maschile."
54. *FG*, 32: "fal-logo, centro erotico del discorso ormai incerto tra maschio e femmina."
55. *FG*, 69: "lunga permanenza nel neutro."
56. *FG*, 77: "A Santa Cruz prese un autobus verso l'università, convinta che fosse una navetta interna al campus. L'autista la richiamò per farle pagare il biglietto e lei si confuse a cercare i soldi. Il giovane uomo la guardava come se fosse affetta da demenza senile. . . . Si rese conto che era stata classificata in un'età più vecchia della sua—a causa non solo dei capelli grigi ma della sua agitazione e confusione, comportamenti che in presenza di segni di giovinezza sarebbero stati interpretati altrimenti."
57. *FG*, 9: "scandalo . . . sfidare le leggi del tempo . . . impunemente . . . andare lontano per inseguire la giovinezza sotto forma di giovane donna."
58. *FG*, 9: "dal mondo che avevano condiviso."
59. *FG*, 24: "tra i rigurgiti di ciò che sarebbe potuto essere e non era stato."
60. *FG*, 22: "vecchie che ricordava dalla sua infanzia."
61. *FG*, 118: "in abiti quattrocenteschi . . . lussuosi e importanti . . . la guardavano dal balcone del vecchio edificio dove avevano abitato per decenni . . . non dal quarto piano, come era stato nella realtà, bensì dal primo. . . . come spia della sua minore distanza dai morti."
62. *FG*, 118: "poteva essere richiamato da elenchi di nomi come quelli del papiro della sua amica artista o anche solo dall'atteggiamento di pietas verso il proprio passato. . . . [nonché dal] rapporto con la morte sereno e consapevole delle vecchie e antiche donne."
63. Woodward points to an alternative to the Lacanian "mirror stage of old age," which she derives from D. W. Winnicot's theories. Although an individual may reject her aging body, she may "find the strength to accept it through a kind of familiarity with its images reflected in the bodies of generations older" (*Aging and Its Discontents*, 71).
64. *FG*, 88: "il suo rapporto con questi giovani non era materno/filiale. . . . due tradizioni di discorso."
65. *FG*, 113: "una sfida alla generazione delle madri femministe."
66. *FG*, 85: "il diritto al sentimento."
67. *FG*, 29: "privo di entusiasmo e di curiosità nel lavoro . . . e come indebolito nella lotta quotidiana."
68. *FG*, 71: "venir meno delle passioni."
69. *FG*, 103: "curvo e rugoso . . . scintillante e paradossale."

70. *FG*, 104: "un po' rigida nel recepire il complimento. . . . nel gioco e nella confusione dell'addio."

71. *FG*, 116: "il retaggio del passato . . . l'avevano gettata fuori di sé, verso gli altri. Ma ora prevalevano le emozioni e il rapporto con se stessa."

72. *FG*, 111: "adesso gli veniva spontaneo vedere il futuro attraverso occhi femminili e in certo modo aprirsi al femminile."

73. *FG*, 111: "rivoluzione del sentire."

74. *FG*, 77: "una seconda vita."

75. *FG*, 89: "a scrutare le possibilità di rivoluzione, come per un riflesso condizionato. . . . i soggetti del cambiamento."

76. *FG*, 93: "dove una giovane donna, ferma sicura e ridente, aiuta una donna più vecchia a entrare nell'acqua."

77. *FG*, 119: "Camminando verso casa le parve per un lampo di tempo che l'aspettasse una presenza, ma subito ricordò che non era così e richiamò indietro, dalla casa a se stessa, quella sensazione. La presenza, che si era profilata quasi per uno scatto automatico, per un'abitudine meccanica che risorgeva dopo molti anni, era una figura dai contorni molto vaghi: la madre? la nonna? un uomo? . . . Ora invece quella presenza era interna—come un sentimento di conciliazione—stava quasi diventando una consuetudine quotidiana."

78. *FG*, 121: "un potere che derivasse dalla conoscenza di molte cose."

79. *FG*, 90: "una certa futilità." This is a reference to Heilbrun, *The Last Gift of Time*, 8. Heilbrun ultimately carried out her plan at age 77, and committed suicide in October 2003.

80. *FG*, 91: "un eccesso di fiducia."

81. Friedan, *The Fountain of Age*, 638.

82. *FG*, 92: "insufficiente riconoscimento del lutto che l'invecchiamento comportava."

83. *FG*, 103: "Che cosa era cambiato? Apparentemente non vedeva cambiamenti rilevanti. Provava un senso di sollievo, come se avesse mollato la presa—su che cosa? Forse sui rimpianti—ne aveva ancora, ma li vedeva come staccati da sé. Aveva lasciato perdere alcune ambizioni—a tutti i costi fare, contestare e protestare oppure promuovere ed essere promossa, basta! Se perdere tutto questo era il prezzo dell'invecchiare, le pareva che ci fosse anche qualche piccolo guadagno: ricuperare briciole di piacere di vivere."

84. *FG*, 102: "pagliuzze di allegria da ragazza."

85. For a discussion of green-world archetypes in both adolescent and mature protagonists' self-definition journeys, see Pratt, *Archetypal Patterns in Women's Fiction*.

86. *FG*, 104: "equanime distacco."

87. *FG*, 107: "dell'ultima o penultima fase della vita . . . un senso di completamento come nell'arrivare a chiudere un cerchio, una soddisfazione maggiore o preferibile a quella che deriva dal raggiungere un punto fisso dopo un percorso lineare o in ascesa, come la vetta di una montagna, da cui comunque bisognerà scendere."

88. *FG*, 110: "la dimensione lineare del tempo [è quella] che alla fine ha la meglio—con la morte . . . c'è anche un'altra dimensione, un'altra forma del tempo dove le cose vanno e vengono e ritornano con movimenti a spirale."

89. *FG*, 110.: "ci sono varie vecchiaie."

90. The term "autogoverno delle stagioni" was used by the journalist Gad Lerner at the book presentation at the Libreria Campus.

91. Piccone Stella, "Un decennio senza cittadinanza," 80: "Siamo disposte anche . . . a passare dalla maturità alla vecchiaia in una notte, ma non a camminare guardando. . . . Dopo tutto sono detestati i capelli grigi, mentre il bianco candido si accetta."

92. *FG*, 59: "consentir[e] qualche scoperta."
93. *FG*, 114: "allestimento del corpo . . . varie forme di lavoro corporale."
94. Virginia Woolf refers to diaristic writing as a way of leaving a legacy to one's "older self": "I fancy this old Virginia putting on her spectacles to read of March 1920 will decidedly wish me to continue. Greetings! my dear ghost; & take heed that I don't think 50 a very great age (9 March 1920)" (*The Diary of Virginia Woolf*, vol. 2, 24); "[T]his diary is to serve the purpose of my memoirs. At 60 I am to sit down & write my life (8 February 1926)" (*The Diary of Virginia Woolf*, vol. 3, 57–58).
95. *FG*, 50: "una piccola casa per sé e le sue cose."
96. *FG*, 48: "immagine di una donna vecchissima—neanche più rassomigliante alla se stessa attuale—che considerava quei simulacri di un passato molto lontano e grazie ad essi vi tornava per qualche attimo . . . gli occhi di quella vegliarda avrebbero ridato un ultimo senso a quegli indumenti."
97. *FG*, 76: "Invecchiare da soli sembrava voler dire rinunciare a tutto questo—il venire meno della speranza, sempre alimentata in un piccolo angolo di sé, che quel mondo condiviso riapparisse in qualche forma."
98. *FG*, 87: "nel contesto di una massa in movimento."
99. *FG*, 10: "capire in quale acqua immergersi."
100. *FG*, 41: "forte e ancora temibile, ancorché allo stremo."
101. *FG*, 65: "quattro direzioni . . . del cammino degli esseri umani sulla terra."
102. This myth appears in Ovid's *Metamorphoses*, Book VIII.
103. *FG*, 101: "come madre, ma come compagna."
104. *FG*, 101: "riconciliazione con se stessi e con il destino di essere vecchi."
105. *FG*, 101: "facce abbronzate da contadini."
106. *FG*, 114: "[r]estare fedeli. . . . al nuovo, alle possibilità di apertura."
107. Passerini, presentation, Libreria Campus: "per non rischiare di trasmettere solo racconti da reduci e storie nostalgiche."

Conclusion

1. See Brunelli," I sani anni della folle saggezza."
2. The first draft of the manuscript of *Una donna* was completed in 1902; the book was published in its final version in 1906. Aleramo's diaries were published in two volumes: *Dal mio diario* in 1945, and *Diario di una donna* in 1978. The first part of Aleramo's diaries was edited by Alba Morino and published by Feltrinelli in 1979 with the title *Un amore insolito*.
3. See Frullini, "La vecchiaia attraverso lo sguardo dei bambini," 89–134; Paltera, "'Ti racconto uno, mille nonni," 135–65; and Spedicato, "Il 'sapere' dei bambini e la vecchiaia," 167–95.
4. The Association De Banfield also asked Italian authors to donate short stories featuring older characters. In 1995, these short stories were collected and published in the volume *Tra le rughe*, the proceeds from which went to benefit the association.
5. See Tamanza, "Fili d'argento a colori."
6. See Wyatt-Brown, "The Future of Literary Gerontology," 48–54.
7. Woodward, "Reminiscence and the Life Review," 153, 160.
8. Gubrium and Holstein, "Narrative Practice and the Coherence of Personal Stories." In his prize-winning discussion of nursing home residents' narratives, Gubrium also concludes that the life narrative is "the subjectively constructed life" and is as fictional as any autobiography or biography (*Speaking of Life*, 178).

Works Cited

Abramovitz, Mimi. *Regulating the Lives of Women: Social Welfare Policy from Colonial Times to the Present.* Boston: South End Press, 1996.

Achenbaum, W. Andrew. "Foreword: Literature's Value in Gerontological Research." In Bagnell and Soper, *Perceptions of Aging in Literature*, xiii–xxii.

———. "Historical Perspective on Aging." In *Handbook of Aging and the Social Sciences*, edited by Robert H. Binstock and Linda K. George, 4th ed., 137–52. San Diego: Academic Press, 1996.

Aleramo, Sibilla. *Un amore insolito: Diario 1940–1944.* Edited by Alba Morino. Milan: Feltrinelli, 1979.

———. *Dal mio diario: 1940–1944.* Rome: Tuminelli, 1945.

———. *Diario di una donna: Inediti 1945–1960.* Edited by Alba Morino. Milan: Feltrinelli, 1978.

———. *Una donna.* Milan: Feltrinelli, 1973. Translated by Rosalind Delmar as *A Woman* (Berkeley: University of California Press, 1983).

Amabile, Lepri, and Masci. "Il nonno mantiene una famiglia su quattro." *La Stampa*, June 13, 2000, 1.

Améry, Jean. *On Aging: Revolt and Resignation.* Translated by John D. Barlow. Bloomington: Indiana University Press, 1994.

"Anche gli anziani vanno a scuola." *Terzaet@News*, April 3, 2000. http://www.terzaeta.com/news.

"Ancora un concorso." *Margherita* 23 (1911): 359.

Antonini, Francesco. "L'età della maturità: Nuove idee sulla vecchiaia." Keynote address, L'anziano protagonista nella città e nella società, Centro Congressi, Turin, May 24–25, 1999.

L'anziano massa. Supplement of *Il manifesto*, November 13, 1983, I–IV.

Arru, Angiolina. "Protezione e legittimazione: Come si usa il mestiere di serva nell'Ottocento." In Ferrante, Palazzi, and Pomata, *Ragnatele di rapporti*, 381–416.

———. *I servi e le serve.* Bologna: Il Mulino, 1988.

Associazione Goffredo De Banfield, ed. *I nonni secondo i ragazzi delle scuole di Trieste.* Udine: Campanotto editore, 1993.

———. *Tra le rughe: Storie di nonni che si fanno ricordare.* Trieste: LINT, 1995.

Baccini, Ida. *Il the delle cinque.* Milan: Agnelli, 1900.

———. "Le vinte: Le vecchie." *Cordelia* 8 (1902): 86.

Bagnell, Priska von Dorotka, and Patricia Spencer Soper, eds. *Perceptions of Aging in Literature: A Cross-Cultural Study.* Westport, CT: Greenwood Press, 1989.

Banner, Lois. *In Full Flower: Aging Women, Power, and Sexuality.* New York: Knopf, 1992.

Banti, Anna. *Un grido lacerante.* Milan: Rizzoli, 1981. Translated by Daria Valentini as *A Piercing Cry* (New York: Lang, 1996).

Barbagli, Marzio. "Asymmetry in Intergenerational Family Relationships in Italy." In *Aging and Generational Relations: Life-Course and Cross-Cultural Perspectives,* edited by Tamara K. Hareven, 139–55. New York: De Gruyter, 1996.

———. *Sotto lo stesso tetto: Mutamenti della famiglia in Italia dal XV al XX secolo.* Bologna: Il Mulino, 1984.

Barberi Squarotti, Giorgio. "Luce D'Eramo pallida luna: Negli inferni della vecchiaia." Review of *Ultima luna,* by L. D'Eramo. *Tuttolibri,* supplement of *La Stampa,* January 15, 1994, 2.

Bartolini, Simonetta. "Luisa Passerini e la sua *Fontana della giovinezza.*" Review of *La fontana della giovinezza,* by L. Passerini. *Il giornale della Toscana,* January 26, 2000, 6.

Bedford, Victoria. "A Comparison of Thematic Apperceptions of Sibling Affiliation, Conflict, and Separation at Two Periods of Adulthood." *International Journal of Aging and Human Development* 1 (1989): 53–66.

Bellassai, Sandro, et al. *Vivencia: Conoscere la vita da una generazione all'altra.* Turin: Rosenberg & Sellier, 2003.

Bellow, Saul. *Mr. Sammler's Planet.* New York: Viking Press, 1964.

Bini, Luigi. "L'immagine dell'anziano nel cinema d'oggi." *Devianza e emarginazione* 6 (1985): 7–24.

Bobbio, Norberto. *De senectute e altri scritti autobiografici.* Turin: Einaudi, 1996.

Bocca, Giorgio. "La carne e lo spirito." *La Repubblica,* January 11, 2000, 1.

Bocolan Parisi, Lia, Marta Bosi, and Marta Ghezzi. *Bisogni, opportunità, servizi per la terza età.* Rome: La Nuova Italia Scientifica, 1992.

Bonomi, Ida. "Le non maritate." *Critica sociale,* March 5, 1895, 74.

Boralevi, Antonella. "Nonne in carriera: Ricerche e storie di vita vissuta dicono che sesso e successo sono per chi sa invecchiare." *L'Europeo* 35 (1993): 68–71.

Bossi Fedrigotti, Isabella. *Di buona famiglia.* Milan: Longanesi, 1991.

Botelho, Lynn, and Pat Thane, eds. *Women and Ageing in British Society since 1500.* Harlow: Longman, 2001.

Braidotti, Rosi. *Nomadic Subjects: Embodiment and Sexual Difference in Contemporary Feminist Theory.* New York: Columbia University Press, 1994.

———. "The Politics of Ontological Difference." In *Between Feminism and Psychoanalysis,* edited by Teresa Brennan, 96–110. London: Routledge, 1989.

Brunelli, Maria. "I sani anni della folle saggezza." *Il Giornale,* March 22, 1993, 5.

Bunyan, John. *The Pilgrim's Progress.* New York: Books, Inc., 1945.

Butler, Robert. "The Life Review: An Interpretation of Reminiscence in the Aged." *Psychiatry* 26 (1963): 65–76.

Buzzi-Donato, Alessandro. *Vediamo passare le stelle: Storie di vita di donne anziane sole.* Milan: Servizi Statistici del Comune, 1992.

Cambria, Adele. "La vecchiaia, l'amore." Interview with L. D'Eramo. *Il Giorno,* November 7, 1993, 16.

Cather, Willa. *The Professor's House.* New York: Knopf, 1925.

Cavarero, Adriana. *Tu che mi guardi, tu che mi racconti: Filosofia della narrazione.* Milan: Feltrinelli, 1997. Translated by Paul A. Kottman as *Relating Narratives: Storytelling and Selfhood* (London: Routledge, 2000).

Cavigioli, Rita. *La fatica di iniziare il libro: Problemi di autorità nei diari di Sibilla Aleramo.* Alessandria: Edizioni dell'Orso, 1995.
Cecconi, Massimo. "Vivere alla grande? Note su cinema e vecchiaia." *Marginalità e società* 16 (1990): 85–107.
Cerati, Carla. *La cattiva figlia.* Piacenza: Frassinelli, 1990.
Cervantes Saavedra, Miguel de. *The Adventures of Don Quixote.* Translated by J. M. Cohen. London: Penguin Books, 1954.
Cesa Bianchi, Marcello. *Giovani per sempre.* Bari: Laterza, 1998.
Chew, Samuel. *The Pilgrimage of Life.* New Haven: Yale University Press, 1962.
Cialente, Fausta. *Le quattro ragazze Wieselberger.* Milan: Mondadori, 1976.
Cicero, Marcus Tullius. *De senectute, De amicitia, De divinatione.* Translated by William A. Falconer. London: Heinemann, 1923.
Cicirelli, Victor. *Sibling Relationships Across the Life Span.* New York: Plenum Press, 1995.
Cole, Jean M., ed. *Handbook on Women and Aging.* Westport, CT: Greenwood Press, 1997.
Cole, Thomas. *The Journey of Life: A Cultural History of Aging in America.* Cambridge: Cambridge University Press, 1992.
———, ed. *Voices and Visions of Aging: Toward a Critical Gerontology.* New York: Springer, 1993.
Cole, Thomas, and Sally Gadow, eds. *What Does It Mean to Grow Old? Reflections from the Humanities.* Durham, NC: Duke University Press, 1986.
Cole, Thomas, Robert Kastenbaum, and Ruth Ray, eds. *Handbook of the Humanities and Aging.* 2nd ed. New York: Springer, 2000.
Cole, Thomas, David Van Tassel, and Robert Kastenbaum, eds. *Handbook of the Humanities and Aging.* 1st ed. New York: Springer, 1992.
Cole, Thomas, and Mary Winkler, eds. *The Oxford Book of Aging.* Oxford: Oxford University Press, 1994.
Colitta, Maria Teresa, and Matilde Panier Bagat. "Gli anziani: Rimpianti e progetti." *Rivista di servizio sociale* 3 (1985): 78–88.
Colombi, Marchesa. *La gente per bene.* Turin: Giornale delle donne, 1877.
Colombo, Furio. "Il mito perduto della giovinezza." *La Repubblica*, June 28, 1999, 31.
Commissione Nazionale per la Parità e le Pari Opportunità. *Quaderni rosa: Elettrici ed elette*, under *Il sito delle streghe*, October 30, 1998. http://www.geocities.com/~tesorino/Il_sito_delle_streghe/p_società.html.
Comune di Roma. Centro studi servizi per enti non profit. "Contro la solitudine . . . meglio la TV." *Sportello etico*, June 16, 2002. http://www.sportelloetico.com/testi/novita/testi6/emegliolatv.htm.
Condorelli, Luigi. "L'elisir di lunga vita." *La nuova scienza* 11 (1990): 64–69.
Coopmans, Marianne. "How Do Older Women Fare in the European Community?" *Ageing International* 16, no. 1 (1990): 38–42.
Coordinamento Nazionale delle Democratiche di Sinistra. "Le età delle donne: In viaggio tra talenti, passioni e libertà." *Più Donne Più*, October 5, 2002. http://www.dsonline.it/partito/aree/donne/inviaggio/età_donne.htm.
Cravenna Brigola, Maddalena. "L'inestimabile beneficio della longevità." *L'azione muliebre* 1 (1923): 14.
Crepaldi, Gaetano, and Stefania Maggi. "Italy." In *Developments and Research on Aging*, edited by Erdman B. Palmore, 187–200. London: Greenwood Press, 1993.

Crispino, Anna Maria, ed. *L'età inventata.* Special issue, *Leggendaria* 15/16 (1999): 4–17.

Cutrufelli, Maria Rosa. "Doris e le sue amiche: Le figure femminili di Elena Gianini Belotti." Review of *Apri le porte all'alba,* by E. Gianini Belotti. *Diario della settimana* 4, no. 9 (1999): 66.

D'Annunzio, Gabriele. *Il fuoco.* Milan: Fratelli Treves, 1909.

D'Eramo, Luce. *Deviazione.* Milan: Mondadori, 1979.

———. *Nucleo zero.* Milan: Mondadori, 1981.

———. *Partiranno.* Milan: Mondadori, 1986.

———. *Ultima luna.* Milan: Mondadori, 1993.

Dauphin, Cécile. "Single Women." Translated by Arthur Goldhammer. In Fraisse and Perrot, *Emerging Feminism from Revolution to World War,* 427–42.

De Beauvoir, Simone. *The Coming of Age.* Translated by Patrick O' Brian. New York: Putnam, 1972.

De Federicis, Lidia. "Generazioni." Review of *La fontana della giovinezza,* by L. Passerini. *L'indice dei libri del mese* 4 (2000): 6.

———. "Vite a perdere." Review of *Adagio un poco mosso,* by E. Gianini Belotti. *L'indice dei libri del mese* 11 (1993): 7.

De Giorgio, Michela. *Le italiane dall'Unità a oggi.* Bari: Laterza, 1992.

———. "Raccontare un matrimonio moderno." In *Storia del matrimonio,* edited by Michela De Giorgio, Christiane Klapisch-Zuber, and Marina Beer, 307–90. Bari: Laterza, 1996.

———. "Signorine e signore italiane fra Otto e Novecento: Modelli culturali e comportamenti sociali regolati da uno stato civile." In Ferrante, Palazzi, and Pomata, *Ragnatele di rapporti,* 454–80.

De Grazia, Victoria. "How Mussolini Ruled Italian Women." In *Toward a Cultural Identity in the Twentieth Century,* edited by François Thébaud, 120–48. Duby, Perrot, and Schmitt Pantel, A History of Women in the West, vol. 5.

De Tomassi, Andreina. "L'allegra vecchiaia." *Il Venerdì,* supplement of *La Repubblica,* March 13, 1998, 18.

Defoe, Daniel. *Moll Flanders.* New York: Modern Library, 1940.

Di Matteo, Gabriele. "Lo spot ha successo se i nonni si amano." *Il Venerdì,* supplement of *La Repubblica,* March 13, 1998, 17.

Dickinson, Emily. *Complete Poems.* Edited by Thomas H. Johnson. Boston: Little, Brown & Co., 1924.

Didion, Joan. *A Book of Common Prayer.* New York: Simon & Schuster, 1977.

Dipartimento Politiche Sociali e Salute. "Euro: Occhio alle truffe." *Comune di Roma,* June 11, 2002. http://www.comune.roma.it/dipsociale/pagine_terza_età/pagina_truffe_euro.htm.

Drake, Emma. *What a Woman of Forty-five Ought to Know.* Philadelphia: The Vir Publishing Company, 1902. Translated as *Quel che la donna di 45 anni deve sapere.* Torino: Sten, 1915.

Duby, Georges, Michele Perrot, and Pauline Schmitt Pantel, eds. A History of Women in the West. 5 vols. Cambridge, MA: Harvard University Press, 1994–96.

Eagleton, Sandra, ed. *Women in Literature: Life Stages Through Stories, Poems, and Plays.* Englewood Cliffs, NJ: Prentice Hall, 1988.

Egidi, Piera. *Vent'anni appena: Diario di una generazione onnipotente.* Pollone: Leone & Griffa, 1999.

Elli, Enrico. "Letteratura femminile degli anni '90: Appunti di lettura sui romanzi di S. Tamaro, M. Mazzantini, L. Facetti." *Vita e pensiero* 2 (1995): 90–102.

Erikson, Erik. *Childhood and Society.* New York: Norton, 1950.

———. *Identity and the Life Cycle: Selected Papers.* New York: International Universities Presses, 1959.

———. *The Life Cycle Completed.* New York: Norton, 1997.

———. "Reflections on Dr. Borg's Life Cycle." In *Aging, Death, and the Completion of Being,* edited by David Van Tassel, 29–67. Philadelphia: University of Pennsylvania Press, 1979.

L'età e gli anni: Riflessioni sull'invecchiare. Special issue, *Memoria: Rivista di storia e cultura delle donne* 1 (1986): 3–85.

Facetti, Laura. *Passeggiate con la nonna.* Milan: Anabasi, 1994.

Faini, Riccardo. "Dove nasce l'euro-disagio." *La Voce,* February 10, 2004. http://www.lavoce.info/news/view.php?id=&cms_pk=907.

Falkner, Thomas M., and Judith de Luce, eds. "A View from Antiquity: Greece, Rome, and Elders." In Cole, Van Tassel, and Kastenbaum, *Handbook of the Humanities and Aging,* 3–39.

Fasolino, Marco. "2050: Cinque milioni di italiani in meno." *Terzaet@News,* April 3, 2001. http://www.terzaeta.com/news/archivio.html.

———. "Donne italiane sempre più longeve, ma per loro si prospetta una vecchiaia di stenti." *Terzaet@News,* April 12, 2002. http://www.terzaeta.com/news/archivio.html.

———. "E' l'Italia il paese più vecchio del mondo." *Terzaet@News,* December 19, 2001. http://www.terzaeta.com/news/archivio.html.

Faulkner, William. *The Mansion.* New York: Random House, 1959.

Featherstone, Michael, and Andrew Wernick, eds. *Images of Aging: Cultural Representations of Later Life.* London: Routledge, 1995.

Ferrante, Lucia, Maura Palazzi, and Gianna Pomata, eds. *Ragnatele di rapporti: Patronage e reti di relazione nella storia delle donne.* Turin: Rosenberg & Sellier, 1988.

Ferrero, Guglielmo. *L'Europa giovane: Studi e viaggi nei paesi del nord.* Milan: Treves, 1897.

Figes, Eva. *Waking.* London: Hamish Hamilton, 1981.

Fofi, Goffredo. "Affari di cuore." Review of *Va' dove ti porta il cuore,* by S. Tamaro. *King,* October 1994, 4–5.

Fortunati, Vita. "Controversial Female Body: New Feminist Perspectives on Ageing." Conference paper, Fourth European Feminist Research Conference, Bologna, September 28–October 1, 2000.

Fraisse, Geneviève, and Michelle Perrot, eds. *Emerging Feminism from Revolution to World War.* Duby, Perrot, and Schmitt Pantel, A History of Women in the West, vol. 4.

Freedman, Richard. "Sufficiently Decayed: Gerontophobia in English Literature." In *Aging and the Elderly: Humanistic Perspectives in Gerontology,* edited by Stuart Spicker, Kathleen Woodward, and David Van Tassel, 49–61. Atlantic Highlands, NJ: Humanities Press Inc., 1978.

Friedan, Betty. *The Fountain of Age.* New York: Simon & Schuster, 1993.

Frullini, Annarita. "La vecchiaia attraverso lo sguardo dei bambini." In Spedicato, *I bambini e la vecchiaia,* 89–134.

Fukasawa, Shichiro. *Le canzoni di Narayama.* Translated by Bianca Garufi. Turin: Einaudi, 1961.

Gadow, Sally. "Subjectivity: Literature, Imagination, and Frailty." In Cole and Gadow, *What Does It Mean to Grow Old*, 131–34.

Gaglianone, Paola, ed. *Conversazioni con Susanna Tamaro: Il respiro quieto*. Rome: Omicron, 1996.

Gardner, John. *October Light*. New York: Knopf, 1976.

George, Diana Hume. "Who is the Double Ghost Whose Head is Smoke? Women Poets on Aging." In Woodward and Schwartz, *Memory and Desire*, 134–53.

Gianini Belotti, Elena. *Adagio un poco mosso*. Milan: Feltrinelli, 1993.

———. *Amore e pregiudizio: Il tabù dell'età nei rapporti sentimentali*. Milan: Mondadori, 1988.

———. *Apri le porte all'alba*. Milan: Feltrinelli, 1999.

———. *Dalla parte delle bambine: L'influenza dei condizionamenti sociali nella formazione del ruolo femminile nei primi anni di vita*. Milan: Feltrinelli, 1973. Translated with an introduction by Margaret Mead as *What are Little Girls Made of? The Roots of Feminine Stereotypes* (New York: Schocken Books, 1976).

———. *Il fiore dell'ibisco*. Milan: Rizzoli, 1985.

Gilligan, Carol. "Visions of Maturity." In *In a Different Voice: Psychological Theory and Women's Development*, 151–74. Cambridge, MA: Harvard University Press, 1982.

Ginzburg, Natalia. "La vecchiaia." In *Mai devi domandarmi: Scritti sulla Stampa 68–70*, 19–23. Turin: Einaudi, 1970.

Giovanardi, Stefano. "Quant'era cattiva nonna Antenora." Review of *Il catino di zinco*, by M. Mazzantini. *La Repubblica*, May 19, 1994, 28.

Girardi, Giampiero, and Guglielmo Giumelli, eds. *Vecchiaia, cinema e audiovisivi: Film e documentari in lingua italiana sulla condizione anziana*. Trento: Guerini Studio, 2000.

Glück, Louise. *Vita Nova*. Hopewell, NJ: Ecco Press, 1999.

Goetting, Ann. "The Developmental Tasks of Siblingship over the Life Cycle." *Journal of Marriage and the Family* 48 (1986): 703–14.

Gold, Deborah. "Sibling Relationships in Old Age: A Typology." *International Journal of Aging and Human Development* 1 (1989): 37–51.

Golini, Antonio. "Profilo demografico della famiglia italiana." In Melograni, *La famiglia italiana dall'Ottocento a oggi*, 327–81.

Golino, Enzo. "Troppo rosolio, signora Bossi Fedrigotti." Review of *Di buona famiglia*, by I. Bossi Fedrigotti. *Millelibri* 46 (1991): 40–41.

Goris, Ria, Anita Harling, and Alvy Derks, eds. *OWN-Europe Bulletin* 5 (October 1999). OWN-Older Women's Network, Europe, 1999–2003. http://www.own-europe.org.

Grasso, Laura. "Madri e figlie nel rapporto fra donne: Dipendenza o reciprocità." In *Il filo di Arianna: Letture della differenza sessuale*, edited by Franca Bimbi, et al., 37–52. Rome: Utopia, 1987.

Greer, Germaine. *The Change: Women, Aging, and the Menopause*. New York: Knopf, 1992.

Groppi, Angela. *I conservatori della virtù: Donne recluse nella Roma dei papi*. Bari: Laterza, 1993.

Grumbach, Doris. *Coming into the End Zone: A Memoir*. New York: Norton, 1991.

Gubrium, Jaber. *Speaking of Life: Horizons of Meaning for Nursing Home Residents*. New York: De Gruyter, 1993.

Gubrium, Jaber, and James Holstein. "Narrative Practice and the Coherence of Personal Stories." *The Sociological Quarterly* 39 (1998): 163–87.

Guidi, Tommasina. *L'amore dei quarant'anni*. Milan: Sandron, 1902.

———. *L'età della moglie*. Milan: Sandron, 1881.
Gullette, Margaret Morganroth. "Age Studies and Gender." In *Encyclopedia of Feminist Theories*, edited by Lorraine Code, 12–14. London: Routledge, 2000.
———. "Age Studies as Cultural Studies." In Cole, Kastenbaum, and Ray, *Handbook of the Humanities and Aging*, 214–34.
———. *Aged by Culture*. Chicago: The University of Chicago Press, 2004.
———. "Creativity, Aging, Gender: A Study of Their Intersections, 1910–1935." In Wyatt-Brown and Rossen, *Aging and Gender in Literature*, 19–48.
———. *Declining to Decline: Cultural Combat and the Politics of the Midlife*. Charlottesville: University Press of Virginia, 1997.
———. *Safe at Last in the Middle Years: The Invention of the Midlife Progress Novel*. Berkeley: University of California Press, 1988.
Gutmann, David. "Beyond Nurture: Developmental Perspectives on the Vital Older Woman." In *In Her Prime: New Views of Middle-Aged Women*, edited by Virginia Kerns and Judith Brown, 221–33. Urbana: University of Illinois Press, 1992.
———. *Reclaimed Powers: Toward a New Psychology of Men and Women in Later Life*. New York: Basic Books, 1987.
Heilbrun, Carolyn. *The Last Gift of Time: Life Beyond Sixty*. New York: The Dial Press, 1997.
———. *Writing a Woman's Life*. New York: Ballantine Books, 1988.
Henderson, John, and Richard Wall, eds. *Poor Women and Children in the European Past*. London: Routledge, 1994.
Herlihy, David. "Growing Old in the Quattrocento." In Stearns, *Old Age in Preindustrial Society*, 104–18.
———. "Old Women in the Italian Renaissance." Conference paper, Conference on Aging and the Life Cycle in the Renaissance, University of Maryland, College Park, April 1988.
Horn, Tamara. *To Grandmother's House We Go*. Ph.D. diss., University of Alabama, 1997.
Hughes, Diane. "Domestic Ideals and Social Behavior: Evidence from Medieval Genoa." In *The Family in History*, edited by Charles Rosenberg, 115–43. Philadelphia: University of Pennsylvania Press, 1975.
Irigaray, Luce. *L'éthique de la différance sexuelle*. Paris: Minuit, 1984.
ISTAT. *Anziani in Italia*. Bologna: Il Mulino, 1997.
"Italia 2001, cosa significa la parola famiglia?" Interview with Marzio Barbagli and Chiara Saraceno. *Rai Educational*, 2001. http://www.educational.rai.it/mat/dr/risp/barbag05.asp.
"Italiani più longevi e numerosi grazie agli immigrati." *La Repubblica.it*, December 10, 2001. http://www.repubblica.it/online/società/istatfigli/annuario/annuario.html.
"Italy: Women's Status." PBS. *Six Billion and Beyond*, 1999. http://www.pbs.org/sixbillion/italy/it-status.html.
James, Henry. *The Ambassadors*. New York: Charles Scribner's Sons, 1909.
Judd, Karen, et al. *Aging in a Gendered World*. Santo Domingo: United Nations International Research and Training Institute for the Advancement of Women/INSTRAW, 1999.
Kertzer, David I., and Nancy Karweit. "The Impact of Widowhood in Nineteenth-Century Italy." In Kertzer and Laslett, *Aging in the Past*, 229–48.

Kertzer, David I., and Peter Laslett, eds. *Aging in the Past: Demography, Society, and Old Age*. Berkeley: University of California Press, 1995.

Kingsley, Amis. *Ending Up*. London: Cape, 1974.

Knibiehler, Yvonne. "Bodies and Hearts." Translated by Arthur Goldhammer. In Fraisse and Perrot, *Emerging Feminism from Revolution to World War*, 325–68.

Kuhn, Maggie. *No Stone Unturned: The Life and Times of Maggie Kuhn*. New York: Ballantine Books, 1991.

La Mendola, Salvatore. "I rapporti di parentela in Veneto." *Polis* 5 (1991): 49–70.

La Porta, Filippo. "Romanzo morale ma molto impudico." Review of *Ultima luna*, by L. D'Eramo. *La talpa libri*, supplement of *Il Manifesto*, November 11, 1993, 3.

Ladimer, Bethany. *Colette, Beauvoir, and Duras: Age and Women Writers*. Gainesville: University of Florida Press, 1999.

Lagorio, Gina. "Addio, famiglia crudele: Clara e Virgina, il fascino discreto dell'ambiguità." Review of *Di buona famiglia*, by I. Bossi Fedrigotti. *Corriere della sera*, May 5, 1991, 23.

Lamura, Giovanni, M. Gabriella Melchiorre, and Massimo Mengani. "Caring for the Caregivers: Challenges for Italian Social Policy." In Judd, *Aging in a Gendered World*, 245–72.

Laslett, Peter. "Necessary Knowledge: Age and Aging in the Societies of the Past." In Kertzer and Laslett, *Aging in the Past*, 3–77.

Laurence, Margaret. *The Stone Angel*. New York: Knopf, 1964.

Lazzarini, Guido. "Analisi sociologica dei risultati della ricerca." Conference paper, L'anziano protagonista nella città e nella società, Centro Congressi, Turin, May 24–25, 1999.

———. *Habitat e lavoro nella città in transizione*. Milan: F. Angeli, 2000.

———. *Risorse e generazioni: La città, la solidarietà, il lavoro*. Milan: F. Angeli, 1997.

Lazzaro-Weis, Carol. *From Margins to Mainstream: Feminism and Fictional Modes in Italian Women's Writing, 1968–1990*. Philadelphia: University of Pennsylvania Press, 1993.

Lefkowitz, Allan, and Barbara Lefkowitz. "Old Age and the Modern Literary Imagination." In *Aging in Literature*, edited by Laurel Porter and Laurence Porter, 129–48. Troy, MI: International Book Publishers, 1984.

"Legittimo sospetto: Ricusazione dei giudici, il Polo accelera." *Il Messaggero Online*, July 25, 2002. http://ilmessaggero.caltanet.it/hermes/20020725/01_NAZIONALE/ POLITICA/ GIUSTI.htm.

Lessing, Doris. *The Diaries of Jane Somers*. London: Michael Joseph, 1984.

Levi, Arrigo. *La vecchiaia può attendere, ovvero, l'arte di restare giovani*. Milan: Mondadori, 1998.

Levi Montalcini, Rita. *L'asso nella manica a brandelli*. Milan: Baldini & Castoldi, 1998.

Levin, Amy. *The Suppressed Sister: A Relationship in Novels by Nineteenth- and Twentieth-Century British Women*. Lewisburg: Bucknell University Press, 1992.

Levinson, Daniel, et al. *The Seasons of a Man's Life*. New York: Knopf, 1978.

Libreria delle donne di Milano. *Non credere di avere dei diritti: La generazione della libertà femminile nell'idea e nella vicende di un gruppo di donne*. Turin: Rosenberg & Sellier, 1987. Translated by Teresa De Lauretis as *Sexual Difference: A Theory of Social-Symbolic Practice* (Bloomington: Indiana University Press, 1990).

Lilli, Laura. "Dalla parte delle nonnine." Review of *Adagio un poco mosso*, by E. Gianini Belotti. *La Repubblica*, September 21, 1993, 28.

———. "Per una vecchia zitella." Review of *Apri le porte all'alba*, by E. Gianini Belotti. *La Repubblica*, February 13, 1999, 30.

Lilli, Virgilio. "Una lunga alterna gara: Ora è più vecchio l'uomo, ora è più vecchia la donna." *Corriere della sera*, November 8, 1959, 3.

Lombardi, Giancarlo. "Thou Shalt Not Break the Mold: Patriarchal Discourse in *Va' dove ti porta il cuore*." *Romance Languages Annual* 9 (1998): 238–43.

Looser, Devoney, and E. Ann Kaplan, eds. *Generations: Academic Feminists in Dialogue*. Minneapolis: University of Minnesota Press, 1997.

Loughman, Celeste. "Novels of Senescence: A New Naturalism." *The Gerontologist* 1 (1977): 79–84.

Lowinsky, Naomi Ruth. "Mothers of Mothers: The Power of the Grandmother in the Female Psyche." In *To Be A Woman: The Birth of the Conscious Feminine*, edited by Connie Zweig, 86–97. New York: St. Martin's Press, 1990.

Lucchetti, Maria. *Invecchiare bene*. Bologna: Il Mulino, 1999.

Mangum, Teresa. "The Aging Female Character in Nineteenth-Century British Children's Literature." In Woodward, *Figuring Age*, 59–87.

Mannheim, Karl. "The Problem of Generations." In *Essays on the Sociology of Knowledge*, edited and translated by Paul Kecskemeti, 276–322. London: Routledge & Kegan, 1952.

Mantegazza, Paolo. *Fisiologia della donna*. Vol. 2. Milan: Treves, 1893.

Manzini, Gianna. *Ritratto in piedi*. Milan: Mondadori, 1971.

———. *Sulla soglia*. Milan: Mondadori, 1973.

Marabini, Claudio. "Mazzantini." Review of *Il catino di zinco*, by M. Mazzantini. *Nuova antologia* 219 (1994): 245–46.

Marcesini, Paolo. "Questo mezzo secolo ci piace: Concorsi bellezza over 50." *L'Europeo* 40 (1994): 104–6.

Marziali, Maria Teresa. "Networking, a way of participating." *Your OWN News: Newsletter of the Older Women's Network, Europe* 5 (1999). http://www.own-europe.org.

Marziali, Maria Teresa, and Alan Topalian, eds. *Older Women Acting: Experiences of Older Women's Drama Groups in Europe and Elsewhere*. Rome: OWN-Europe, 1997.

Masci, Raffaello. "Bravi ragazzi, eterni adolescenti." *La Stampa*, June 15, 2002, 17.

Masi, Paola. "Donne senza precedenti." In *Politica, sull'orlo del tempo*, special issue, *DWF* 4 (1997): 9–16.

Maucci, Chiara. "L'amore autunnale è colmo di vita." Review of *Ultima luna*, by L. D'Eramo. *Il Piccolo*, February 1, 1994, 9.

Mazzantini, Margaret. *Il catino di zinco*. Venezia: Marsilio, 1994.

———. *Non ti muovere*. Milan: Mondadori, 2001.

Melograni, Piero, et al. *La famiglia italiana dall'Ottocento a oggi*. Bari: Laterza, 1988.

Mengani, Massimo, and Cristina Gagliardi. *Older Women in the European Community: Social and Economical Conditions*. Ancona: INRCA, 1993.

Michaelis, Karen. *The Dangerous Age: Letters and Fragments from a Woman's Diary*. Translated by Phyllis Lassner. New York: John Lane Company, 1911.

Mill, John Stuart. *The Subjection of Women*. Translated by Anna Maria Mozzoni as *La servitù delle donne* (Milan: Legros, 1870).

Minerva, Daniela. "Susanna? Non parlava quasi mai: Colloquio con Giovanni Tamaro." Interview with G. Tamaro. *L'Espresso*, June 24, 1994, 108.

Minois, George. *History of Old Age: From Antiquity to the Renaissance.* Translated by Sarah Hanbury Tenison. Chicago: University of Chicago Press, 1989.

Mirabile, Maria Luisa. "The Politics of Old Age in Italy." In *The Politics of Old Age in Europe*, edited by Alan Walker and Gerhard Naegele, 110–21. Buckingham: Open University Press, 1999.

Molho, Anthony. "Deception and Marriage Strategy in Renaissance Florence: The Case of Women's Ages." *Renaissance Quarterly* 2 (1988): 193–217.

Mondo, Lorenzo. "Nei segreti del cuore." Review of *Va' dove ti porta il cuore*, by S. Tamaro. *Tuttolibri*, supplement of *La Stampa*, January 29, 1994, 2.

Moody, Harry. "The Collector." *Human Values and Aging Newsletter* 8, no. 1 (1985): 1–2.

———. "The Meaning of Life and the Meaning of Old Age." In Cole and Gadow, *What Does It Mean to Grow Old*, 11–40.

———. "Overview: What is Critical Gerontology and Why Is It Important?" In Cole, *Voices and Visions of Aging*, xv–xli.

Moretti, Daniele. "Senilità e disimpegno: Riflessioni sugli anziani di un centro sociale." *Prospettive sociali e sanitarie* 1 (1987): 14–16.

Moretti, Franco. *Il romanzo di formazione.* Milan: Garzanti, 1986.

Moroli, Emanuela. "Nasce dalla donna un nuovo genere letterario." Interview with E. Gianini Belotti. *Paese sera*, March 15, 1986, 5.

Morrison, Toni. *Jazz.* New York: Knopf, 1992.

Müller, Reinhold C. "Charitable Institutions, the Jewish Community, and Venetian Society." *Studi Veneziani* 14 (1972): 52–60.

Napione, E. *Varcando i quarant'anni: Igiene dell'età critica.* Turin: Praxis, 1911.

Nation by nation.com, 2003. http://www.nationbynation.com/Italy/Population.html.

Nielsen, Anne Maj. *Older Women in the European Community: Social and Economical Conditions and Differences.* Copenhagen: Dane Age Association, 1994.

"I nonni italiani sono superattivi: Battono tutti i colleghi europei." *La Repubblica*, July 29, 2002, 23.

Older Women's Network, Europe. *Integrating the European Dimension: Contributions to Conferences of the European Platform for Senior Organisations during 1994–5.* N.p.: OWN-Europe, 1995.

———. *Recognising Older Women's Experience: Report of the Inaugural Meeting of the Older Women's Network, Europe held in Ireland, 19–24 June 1995.* N.p.: OWN-Europe, 1995.

Olsen, Tillie. *Tell Me a Riddle.* New York: Dell, 1961.

Oppo, Anna. "Madri, figlie e sorelle: Solidarietà parentali in Sardegna." *Polis* 5 (1991): 21–48.

Ortoleva, Peppino. *Saggio sui movimenti del 1968 in Europa e in America.* Rome: Editori Riuniti, 1988.

Ottone, Piero. *Il grande gioco: Lettera ai nipoti.* Milan: Longanesi, 2000.

Ovid. *The Metamorphoses.* Edited and translated by Horace Gregory. New York: Viking Press, 1958.

Paci, Massimo. *Famiglie e mercato del lavoro in un'economia periferica.* Milan: F. Angeli, 1980.

Pallavicini, Paola. "Ritorno al presente: Aspetti virtuali delle relazioni inter-generazionali nel femminismo italiano." Conference paper, Sconvegno: Quali soggettività femministe oggi, Sala dell'Unione femminile, Milan, May 4, 2002. *Unione femminile nazionale*, 1999–2002. http://www.unionefemminile.it/ospiti/sconvegno/pallavicini.htm.

Palma, Ester. "Terza età, nuovo record italiano." *Corriere della sera*, April 7, 1998, 19.

Paltera, Anna. "'Ti racconto uno, mille nonni': Un'esperienza didattica." In Spedicato, *I bambini e la vecchiaia*, 135–65.

Paoletti, Isabella. *Being an Older Woman: A Study in the Social Production of Identity.* Mahwah, NJ: Erlbaum, 1998.

———. "Caring Women, Cared-for Women: The Discourse of Caregiving in Italy.' In Judd, *Aging in a Gendered World*, 133–54.

———. "A Half Life: Women Caregivers of Older Disabled Relatives." *Journal of Women and Aging* 1 (1999): 53–67.

Paoletti, Isabella, and Maria Teresa Marziali. *Generazioni di donne.* Perugia: Associazione Generazioni, 2001.

Parini, Silvia. "Giovani navigatori crescono. . . ." *Terzaet@News*, February 1, 2002. http://www.terzaeta.com/news/archivio.html.

Passerini, Luisa. *Autoritratto di gruppo.* Firenze: Giunti, 1988. Translated by Lisa Erdberg as *Autobiography of a Generation: Italy, 1968* (Hanover, NH: University Press of New England, 1996).

———. *La fontana della giovinezza.* Firenze: Giunti, 1999.

———. Presentation of *La fontana della giovinezza.* Libreria Campus, Turin, March 27, 2000.

Pedemonte, Enrico. "La vecchiaia non c'è più." *L'Espresso* 27 (2002): 44–47.

Petraglia, Angelina. "Anziani: Il nuovo tempo libero." *Terzaet@News*, March 12, 2001. http://www.terzaeta.com/news/archivio.html.

Petrignani, Sandra. *Vecchi.* Rome: Theoria, 1994.

Piazza, Marina. *Le ragazze di cinquant'anni: Amori, lavori, famiglie e nuove libertà.* Milan: Mondadori, 1999.

Piccone Stella, Simonetta. "Un decennio senza cittadinanza." In *L'età e gli anni*, 79–85.

Pinnelli, Antonella. "La longevità femminile: Cifre, dimensioni, valori." In *L'età e gli anni*, 38–60.

Pinnelli, Antonella, and Paola Mancini. "Un indicatore forte dell'ineguaglianza fra i sessi: Le differenze di mortalità nell'infanzia." *Memoria* 32 (1991): 99–115.

Pisu, Renata. "Vita dura con la bisnonna." *La Stampa*, June 27, 1990, 13.

Pizzo, Anna. "Una nuova scienza per il mondo: E' la geriatria." In *Senilità*, special issue, *Il manifesto*, September 28, 1987, I.

Politi, Marco. "La volontà di Woytyla: 'Dio mi dà la forza.'" *La Repubblica*, January 11, 2000, 10.

Prandin, Ivo. "Tracce del nostro tempo." Review of *Di buona famiglia*, by I. Bossi Fedrigotti. *Il Gazzettino*, August 10, 1991, 3.

Prato, Dolores. *Giù la piazza non c'è nessuno.* Milan: Mondadori, 1980.

Pratt, Annis. *Archetypal Patterns in Women's Fiction.* Bloomington: Indiana University Press, 1981.

Premo, Terri. *Winter Friends: Women Growing Old in the New Republic, 1785–1835.* Urbana: University of Illinois Press, 1990.

Prince, Gerald. *Narratology: The Form and Functioning of Narrative.* Berlin: Mouton Publ., 1982.

Pym, Barbara. *Quartet in Autumn.* London: Macmillan, 1977.

Quaranta, Bruno. "Margaret Mazzantini: Un altare per la nonna." Review of *Il catino di zinco*, by M. Mazzantini. *Tuttolibri*, supplement of *La Stampa*, April 2, 1994, 4.

Ravera, Lidia. *Né giovani né vecchi*. Milan: Mondadori, 2000.

Rüschmann, Eva. *Those Precious Bonds: A Psychoanalytic Study of Sister Relationships in Twentieth-Century Literature*. Ph.D. diss., University of Massachussets-Amherst, 1994.

Ricci, Bruno. "Images of Ageing Around the World: Italy." *International Federation on Ageing Publications* 2 (1984): 9–10.

Riemer, Eleanor. "Women, Dowries, and Capital Investment in Thirteenth-Century Siena." In *The Marriage Bargain: Women and Dowries in European History*, edited by Marion Kaplan, 59–80. New York: Haworth Press, 1985.

Rollo Bancale, Luciana. "All'ombra di donne non tanto in fiore." Review of *Di buona famiglia*, by I. Bossi Fedrigotti. *Il mattino*, June 25, 1991, 16.

Romano, Lalla. *Dall'ombra*. Turin: Einaudi, 1999.

———. *Le parole tra noi leggere*. Turin: Einaudi, 1969.

Romé, Franca. *Per una ruga in più*. Milan: Rizzoli, 1982.

Rooke, Constance. "Hagar's Old Age: *The Stone Angel* as *Vollendungsroman*." In *Fear of the Open Heart*, 70–81. Toronto: Coach House Press, 1989.

———. "Old Age in Contemporary Fiction: A New Paradigm of Hope." In Cole, Van Tassel, and Kastenbaum, *Handbook of the Humanities and Aging*, 241–57.

Ros, Teresa. "La nonna." *La donna italiana* 6 (1930): 14.

Russo, Mary. "Aging and the Scandal of Anachronism." In Woodward, *Figuring Age*, 20–33.

Rutigliano, Rita. "Basta con la solita maglia e cucito." Interview with Clara Aprà, Associazione Ragazze di ieri. *L'Unità*, November 27, 1984, under *La Gazzetta Web di Rita Rutigliano*, February 9, 2002. http://www.lagazzettaweb.it/Pages/art_port/tutti/portfolio/basta.html.

Sala, Rita. "Romanzi, ricami e karate." Interview with S. Tamaro. *Il messaggero*, June 10, 1994, 19.

Saletti, Bianca. "I seni di Eva: Immagini di vecchie nella pittura." In *L'età e gli anni*, 71–78.

Sansone, Vito. *La quarta età: Inchiesta sul secolo dai capelli bianchi*. Rome: Editori Riuniti, 2000.

Sanvitale, Francesca. *Madre e figlia*. Turin: Einaudi, 1980.

Saraceno, Chiara. *Sociologia della famiglia*. Bologna: Il Mulino, 1988.

Sarton, May. *After the Stroke: A Journal*. New York: Norton, 1988.

Sasso, Eleonora. "La terza età multimediale: Gli ultrasessantenni, protagonisti e nuovo target del mondo pubblicitario." In Spedicato, *I bambini e la vecchiaia*, 53–77.

Scadron, Arlene, ed. *On Their Own: Widows and Widowhood in the American Southwest, 1848–1939*. Urbana: University of Illinois Press, 1988.

Scaparro, Fulvio. *Storie del mese azzurro: La vecchiaia narrata ai giovani*. Milan: Rizzoli, 1998.

Scaraffia, Lucetta. "Essere uomo, essere donna." In Melograni, *La famiglia italiana dall'Ottocento a oggi*, 193–258.

Scarpa, Paola. "Quell'amata nonna-donna." Interview with M. Mazzantini. *Il gazzettino*, June 10, 1994, 19.

Schisa, Brunella. "Ricomincio da 50." *Il Venerdì*, supplement of *La Repubblica*, June 14, 1996, 82–85.

Scortegagna, Renzo. *Invecchiare.* Bologna: Il Mulino, 1999.
Scurani, Alessandro. Review of *Ultima luna,* by L. D'Eramo. *Letture* 49 (1994): 22–24.
Senardi, Fulvio. "Nonne e giardini: La narrativa di Susanna Tamaro, ovvero come si costruisce il successo letterario." *Problemi* 102 (1995): 180–99.
Serao, Matilde. *Saper vivere.* Firenze: Laudi, 1900.
Skord, Virginia. "'Withered Blossoms': Aging in Japanese Literature." In Bagnell and Soper, *Perceptions of Aging in Literature,* 131–44.
Smith-Rosenberg, Carroll. "The Female World of Love and Ritual: Relations Between Women in Nineteenth-Century America." In *Disorderly Conduct: Visions of Gender in Victorian America,* 53–76. New York: Knopf, 1985.
Sokoloff, Janice. "Character and Aging in *Moll Flanders.*" *The Gerontologist* 6 (1986): 681–85.
———. *The Margin that Remains: A Study of Aging in Literature.* New York: Lang, 1987.
Søland, Birgitte, ed. *Ages of Women: Age as a Category of Analysis in Women's History.* Special issue, *Journal of Women's History* 4 (2001): 1–237.
Sontag, Susan. "The Double Standard of Aging." In *The Other Within Us: Feminist Explorations of Women and Aging,* edited by Marilyn Pearsall, 19–24. Boulder, CO: Westview Press, 1997.
Spark, Muriel. *Memento mori.* Philadelphia: Lippincott, 1958.
Spedicato, Eide, et al. *I bambini e la vecchiaia: Quadri di un immaginario.* Pescara: Tracce, 1998.
Spedicato, Eide. "Il 'sapere' dei bambini e la vecchiaia: Dalla diffidenza alla confidenza alla virtualità." In Spedicato, *I bambini e la vecchiaia,* 167–95.
———. *Vecchiaia e pregiudizio: La donna anziana nella stampa quotidiana.* Rome: Ediesse, 1995.
SPI-CGIL. "Gli anziani spesso mantengono un'intera famiglia." *Terzaet@News,* June 22, 2000. http://www.terzaeta.com/news/archivio.html.
Stearns, Peter N., ed. *Old Age in Preindustrial Society.* New York: Holmes & Meier, 1982.
Stegner, Wallace. *Angle of Repose.* Garden City, NY: Doubleday, 1971.
Suardi, Teresa. *Invecchiare al femminile.* Rome: La Nuova Italia Scientifica, 1993.
Swindell, Richard, and Jean Thompson. "An International Perspective on the University of the Third Age." *Educational Gerontology* 5 (1995): 429–48.
Tamanza, Giancarlo. "Fili d'argento a colori: Il ruolo dei nonni nelle rappresentazioni dei nipoti." In *Rappresentazioni e transizioni dell'ultima età della vita,* 48–63. Rome: F. Angeli, 2001.
Tamaro, Susanna. *Chissene. . . .* Parola di donne. Milan: Piccola Biblioteca Millelire, 1994.
———. *Per voce sola.* Venezia: Marsilio, 1991. Translated by Sharon Wood as *For Solo Voice* (Manchester: Carcanet, 1995).
———. *Va' dove ti porta il cuore.* Milan: Rizzoli, 2000. First published in 1994 by Baldini & Castoldi. Translated by John Cullen as *Follow Your Heart* (New York: Dell Publishing Group, 1996).
Tanizaki, Jun'ichirō. *Diary of a Mad Old Man.* Translated by Howard Hibbett. New York: Knopf, 1965.
Tarquini, Andrea. "Un Papa può rinunciare per il bene della Chiesa." *La Repubblica,* January 11, 2000, 10.
"Il tema." In *L'età e gli anni,* 3.

Terza età. Supplement of *La Stampa*, May 28, 2001, 1–30.

Thane, Pat. "The History of Aging in the West." In Cole, Kastenbaum, and Ray, *Handbook of the Humanities and Aging*, 3–24.

Todisco, Alfredo. "Tanto di Campiello." Interview with M. Mazzantini. *Sette*, supplement of *Il Corriere della sera*, June 30, 1994, 69–71.

Trecca, Michele. "Grazie nonna crudele." Interview with M. Mazzantini. *La Gazzetta del Mezzogiorno*, July 31, 1994, 21.

Trexler, Richard. "Une Table Florentine d'Espérance de Vie." *Annales E.S.C.* 26 (1971): 138.

———. "A Widow's Asylum of the Renaissance: The Orbatello of Florence." In Stearns, *Old Age in Preindustrial Society*, 119–49.

Troyansky, David. "History of Old Age in the Western World." *Ageing and Society* 2 (1996): 234–35.

Updike, John. *The Poorhouse Fair*. Greenwich, CT: Fawcett Publication, Inc., 1958.

"Vacanze, dieci milioni di anziani le trascorrono a casa." *La Stampa*, July 15, 2002, 13.

Valentini, Chiara. "Badanti nella bufera." *L'Espresso Online*, July 4, 2002. http://www.espressonline.it/ESW_articolo/0,2393,35483,00.html.

Vasari, Giorgio. *Le vite dei più eccellenti pittori, scultori e architetti*. Rome: Newton & Compton, 2001.

Il vecchio e il male. Special issue, *Il manifesto*, June 26, 1990: I–IV.

Vera. "Per essere belle." *Almanacco della donna italiana* 14 (1936): 342–46; 19 (1941): 312–14.

Vertua Gentile, Anna. *Come devo comportarmi?* Milan: Hoepli, 1897.

Vitale, Giovanna, "Cinquant'anni senza paura: Qual è la carta da giocare? L'esperienza." *La Repubblica*, September 26, 1994, 21.

Wada, Shuichi. "The Status and Image of the Elderly in Japan: Understanding the Paternalistic Ideology." In Featherstone and Wernick, *Images of Aging*, 48–60.

Walker, Barbara G. *The Crone: Woman of Age, Wisdom, and Power*. San Francisco: Harper & Row, 1985.

Waxman, Barbara Frey. *From the Hearth to the Open Road: A Feminist Study of Aging in Contemporary Literature*. Westport, CT: Greenwood Press, 1990.

———. *To Live in the Center of the Moment: Literary Autobiographies of Aging*. Charlottesville: University Press of Virginia, 1997.

Weiland, Steven. "Criticism Between Literature and Gerontology." In Cole, *Voices and Visions of Aging*, 76–104.

Wernick, Andrew. "Selling Funerals, Imaging Death." In Featherstone and Wernick, *Images of Aging*, 280–86.

Westerwelt, Linda. *Beyond Innocence, or the Altersroman in Modern Fiction*. Columbia: University of Missouri Press, 1997.

Woodward, Kathleen. *Aging and Its Discontents: Freud and Other Fictions*. Bloomington: Indiana University Press, 1991.

———. "Instant Repulsion: Decrepitude, the Mirror Stage, and the Literary Imagination." *The Kenyon Review* 4 (1983): 43–66.

———. Introduction. In Woodward, *Figuring Age*, ix–xxix.

———. "Inventing Generational Models." In Woodward, *Figuring Age*, 149–68.

——. "Reminiscence and the Life Review: Prospects and Retrospects." In Cole and Gadow, *What Does It Mean to Grow Old*, 135–61.

——, ed. *Figuring Age: Women, Bodies, Generations*. Bloomington: Indiana University Press, 1999.

Woodward, Kathleen, and Murray Schwartz, eds. *Memory and Desire: Aging, Literature, Psychoanalysis*. Bloomington: Indiana University Press, 1986.

Woolf, Virginia. *The Diary of Virginia Woolf*. Edited by Anne Olivier Bell. Vols. 2 and 3. New York: Harcourt Brace, 1977–84.

Wyatt-Brown, Anne. "The Future of Literary Gerontology." In Cole, Kastenbaum, and Ray, *Handbook of the Humanities and Aging*, 41–61.

——. "Introduction: Aging, Gender, and Creativity." In Wyatt-Brown and Rossen, *Aging and Gender in Literature*, 1–17.

——. "Literary Gerontology Comes of Age." In Cole, Van Tassel, and Kastenbaum, *Handbook of the Humanities and Aging*, 331–51.

Wyatt-Brown, Anne, and Janice Rossen, eds. *Aging and Gender in Literature: Studies in Creativity*. Charlottesville: University Press of Virginia, 1993.

Wyatt-Brown, Anne, and Barbara Frey Waxman. *Aging in Literature. Brief Bibliography: A Selected Bibliography for Gerontological Instruction*. Washington, DC: Association for Gerontology in Higher Education, 1999.

Yahnke, Robert, and Richard Eastman. *Aging in Literature: A Reader's Guide*. Chicago: American Library Association, 1990.

——. *Literature and Gerontology: A Research Guide*. Westport, CT: Greenwood Press, 1995.

Zanuso, Lorenza. "Lavoro e generazioni." *Politiche del lavoro* 1 (1986): 15–22.

Zuccino, Angela. "The Three-Generation Rural Family in Italy." In *Aging in Western Societies*, edited by Ernest W. Burgess, 439–40. Chicago: University of Chicago Press, 1960.

Index

Abramovitz, Mimi, 204 n. 2
Achenbaum, W. Andrew, 200 n. 19, 204 n. 1
Adagio un poco mosso (Gianini Belotti), 131, 156, 165
affidamento, 75
afterlife, 26, 27, 56–57, 105
age, 19, 20, 26; allegorization of female, 36; appropriateness, 30, 37, 117–18; authority, 58; "awakening" at the threshold of, 170; boundaries, 46; case studies in *Apri le porte all'alba*, 164; categories for Italian women, 44; classes, 21–23, 36, 42; and creativity, 23; and consumerism, 56; as cultural construct, 18; definition of, 26; and difference, 19; fictions, 20, 21; fictionalizing, 19, 39, 102; experience, 19, 173; historiography, 37; identities, 15, 19, 80–83; images, 48; issues, 15, 18, 43, 48, 50, 52, 54–56, 59, 70–76, 129, 145–46; issues, for women, 70–73; legacies, 48; and the media, 60–63; in novel analyses, 87–193; old, and culture, 54–59; patriarchal discourses of, 64–70; patriarchal views of, 164; and role reversal, 131, 160, 170; scenarios, 18, 163; reinvention of, 18; roles, 37–42; shifting markers of, for women, 48; static condition of, 20–21; stereotypes, 21; studies, 19–25; and taking stock, 133; utopias, 21; Woodward's theory of "figuring," 19. *See also* aging
age-conscious: critique of contemporary narratives, 16, 173; genre, 23; perspective, 21; reading and literary criticism, 16, 21, 22
age consciousness: and "age-consciousness raising," 16, 27; and children, 87; in *La fontana della giovinezza*, 181–93; and narrative strategies, 16; study of authors', 24; transitional state of, in Italy, 47
"Age Studies as Cultural Studies" (Gullette), 21
Aged by Culture (Gullette), 16
ageism: anti-youth, 99; and discourses, 21; in Italian culture, 67; in *La fontana della giovinezza*, 187–88, 191; older Italians' recognition of, 54; and periodization, 37
aging: analysis of dynamics in, 24; discourses, Italian, 173; experiences, 18; experiences of, in present-day Italy, 25; gender stereotypes of, 68–70; literary attitudes toward, 20; in novel analyses, 87–193; and patriarchal discourses, 67–68; phenomenology of, 24; positive view of, in women's magazines, 63; processes, 19; and social freedom for women, 44, 164; universal attitudes toward, 24
Aging and Gender in Literature (Wyatt-Brown), 24
AIDA (Association of Older Active Women), 73
Aleramo, Sibilla (Rina Faccio), 16, 28, 58, 59, 195, 199 n. 5
alienation, 27, 28, 81; from offspring, 119–20, 163
Almanacco della donna italiana, 46
Altersroman(e), 23
Altman, Robert, 63
Améry, Jean, 26, 182
Amore e pregiudizio (Gianini Belotti), 131, 160
anachronism, 15, 21; in *Apri le porte all'alba*, 161–62; in *Di buona famiglia*, 112, 120, 122, 125; in *La fontana della giovinezza*, 172–73
Angelou, Maya, 203 n. 48
animals, 29, 102, 109, 153, 158

261

Antonini, Francesco, 70
anziano protagonista nella città e nella società, L', 211 nn. 39 and 42
Apri le porte all'alba (Gianini Belotti), 29, 128–31, 153–71
Archibugi, Francesca, 215 n. 10
Ariosto, Ludovico, 194
Arru, Angiolina, 206 n. 29
Association for Gerontology in Higher Education, 201 n. 34
Associazione De Banfield, 66, 194, 196, 245 n. 4
asso nella manica a brandelli, L' (Levi Montalcini), 58, 194
autobiography: in *Apri le porte all'alba*, 157; in *Il catino di zinco*, 107; and consciousness, 16; female, 16; fictional, in novels, 87–127; in *La fontana della giovinezza*, 25, 172, 173; literary, of aging, 23; secret, 16; in *Ultima luna*, 132–33, 147
Autoritratto di gruppo [Autobiography of a Generation] (Passerini), 174

Baccini, Ida, 42, 45
bambini e la vecchiaia, I (Spedicato), 196
Banner, Lois, 38, 204 n. 2, 205 n. 14
Banti, Anna (Lucia Lopresti Longhi), 195
Barbagli, Marzio, 205 nn. 24 and 25
Barberi Squarotti, Giorgio, 233 n. 24
Bartolini, Simonetta, 241 n. 3
Bedford, Victoria, 228 n. 127
Being an Older Woman (Paoletti), 71
bella figura mystique, 19, 37
Bellow, Saul, 202 n. 45
Bertelli, Christoforo, 205 n. 7
Bildungsroman(e), 24; *Apri le porte all'alba* as, 155; female, 23; *Ultima luna* as, 133–34, 139
Bini, Luigi, 215 n. 9
Bisogni, opportunità, servizi per la terza età (Bocolan Parisi, Bosi, and Ghezzi), 69
Blumenschein, Ernest, 176
Bobbio, Norberto, 56, 212 n. 44, 213 n. 52
Bocca, Giorgio, 58, 213 n. 50
Bocolan Parisi, Lia, 217 nn. 33 and 42, 219 n. 75, 220 n. 98, 221 n. 106
body(ies), 16, 19, 159–60; compassion toward, 111; decline of, 45–46, 103–4, 106, 146; in *Di buona famiglia*, 117–19; house as projection of, 28; new aging modes of, 44–49; parents', 169; and sex, 96; women's, 24, 28, 108
Bollas, Christopher, 28
Bonomi, Ida, 207 n. 46
Boralevi, Antonella, 215 n. 12
Borboni, Paola, 58
Bosi, Marta, 217 n. 33
Bossi Fedrigotti, Isabella, 89, 111–27
Botelho, Lynn, 204 n. 2
Bottoni, Gianluca, 213 n. 53
Braidotti, Rosi, 74, 200 n. 14
Brunelli, Maria, 245 n. 1
Bunyan, John, 36
Buon Natale, Buon Anno (L. Comencini), 61
Butler, Robert, 92, 197, 199 n. 6, 222 n. 17
Buzzi-Donato, Alessandro, 221 n. 109

Calvi, Chiara, 214 n. 1
Cambria, Adele, 147
Camon, Ferdinando, 112
caregiving, 30, 51, 77; in *Il catino di zinco*, 105; daughter's, of father, in *Apri le porte all'alba*, 169; and immigrants, 51, 154, 162, 165–67; in Italian families, 40; in *Ultima luna*, 128–29
"carne e lo spirito, La" (Bocca), 58
Carpi, Fabio, 215 n. 8
casa del sorriso, La (Ferreri), 62
Cather, Willa, 203 n. 50
Catholic: church, 58; women's affiliation, 47
catino di zinco, Il (Mazzantini), 29, 87, 89, 99–111
Cavarero, Adriana, 73, 241 n. 10
Cavigioli, Rita, 199 n. 5
Cecconi, Massimo, 215 n. 9
Cerati, Carla, 215 n. 14, 240 n. 150
Cervantes Saavedra, Miguel de, 203 n. 50
Cesa Bianchi, Marcello, 217 n. 42, 221 n. 106
character(s): development, 21; development of male, 101; and extrafamilial communities, 17; female, 21; maturing of female, 15; in novel analyses, 87–193; older, 25–31
characterization: modes of, 20; in textual analyses, 18; of women protagonists, 48–49
Cherchi, Grazia, 241 n. 8
Chew, Samuel, 205 n. 7
child(ren): and bond with elderly, 29; and

grandparents, 55, 64–67; immigrants as replacements for, 155, 165–66; lack of, in *Apri le porte all'alba*, 163; role of, in *Di buona famiglia*, 126; role of, in Tamaro's works, 93; role of, in *Ultima luna*, 144–45
"Chissene...." (Tamaro), 167
Chodorow, Nancy, 202 n. 43, 228 n. 126
Cialente, Fausta, 195
Cicero, Marcus Tullius, 36
Cicirelli, Victor, 228 n. 127
Cixous, Hélène, 28, 228 n. 126
class: and cultural models, 42–45; and economic status, 82; and education, 41; and Fascism, 47; identity, in *Di buona famiglia*, 114; social, of writer, 24
Clifton, Lucille, 203 n. 48
codes: age, 72; age-appropriateness, 30, 37; age-based, 35, 42–45; behavioral, female, 20, 37; and Fascism, 47; violation of propriety, 118; violation of sexual, 59
Cole, Jean, 204 n. 3
Cole, Thomas, 36, 202 n. 34, 205 nn. 5 and 7
Colitta, Maria Teresa, 217 n. 35, 221 n. 107
"Collector, The" (Moody), 28
Colombi, Marchesa (Maria Antonietta Torriani Torelli), 206 n. 36
Colombo, Furio, 68
Comencini, Cristina, 62, 215 n. 10
Comencini, Luigi, 61, 215 n. 8
community(ies): in *Apri le porte all'alba*, 153, 163, 170–71; extrafamilial, 17; old-age, in *Ultima luna*, 128–30
Condorelli, Luigi, 209 n. 7
Coopmans, Marianne, 218 n. 50, 220 nn. 77 and 99
Corriere della sera, 67
Cranach, Lucas, 176
Cravenna Brigola, Maddalena, 213 n. 49
creativity: and aging and gender, 21; late-life, 15, 23, 194; women's late-life, 16, 23, 24, 59, 195–96
Crepaldi, Gaetano, 208 n. 2
cultural: construct, age as, 18; -history focus in literary analysis, 21; -history survey, 172; discourses of difference, 19; revolutions, 15; studies of gender and aging, 18
Cutrufelli, Rosa, 161

D'Annunzio, Gabriele, 45
D'Eramo, Luce, 131, 132–53
dailiness, 25, 82, 114, 156. *See also* domestic
Dalla parte delle bambine [What are Little Girls Made of?] (Gianini Belotti), 131, 163
Dall'ombra (Romano), 195
Dangerous Age, The (Michaelis), 45
daughters: aging, in contemporary Italy, 74; as caregivers, 40, 71, 77; and marriage in Renaissance Italy, 39; in novel analyses, 87–193
Dauphin, Cécile, 206 n. 29
De Beauvoir, Simone, 173, 188, 241 n. 6
De Federicis, Lidia, 237 n. 87, 241 n. 7
De Giorgio, Michela, 43, 206 nn. 32, 33, and 34, 206 n. 36, 207 nn. 42, 44–50, and 56, 208 n. 65, 216 n. 15
De Grazia, Victoria, 208 n. 60
De Luce, Judith, 205 n. 10
"De senectute" (Bobbio), 56
De senectute, De amicitia, De divinatione (Cicero), 36
De Sica, Vittorio, 215 n. 8
De Tomassi, Andreina, 211 n. 37, 213 n. 53
death: in *Apri le porte all'alba*, 157; in *Il catino di zinco*, 100; in *Di buona famiglia*, 127; expenses of, in *Ultima luna*, 140, 142–43; fear of, 29; preparation for, 168; protagonist's, 26, 27; realization of impending, 16, 130; in *Ultima luna*, 134; viewed as stage in life cycle, 82
decline, 29; discourses, 16; fear of, 26; of female body, 45–46, 103, 108; of formal society in *Di buona famiglia*, 112, 118; mentality about aging, 21; in novel analyses, 87–193
Declining to Decline (Gullette), 16
Defoe, Daniel, 21
demographic: figures and Italian aging, 50–51; imbalance, and Italian old-age culture, 57; patterns, Italian, 17; presence of older women in contemporary Italy, 76–78; revolutions, 15
development: of female characters across the life span, 15; of women protagonists, in novel analyses, 87–193
Deviazione (D'Eramo), 131
Di buona famiglia (Bossi Fedrigotti), 29, 87, 89, 90, 111–27

Dickinson, Emily, 154
Didion, Joan, 203 n. 50
Di Matteo, Gabriele, 214 n. 2
Dipingere in tarda età, 194
domestic: routine in novels, 88; routine and women, 27, 28, 79; service as a career for poor women, 41, 123, 166
donna, Una (Aleramo), 195
donnawomanfemme, 74
Drake, Emma, 45
Duse, Eleonora, 49

Eagleton, Sandra, 202 n. 34
Eastman, Richard, 202 n. 34
education, 48; democratization of, 54; in *Di buona famiglia*, 115–16; and gender gap, 78; in post-Unification Italy, 41; in *Va' dove ti porta il cuore*, 91, 93–95
Egidi, Piera, 218 n. 46
Elli, Enrico, 221 n. 5
employment: and pension reform, 51, 77–78; women's, 44, 48, 77–78
Erikson, Erik, 22–24, 202 n. 39, 228 n. 129
età e gli anni, L', 73–74
età inventata, L', 73
EUROTRE (European School for the Third Age), 212 n. 39

Facetti, Laura, 224 n. 55
Faini, Gianfranco, 210 n. 29
Falkner, Thomas M., 205 n. 10
family, 25; and age-consciousness, 27; ceremonies and traditions in *Di buona famiglia*, 121; dynamics of, 37; dynamics in nineteenth- and twentieth-century rural communities, 39; extended, 39; gender and age roles in, 40; and generational models, 16; histories, in novels, 87–127; household income of, 52, 53; Italian, medieval and modern, 37; kinship patterns in, 40; legacy, in *Apri le porte all'alba*, 168; loosening of ties, 105, 170; narratives, 29, 30; in novel analyses, 87–193; and old-age studies, 36; property and power, in *Di buona famiglia*, 112, 124; reestablishment of new adoptive in *Apri le porte all'alba*, 166; replaced by Fascist state, 47; roles, 29–30; rules, in *Di buona famiglia*, 114
Fascism: in *Il catino di zinco*, 102–3; and generational identity, 47; and women's roles, 47
Fasolino, Marco, 208 nn. 1 and 4, 209 n. 6, 210 n. 21
father: adultery of, in *Di buona famiglia*, 115; in *Apri le porte all'alba*, 166–71; in *Il catino di zinco*, 101–2; role of, in childraising, 38
Faulkner, William, 203 n. 50
feminism: and age studies, 173; in *Apri le porte all'alba*, 157; in *La fontana della giovinezza*, 173, 175, 183–88; impact of, on characters, 30; Italian, and age studies, 73–77; as lens for autobiography, 23; and scholarship, 23; in *Va' dove ti porta il cuore*, 96–97; and youth protest movement, 48
Ferreri, Marco, 62, 215 n. 8
Ferrero, Guglielmo, 207 n. 43
Figes, Eva, 203 n. 49
Figuring Age (Woodward), 19, 24
fiore dell'ibisco, Il (Gianini Belotti), 131, 157, 160
Fisiologia della donna (Mantegazza), 45
Fofi, Goffredo, 99
fontana della giovinezza, La (Passerini), 25, 29, 157, 172–93
Fortunati, Vita, 218 n. 50
Freedman, Richard, 24, 201 n. 32
Freud, Sigmund, 24
Friedan, Betty, 173, 187, 188, 241 n. 6
Frullini, Annarita, 245 n. 3
Fukasawa, Shichiro, 149
fuoco, Il (D'Annunzio), 45

Gadow, Sally, 200 n. 8, 204 n. 60, 231 n. 1
Gaglianone, Paola, 222 n. 23
Gagliardi, Cristina, 218 n. 50, 220 n. 85
Gallen-Kallela, Akseli, 176
Gardner, John, 203 n. 49
gaze: in *Apri le porte all'alba*, 159–69; male, in *Di buona famiglia*, 116, 117; and mirror stage of old age, in *La fontana della giovinezza*, 183–84; of past generations, 108; patriarchal, 19
gender: and gerontology, 15; and perspective, 19, 20, 24, 30; and perspective of life cycles, 23; studies, 19–20; and subject, 19
genealogy, 29; in *Il catino di zinco*, 100–101, 110; disinvestment from, 163, 165;

guilt and purification of, in *Va' dove ti porta il cuore*, 96–97; and revenge, 109; transmission of, in *Di buona famiglia*, 122
generation(s), 19, 24, 25, 30, 72, 74; of 1968, 30, 57, 71, 73–74, 99, 172–93; 30something, 75–76; in Italian age studies, 196–97
generational: alliances as an alternative to genealogy, 165; authority, 46–47; consciousness of older women, 28; debates, 17; heritage, in novel analyses, 87–193; inter- and intragenerational patterns within the family 17; intergenerational power relations, 35; models, 15–16; perspective, in *La fontana della giovinezza*, 174; relations, 30, 31
Generazioni di donne (Paoletti and Marziali), 72
genre(s): debate, 22; new, from life-course perspective, 22; studies, 23; theories, 22; old-age, 130, 196–98
Gentili signore (Monti), 63
George, Diana Hume, 24
gerontology, 15, 16, 18, 22; humanistic, 16, 18, 31, 35; literary, 20; sources of information, 35, 67
Ghezzi, Marta, 217 n. 33
Gianini Belotti, Elena, 71, 72, 131, 137, 153–71
Gilligan, Carol, 23, 202 n. 43, 228 n. 126
Ginzburg, Natalia, 57
giorno più bello della mia vita, Il (C. Comencini), 62
Giotto (Ambrogio Bondone), 36
Giovanardi, Stefano, 226 n. 100
Girardi, Giampiero, 215 n. 9
Giù la piazza non c'è nessuno (Prato), 195
Giumelli, Guglielmo, 215 n. 9
Glück, Louise, 177
Goethe, Johann Wolfgang, von, 193
Goetting, Ann, 228 n. 128
Gold, Deborah, 228 n. 127
Golini, Antonio, 209 n. 7
Golino, Enzo, 228 n. 119
Gordimer, Nadine, 202 n. 46
Gramatica, Emma and Irma, 62
grandchild(ren): in *Il catino di zinco*, 105–11; and grandfathers, 61, 64–66; and grandmothers, 64–66; in *Va' dove ti porta il cuore*, 90–99. *See also* children

grandi vecchi, I, 194
grandmother(s): in *Il catino di zinco*, 105–11; in *Va' dove ti porta il cuore*, 90–99; as source of wounded feminine, 88–89
grandparents, 55; in children's drawings and essays, 64–67; in *Il catino di zinco*, 99–111; as family providers, 52; and grandmother-mother-granddaughter line, 17, 88; in the media, 60–64; in novels, 89; as resource, 55–56; role of, in *Apri le porte all'alba*, 164; in *Va' dove ti porta il cuore*, 90–99
Grasso, Laura, 219 n. 67
Greer, Germaine, 173, 187, 241 n. 6
grido lacerante, Un (Banti), 195
Groppi, Angela, 207 n. 48
"Growing Old in the Quattrocento" (Herlihy), 38
Grumbach, Doris, 173, 187, 189, 203 n. 48, 241 n. 6
Gubrium, Jaber, 245 n. 8
Guidi, Tommasina, 207 n. 55
Gullette, Margaret Morganroth, 16, 19, 21, 23, 173, 194, 201 nn. 28 and 30, 202 nn. 34 and 46, 241 n. 6
Gutmann, David, 23, 202 n. 41

Heilbrun, Carolyn, 24, 173, 188, 241 n. 6
Henderson, John, 204 n. 2
Herlihy, David, 38, 39
historical: developments evident in twentieth century, 16; perspective on Italian women's life courses, 35–49; subjects, women's growth as, 15
history: in *Apri le porte all'alba*, 167; in *Di buona famiglia*, 113–14; in *La fontana della giovinezza*, 173; Italian, and representations of women's bodies, 17
Holstein, James, 245 n. 8
home: in *Apri le porte all'alba*, 168; as central setting, 27; as primary location for older people's lives, 79; as projection of body, 28; and undesirable environment, 28, 154
Horn, Tamara, 223 n. 45
Hughes, Diane, 205 n. 16

identity(ies): age, 15, 136; and age-identity gap in *Ultima luna*, 139; character, 25; confusion of, in *Di buona famiglia*,

127; development of a national female, 42; of old-age, for women, 80–83; private and public, 25; suppression and appropriation of, 89; theory, 19; women's search for, 15, 19
imaginary(ies): age and the Italian cultural, 16, 24; collective, 21, 137; female middle- and young-old-age, 63; older people's and children's, 28; western old-age, 173
INRCA (National Institute for the Cure and Care of Older People), 217 n. 45, 218 n. 52
Iotti, Nilde, 58, 213 n. 55
Irigaray, Luce, 219 n. 65, 228 n. 126
ISTAT (National Institute of Statistics), 79, 209 n. 8, 210 n. 26, 212 n. 43, 217 n. 43, 220 n. 83

James, Henry, 203 n. 50
John Paul II (Karol Wojtyla), 58, 213 n. 50
journals: and diary of Sibilla Aleramo, 16; as primary research material, 24; of a woman writer, 23
Jung, Carl Gustav, 24

Kaplan, E. Ann, 203 n. 51
Karweit, Nancy, 40, 205 n. 22, 206 n. 26
Kertzer, David I., 40, 205 n. 22, 206 n. 26
Kingsley, Amis, 202 n. 45
Knibiehler, Yvonne, 41
Kohut, Heinz, 24
Kristeva, Julia, 228 n. 126
Kuhn, Maggie, 173, 187, 241 n. 6

L'Engle, Madeleine, 203 n. 48
La Mendola, Salvatore, 205 n. 25
La Porta, Filippo, 133, 231 n. 4
Lacan, Jacques, 24
Ladimer, Bethany, 204 n. 52
Lagorio, Gina, 228 n. 121
Lamura, Giovanni, 218 n. 45
language: in *Il catino di zinco*, 106, 110; critical, 22; fictionalized, in *Di buona famiglia*, 112; in *Ultima luna*, 133; of visual arts in *La fontana della giovinezza*, 172
Laslett, Peter, 219 n. 71
late-life: achievement, 58–59; awakening, 23; creativity, 15, 23, 24, 59; development, 22; empowerment, late-life psychoanthropological theories of, 24; reengagement, 23, 29; sex and intimacy, 146–53; travel, 54, 105, 157
Laurence, Margaret, 23
Lazzarini, Guido, 210 n. 25
Lazzaro-Weis, Carol, 75, 219 n. 67
Lefkowitz, Allan and Barbara, 20, 99
Leggendaria, 73
Lehmann, Karl, 58
Lerner, Gad, 244 n. 90
Lessing, Doris, 202 n. 46, 203 n. 49
Levi, Arrigo, 69, 213 n. 52
Levi Montalcini, Rita, 58, 73, 194, 213 n. 54, 213–94 n. 55
Levin, Amy, 228 n. 125
Levinson, Daniel, 23, 24, 202 n. 39
Libreria delle donne di Milano, 75, 219 n. 66
life course, 21; impact of demographic and cultural changes on women's, 15; genres, 20, 24, 30, 133; medieval and early-modern, 36; perspective, 16; portrayal of, in novels, 87–193; women's, in Italy, 37
life expectancy: of artists and religious people, 57; changes in, 50, 78; women's 15
life review, 16, 197; final authorized version of, 25; in novels, 87; of older women, 81; parallel, in *Di buona famiglia*, 115, 127; revision of, 25; versions of, 25; 26
Lilli, Laura, 155, 238 n. 105
Lilli, Virgilio, 67
Lisi, Virna, 61, 62, 215 n. 11
literary: authority issues, 16; criticism and aging, 18; imaginations, impact of demographic and cultural change on, 15; representations and American debates, 18
living conditions: of Italian elderly 52–53, 77–83; in *Apri le porte all'alba*, 164
Livy (Titus Livius), 38
Lombardi, Giancarlo, 97
Looser, Devoney, 203 n. 51
Lorde, Audre, 203 n. 48
Loren, Sofia, 63
Loughman, Celeste, 202 n. 45, 203 n. 49
Lowinsky, Naomi Ruth, 88, 89, 108
Loy, Nanni, 214 n. 8

Lozano, Margherita, 61
Lucchetti, Maria, 217 n. 42, 220 nn. 84 and 99, 221 nn. 103 and 105
"lunga alterna gara, Una" (Lilli), 67–68

Maggi, Stefania, 208 n. 2
male: life cycle, 23; cycle as archetypal, 3
Mancini, Paola, 219 n. 75
Mangum, Teresa, 21
manifesto, Il, 69, 217 n. 37
Mannheim, Karl, 240 n. 2
Mantegazza, Paolo, 45, 206 n. 32
Manzini, Gianna, 195
Marabini, Claudio, 224 n. 54
Marcesini, Paolo, 215 n. 12
Margherita, 44, 206 n. 36
Margin that Remains, The (Sokoloff), 20
marginalization: 28; and children, 28; of elderly in *Apri le porte all'alba*, 165; and immigrants, 28
marriage: and age distribution, 43; moralization of, 43; prospects for women, 17; and women's regrets, 81; vs. women's single status, 43, 80, 83, 158
Marshall, Paule, 202 n. 46
Marziali, Maria Teresa, 72
Masci, Raffaello, 210 n. 18, 213 n. 46
Masi, Paola, 74
Mastroianni, Marcello, 63
materialism, 29; in *Apri le porte all'alba*, 167, 168; and collecting, 28–29; in *Di buona famiglia*, 120, 123; and objects, in *Il catino di zinco*, 100–101, 106–7; and relationship with "things," 82; in *Va' dove ti porta il cuore*, 99
Maucci, Chiara, 134
Mazzantini, Margaret, 89, 99–111, 221 n. 3
media: and consumerism, 28; portrayals of female old age in, 60–64
Melchiorre, M. Gabriella, 218 n. 45
Memoria: Rivista di storia e cultura delle donne, 73
memories: characters' attachment to, 27; in *Il catino di zinco*, 100–111; childhood, in *Apri le porte all'alba*, 167; of father in *Apri le porte all'alba*, 166; in novels, 87; in *Ultima luna*, 138
Mengani, Massimo, 218 nn. 45 and 50, 220 n. 85

menopause: women's growth and fulfillment after, 23, 45, 70–71
Michaelis, Karen, 45
Michelangelo (Michelangelo Buonarroti), 194
Milan Women's Bookshop Collective. *See* Libreria delle donne di Milano
Miller, Jean Baker, 202 n. 43, 228 n. 126
Millet, Kate, 237 n. 88
Minerva, Daniela, 221 n. 10
Minois, George, 38, 213 n. 48
Mirabile, Luisa, 209 nn. 10, 11, and 12, 210 nn. 15, 19, and 28, 211 n. 32
"mito perduto della giovinezza, Il" (Colombo), 68
model(s): age, and female identity, 42–44; female, 88, 163; old-age, 58; real-life, for characters, 24, 90; rejection of, 74
Molho, Anthony, 39
Moll Flanders (Defoe), 21
Mondo, Lorenzo, 222 n. 8
Monicelli, Mario, 62, 214–15 n. 8
Monti, Adriana, 63
Moody, Harry, 18, 28, 199 n. 6, 202 n. 38
Moretti, Daniele, 217 n. 34
Moretti, Franco, 23
Moroli, Emanuela, 237 n. 88
Morrison, Toni, 202 n. 46, 203 n. 50
mother: -daughter line, in Italian feminism, 73, 75; figure of, in *Ultima luna*, 139, 143; in novel analyses, 87–193; role of, in childraising, 38
Mozzoni, Anna Maria, 207 n. 43
Muccino, Gabriele, 63
Müller, Reinhold C., 205 n. 17
Muraro, Luisa, 73

Napione, E., 207 n. 54
Narayama (Fukusawa), 149
narrative(s): of aging, 15, 21, 22, 24, 26, 49; best-selling, and new reading audiences, 16; confessional, in *Di buona famiglia*, 112; as connection between literature and gerontology, 18; defined, 18; developments of the twentieth century in, 16; elements and novel analyses, 18; female-development, 24; focus on generations and women's bodies, 24; frame, provided by characters, 25; life, 16, 197; midlife-progress, 173; patterns, 22; patterns of response, 20; strategies,

17; structure, 18, 26, 115; technique, 18, 156; women's, 23
Nielsen, Anne Maj, 218 n. 50
Nomadic Subjects (Braidotti), 74
normative periodization, 36–37
notte di San Lorenzo, La (Taviani), 61
novel(s) of senescence, 23, 130, 133, 144
Nucleo zero (D'Eramo), 131
nursing home: in *Il catino di zinco*, 105; percentage of elderly in, 51; scenario examined, 17, 27, 128; in *Ultima luna*, 130, 132, 134–40

"Old Age and the Modern Literary Imagination" (Lefkowitz and Lefkowitz), 20–21
Older Women Acting (Marziali and Topalian), 72, 73
Older Women's Network, 72, 218 nn. 50, 51, and 52
Olsen, Tillie, 203 n. 49
Oppo, Anna, 205 n. 25
Ortoleva, Peppino, 218 n. 55
Ottone, Piero, 213 n. 52
Ovid (Publius Ovidius Naso), 192
OWN-Europe. *See* Older Women's Network

Paci, Massimo, 205 n. 25
Palazzeschi, Aldo, 62
Pallavicini, Paola, 75
Palma, Ester, 208 n. 6, 210 n. 27, 211 nn. 33 and 35, 219 n. 72, 220 n. 91
Paltera, Anna, 245 n. 3
Panier Bagat, Matilde, 217 n. 35, 221 n. 107
Paoletti, Isabella, 71, 217–18 n. 45, 218 n. 52
Parenti serpenti (Monicelli), 62
Parini, Silvia, 211 n. 38
parole tra noi leggere, Le (Romano), 195
Partiranno (D'Eramo), 131
Passerini, Luisa, 157, 172–93
Pedemonte, Enrico, 210 n. 14
Per voce sola [For Solo Voice] (Tamaro), 92–93
Petraglia, Angelina, 212 n. 43
Petri, Elio, 215 n. 8
Petrignani, Sandra, 197
physical immobililty, 27; of grandmother, in *Il catino di zinco*, 110–11

Piazza, Marina, 71
Picasso, Pablo, 194, 214 n. 1
Piccone Stella, Simonetta, 74, 244 n. 91
Pilgrim's Progress, The (Bunyan), 36–37
Pinnelli, Antonella, 73, 219 n. 75
Pisu, Renata, 215 n. 13
Pitré, Giuseppe, 209 n. 7
Pizzo, Anna, 217 n. 37
Poggioli, Ferdinando Maria, 62
Pogliani, Milka, 214 n. 1
Politi, Marco, 213 n. 50
Prandin, Ivo, 227 n. 115, 228 n. 118
Prato, Dolores, 195
Pratt, Annis, 244 n. 85
Premo, Terri, 204 n. 2
Prince, Gerald, 200 n. 11
protagonist(s): and death, 25; and memories, 25; as older women, 25; older women as, in film, 61–63; and relations with other age groups, 25
Pym, Barbara, 203 n. 49

Quaranta, Bruno, 224 n. 56
quattro ragazze Wieselberger, Le (Cialente), 195

ragazze di cinquant'anni, Le (Piazza), 71
Ravera, Lidia, 218 n. 46
Ready to Wear (Altman), 63
Reifungsroman(e) (novel of ripening), 23, 31, 130, 145
religion: longing for, 27; in *Il catino di zinco*, 103; in old age, 79; in *Ultima luna*, 130, 141–43; in *Va' dove ti porta il cuore*, 95
representation(s): of grandparents in children's drawings, 64–67; literary, of gender and aging, 18, 20, 55–56, 87–193; of older women in media, 60–64; and self-representation of older women, 19; of single women, 43–44; stereotypical roles of, 64–67; of women's aging bodies, 17; of women's life as punishment, 109; of women subjects' vitality, 161
reproduction: as age marker for women, 48; liberation from sex and, 104; reproductive years, outliving, 15
Repubblica, La, 58, 68, 212 n. 39
retirement home. *See* nursing home
Ricci, Bruno, 210 n. 22

Riemer, Eleanor, 205 n. 15
Ritratto in piedi (Manzini), 195
Rollo Bancale, Luciana, 228 n. 117
Romano, Lalla, 59, 195
Romé, Franca, 217 n. 44
Rooke, Constance, 23, 25, 27, 29, 200 n. 7, 203 n. 49
Ros, Teresa, 208 n. 63
Roth, Philip, 203 n. 48
Rubens, Peter Paul, 176
Rüschmann, Eva, 228 n. 126
Russo, Mary, 161, 199 n. 1, 200 n. 18, 218 n. 53
Rutigliano, Rita, 220 n. 81

Safe at Last in the Middle Years (Gullette), 21
Sala, Rita, 222 n. 19
Saletti, Bianca, 205 n. 4
Sandrelli, Stefania, 63
Sansone, Vito, 208 n. 3, 209 n. 11, 210 nn. 23 and 26, 211 n. 33, 212 n. 45, 217 n. 43, 219 n. 72, 220 nn. 78, 80, 86, 91, and 97
Sanvitale, Francesca, 240 n. 150
Saraceno, Chiara, 205 n. 23, 220 n. 82
Sarton, May, 173, 187, 189, 202 n. 46, 241 n. 6
Sasso, Eleonora, 214 n. 4
Scadron, Arlene, 205 n. 3
Scaparro, Fulvio, 196
Scaraffia, Lucetta, 206 n. 28, 208 nn. 59 and 64
Scarpa, Paola, 227 n. 109
Schisa, Brunella, 215 n. 12
Schwartz, Murray, 204 n. 55
Scola, Ettore, 215 n. 8
Scortegagna, Renzo, 209 n. 11, 212 n. 39, 217 nn. 36 and 41
Scott-Maxwell, Florida, 203 n. 48
Scurani, Alessandro, 231 n. 3, 233 n. 30
Segre, Daniele, 215 n. 9
Senardi, Flavio, 221 n. 7, 222 n. 13
senility, 25; of protagonist, 25, 26; in *Ultima luna*, 136; in *Va' dove ti porta il cuore*, 92
Serao, Matilde, 44
sex: and mature intimacy, 159; sexual initiation 116; sexual orientation, 24; sexual transgression, 118
Sidorenko, Alexander, 212 n. 39

sisters: in *Di buona famiglia*, 111–27; rivalry of, 126–27
Skord, Virginia, 232 n. 7
smells, 29; in *Di buona famiglia*, 121; in *Ultima luna*, 148
Smith-Rosenberg, Carroll, 206 n. 30
socialization: in nineteenth-century Italy, 41; new terrains of, for older women, 170; in *Ultima luna*, 128–29, 137
Sokoloff, Janice, 20, 21, 200 n. 23
Sontag, Susan, 200 n. 17
Sordi, Alberto, 215 n. 8
sorelle Materassi, Le (Poggioli), 62
Soseki, Natsume, 234 n. 47
Spark, Muriel, 202 n. 45
Spedicato, Eide, 63, 216 n. 22, 245 n. 3
Stampa, La, 52, 61, 214 n. 6
Stegner, Wallace, 203 n. 50
Stone Angel, The (Laurence), 23
Storie del mese azzurro (Scaparro), 196
Strozzi, Bernardo, 33
Stuart Mill, John, 207 n. 43
Suardi, Teresa, 217 n. 44
Sulla soglia (Manzini), 195
Svevo, Italo (Ettore Schmitz), 91
Swindell, Richard, 211 n. 37

Tacitus (Cornelius Tacitus), 38
Tamanza, Giancarlo, 64, 66, 196, 212 n. 40
Tamaro, Susanna, 89–99, 101, 102, 105, 106, 167, 221 n. 7
Tanizaki, Jun'ichirō, 202 n. 45
Tarquini, Andrea, 213 n. 50
Taviani, Paolo and Vittorio, 61
Thane, Pat, 204 nn. 1 and 2
Thompson, Jean, 211 n. 37
Thulin, Ingrid, 62
time: consciousness of, 18; in *La fontana della giovinezza*, 172; gerontology as study of, 18; of paternal house, in *Di buona famiglia*, 119, 121–22; prospective and retrospective, 18, 198; representations based on, 27; and space, 27, 29, 78–79; use of in old age, 79–80; women's relationship to, 82
Titian (Tiziano Vecellio), 36
Todisco, Alfredo, 108
Togliatti, Palmiro, 73
Tognazzi, Ugo, 62
transmission, 27, 30; along female family

lines, 20, 38, 41, 74–75, 89, 94–95, 109; genealogical, in novel analyses, 87–193
Trecca, Michele, 225 n. 88, 226 n. 99
Trexler, Richard, 39, 205 n. 17
Troyansky, David, 204 n. 1
Turco, Livia, 219 n. 74

Ultima luna (D'Eramo), 29, 128–53, 158, 164, 168
ultimo bacio, L' (Muccino), 63
Updike, John, 203 n. 49
UPTER (Popular University of the Third Age), 211 n. 37
Usai, Grazia, 214 n. 1

Va' dove ti porta il cuore [Follow Your Heart] (Tamaro), 29, 62, 87, 89–99, 103, 106, 110, 133
Valentini, Chiara, 209 n. 9
Vallotton, Felix, 188
Vanoni, Ornella, 62
Vasari, Giorgio, 213 n. 48
Vecchi (Petrignani), 197
Vecchiaia e pregiudizio (Spedicato), 63
vecchiaia può attendere, La (Levi), 69
Vediamo passare le stelle (Buzzi-Donato), 71, 81–83, 197, 198
Velsi, Pia, 62
Vertua Gentile, Anna, 43
viaggiatori della sera, I (Tognazzi), 62
Visconti, Luchino, 215 n. 8
Vitale, Giovanna, 220 n. 90
Vivencia (Bellassai), 196
Vollendungsroman(e) (novel of completion), 23, 25, 27, 31, 130

Wada, Shuichi, 232 n. 7
Walker, Alice, 202 n. 46
Walker, Barbara, 173, 188, 241 n. 6
Wall, Richard, 204 n. 2
Waxman, Barbara Frey, 21, 23, 28, 201 n. 31, 202 n. 34, 202–3 n. 47, 203 n. 48

Weiland, Steven, 18, 22
Wernick, Andrew, 233 n. 38
Westerwelt, Linda, 23, 203 n. 50
What a Woman of Forty-five Ought to Know (Drake), 45
Winkler, Mary, 202 n. 34
Winnicott, Donald W., 24, 29, 243 n. 63
women: and adaptation to aging, 67–70, 74; age history of, 48; and age-related issues, 70–73; age roles of, 37; bodies of, 24; communication between young and old, 164; education, 17; geographical locations of, 17; growth as historical subjects 15; life conditions of older, 37; life expectancy of, 15; narratives of, 23; in novel analyses, 87–193; professional opportunities for, 17; relationships to social institutions 15; relationships to time, 18; social status of, 16; subjectivity of older, 15; writing women's lives, innovations in, 24
women's movement, 17. *See also* feminism
Woodward, Kathleen, 18, 19, 24, 28, 74, 183, 198, 202 n. 34, 203 n. 51, 204 n. 55, 243 n. 63, 245 n. 7
Woolf, Virginia, 21, 246 n. 94
Writing a Woman's Life (Heilbrun), 24
Wyatt-Brown, Anne, 20, 22–24, 197, 200 n. 19, 201 n. 33

Yahnke, Robert, 202 n. 34
youth(young): characters, 25; older women's view of, 82; promotion of, 56; and seduction, 117–18; significance of old-age cultures, for, 196

Zaccaro, Maurizio, 215 n. 8
Zanuso, Lorenza, 220 n. 87
Zuccino, Angela, 206 n. 27